With Best Wishes
For Good Reading

To: _____

From: _____

God's Way of Salvation

VOLUME 1

Loewen's Selections
of Bible Readings
for Daily Devotions

HERITAGECLASSICS

Library of Congress Catalog Card Number: 94-75579

ISBN: 0-9640876-0-X

Cover design by Gwen Stamm

Printed in the United States of America

FOREWORD

The preparation of these two volumes of Bible readings grew out of a long tradition of family devotions. My wife Elfrieda's father and grandfather were farmers and preachers in the American west. Daily devotional readings were a matter of course. My own forebears on the prairies of western Canada were entrepreneurs with threshing crews, sawmills and construction gangs, yet they had time for Bible reading and prayer.

It was therefore natural that in our own growing family with six children we maintained that happy tradition of family devotions. Yet, even good habits can become routine and perfunctory. We tried a variety of devotional materials to keep the attention of several age-groups: Bible verses assembled on a theme, comments on short passages, and, of course, the popularized Bible stories, mainly about Old Testament heroes. All were useful at certain periods of the family's development. Essentially, these readings needed to attract attention and provoke discussion, then move to reflection and prayer. Morning devotions were short and brisk as the family dashed off to school and work. Evening readings - between supper's main dish and dessert - were more paced, prompting comments and personal resolve.

Reading the entire Bible cannot be improved upon, for God's word is the believer's ultimate guideline for faith and practice. But for families with children, even for adults in their private readings, long genealogies, reenforcing repetitions, and the symbolisms of some prophecies can become wearying. We began to wonder whether a series of Bible readings could be related to a theme (or themes) and gathered into a meaningful sequence. Could perhaps a one-page selection for a day tell of an incident or relate an event with consequent impact on life? Could those teachings be tied together for 365 pages and become a year's daily readings? Could we be selective yet offer an introduction to each of the sixty-six books of the Bible? Hopefully, the readings would draw the reader to the Bible itself for a fuller study of God's revelation.

So we set the following guidelines in choosing the selections:
    i) A reading would not be more than one page in length;
    ii) Though some verses might be skipped in a reading, the narrative had to stand by itself; there would be no backtracking or rearranging of verses;

iii) The sequence of readings would be progressive, i.e. move in the direction of the Books in the Bible from Genesis to Revelation;

iv) When all the selections had been read, the reader would have read something from each book of the Bible.

We eventually selected 660 passages. Many remained intact as in the original text; some retained a natural flow even when verses needed to be deleted; a few, unfortunately, were held together more for convenience than by logic. For these latter, we beg the reader's understanding. But each reading has enough material to sketch an event, to relay a teaching; something on which to meditate, to pray and to act.

What about the overriding themes? Are there major threads that weave through the Scriptures? We found two, and used them for the two volumes. First, God's Way of Salvation traces the creation of man to his ultimate redemption from the Fall via the choosing of a people who were to be models and who were to present the Savior, a people at once obedient and rebellious. Throughout, God is preparing the way of salvation for all mankind through His Son Jesus.

The other theme is a corollary to the first. Having accepted THE WAY what then will be the Believer's Way of Life? Are there not many examples of how faithful men and women walked with God? How did this earlier cloud of witnesses handle their situations? We read with joy their magnificent psalms of victory. Alas, we see also the torment of their souls as they agonized in defeat and sought forgiveness and restoration with the Father.

It was not always easy to separate these two streams. Indeed, seventy readings of the first volume also relate to the theme of the second volume.

We hope that as you meditate on these pages from God's word you will catch the majesty of His ways in the believer's life.

Melvin J. Loewen
at Old Oaks
Easter Sunday, 1994

CONTENTS

Bible Readings Found in the
Two Volumes of
Loewen's Selections of
Bible Readings

		Volume 1	Volume 2
			The
		God's	Believer's
		Way of	Way of
		Salvation	Life
		Page	Page
Genesis 1:1-23	God Creates The Heavens And The Earth	1	
Gen 1:24-2:3	And God Made Man	2	1
Gen 2:15-3:7	"Did God Really Say You Must Not Eat Of The Fruit?"	3	
Gen 3:8-24	So God Banished Them From The Garden	4	
Gen 4:1-15;5:3-5	Cain Kills Abel	5	2
Gen 6:9-7:6	Noah Was A Righteous Man		3
Gen 7:7-8:4	The Floods Covered The Earth		4
Gen 8:21-9:17	God Gives The Rainbow		5
Gen 11:1-9	The Tower Of Babel		
11:27-32	Terah, Father Of Abram	6	
Gen 12:1-8a;13:1-12	Abram And Lot	7	
Gen 15:1-21	Abram's Descendants Will Have A Land	8	6
Gen 16:1-16	Sarai Gives Hagar To Be Abram's Wife	9	
Gen 17:1-20a	No Longer Abram, Your Name Will Be Abraham		7
Gen 18:1-19	Sarah Is Promised A Son	10	8
Gen 18:20-33;19:15-17	Abraham Pleads For Sodom And Gomorrah	11	
Gen 21:1-21	Isaac Is Born, Ishmael Sent Away	12	9
Gen 22:1-18	Abraham Told To Sacrifice Isaac	13	
Gen 23:1-20	Sarah Dies	14	

		Vol. 1	Vol. 2
Gen 24:10-26	Rebekah Waters The Camels	15	
Gen 24:50-67	Isaac Marries Rebekah	16	
Gen 25:1-18a	Abraham Dies		
	And Is Buried By Isaac And Ishmael	17	10
Gen 25:19-34;26:34-35	Jacob And Esau	18	11
Gen 27:1-24	Deception By Rebekah and Jacob	19	
Gen 27:25-40	Isaac Blesses Jacob	20	12
Gen 27:41-28:9	Jacob Leaves Home	21	
Gen 28:10-29:6	Jacob Has A Dream	22	
Gen 29:13-28	Jacob Marries Leah And Rachel	23	
Gen 31:17-36	Jacob Leaves For Canaan	24	13
Gen 31:38-55	Laban And Jacob Separate In Peace	25	
Gen 32:8-28	Jacob's Name Changed To Israel	26	
Gen 33:1-18	Jacob And Esau Meet In Peace	27	14
Gen 35:9-20,22c-29	Rachel Dies		
	Isaac Dies And Is Buried By Esau And Jacob	28	15
Gen 36:2-14,40-43	Esau's Descendants	29	
Gen 37:2b-18	Young Joseph Has Dreams	30	16
Gen 37:19-36	Joseph Is Sold To Traders	31	17
Gen 39:1-21	Joseph Is Bought By Potiphar	32	
Gen 40:1-22a			
Gen 41:1-24	Pharaoh Has A Dream	34	
Gen 41:26-46	Joseph Becomes Prime Minister	35	18
Gen 42:1-21	Joseph's Brothers Seek Food In Egypt	36	
Gen 42:35-43:14			
	Joseph's Brothers Prepare Second Trip To Egypt	37	
Gen 43:15-33	Benjamin Goes Along To Egypt	38	
Gen 44:10-31	Silver Cup Found In Benjamin's Bag	39	
Gen 45:1-20	Joseph Reveals Himself To His Brothers	40	
Gen 46:1-6,26-47:3			
	Jacob And His Descendants Move To Egypt	41	19
Gen 47:28-48:9;49:29-33	Jacob Dies	42	20
Gen 50:2-20	Joseph And His Brothers Bury Jacob	43	21
Exodus 1:6-22	A New King Oppresses The Israelites	44	22
Exo 2:1-21	Moses Is Born; Later Flees To Midian	45	
Exo 3:1-17a			
	Moses Is Called To Lead Israel Out Of Egypt	46	23
Exo 4:1-20	Moses Returns To Egypt	47	
Exo 5:1-21a	Moses' Appeal Rejected By Pharaoh	48	24
Exo 6:28-7:13;11:1-3	Aaron Helps Moses	49	25

		Vol. 1	Vol. 2
Exo 12:21-36,50-51	Passover And Exodus	50	26
Exo 13:17-22;14:5-14	Pharaoh Pursues The Israelites	51	
Exo 14:19-31;15:19-21	Crossing The Red Sea	52	
Exo 15:27-16:15	Water And Bread	53	
Exo 17:1-15	Moses Strikes Rock For Water, And Raises Hands For Victory	54	
Exo 18:6-24	Moses Accepts Advice From His Father-in-law	55	
Exo 19:3-19	Moses Meets God On Mt.Sinai	56	27
Exo 20:1-19	The Ten Commandments	57	28
Exo 24:3-25:2;25:8-9	God Confirms His Covenant	58	
Exo 32:1-7,15-24	The Israelites Build The Golden Calf	59	
Exo 34:1-16	Moses Chisels Two Stone Tablets	60	29
Exo 36:2-6;37:1-9,25-29	Building the Tabernacle, The Ark And The Altar Of Incense	61	
Exo 40:1-17,34-38	Moses Sets Up The Tabernacle And The Tent Of Meeting	62	
Leviticus 4:5-21	The Sin Offering	63	30
Lev 8:1-21	Aaron And His Sons Anointed As Priests	64	
Lev 9:5-23	The Priests Begin Their Ministry	65	31
Lev 19:1-4,9-18,30-37	Rules For Daily Living	66	32
Lev 25:3-23	The Sabbatical Year; The Year Of Jubilee	67	33
Lev 26:3-21	The Rewards Of Obedience, And The Punishments For Disobedience	68	34
Lev 27:16-28,30-34	A Tithe Belongs To The Lord	69	35
Numbers 1:20,21,23,25,27,29,31, 33,35,37,39,41,43,45-50	A Census Of Israel	70	
Num 3:1-16,39-43	Aaron And Sons Appointed As Priests	71	
Num 8:5-25	Levites Set Apart	72	
Num 10:11-17,29-36	Israelites Leave Sinai	73	
Num 11:11-17	Seventy Elders Appointed		
11:31-34	The People Complain And Get Quail	74	36
Num 12:1-15	Miriam And Aaron Talk Against Moses	75	
Num 13:1-2,17-33	Scouts Look At Canaan	76	
Num 14:7-24	Again The People Grumble	77	37
Num 20:2-12	Moses Strikes Rock For Water		
20:15-21	Edom Refuses Passage To Israel	78	

		Vol. 1	Vol. 2
Num 20:22-29	Aaron Dies		
21:4-9	Bronze Snake On A Pole	79	
Num 22:21-38	Balaam Is Asked To Prophecy	80	
Num 23:7-12;24:1-9	Balaam Blesses Israel	81	
Num 26:1-4,51-56,62-65			
	Another Census Before Entering Canaan	82	
Num 27:18-23	Joshua Succeeds Moses As Leader		
32:6-17	Reuben And Gad Stay East Of Jordan	83	
Num 33:51b-56	Instructions On How To Take Canaan		
35:2-14	Towns For Levites And		
	Cities Of Refuge	84	38
Deuteronomy 4:23-38			
	God Makes For Himself One Nation	85	
Deu 5:4-22	The Ten Commandments	86	
Deu 6:3-25	Fear The Lord And Serve Him Only	87	39
Deu 7:7-19,25-26	A Special People Loved Of God	88	
Deu 14:22-23,27-29;15:1-11			
	Give A Tithe; Help The Poor	89	40
Deu 23:7-8	Respect Edomites And Egyptians		
24:5	Newly-Married Should Stay At Home		
24:10-15,19-22;25:13-16	Loans, Weights, Measures	90	41
Deu 28:1-14,20-24	Blessings And Curses	91	42
Deu 30:1-18a	Prosperity When You Obey The Lord	92	43
Deu 31:1-8,19-26a	Joshua Succeeds Moses	93	
Deu 32:48-52;34:1-12	Moses Dies	94	
Joshua 1:1-18	Instructions To Joshua	95	
Josh 2:1-18	Spies Make A Deal With Rahab	96	
Josh 3:1-17	Israelites Cross The Jordan Into Canaan	97	
Josh 6:10-23	The Fall Of Jericho	98	
Josh 9:3-21	The Gibeonites Deceive The Israelites	99	
Josh 10:1-15	The Sun Stands Still At Gibeon	100	
Josh 21:43-45	All Of Canaan Given To Israelites;		
22:1-9			
Reuben, Gad And Manasseh Return To East Of Jordan		101	
Josh 24:19-24,29-33	Death Of Joshua And Of Eleazar	102	
Judges 1:1-3,8-18,27-29			
	Israel Fights The Canaanite Tribes	103	

		Vol. 1	Vol. 2
Judg 2:1-3,14-23;3:5-6			
	Israel Lives With The Canaanites	104	
Judg 4:1-16;5:1-3	Deborah Leads Israel	105	
Judg 6:14-23,33-40	Gideon Puts Out A Fleece	106	44
Judg 7:5b-20	Gideon's Three Hundred Fight Midian	107	45
Judg 8:22-35	Gideon Dies	108	
Judg 11:1-6,9-10,29-39a			
	Jephthah Sacrifices His Daughter	109	
Judg 13:6-24	Samson Is Born	110	
Judg 14:1-3,10-20	Samson Marries A Philistine Woman	111	
Judg 16:8-22	Delilah Betrays Samson	112	
Judg 16:23-31	Death of Samson	113	
Ruth 1:1-19	Ruth Migrates With Naomi	114	46
Ruth 2:8-20a	Ruth Meets Boaz	115	
Ruth 3:1-18			
	Boaz Promises To Find A Husband For Ruth	116	
Ruth 4:2-17	Boaz Marries Ruth	117	
1 Samuel 1:3-20	Birth Of Samuel	118	
1 Sam 1:21-28;2:19-21,26			
	Samuel Is Dedicated To The Lord	119	47
1 Sam 2:22-36	The Sons Of Eli Are Wicked	120	
1 Sam 3:1-21	The Lord Calls Samuel	121	48
1 Sam 4:5-21	Eli's Sons Are Killed And Eli Dies	122	
1 Sam 5:10b-6:12			
	Philistines Return The Ark Of The Covenant	123	
1 Sam 7:2-17	Peace In Israel While Samuel Is Judge	124	49
1 Sam 8:1-22	Israel Asks For A King	125	
1 Sam 9:1-17	Samuel Looks For A King	126	
1 Sam 9:22-10:8	Samuel Anoints Saul As King	127	
1 Sam 10:11-27;13:1	Saul Becomes King Of Israel	128	
1 Sam 14:4-15,20-23			
	Jonathan Attacks The Philistines	129	
1 Sam 15:10-26	Saul Rejected As King	130	
1 Sam 16:5b-23	Samuel Anoints David As The New King Yet David Serves Saul	131	50
1 Sam 17:4-10,32,41-50	David And Goliath	132	
1 Sam 18:9-16,20-30	David Marries Saul's Daughter	133	
1 Sam 19:1b-20	Saul Pursues David	134	
1 Sam 20:24-42a	David And Jonathan	135	51

		Vol. 1	Vol. 2
1 Sam 24:7-22	David Could Have Killed Saul		
25:1	Samuel Dies	136	
1 Sam 28:3-20	Saul Consults A Witch	137	
1 Sam 31:1-13	Saul Takes His Own Life	138	
2 Sam 2:1-17	David Becomes King Of Judah	139	
2 Sam 3:12-27			
	Abner Joins David And Is Murdered By Joab	140	
2 Sam 4:5-5:5	David Becomes King of Israel	141	52
2 Sam 5:6-12,17-25			
	Jerusalem Becomes City Of David	142	
2 Sam 6:2-19			
	David Returns Ark Of The Lord To Jerusalem	143	
2 Sam 7:1-17			
	David's Son To Build A House For The Lord	144	
2 Sam 9:1-13	David Shows Kindness To Jonathan's Son	145	53
2 Sam 11:2b-21	David, Bathsheba And Uriah	146	
2 Sam 12:1-18a	David Repents	147	54
2 Sam 15:1-17a			
	Absalom Leads A Rebellion And David Flees	148	
2 Sam 17:1-16			
	Ahitophel And Hushai Davise Absalom	149	
2 Sam 18:1-17	Absalom Dies	150	
2 Sam 18:32b-19:14	David Returns To Jerusalem	151	
2 Sam 20:1-15a	Sheba Leads A Rebellion	152	
2 Sam 22:31-51	David's Song Of Praise	153	
2 Sam 24:1-4,8-17			
	God Punishes David For Counting His Forces	154	
1 Kings 1:11-30a	Adonijah Usurps The Throne	155	
1 King 1:36-53	Solomon Is Anointed King	156	
1 King 2:1-11	David's Final Instructions To Solomon	157	55
1 King 2:30-46			
	Solomon Establishes His Own Administration	158	
1 King 3:11-28	Solomon The Wise	159	56
1 King 5:1-18			
	Solomon Prepares To Build The Temple	160	
1 King 6:11-18	Solomon Builds The Temple	161	
1 King 7:1-11	Solomon Builds His Palace	162	
1 King 8:15-30	Dedication Of The Temple	163	
1 King 9:1-14,24-25	God's Promise To Solomon	164	57

		Vol. 1	Vol. 2
1 King 10:1-10,23-29			
	Solomon Is Rich, Visited By The Queen Of Sheba	165	
1 King 11:1-18			
	Solomon's Many Wives Increase His Difficulties	166	58
1 King 11:27-43	Rebellion Of Jeroboam;		
	Death Of Solomon	167	
1 King 12:3-20	Israel Rebels Against Rehoboam	168	
1 King 14:7-9,19-20,21-31a			
	Jeroboam King Of Israel; Rehoboam King Of Judah	169	
1 King 17:5-24			
	Elijah Is Fed By Ravens; A Widow Has Flour And Oil	170	59
1 King 18:1-20	Elijah And Obadiah, Men Of God	171	
1 King 18:30-46			
	Elijah Sacrifices To God And Ends The Drought	172	60
1 King 19:7-21	Elijah Flees And Calls Elisha	173	61
1 King 21:5-23	Jezebel Gets A Vineyard For Ahab	174	
1 King 22:7-9,17-28,34a,37			
	Micaiah, A Prophet Of God; Ahab Dies	175	
2 King 2:1-15	Elijah Is Taken To Heaven	176	
2 King 4:14-21,27-37			
	Elisha Raises A Boy From The Dead	177	
2 King 5:1-16	Naaman Is Healed	178	
2 King 17:6-20	Israel Is Taken In Exile To Assyria	179	
2 King 18:13-25			
	Sennacherib Of Assyria Threatens Judah	180	
2 King 19:5-19,35-36			
	Isaiah Foresees The Withdrawal Of Sennecharib	181	
2 King 20:1-17			
	Isaiah Foresees Judah's Captivity In Babylon	182	
2 King 25:5-21			
	Nebuchadnezzar Of Babylon Captures Jerusalem	183	
1 Chronicles 13:7-14;15:1-3,25-16:1a			
	The Ark Brought Back To Jerusalem		62
1 Chron 16:17-29,34-36	David's Song Of Praise		63
1 Chron 17:1-19	God Promises Blessings To David		64
1 Chron 21:5-18,26-27			
	God Is Angry Because David Counts His Troops		65
1 Chron 22:1-17	David Prepares To Build The Temple		66

		Vol. 1	Vol. 2
1 Chron 29:6-20			
	The People Bring Gifts For the Temple		67
1 Chron 29:21-30	Solomon The New King; David Dies		68
2 Chron 1:1-17	God Gives Wisdom To Solomon		69
2 Chron 3:1-17	Solomon Builds The Temple		70
2 Chron 6:12-21;7:1-5	Solomon Dedicates The Temple		71
2 Chron 8:1-16	Solomon Consolidates His Kingdom		72
2 Chron 9:1-14	The Queen Of Sheba Comes To Jerusalem		73
2 Chron 28:1-11,22-25			
	King Ahaz Does Not Honor The Lord		74
2 Chron 29:1-11,25-30			
	Ahaz' Son Hezekiah Honors The Lord		75
2 Chron 31:3-12a,20-21			
	Hezekiah Encourages Gifts To The Lord		76
2 Chron 34:1-3,16b-28a	Josiah Seeks The Ways Of God		77
Ezra 1:1-8;2:64-70;3:1	Exiles Return To Jerusalem	184	
Ezra 3:7-4:5	The Jews Start To Rebuild The Temple	185	
Ezra 5:3-17	The Jews Appeal To Cyrus' Earlier Decree	186	
Ezra 6:2-16	Cyrus' Decree Is Confirmed By Darius;		
	The Temple Is Rebuilt	187	
Ezra 7:8-23a	Ezra Returns To Jerusalem	188	78
Ezra 9:1-12	Ezra Disturbed About Mixed Marriages	189	79
Nehemiah 1:1-2:3	Nehemiah Weeps For Jerusalem		80
Neh 2:6-20	Nehemiah Goes To Jerusalem	190	
Neh 4:1-18a	Jews Rebuild The Wall While Under Attack	191	
Neh 5:1-15	Nehemiah Helps The Poor	192	
Neh 6:1-16	The Wall Of Jerusalem Is Rebuilt	193	
Neh 8:1b-3,15-18			
	Ezra, Nehemiah, and the Levites Instruct the People	194	
Neh 13:1-13,15	Nehemiah's Final Instructions	195	
Esther 1:9-22	Queen Vashti Is Banished	196	
Esther 2:5-18	Esther Becomes Queen	197	
Esther 3:2-15	Mordecai Discovers Haman's Plot	198	
Esther 4:7-5:6	Esther Prepares A Banquet	199	
Esther 5:9-6:10	Mordecai Is Honored By The King	200	
Esther 7:3-8:8a			
	Haman Is Hanged, And The Jews Protected	201	

		Vol. 1	Vol. 2
Esther 9:18-32	The Jews Observe Purim	202	
Job 1:1-12,18-22	Job's Children Are Killed		81
Job 2:1-3:2;3:23-26	Job Becomes Ill And Complains		82
Job 4:1-5;5:8-11,17-27	Eliphaz Gives Counsel		83
Job 6:8-10,24-26;7:11-21	Job Replies To Eliphaz		84
Job 8:1-10,20-22;9:1-4;10:1-9	Bildad Gives Counsel And Job Replies		85
Job 11:1-5,13-18;13:1-3;14:1-2,14-16	Zaphar Gives Counsel And Job Replies		86
Job 32:1-6;33:8-15,19,26-28	Elihu Gives Counsel		87
Job 35:1-12;36:1-12,15-16	Elihu Continues His Counsel		88
Job 38:4-8,12-13,19-22,31-35; 39:26-27;40:1-5	God Replies		89
Job 42:1-17	Job Restored To Health And Wealth		90
Psalms 1 and 2			91
Psalms 4 and 5:1-8		203	92
Psalm 8			93
Psalms 14 and 16:5-11			94
Psalm 18:1-19			95
Psalm 19			96
Psalm 22:1-8,22-31			97
Psalms 23 and 24			98
Psalm 27			99
Psalm 32			100
Psalm 33			101
Psalm 34			102
Psalm 37:1-20			103
Psalm 37:21-40		204	104
Psalm 38			105
Psalm 40			106
Psalm 41			107
Psalm 42			108
Psalms 46 and 47:1-6			109
Psalm 49			110
Psalm 51			111
Psalms 53 and 54		205	112
Psalm 56			113
Psalm 66			114
Psalms 67 and 68:1-10			115

	Vol. 1	Vol. 2
Psalm 71:1-18		116
Psalm 84		117
Psalm 90	206	
Psalm 91		118
Psalms 95 and 96		119
Psalms 100 and 101		120
Psalm 103		121
Psalm 107:1-22		122
Psalms 112 and 113		123
Psalm 115		124
Psalm 116		125
Psalms 117 and 118:1-14		126
Psalm 118:15-29		127
Psalm 119:1-24		128
Psalm 119:33-40,57-64,73-80		129
Psalms 121 and 124		130
Psalms 127 and 128		131
Psalms 133 and 134 and 135:1-9		132
Psalms 137 and 138		133
Psalm 139:1-19		134
Psalms 141 and 142		135
Psalm 145		136
Psalm 147		137
Psalms 149 and 150		138
Proverbs 1:7-19;2:1-6		139
Prov 3:1-14,27-29	207	
Prov 5:1-23		140
Prov 6:1-19		141
Prov 10:1-5,12-22		142
Prov 11:1-8,16-28		143
Prov 15:1-18		144
Prov 16:3-21		145
Prov 17:1,5-6,9-10,12-16	208	146
Prov 21:1-21		147
Prov 22:1-19		148
Prov 23:4-25		149
Prov 24:3-7,23b-34		150
Prov 27:1-2,17-21;28:5-9		151
Prov 30:7-8,15b-16,18-19;31:1-9		152
Prov 31:10-31		153

		Vol. 1	Vol. 2
Ecclesiastes 2:1-18			
	The Things I Toiled For I Must Leave Behind		154
Eccles 3:1-22	Every Activity Has Its Time		155
Eccles 5:4-20			
	Let Man Labor And Enjoy God's Blessings		156
Eccles 11:1-2,6,9;12:1-7,13-14			
	Cast Your Bread Upon The Waters		157
Song of Solomon 4:1-7;7:10-13;8:6-7			
	How Beautiful Is My Beloved		158
Isaiah 1:1-4,13-20	If You Rebel You Will Be Destroyed		159
Isa 3:8-26	Judgment Pronounced On The Wicked		160
Isa 6:1-12;8:5-8	God Commissions Isaiah	209	
Isa 8:18-9:7	The Promise Of The Savior	210	
Isa 10:5-19	Woe To Assyria	211	
Isa 10:20-25;11:1-11			
	A Remnant Of Israel Will Trust In God	212	161
Isa 14:3-15	Babylon Too Will Be Destroyed	213	
Isa 25:1-12	A Song Of Praise To God		162
Isa 30:15-26;31:6-9	A Call For Repentance		163
Isa 36:1-10;37:14-20			
	Sennecharib, King Of Assyria, Threatens To Attack	214	
Isa 38:1-19	Hezekiah's Life Prolonged	215	
Isa 40:1-15a	Good Tidings For God's People		164
Isa 49:8-18,22-23	God Promises To Remember Israel		165
Isa 53:1-12	The Messiah Will Come In Sacrifice	216	
Isa 55:1-13	God's Ways Are Above Man's Ways		166
Isa 58:5-14	True Fasting Is To Help The Poor		167
Isa 61:1-11	The Year Of The Lord		168
Isa 62:1-12	The Nations Will See Your Righteousness		169
Isa 65:16-25	A New Creation		170
Isa 66:1-2,5-6,12-14	A Blessed Hope For God's People		171
Jeremiah 1:1-19	Jeremiah Is Called To Prophesy	217	
Jer 2:13-26a	Israel Has Turned Away From God	218	
Jer 3:6-20			
	Both Israel And Judah Have Been Unfaithful	219	
Jer 5:14-29	God Will Punish His Unfaithful Children		172
Jer 7:8-26	God Will Help If Israel Changes Its Ways	220	

		Vol. 1	Vol. 2
Jer 10:11-25	God Is The Maker Of All And Will Judge All		173
Jer 11:1-17a	Judah Has Broken The Covenant	221	
Jer 18:1-20	The Potter's Clay		174
Jer 21:1-14	Zedekiah Seeks God's Help And Is Rejected	222	
Jer 23:1-8;24:1-7	God Will Gather A Remnant		175
Jer 26:5-19	Priests Want Jeremiah Killed	223	
Jer 27:8-22	Nebuchadnezzar Will Carry Away Judah	224	
Jer 28:1-17	But Nebuchadnezzar's Yoke Will Be Broken	225	
Jer 29:3-19	Jeremiah's Letter To The Elders In Exile	226	
Jer 30:1-3;31:1-10	Israel And Judah Will Return In Joy		176
Jer 31:23-33,38-40	God Will Bring Them Back To Rebuild The City		177
Jer 33:1-11,14-17	Call Upon Me And I Will Show You Great And Mighty Things		178
Jer 34:2b-17	Freedom To The Slaves		179
Jer 36:8,16-31a	Jehoiakim Burns Jeremiah's Scroll	227	
Jer 38:2-4,14-23	Jeremiah Foresees The Fall Of Jerusalem	228	
Jer 39:1-17a	Jersualem Is Taken By Babylon	229	
Jer 42:5-22	A Remnant Goes To Egypt In Spite Of God's Warning	230	
Jer 44:14-27a	The Remnant In Egypt To Be Destroyed	231	
Jer 51:49-64	And Babylon Will Also Be Destroyed	232	
Jer 52:4-16,27b-30	Jerusalem Is Destroyed	233	
Lamentations 1:1-8	How Deserted Lies The City		180
Lament 2:11-19a	My Eyes Fail From Weeping		181
Lament 3:19-42	Yet, We Have Hope		182
Lament 4:22-5:22	Restore Us Lord To Yourself		183
Ezekiel 1:1-3,19-28	God's Glory Appears To Ezekiel	234	
Ezek 3:3-19	Ezekiel Is Asked To Eat The Scroll And Warn Israel	235	
Ezek 4:16-5:14	Siege Of Jerusalem Is Foretold	236	
Ezek 8:17-9:8	There Is Sin In The Temple	237	
Ezek 11:14-12:7a	God Will Again Gather His People		184
Ezek 16:43-59	The Sin Of Israel		185

		Vol. 1	Vol. 2
Ezek 17:1-19	Parable Of The Eagles And A Vine		186
Ezek 18:4-20			
	Each Generation Will Have Its Own Reward		187
Ezek 20:28-42			
	Israel Will Be Punished, Then Restored	238	
Ezek 33:1-16	Ezekiel Is The Watchman To Warn Israel	239	
Ezek 34:2b-17	Shepherds Care For Their Flocks		188
Ezek 37:1b-19	Valley Of Dry Bones		189
Ezek 39:1-8,17-25			
	Gog, From The North, Will Be Destroyed		190
Ezek 45:18-25;46:11-15	Offerings To The Lord		191
Daniel 1:1-19	Daniel And Friends Go On Vegetable Diet	240	
Dan 2:3-19a	Nebuchadnezzar Had A Dream,		
	But Wouldn't Say What He Dreamt	241	
Dan 2:24-40			
	Daniel Recounts The Dream And Interprets It	242	
Dan 3:3-19	Nebuchadnezzar Casts Daniel's Friends		
	Into The Fiery Furnace	243	
Dan 4:1-18a	Nebuchadnezzar Dreams Of A Tree	244	
Dan 4:19b-33	The King's Dream Comes True	245	
Dan 5:1-16a			
	A New King, Belshazzar, Sees Writing On The Wall	246	
Dan 5:17-31	Daniel Interprets The Writing	247	
Dan 6:7b-23a			
	A New King, Darius, Throws David To The Lions	248	
Dan 7:1-14b	Daniel Also Dreams - Of Four Beasts		192
Dan 7:15-28			
	Daniel Is Offered An Interpretation Of His Dream		193
Dan 8:1-17	Daniel Has A Vision Of A Ram And A Goat		194
Dan 9:1-17a	Daniel Prays For The Restoration of Israel		195
Dan 9:20-27	Gabriel Speaks Of Seventy Sevens		196
Dan 11:40-12:10	At The Time Of The End		197
Hosea 1:1-2:5a	Hosea's Adulterous Wife	249	198
Hosea 2:14-3:5			
	But God Will Love Even An Adulterous Wife		199
Hosea 11:1-11;14:9	God Will Heal Israel		200
Joel 1:1-3;2:12-19,26-27	Repent And God Will Hear		201

	Vol. 1	Vol. 2
Joel 3:1-2,9-12,16-21		
Judah Will Be Restored, And The Nations Judged	250	202
Amos 2:4-16		
Judgment Pronounced On Judah And Israel	251	
Amos 3:1-8;4:10-13		
God's Chosen People Will Be Punished	252	203
Amos 5:4-15,21-24		
Israel Will Live When It Seeks God	253	204
Amos 7:1-17		
Amos The Shepherd Rebukes Amaziah The Priest	254	
Amos 8:1-12		
The Lord Will Tremble Because Of Israel's Sin	255	
Amos 9:8-15 Yet, God Will Not Totally Destroy Israel	256	
Obadiah 1:10-21 Punishment Promised To		
Those Nations Who Do Not Defend Israel		205
Jonah 1:1-17 Jonah Tries To Run Away From God		206
Jonah 2:1-10		
Jonah, Inside The Giant Fish, Prays To God		207
Jonah 3:3-4:11 Jonah Obeys God		208
Micah 1:1-5;2:1-5,12-13		
Punishment Promised To Israel, But Also Deliverance	257	209
Micah 4:1-8;5:2-5a God's Temple Will Be Restored		
And Bethlehem Will Be Proud	258	
Micah 6:1-15 God's Accusation Against Israel	259	
Micah 7:8-13,15-20 But Israel Will Be Restored	260	
Nahum 1:1-15		
Condemnation of Nineveh; Judah To Be Rescued	261	
Habakkuk 1:1-6,12-13;2:2-3,20;3:1-2		
Why, Oh Lord, Do You Tolerate The Wicked?	262	210
Zephaniah 1:14-2:3		
Repent, The Day Of The Lord Is Near		211
Zeph 3:8b-20 Jerusalem Will Be Restored		212
Haggai 1:1-15 God's Call To Rebuild The Temple	263	

		Vol. 1	Vol. 2
Haggai 2:6-23	God Will Again Bless His People		213
Zechariah 1:1-17	God Promises Restoration		214
Zech 2:1-13;3:1-7	Measurements For Jerusalem;		
	Garments For The Priests	264	
Zech 4:1-9;5:1-11	Not By Might, Nor By Power,		
	But By My Spirit		215
Zech 7:4-14;8:1-8	Blessings Promised To Jerusalem		216
Zech 11:7-17;12:1-5	Thirty Pieces Of Silver	265	
Zech 14:1-16			
	God Will Gather Nations Against Jerusalem	266	
Malachi 1:1-14	Sacrifices Defiled	267	
Mal 2:7-3:4	He Will Be Like A Refiner's Fire	268	
Mal 3:7-4:6a	Bring All The Tithe		217
Matthew 1:18-2:12	Birth Of Jesus		218
Mat 3:1-17	John Presents Jesus		219
Mat 4:1-22	Jesus Is Tempted, Calls His Disciples		220
Mat 5:1-12,38-48	The Beatitudes; Love Your Enemies		221
Mat 6:5-15,25-34			
	The Lord's Prayer; Trust Him For Your Needs		222
Mat 7:1-6,15-29	Do Not Judge Others;		
	Watch For False Prophets; Build On Rock		223
Mat 8:1-22	Jesus Begins Healing Ministry		224
Mat 9:1-17			
	Jesus Heals; Calls Matthew; Comments On Fasting		225
Mat 10:1-25a	Jesus Sends Out His Disciples		226
Mat 12:1-14,22-27,33-34	Jesus Heals On Sabbath		227
Mat 13:2-23a	Parable Of The Sower		228
Mat 13:31-50	Parables Of Mustard Seed, Yeast,		
	Weeds, And Hidden Treasure		229
Mat 14:13-36			
	Jesus Feeds Five Thousand, Walks On Water		230
Mat 16:1-20	Pharisees Want Proof; Peter's Witness		231
Mat 17:1-13;18:1-9a			
	Transfiguration; Lesson On Greatness		232
Mat 18:10-14,21-35			
	Parables Of Lost Sheep And The Unmerciful Servant		233

		Vol. 1	Vol. 2
Mat 19:1-21	Jesus Teaches On Divorce,		
	Receives Little Children, Talks To Rich Young Man		234
Mat 20:1-16,23-28	Parable Of Workers In Vineyard;		
	Mrs. Zebedee Wants A Favor		235
Mat 21:1-17	Jesus' Triumphal Entry Into Jerusalem		236
Mat 21:23-41a	Jesus' Authority Questioned;		
	Parables Of Two Sons, And Of Landowner		237
Mat 22:1-14,34-46			
	Parable Of A Wedding; The Great Commandment		238
Mat 23:2-25	Woes To False Teachers		239
Mat 24:2-27	Signs Of The End		240
Mat 25:1-13,16-26a			
	Parables Of Virgins, And Of Talents		241
Mat 26:6-30	Perfume For Jesus; The Last Supper		242
Mat 26:33-54			
	Jesus Predicts Peter's Denial And Jesus' Arrest		243
Mat 26:59-27:5	Jesus Before The Sanhedrin;		
	Peter Denies Jesus; Judas Hangs Himself		244
Mat 27:15-37	Pilate Interrogates Jesus;		
	Soldiers Mock Him And Crucify Him		245
Mat 27:45-66	Jesus' Death And Burial		246
Mat 28:1-20			
	Jesus' Resurrection; The Great Commission		247
Mark 1:1-20			
	Jesus Is Baptized, Calls His First Disciples	269	
Mark 1:21-45	Jesus Heals The Sick, Prays Alone	270	
Mark 2:18-27;3:8-19			
	Jesus Comments On Fasting, Calls Twelve Diciples	271	
Mark 4:1-20	Parable Of The Sower And The Seed	272	
Mark 5:1-20	Jesus Heals Demon-Possessed	273	
Mark 6:7-28	Jesus Sends Out His Disciples		
	John The Baptist Is Beheaded	274	
Mark 6:30-51			
	Jesus Feeds Five Thousand, Walks On Water	275	
Mark 7:7-30	The Pharisees' Laws Condemned;		
	Exemplary Faith Of The Phoenician Woman	276	
Mark 8:14-36	The Pharisees' Leaven;		
	Jesus Heals A Blind Man; Peter's Witness	277	
Mark 9:2-9	Jesus' Transfiguration		
9:17-27	Jesus Heals Boy With Evil Spirit	278	

	Vol. 1	Vol. 2
Mark 10:1-25 Jesus Comments On Divorce, And Little Children; And Has Conversation With Rich Young Man	279	
Mark 10:32-52 Jesus Predicts His Death; John And James Want Privileges; Bartimaeus Is Healed	280	
Mark 11:1-19 Jesus Enters Jerusalem In Triumph, And Clears The Temple	281	
Mark 11:28b-12:11;12:13-17 Chief Priests Question Jesus' Authority; Parable Of Tenants; On Paying Taxes	282	
Mark 12:28-44 The Great Commandment; The Widow's Offering	283	
Mark 13:4-27 The End Days	284	
Mark 14:3-24 Jesus Anointed; The Last Supper	285	
Mark 14:29-51 Peter's Denial Predicted; Gethsemane; Jesus Arrested	286	
Mark 15:22-46 Crucifixion And Burial Of Jesus	287	
Mark 16:1-20 Resurrection Of Jesus	288	
Luke 1:5-25 The Birth Of John Foretold		248
Luke 1:26-38,46-55 Birth Of Jesus Foretold; Mary's Praise		249
Luke 2:1-24 Jesus Is Born, And Presented In The Temple		250
Luke 2:41-3:6,15-16 Young Jesus In The Temple; John The Baptist's Announcement		251
Luke 4:1-24 Temptation Of Jesus; Jesus Rejected in Nazareth		252
Luke 5:1-20 Jesus Calls His First Disciples; And Heals Leper And Paralytic		253
Luke 6:1-22 Jesus' Teaching About The Sabbath; Chooses Twelve; Teaches About Blessings And Woes		254
Luke 6:27-48 Love Your Enemies; Do Not Judge; Build On Rock		255
Luke 7:1-17,20-23 Faith Of The Centurion; Widow's Son Revived; John The Baptist Has Doubts		256
Luke 8:1-18 Parable Of The Sower; A Lamp On A Stand		257
Luke 8:22-39 Jesus Calms The Storm, Heals A Demon-Possessed		258
Luke 9:1-21 Jesus Sends Out Twelve, Feeds Five Thousand; Peter's Witness		259

	Vol. 1	Vol. 2
Luke 9:28-48 Transfiguration; Jesus Heals A Boy; A Question Of Greatness		260
Luke 9:57b-10:20 The Cost Of Discipleship		261
Luke 10:25-42 The Good Samaritan; Mary And Martha		262
Luke 11:1-10,33-36 Jesus Comments On Prayer; A Lamp On A Stand		263
Luke 11:37-12:2 Warnings On Hypocrisy		264
Luke 12:13-35 The Foolish Rich Man; Cast Your Cares On God		265
Luke 13: 1-8,18-29 Repent! Of Mustard Seed, Yeast, And The Narrow Door		266
Luke 14:13-35a Parable Of The Banquet; On The Cost Of Discipleship		267
Luke 15:11-32 The Lost Son		268
Luke 16:1-8a,19-31 Parable of the Good Manager; The Rich Man and Lazarus		269
Luke 17:11-19;18:1-14 Ten Lepers Healed; Parable Of The Persistent Widow; The Tax Collector		270
Luke 19:1-23 Zacchaeus The Tax Collector; Parable On Stewardship		271
Luke 19:32-20:8 Jesus' Triumphal Entry Into Jerusalem; Jesus' Authority Is Questioned		272
Luke 20:9-26 Parable Of Tenants; On Paying Taxes		273
Luke 21:8-31 Signs Of The End		274
Luke 22:13b-38 The Last Supper		275
Luke 22:39-62 Jesus On The Mount Of Olives; Betrayal By Peter		276
Luke 22:70-23:25 Jesus Before Pilate		277
Luke 23:32-56 Jesus' Crucifixion, Death And Burial		278
Luke 24:1-16,30-32,48-53 Jesus' Resurrection; Appears To His Disciples; His Ascension		279
John 1:1-27 The Word Became Flesh; Ministry Of John The Baptist	289	
John 1:35-51 Jesus' First Disciples	290	
John 2:1-23 Jesus At A Wedding; And Clears Out The Temple	291	
John 3:1-22 Jesus And Nicodemus	292	
John 4:5-26 Jesus Talks To Samaritan Woman	293	

	Vol. 1	Vol. 2
John 4:45-5:14 Jesus Heals Official's Son, And Heals An Invalid On The Sabbath	294	
John 5:17-39 Eternal Life Through Jesus	295	
John 6:2-24 Jesus Feeds Five Thousand, Walks On Water	296	
John 6:32b-58 Jesus The Bread Of Life	297	
John 7:1-24 Jesus At Feast Of The Tabernacle	298	
John 7:31-52 "Is This The Christ?"	299	
John 8:13-36 Jesus' Testimony Is True	300	
John 9:2-25 Man Born Blind Is Healed	301	
John 10:1b-27 Jesus, Shepherd Of His Flock	302	
John 11:1-27,43-44a Death And Raising Of Lazarus	303	
John 12:1-19 Jesus' Anointing At Bethany; Jesus' Triumphal Entry Into Jerusalem	304	
John 13:5-28 Jesus Washes Disciples Feet, Foresees His Betrayal	305	
John 14:4-27a Jesus Promises The Comforter, The Holy Spirit	306	
John 15:1-24 Vine And Branches	307	
John 16:15-33 Sorrow Will Turn To Joy	308	
John 17:1b-24 Jesus Prays For His Own	309	
John 18:1-11,17-27 Jesus Arrested, Denied By Peter	310	
John 18:35b-19:14 Jesus Before Pilate	311	
John 19:23-40 Crucifixion, Death And Burial Of Jesus	312	
John 20:1-22 Resurrection Of Jesus; He Appears To Mary Magdalene And To Disciples	313	
John 20:24-21:12 Jesus Talks To Thomas, And Helps Peter Cook Fish	314	
John 21:15-25 Fellowship Of Jesus And Peter Restored	315	
Acts 1:1-11;2:1-11 Jesus Is Taken To Heaven; The Holy Spirit Comes	316	
Acts 2:14-24,36-41 Peter's Sermon In Jerusalem	317	
Acts 2:44-3:19a The Works And Preaching Of The New Believers	318	
Acts 4:7-23 Peter And John Testify Before The Sanhedrin	319	
Acts 4:32-5:15 The Believers Share Everything	320	
Acts 5:22-41 Apostles Arrested Again	321	
Acts 6:1-15 Stephen And Other Deacons Chosen	322	
Acts 7:1-18,51 Stephen Preaches to Sanhedrin	323	

		Vol. 1	Vol. 2
Acts 8:4-8,26-40	Ministry Of Philip	324	
Acts 9:3-26	Saul Becomes A Christian	325	
Acts 10:1-23a	Cornelius Sends for Peter	326	
Acts 10:28-48a	Peter Baptizes Cornelius	327	
Acts 11:1-24	Peter Defends His Actions	328	
Acts 12:1-19a	Peter Escapes From Prison	329	
Acts 13:7b-25	Barnabas And Paul Go West And Preach	330	
Acts 13:32-52	Paul Continues Sermon In Antioch	331	
Acts 14:2-22a			
	Paul And Barnabas Visit Other Towns In Asia Minor	332	
Acts 15:1-20			
	Jerusalem Council Accepts Gentile Believers	333	
Acts 15:22-35			
	Letter From Jerusalem Council To Gentile Believers	334	
Acts 15:36-41			
	Disagreement Between Paul And Barnabas;		
16:1-10	Paul Has Vision To Go To Macedonia	335	
Acts 16:14-33a	Lydia Becomes A Believer In Philippi;		
	Paul And Silas In Prison	336	
Acts 16:35-17:12	Paul And Silas Released From Prison,		
	And Go To Thessalonica And Berea	337	
Acts 17:15-32	Paul Preaches In Athens	338	
Acts 18:1-22			
	Paul Stays With Priscilla And Aquila In Corinth	339	
Acts 19:1-21	Paul At Ephesus	340	
Acts 19:23-41			
	Demetrius, The Silversmith, Stirs Up A Riot	341	
Acts 20:17-38			
	Paul Says Farewell To Ephesian Believers	342	
Acts 21:3-24a	Paul Goes To Jerusalem	343	
Acts 21:27-22:2a			
	Angry Crowd Incites Paul's Arrest In Jerusalem	344	
Acts 22:2-22	Paul Tells Of His Conversion	345	
Acts 22:30-23:11	Paul Before The Sanhedrin	346	
Acts 23:12-32	Jews Plot To Kill Paul	347	
Acts 24:1-22	Paul Before Governor Felix	348	
Acts 25:4-22			
	Paul Is Tried Before Festus Who Consults Agrippa	349	
Acts 25:23-26:11			
	Paul Begins Testimony Before King Agrippa	350	

		Vol. 1	Vol. 2
Acts 26:12-31	Paul Ends Testimony Before King Agrippa	351	
Acts 27:3-22	Paul Sails For Rome	352	
Acts 27:29-28:5	Paul Shipwrecked On Malta	353	
Acts 28:13-31	Paul Preaches In Rome	354	
Romans 1:1-20	Paul Called To Preach To Jews And Gentiles	355	280
Rom 1:21-2:8	All Men Have A Knowledge Of God		281
Rom 3:9-31	Believers Are Justified By Faith		282
Rom 4:3-22	Abraham Was Justified By Faith		283
Rom 5:1-19	As By One Man Came Death, So By Christ Came Life		284
Rom 7:7b-8:3a	The Christian's Struggle With Sin		285
Rom 8:18,22-39	Christians Will Overcome		286
Rom 9:1-21	God Has Mercy On His Chosen people		287
Rom 9:22-33	Gentile Believers Are Also Heirs Of God's Promise		288
Rom 10:1-21	Christ Is The End Of The Law		289
Rom 11:1-21	Gentiles Are Blessed Through Israel		290
Rom 11:22-36	Both Gentiles And Israel Are Blessed By A Sovereign God		291
Rom 12:1-21	Paul Calls For Living Sacrifices		292
Rom 13:1-14:1,13	Submit To Authorities; Do Not Judge		293
1 Corinthians 1:10-31	Let There Be No Divisions Among Christians		294
1 Cor 3:16-23	Christians Are Temples Of God's Spirit		
5:9-6:9a	Do Not Take A Brother To Court		295
1 Cor 6:12-7:13	On Sex And Marriage		296
1 Cor 7:15-35	On Marriage		297
1 Cor 10:9-33a	Lessons From Israel; The Earth Is The Lord's		298
1 Cor 11:17-34	On The Lord's Supper		299
1 Cor 12:1-24	Different Gifts		300
1 Cor 13:1-13	Love, The Perfect Way		301
1 Cor 14:2-22	Speaking In Tongues		302
1 Cor 15:3-27a	Christ Is Risen		303
1 Cor 15:35-58	The Dead Will Be Raised		304
2 Cor 4:1-5:10	A Treasure In Earthen Vessels		305

		Vol. 1	Vol. 2
2 Cor 5:11-6:2	A Ministry Of Reconciliation		
6:14-18	Be Not Yoked With Unbelievers		306
2 Cor 8:1-15;9:6-10	Believers To Be Generous		307
2 Cor 11:1-13,23-28	Warning About False Teachers		308
2 Cor 12:15-13:11	Paul's Concern For Corinthian Believers		309
Galatians 1:11-2:2,15-21	Paul's Message From God		310
Gal 3:6-25	Of Faith And The Law		311
Gal 3:26-4:7,21-31	Heirs Of God		312
Gal 5:1-25	Freedom In Christ		313
Ephesians 1:3-23	Blessings In Christ		314
Eph 2:1-22	Christ Is Our Peace		315
Eph 4:4-28a	One Body And One Spirit		316
Eph 5:22-6:9	Of Wives, Husbands And Children, Servants And Masters		317
Eph 6:10-18	Put On The Armour Of God		318
Philippians 2:1-18	Consider Others Better Than Yourselves		319
Phil 3:2-4:1	Press On Toward The Goal In Christ Jesus		320
Phil 4:4-20	Rejoice In The Lord, And Share With Others		321
Col 1:19-23;2:6-18	All The Fulness Of God Is In Christ; Live In The Freedom Of Christ		322
Col 3:1-24	Set Your Affection On Things Above; Wives Submit, Husbands Love, Children Obey		323
1 Thessalonians 1:2-10;4:1-12	Living To God's Glory		324
1 Thess 4:15-5:24	Work, For The Lord Is Coming		325
2 Thess 1:5b-2:12	Work And Keep The Faith		326
2 Thess 2:13-3:16	Keep The Faith And Work		327
1 Timothy 2:2b-3:13	How To Select Church Leaders		328
1 Tim 5:1-20	Of Widows and Elders		329
1 Tim 6:3-21	Godliness With Contentment		330
2 Tim 1:3-2:6	Be Strong In God's Grace		331

		Vol. 1	Vol. 2
2 Tim 2:15-26;3:10-17	A Workman Approved Of God		332
Titus 2:1-3:7	Conduct Of The Believers		333
Philemon 1:1-25	Paul's Plea For His Friend		334
Hebrews 2:1-18	Jesus Is Like A Brother	356	
Heb 3:1-6;4:14-5:10	Jesus, The Apostle And High Priest	357	
Heb 6:1-20	Go On To Maturity	358	
Heb 7:1-22	Jesus Is Like Melchizedek	359	
Heb 8:1-13	Jesus, The High Priest Of A New Covenant	360	
Heb 9:12-28	Christ, The Mediator Of A New Covenant	361	
Heb 11:1-19a	Heroes Of The Faith	362	
Heb 11:20-40	More Heroes Of The Faith	363	
Heb 12:4-25a	Live At Peace With All Men	364	
Heb 13:1-21	Keep On Loving Each Other	365	
James 1:5-27	Christians Should Act On What They Know		335
James 2:1-24	Deeds Must Be Consistent With Confession Of Faith		336
James 3:1-18	The Tongue Can Be Both Curse And Praise		337
James 4:1-17	No One Knows About Tomorrow		338
James 5:1-20	Warning To The Rich; Pray For One Another		339
1 Peter 1:6-25	Be Holy In All You Do		340
1 Peter 2:6-25	You Are A Chosen People		341
1 Peter 3:1-18	Wives Submit, Husbands Be Considerate; Repay Evil With Blessing		342
1 Peter 4:1-19	Live For God's Glory		343
1 Peter 5:1-12	Elders, Eager To Serve; Young Men, Submissive		344
2 Peter 1:3-21	Make Your Salvation Sure; Prophets Speak God's Word		345
2 Peter 2:3-19	False Teachers Will Be Destroyed		346
2 Peter 3:1-18	Scoffers Will Come In The Last Days		347

		Vol. 1	Vol. 2
1 John 1:1-2:12	The Word Of Life Was From The Beginning; Those In The Light Have Fellowship		348
1 John 2:15-3:7a	Be Not Led Astray		349
1 John 3:11-24;4:7-16	Love One Another		350
1 John 5:1-21	To Love God Is To Obey Him		351
2 John	Walk In Love		352
3 John	Imitate The Good		353
Jude 1:8-25	Godless Men Are Condemned; God Can Keep Us From Falling		354
Revelation 1:1-16	I Heard A Loud Voice Like A Trumpet		355
Rev 1:17-2:11	Messages To Ephesus And Smyrna		356
Rev 2:12-29	Messages To Pergamum And Thyatira		357
Rev 3:1-17	Messages To Sardis, Philadelphia and Laodicea		358
Rev 4:6-5:10	I Will Tell You What Will Happen		359
Rev 7:1-4,9-17	A Great Multitude In White Robes		360
Rev 11:15-19;12:7-12	The Seventh Angel Sounds The Trumpet		361
Rev 19:6-21	Our Lord God Almighty Reigns		362
Rev 20:1-15	The Righteous Will Reign With Christ For A Thousand Years; Satan Is Doomed; The Books Are Opened		363
Rev 21:6-25	Then I Saw A New Heaven And A New Earth		364
Rev 22:3-21	The Spirit And The Bride Say, "Come"		365

GOD CREATES THE HEAVENS AND THE EARTH

Gen 1:1-23

In the beginning God created the heavens and the earth. {2} Now the earth was formless and empty, darkness was over the surface of the deep, and the Spirit of God was hovering over the waters. {3} And God said, "Let there be light," and there was light. {4} God saw that the light was good, and he separated the light from the darkness. {5} God called the light "day," and the darkness he called "night." And there was evening, and there was morning–the first day.

{6} And God said, "Let there be an expanse between the waters to separate water from water." {7} So God made the expanse and separated the water under the expanse from the water above it. And it was so. {8} God called the expanse "sky." And there was evening, and there was morning–the second day.

{9} And God said, "Let the water under the sky be gathered to one place, and let dry ground appear." And it was so. {10} God called the dry ground "land," and the gathered waters he called "seas." And God saw that it was good. {11} Then God said, "Let the land produce vegetation: seed-bearing plants and trees on the land that bear fruit with seed in it, according to their various kinds." And it was so. {12} The land produced vegetation: plants bearing seed according to their kinds and trees bearing fruit with seed in it according to their kinds. And God saw that it was good. {13} And there was evening, and there was morning–the third day.

{14} And God said, "Let there be lights in the expanse of the sky to separate the day from the night, and let them serve as signs to mark seasons and days and years, {15} and let them be lights in the expanse of the sky to give light on the earth." And it was so. {16} God made two great lights–the greater light to govern the day and the lesser light to govern the night. He also made the stars. {17} God set them in the expanse of the sky to give light on the earth, {18} to govern the day and the night, and to separate light from darkness. And God saw that it was good. {19} And there was evening, and there was morning–the fourth day.

{20} And God said, "Let the water teem with living creatures, and let birds fly above the earth across the expanse of the sky." {21} So God created the great creatures of the sea and every living and moving thing with which the water teems, according to their kinds, and every winged bird according to its kind. And God saw that it was good. {22} God blessed them and said, "Be fruitful and increase in number and fill the water in the seas, and let the birds increase on the earth." {23} And there was evening, and there was morning–the fifth day.

AND GOD MADE MAN

Gen 1:24-2:3

And God said, "Let the land produce living creatures according to their kinds: livestock, creatures that move along the ground, and wild animals, each according to its kind." And it was so. {25} God made the wild animals according to their kinds, the livestock according to their kinds, and all the creatures that move along the ground according to their kinds. And God saw that it was good. {26} Then God said, "Let us make man in our image, in our likeness, and let them rule over the fish of the sea and the birds of the air, over the livestock, over all the earth, and over all the creatures that move along the ground." {27} So God created man in his own image, in the image of God he created him; male and female he created them. {28} God blessed them and said to them, "Be fruitful and increase in number; fill the earth and subdue it. Rule over the fish of the sea and the birds of the air and over every living creature that moves on the ground." {29} Then God said, "I give you every seed-bearing plant on the face of the whole earth and every tree that has fruit with seed in it. They will be yours for food. {30} And to all the beasts of the earth and all the birds of the air and all the creatures that move on the ground–everything that has the breath of life in it–I give every green plant for food." And it was so. {31} God saw all that he had made, and it was very good. And there was evening, and there was morning–the sixth day.

{2:1} Thus the heavens and the earth were completed in all their vast array. {2} By the seventh day God had finished the work he had been doing; so on the seventh day he rested from all his work. {3} And God blessed the seventh day and made it holy, because on it he rested from all the work of creating that he had done.

"DID GOD REALLY SAY YOU MUST NOT EAT OF THE FRUIT?"

Gen 2:15-3:7

The LORD God took the man and put him in the Garden of Eden to work it and take care of it. {16} And the LORD God commanded the man, "You are free to eat from any tree in the garden; {17} but you must not eat from the tree of the knowledge of good and evil, for when you eat of it you will surely die." {18} The LORD God said, "It is not good for the man to be alone. I will make a helper suitable for him." {19} Now the LORD God had formed out of the ground all the beasts of the field and all the birds of the air. He brought them to the man to see what he would name them; and whatever the man called each living creature, that was its name. {20} So the man gave names to all the livestock, the birds of the air and all the beasts of the field.

But for Adam no suitable helper was found. {21} So the LORD God caused the man to fall into a deep sleep; and while he was sleeping, he took one of the man's ribs and closed up the place with flesh. {22} Then the LORD God made a woman from the rib he had taken out of the man, and he brought her to the man. {23} The man said, "This is now bone of my bones and flesh of my flesh; she shall be called 'woman,' for she was taken out of man." {24} For this reason a man will leave his father and mother and be united to his wife, and they will become one flesh. {25} The man and his wife were both naked, and they felt no shame. {3:1} Now the serpent was more crafty than any of the wild animals the LORD God had made. He said to the woman,' Did God really say, 'You must not eat from any tree in the garden'?" {2} The woman said to the serpent, "We may eat fruit from the trees in the garden, {3} but God did say, 'You must not eat fruit from the tree that is in the middle of the garden, and you must not touch it, or you will die.'" {4} "You will not surely die," the serpent said to the woman. {5} "For God knows that when you eat of it your eyes will be opened, and you will be like God, knowing good and evil." {6} When the woman saw that the fruit of the tree was good for food and pleasing to the eye, and also desirable for gaining wisdom, she took some and ate it. She also gave some to her husband, who was with her, and he ate it. {7} Then the eyes of both of them were opened, and they realized they were naked; so they sewed fig leaves together and made coverings for themselves.

SO GOD BANISHED THEM FROM THE GARDEN

Gen 3:8-24

Then the man and his wife heard the sound of the LORD God as he was walking in the garden in the cool of the day, and they hid from the LORD God among the trees of the garden. {9} But the LORD God called to the man, "Where are you?" {10} He answered, "I heard you in the garden, and I was afraid because I was naked; so I hid." {11} And he said, "Who told you that you were naked? Have you eaten from the tree that I commanded you not to eat from?" {12} The man said, "The woman you put here with me–she gave me some fruit from the tree, and I ate it." {13} Then the LORD God said to the woman, "What is this you have done?" The woman said, "The serpent deceived me, and I ate." {14} So the LORD God said to the serpent, "Because you have done this, "Cursed are you above all the livestock and all the wild animals! You will crawl on your belly and you will eat dust all the days of your life. {15} And I will put enmity between you and the woman, and between your offspring and hers; he will crush your head, and you will strike his heel." {16} To the woman he said, "I will greatly increase your pains in childbearing; with pain you will give birth to children. Your desire will be for your husband, and he will rule over you."

{17} To Adam he said, "Because you listened to your wife and ate from the tree about which I commanded you, 'You must not eat of it,' "Cursed is the ground because of you; through painful toil you will eat of it all the days of your life. {18} It will produce thorns and thistles for you, and you will eat the plants of the field. {19} By the sweat of your brow you will eat your food until you return to the ground, since from it you were taken; for dust you are and to dust you will return." {20} Adam named his wife Eve, because she would become the mother of all the living.

{21} The LORD God made garments of skin for Adam and his wife and clothed them. {22} And the LORD God said, "The man has now become like one of us, knowing good and evil. He must not be allowed to reach out his hand and take also from the tree of life and eat, and live forever." {23} So the LORD God banished him from the Garden of Eden to work the ground from which he had been taken. {24} After he drove the man out, he placed on the east side of the Garden of Eden cherubim and a flaming sword flashing back and forth to guard the way to the tree of life.

CAIN KILLS ABEL

Gen 4:1-15

Adam lay with his wife Eve, and she became pregnant and gave birth to Cain. She said, "With the help of the LORD I have brought forth a man." {2} Later she gave birth to his brother Abel. Now Abel kept flocks, and Cain worked the soil. {3} In the course of time Cain brought some of the fruits of the soil as an offering to the LORD. {4} But Abel brought fat portions from some of the firstborn of his flock. The LORD looked with favor on Abel and his offering, {5} but on Cain and his offering he did not look with favor. So Cain was very angry, and his face was downcast. {6} Then the LORD said to Cain, "Why are you angry? Why is your face downcast? {7} If you do what is right, will you not be accepted? But if you do not do what is right, sin is crouching at your door; it desires to have you, but you must master it." {8} Now Cain said to his brother Abel, "Let's go out to the field." And while they were in the field, Cain attacked his brother Abel and killed him. {9} Then the LORD said to Cain, "Where is your brother Abel?" "I don't know," he replied. "Am I my brother's keeper?" {10} The LORD said, "What have you done? Listen! Your brother's blood cries out to me from the ground. {11} Now you are under a curse and driven from the ground, which opened its mouth to receive your brother's blood from your hand. {12} When you work the ground, it will no longer yield its crops for you. You will be a restless wanderer on the earth." {13} Cain said to the LORD, "My punishment is more than I can bear. {14} Today you are driving me from the land, and I will be hidden from your presence; I will be a restless wanderer on the earth, and whoever finds me will kill me." {15} But the LORD said to him, "Not so; if anyone kills Cain, he will suffer vengeance seven times over." Then the LORD put a mark on Cain so that no one who found him would kill him.

Genesis 5:3-5

When Adam had lived 130 years, he had a son in his own likeness, in his own image; and he named him Seth. {4} After Seth was born, Adam lived 800 years and had other sons and daughters. {5} Altogether, Adam lived 930 years, and then he died.

THE TOWER OF BABEL

Gen 11:1-9

Now the whole world had one language and a common speech. {2} As men moved eastward, they found a plain in Shinar and settled there. {3} They said to each other, "Come, let's make bricks and bake them thoroughly." They used brick instead of stone, and tar for mortar. {4} Then they said, "Come, let us build ourselves a city, with a tower that reaches to the heavens, so that we may make a name for ourselves and not be scattered over the face of the whole earth." {5} But the LORD came down to see the city and the tower that the men were building. {6} The LORD said, "If as one people speaking the same language they have begun to do this, then nothing they plan to do will be impossible for them. {7} Come, let us go down and confuse their language so they will not understand each other." {8} So the LORD scattered them from there over all the earth, and they stopped building the city. {9} That is why it was called Babel —because there the LORD confused the language of the whole world. From there the LORD scattered them over the face of the whole earth.

TERAH, FATHER OF ABRAM

Genesis 11:27-32

This is the account of Terah. Terah became the father of Abram, Nahor and Haran. And Haran became the father of Lot. {28} While his father Terah was still alive, Haran died in Ur of the Chaldeans, in the land of his birth. {29} Abram and Nahor both married. The name of Abram's wife was Sarai, and the name of Nahor's wife was Milcah; she was the daughter of Haran, the father of both Milcah and Iscah. {30} Now Sarai was barren; she had no children. {31} Terah took his son Abram, his grandson Lot son of Haran, and his daughter-in-law Sarai, the wife of his son Abram, and together they set out from Ur of the Chaldeans to go to Canaan. But when they came to Haran, they settled there. {32} Terah lived 205 years, and he died in Haran.

ABRAM AND LOT

Gen 12:1-8a

The LORD had said to Abram, "Leave your country, your people and your father's household and go to the land I will show you. {2} "I will make you into a great nation and I will bless you; I will make your name great, and you will be a blessing. {3} I will bless those who bless you, and whoever curses you I will curse; and all peoples on earth will be blessed through you." {4} So Abram left, as the LORD had told him; and Lot went with him. Abram was seventy-five years old when he set out from Haran. {5} He took his wife Sarai, his nephew Lot, all the possessions they had accumulated and the people they had acquired in Haran, and they set out for the land of Canaan, and they arrived there. {6} Abram traveled through the land as far as the site of the great tree of Moreh at Shechem. At that time the Canaanites were in the land. {7} The LORD appeared to Abram and said, "To your offspring I will give this land." So he built an altar there to the LORD, who had appeared to him. {8} From there he went on toward the hills east of Bethel and pitched his tent....

Genesis 13:1-12

So Abram went up from Egypt to the Negev, with his wife and everything he had, and Lot went with him. {2} Abram had become very wealthy in livestock and in silver and gold. {3} From the Negev he went from place to place until he came to Bethel, to the place between Bethel and Ai where his tent had been earlier {4} and where he had first built an altar. There Abram called on the name of the LORD. {5} Now Lot, who was moving about with Abram, also had flocks and herds and tents. {6} But the land could not support them while they stayed together, for their possessions were so great that they were not able to stay together. {7} And quarreling arose between Abram's herdsmen and the herdsmen of Lot. The Canaanites and Perizzites were also living in the land at that time. {8} So Abram said to Lot, "Let's not have any quarreling between you and me, or between your herdsmen and mine, for we are brothers. {9} Is not the whole land before you? Let's part company. If you go to the left, I'll go to the right; if you go to the right, I'll go to the left." {10} Lot looked up and saw that the whole plain of the Jordan was well watered, like the garden of the LORD, like the land of Egypt, toward Zoar. (This was before the LORD destroyed Sodom and Gomorrah.) {11} So Lot chose for himself the whole plain of the Jordan and set out toward the east. The two men parted company: {12} Abram lived in the land of Canaan, while Lot lived among the cities of the plain and pitched his tents near Sodom.

ABRAM'S DESCENDANTS WILL HAVE A LAND

Gen 15:1-21

After this, the word of the LORD came to Abram in a vision: "Do not be afraid, Abram. I am your shield, your very great reward." {2} But Abram said, "O Sovereign LORD, what can you give me since I remain childless and the one who will inherit my estate is Eliezer of Damascus?" {3} And Abram said, "You have given me no children; so a servant in my household will be my heir." {4} Then the word of the LORD came to him: "This man will not be your heir, but a son coming from your own body will be your heir." {5} He took him outside and said, "Look up at the heavens and count the stars–if indeed you can count them." Then he said to him, "So shall your offspring be." {6} Abram believed the LORD, and he credited it to him as righteousness. {7} He also said to him, "I am the LORD, who brought you out of Ur of the Chaldeans to give you this land to take possession of it." {8} But Abram said, "O Sovereign LORD, how can I know that I will gain possession of it?" {9} So the LORD said to him, "Bring me a heifer, a goat and a ram, each three years old, along with a dove and a young pigeon." {10} Abram brought all these to him, cut them in two and arranged the halves opposite each other; the birds, however, he did not cut in half. {11} Then birds of prey came down on the carcasses, but Abram drove them away. {12} As the sun was setting, Abram fell into a deep sleep, and a thick and dreadful darkness came over him. {13} Then the LORD said to him, "Know for certain that your descendants will be strangers in a country not their own, and they will be enslaved and mistreated four hundred years. {14} But I will punish the nation they serve as slaves, and afterward they will come out with great possessions. {15} You, however, will go to your fathers in peace and be buried at a good old age. {16} In the fourth generation your descendants will come back here, for the sin of the Amorites has not yet reached its full measure." {17} When the sun had set and darkness had fallen, a smoking firepot with a blazing torch appeared and passed between the pieces.

{18} On that day the LORD made a covenant with Abram and said, "To your descendants I give this land, from the river of Egypt to the great river, the Euphrates– {19} the land of the Kenites, Kenizzites, Kadmonites, {20} Hittites, Perizzites, Rephaites, {21} Amorites, Canaanites, Girgashites and Jebusites."

SARAI GIVES HAGAR TO BE ABRAM'S WIFE

Gen 16:1-16

Now Sarai, Abram's wife, had borne him no children. But she had an Egyptian maidservant named Hagar; {2} so she said to Abram, "The LORD has kept me from having children. Go, sleep with my maidservant; perhaps I can build a family through her." Abram agreed to what Sarai said. {3} So after Abram had been living in Canaan ten years, Sarai his wife took her Egyptian maidservant Hagar and gave her to her husband to be his wife. {4} He slept with Hagar, and she conceived. When she knew she was pregnant, she began to despise her mistress. {5} Then Sarai said to Abram, "You are responsible for the wrong I am suffering. I put my servant in your arms, and now that she knows she is pregnant, she despises me. May the LORD judge between you and me." {6} "Your servant is in your hands," Abram said. "Do with her whatever you think best." Then Sarai mistreated Hagar; so she fled from her. {7} The angel of the LORD found Hagar near a spring in the desert; it was the spring that is beside the road to Shur. {8} And he said, "Hagar, servant of Sarai, where have you come from, and where are you going?" "I'm running away from my mistress Sarai," she answered. {9} Then the angel of the LORD told her, "Go back to your mistress and submit to her." {10} The angel added, "I will so increase your descendants that they will be too numerous to count." {11} The angel of the LORD also said to her: "You are now with child and you will have a son. You shall name him Ishmael, for the LORD has heard of your misery. {12} He will be a wild donkey of a man; his hand will be against everyone and everyone's hand against him, and he will live in hostility toward all his brothers." {13} She gave this name to the LORD who spoke to her: "You are the God who sees me," for she said, "I have now seen the One who sees me." {14} That is why the well was called Beer Lahai Roi; it is still there, between Kadesh and Bered. {15} So Hagar bore Abram a son, and Abram gave the name Ishmael to the son she had borne. {16} Abram was eighty-six years old when Hagar bore him Ishmael.

SARAH IS PROMISED A SON

Gen 18:1-19

The LORD appeared to Abraham near the great trees of Mamre while he was sitting at the entrance to his tent in the heat of the day. {2} Abraham looked up and saw three men standing nearby. When he saw them, he hurried from the entrance of his tent to meet them and bowed low to the ground. {3} He said, "If I have found favor in your eyes, my lord, do not pass your servant by. {4} Let a little water be brought, and then you may all wash your feet and rest under this tree. {5} Let me get you something to eat, so you can be refreshed and then go on your way—now that you have come to your servant." "Very well," they answered, "do as you say." {6} So Abraham hurried into the tent to Sarah. "Quick," he said, "get three seahs of fine flour and knead it and bake some bread." {7} Then he ran to the herd and selected a choice, tender calf and gave it to a servant, who hurried to prepare it. {8} He then brought some curds and milk and the calf that had been prepared, and set these before them. While they ate, he stood near them under a tree.

{9} "Where is your wife Sarah?" they asked him. "There, in the tent," he said. {10} Then the LORD said, "I will surely return to you about this time next year, and Sarah your wife will have a son." Now Sarah was listening at the entrance to the tent, which was behind him. {11} Abraham and Sarah were already old and well advanced in years, and Sarah was past the age of childbearing. {12} So Sarah laughed to herself as she thought, "After I am worn out and my master is old, will I now have this pleasure?" {13} Then the LORD said to Abraham, "Why did Sarah laugh and say, 'Will I really have a child, now that I am old?' {14} Is anything too hard for the LORD? I will return to you at the appointed time next year and Sarah will have a son." {15} Sarah was afraid, so she lied and said, "I did not laugh." But he said, "Yes, you did laugh." {16} When the men got up to leave, they looked down toward Sodom, and Abraham walked along with them to see them on their way. {17} Then the LORD said, "Shall I hide from Abraham what I am about to do? {18} Abraham will surely become a great and powerful nation, and all nations on earth will be blessed through him. {19} For I have chosen him, so that he will direct his children and his household after him to keep the way of the LORD by doing what is right and just, so that the LORD will bring about for Abraham what he has promised him."

ABRAHAM PLEADS FOR SODOM AND GOMORRAH

Gen 18:20-33

Then the LORD said, "The outcry against Sodom and Gomorrah is so great and their sin so grievous {21} that I will go down and see if what they have done is as bad as the outcry that has reached me. If not, I will know." {22} The men turned away and went toward Sodom, but Abraham remained standing before the LORD. {23} Then Abraham approached him and said: "Will you sweep away the righteous with the wicked? {24} What if there are fifty righteous people in the city? Will you really sweep it away and not spare the place for the sake of the fifty righteous people in it? {25} Far be it from you to do such a thing—to kill the righteous with the wicked, treating the righteous and the wicked alike. Far be it from you! Will not the Judge of all the earth do right?" {26} The LORD said, "If I find fifty righteous people in the city of Sodom, I will spare the whole place for their sake." {27} Then Abraham spoke up again: "Now that I have been so bold as to speak to the Lord, though I am nothing but dust and ashes, {28} what if the number of the righteous is five less than fifty? Will you destroy the whole city because of five people?" "If I find forty-five there," he said, "I will not destroy it." {29} Once again he spoke to him, "What if only forty are found there?" He said, "For the sake of forty, I will not do it." {30} Then he said, "May the Lord not be angry, but let me speak. What if only thirty can be found there?" He answered, "I will not do it if I find thirty there." {31} Abraham said, "Now that I have been so bold as to speak to the Lord, what if only twenty can be found there?" He said, "For the sake of twenty, I will not destroy it." {32} Then he said, "May the Lord not be angry, but let me speak just once more. What if only ten can be found there?" He answered, "For the sake of ten, I will not destroy it." {33} When the LORD had finished speaking with Abraham, he left, and Abraham returned home.

Genesis 19:15-17

With the coming of dawn, the angels urged Lot, saying, "Hurry! Take your wife and your two daughters who are here, or you will be swept away when the city is punished." {16} When he hesitated, the men grasped his hand and the hands of his wife and of his two daughters and led them safely out of the city, for the LORD was merciful to them. {17} As soon as they had brought them out, one of them said, "Flee for your lives! Don't look back, and don't stop anywhere in the plain! Flee to the mountains or you will be swept away!"

ISAAC IS BORN, ISHMAEL SENT AWAY

Gen 21:1-21

Now the LORD was gracious to Sarah as he had said, and the LORD did for Sarah what he had promised. {2} Sarah became pregnant and bore a son to Abraham in his old age, at the very time God had promised him. {3} Abraham gave the name Isaac to the son Sarah bore him. {4} When his son Isaac was eight days old, Abraham circumcised him, as God commanded him. {5} Abraham was a hundred years old when his son Isaac was born to him. {6} Sarah said, "God has brought me laughter, and everyone who hears about this will laugh with me." {7} And she added, "Who would have said to Abraham that Sarah would nurse children? Yet I have borne him a son in his old age." {8} The child grew and was weaned, and on the day Isaac was weaned Abraham held a great feast.

{9} But Sarah saw that the son whom Hagar the Egyptian had borne to Abraham was mocking, {10} and she said to Abraham, "Get rid of that slave woman and her son, for that slave woman's son will never share in the inheritance with my son Isaac." {11} The matter distressed Abraham greatly because it concerned his son. {12} But God said to him, "Do not be so distressed about the boy and your maidservant. Listen to whatever Sarah tells you, because it is through Isaac that your offspring will be reckoned.

{13} I will make the son of the maidservant into a nation also, because he is your offspring." {14} Early the next morning Abraham took some food and a skin of water and gave them to Hagar. He set them on her shoulders and then sent her off with the boy. She went on her way and wandered in the desert of Beersheba. {15} When the water in the skin was gone, she put the boy under one of the bushes. {16} Then she went off and sat down nearby, about a bowshot away, for she thought, "I cannot watch the boy die." And as she sat there nearby, she began to sob. {17} God heard the boy crying, and the angel of God called to Hagar from heaven and said to her, "What is the matter, Hagar? Do not be afraid; God has heard the boy crying as he lies there. {18} Lift the boy up and take him by the hand, for I will make him into a great nation." {19} Then God opened her eyes and she saw a well of water. So she went and filled the skin with water and gave the boy a drink. {20} God was with the boy as he grew up. He lived in the desert and became an archer. {21} While he was living in the Desert of Paran, his mother got a wife for him from Egypt.

ABRAHAM TOLD TO SACRIFICE ISAAC

Gen 22:1-18

Some time later God tested Abraham. He said to him, "Abraham!" "Here I am," he replied. {2} Then God said, "Take your son, your only son, Isaac, whom you love, and go to the region of Moriah. Sacrifice him there as a burnt offering on one of the mountains I will tell you about." {3} Early the next morning Abraham got up and saddled his donkey. He took with him two of his servants and his son Isaac. When he had cut enough wood for the burnt offering, he set out for the place God had told him about. {4} On the third day Abraham looked up and saw the place in the distance. {5} He said to his servants, "Stay here with the donkey while I and the boy go over there. We will worship and then we will come back to you." {6} Abraham took the wood for the burnt offering and placed it on his son Isaac, and he himself carried the fire and the knife.

As the two of them went on together, {7} Isaac spoke up and said to his father Abraham, "Father?" "Yes, my son?" Abraham replied. "The fire and wood are here," Isaac said, "but where is the lamb for the burnt offering?" {8} Abraham answered, "God himself will provide the lamb for the burnt offering, my son." And the two of them went on together.

{9} When they reached the place God had told him about, Abraham built an altar there and arranged the wood on it. He bound his son Isaac and laid him on the altar, on top of the wood. {10} Then he reached out his hand and took the knife to slay his son. {11} But the angel of the LORD called out to him from heaven, "Abraham! Abraham!" "Here I am," he replied. {12} "Do not lay a hand on the boy," he said. "Do not do anything to him. Now I know that you fear God, because you have not withheld from me your son, your only son." {13} Abraham looked up and there in a thicket he saw a ram caught by its horns. He went over and took the ram and sacrificed it as a burnt offering instead of his son.

{14} So Abraham called that place The LORD Will Provide. And to this day it is said, "On the mountain of the LORD it will be provided." {15} The angel of the LORD called to Abraham from heaven a second time {16} and said, "I swear by myself, declares the LORD, that because you have done this and have not withheld your son, your only son, {17} I will surely bless you and make your descendants as numerous as the stars in the sky and as the sand on the seashore. Your descendants will take possession of the cities of their enemies, {18} and through your offspring all nations on earth will be blessed, because you have obeyed me."

SARAH DIES

Gen 23:1-20

Sarah lived to be a hundred and twenty-seven years old. {2} She died at Kiriath Arba (that is, Hebron) in the land of Canaan, and Abraham went to mourn for Sarah and to weep over her.

{3} Then Abraham rose from beside his dead wife and spoke to the Hittites. He said, {4} "I am an alien and a stranger among you. Sell me some property for a burial site here so I can bury my dead." {5} The Hittites replied to Abraham, {6} "Sir, listen to us. You are a mighty prince among us. Bury your dead in the choicest of our tombs. None of us will refuse you his tomb for burying your dead." {7} Then Abraham rose and bowed down before the people of the land, the Hittites. {8} He said to them, "If you are willing to let me bury my dead, then listen to me and intercede with Ephron son of Zohar on my behalf {9} so he will sell me the cave of Machpelah, which belongs to him and is at the end of his field. Ask him to sell it to me for the full price as a burial site among you." {10} Ephron the Hittite was sitting among his people and he replied to Abraham in the hearing of all the Hittites who had come to the gate of his city. {11} "No, my lord," he said. "Listen to me; I give you the field, and I give you the cave that is in it. I give it to you in the presence of my people. Bury your dead." {12} Again Abraham bowed down before the people of the land {13} and he said to Ephron in their hearing, "Listen to me, if you will. I will pay the price of the field. Accept it from me so I can bury my dead there." {14} Ephron answered Abraham, {15} "Listen to me, my lord; the land is worth four hundred shekels of silver, but what is that between me and you? Bury your dead." {16} Abraham agreed to Ephron's terms and weighed out for him the price he had named in the hearing of the Hittites: four hundred shekels of silver, according to the weight current among the merchants. {17} So Ephron's field in Machpelah near Mamre–both the field and the cave in it, and all the trees within the borders of the field–was deeded {18} to Abraham as his property in the presence of all the Hittites who had come to the gate of the city.

{19} Afterward Abraham buried his wife Sarah in the cave in the field of Machpelah near Mamre (which is at Hebron) in the land of Canaan. {20} So the field and the cave in it were deeded to Abraham by the Hittites as a burial site.

REBEKAH WATERS THE CAMELS

Gen 24:10-26

Then the servant took ten of his master's camels and left, taking with him all kinds of good things from his master. He set out for Aram Naharaim and made his way to the town of Nahor. {11} He had the camels kneel down near the well outside the town; it was toward evening, the time the women go out to draw water. {12} Then he prayed, "O LORD, God of my master Abraham, give me success today, and show kindness to my master Abraham. {13} See, I am standing beside this spring, and the daughters of the townspeople are coming out to draw water. {14} May it be that when I say to a girl, 'Please let down your jar that I may have a drink,' and she says, 'Drink, and I'll water your camels too'–let her be the one you have chosen for your servant Isaac. By this I will know that you have shown kindness to my master." {15} Before he had finished praying, Rebekah came out with her jar on her shoulder. She was the daughter of Bethuel son of Milcah, who was the wife of Abraham's brother Nahor. {16} The girl was very beautiful, a virgin; no man had ever lain with her. She went down to the spring, filled her jar and came up again. {17} The servant hurried to meet her and said, "Please give me a little water from your jar." {18} "Drink, my lord," she said, and quickly lowered the jar to her hands and gave him a drink. {19} After she had given him a drink, she said, "I'll draw water for your camels too, until they have finished drinking." {20} So she quickly emptied her jar into the trough, ran back to the well to draw more water, and drew enough for all his camels. {21} Without saying a word, the man watched her closely to learn whether or 2not the LORD had made his journey successful. {22} When the camels had finished drinking, the man took out a gold nose ring weighing a beka and two gold bracelets weighing ten shekels. {23} Then he asked, "Whose daughter are you? Please tell me, is there room in your father's house for us to spend the night?" {24} She answered him, "I am the daughter of Bethuel, the son that Milcah bore to Nahor." {25} And she added, "We have plenty of straw and fodder, as well as room for you to spend the night." {26} Then the man bowed down and worshiped the LORD....

ISAAC MARRIES REBEKAH

Gen 24:50-67

Laban and Bethuel answered, "This is from the LORD; we can say nothing to you one way or the other. {51} Here is Rebekah; take her and go, and let her become the wife of your master's son, as the LORD has directed." {52} When Abraham's servant heard what they said, he bowed down to the ground before the LORD. {53} Then the servant brought out gold and silver jewelry and articles of clothing and gave them to Rebekah; he also gave costly gifts to her brother and to her mother. {54} Then he and the men who were with him ate and drank and spent the night there. When they got up the next morning, he said, "Send me on my way to my master." {55} But her brother and her mother replied, "Let the girl remain with us ten days or so; then you may go." {56} But he said to them, "Do not detain me, now that the LORD has granted success to my journey. Send me on my way so I may go to my master." {57} Then they said, "Let's call the girl and ask her about it."

{58} So they called Rebekah and asked her, "Will you go with this man?" "I will go," she said. {59} So they sent their sister Rebekah on her way, along with her nurse and Abraham's servant and his men. {60} And they blessed Rebekah and said to her, "Our sister, may you increase to thousands upon thousands; may your offspring possess the gates of their enemies." {61} Then Rebekah and her maids got ready and mounted their camels and went back with the man. So the servant took Rebekah and left.

{62} Now Isaac had come from Beer Lahai Roi, for he was living in the Negev. {63} He went out to the field one evening to meditate, and as he looked up, he saw camels approaching. {64} Rebekah also looked up and saw Isaac. She got down from her camel {65} and asked the servant, "Who is that man in the field coming to meet us?" "He is my master," the servant answered. So she took her veil and covered herself. {66} Then the servant told Isaac all he had done. {67} Isaac brought her into the tent of his mother Sarah, and he married Rebekah. So she became his wife, and he loved her; and Isaac was comforted after his mother's death.

ABRAHAM DIES AND IS BURIED
BY ISAAC AND ISHMAEL

Gen 25:1-18a

Abraham took another wife, whose name was Keturah. {2} She bore him Zimran, Jokshan, Medan, Midian, Ishbak and Shuah. {3} Jokshan was the father of Sheba and Dedan; the descendants of Dedan were the Asshurites, the Letushites and the Leummites. {4} The sons of Midian were Ephah, Epher, Hanoch, Abida and Eldaah. All these were descendants of Keturah. {5} Abraham left everything he owned to Isaac. {6} But while he was still living, he gave gifts to the sons of his concubines and sent them away from his son Isaac to the land of the east.

{7} Altogether, Abraham lived a hundred and seventy-five years. {8} Then Abraham breathed his last and died at a good old age, an old man and full of years; and he was gathered to his people. {9} His sons Isaac and Ishmael buried him in the cave of Machpelah near Mamre, in the field of Ephron son of Zohar the Hittite, {10} the field Abraham had bought from the Hittites. There Abraham was buried with his wife Sarah.

{11} After Abraham's death, God blessed his son Isaac, who then lived near Beer Lahai Roi. {12} This is the account of Abraham's son Ishmael, whom Sarah's maidservant, Hagar the Egyptian, bore to Abraham. {13} These are the names of the sons of Ishmael, listed in the order of their birth: Nebaioth the firstborn of Ishmael, Kedar, Adbeel, Mibsam, {14} Mishma, Dumah, Massa, {15} Hadad, Tema, Jetur, Naphish and Kedemah. {16} These were the sons of Ishmael, and these are the names of the twelve tribal rulers according to their settlements and camps. {17} Altogether, Ishmael lived a hundred and thirty-seven years. He breathed his last and died, and he was gathered to his people. {18} His descendants settled in the area from Havilah to Shur, near the border of Egypt, as you go toward Asshur.

18

JACOB AND ESAU

Gen 25:19-34

This is the account of Abraham's son Isaac. Abraham became the father of Isaac, {20} and Isaac was forty years old when he married Rebekah daughter of Bethuel the Aramean from Paddan Aram and sister of Laban the Aramean. {21} Isaac prayed to the LORD on behalf of his wife, because she was barren. The LORD answered his prayer, and his wife Rebekah became pregnant. {22} The babies jostled each other within her, and she said, "Why is this happening to me?" So she went to inquire of the LORD. {23} The LORD said to her, "Two nations are in your womb, and two peoples from within you will be separated; one people will be stronger than the other, and the older will serve the younger." {24} When the time came for her to give birth, there were twin boys in her womb. {25} The first to come out was red, and his whole body was like a hairy garment; so they named him Esau. {26} After this, his brother came out, with his hand grasping Esau's heel; so he was named Jacob. Isaac was sixty years old when Rebekah gave birth to them.

{27} The boys grew up, and Esau became a skillful hunter, a man of the open country, while Jacob was a quiet man, staying among the tents. {28} Isaac, who had a taste for wild game, loved Esau, but Rebekah loved Jacob.

{29} Once when Jacob was cooking some stew, Esau came in from the open country, famished. {30} He said to Jacob, "Quick, let me have some of that red stew! I'm famished!" (That is why he was also called Edom.) {31} Jacob replied, "First sell me your birthright." {32} "Look, I am about to die," Esau said. "What good is the birthright to me?" {33} But Jacob said, "Swear to me first." So he swore an oath to him, selling his birthright to Jacob. {34} Then Jacob gave Esau some bread and some lentil stew. He ate and drank, and then got up and left. So Esau despised his birthright.

Gen 26:34-35

When Esau was forty years old, he married Judith daughter of Beeri the Hittite, and also Basemath daughter of Elon the Hittite. {35} They were a source of grief to Isaac and Rebekah.

DECEPTION BY REBEKAH AND JACOB

Gen 27:1-24

When Isaac was old and his eyes were so weak that he could no longer see, he called for Esau his older son and said to him, "My son." "Here I am," he answered. {2} Isaac said, "I am now an old man and don't know the day of my death. {3} Now then, get your weapons–your quiver and bow–and go out to the open country to hunt some wild game for me. {4} Prepare me the kind of tasty food I like and bring it to me to eat, so that I may give you my blessing before I die." {5} Now Rebekah was listening as Isaac spoke to his son Esau. When Esau left for the open country to hunt game and bring it back, {6} Rebekah said to her son Jacob, "Look, I overheard your father say to your brother Esau, {7} 'Bring me some game and prepare me some tasty food to eat, so that I may give you my blessing in the presence of the LORD before I die.' {8} Now, my son, listen carefully and do what I tell you: {9} Go out to the flock and bring me two choice young goats, so I can prepare some tasty food for your father, just the way he likes it. {10} Then take it to your father to eat, so that he may give you his blessing before he dies." {11} Jacob said to Rebekah his mother, "But my brother Esau is a hairy man, and I'm a man with smooth skin. {12} What if my father touches me? I would appear to be tricking him and would bring down a curse on myself rather than a blessing." {13} His mother said to him, "My son, let the curse fall on me. Just do what I say; go and get them for me." {14} So he went and got them and brought them to his mother, and she prepared some tasty food, just the way his father liked it. {15} Then Rebekah took the best clothes of Esau her older son, which she had in the house, and put them on her younger son Jacob. {16} She also covered his hands and the smooth part of his neck with the goatskins. {17} Then she handed to her son Jacob the tasty food and the bread she had made. {18} He went to his father and said, "My father." "Yes, my son," he answered. "Who is it?" {19} Jacob said to his father, "I am Esau your firstborn. I have done as you told me. Please sit up and eat some of my game so that you may give me your blessing." {20} Isaac asked his son, "How did you find it so quickly, my son?" "The LORD your God gave me success," he replied. {21} Then Isaac said to Jacob, "Come near so I can touch you, my son, to know whether you really are my son Esau or not." {22} Jacob went close to his father Isaac, who touched him and said, "The voice is the voice of Jacob, but the hands are the hands of Esau." {23} He did not recognize him, for his hands were hairy like those of his brother Esau; so he blessed him. {24} "Are you really my son Esau?" he asked. "I am," he replied.

ISAAC BLESSES JACOB

Gen 27:25-40

Then he said, "My son, bring me some of your game to eat, so that I may give you my blessing." Jacob brought it to him and he ate; and he brought some wine and he drank. {26} Then his father Isaac said to him, "Come here, my son, and kiss me." {27} So he went to him and kissed him. When Isaac caught the smell of his clothes, he blessed him and said, "Ah, the smell of my son is like the smell of a field that the LORD has blessed. {28} May God give you of heaven's dew and of earth's richness– an abundance of grain and new wine. {29} May nations serve you and peoples bow down to you. Be lord over your brothers, and may the sons of your mother bow down to you. May those who curse you be cursed and those who bless you be blessed."

{30} After Isaac finished blessing him and Jacob had scarcely left his father's presence, his brother Esau came in from hunting. {31} He too prepared some tasty food and brought it to his father. Then he said to him, "My father, sit up and eat some of my game, so that you may give me your blessing." {32} His father Isaac asked him, "Who are you?" "I am your son," he answered, "your firstborn, Esau." {33} Isaac trembled violently and said, "Who was it, then, that hunted game and brought it to me? I ate it just before you came and I blessed him–and indeed he will be blessed!" {34} When Esau heard his father's words, he burst out with a loud and bitter cry and said to his father, "Bless me–me too, my father!" {35} But he said, "Your brother came deceitfully and took your blessing." {36} Esau said, "Isn't he rightly named Jacob ? He has deceived me these two times: He took my birthright, and now he's taken my blessing!" Then he asked, "Haven't you reserved any blessing for me?" {37} Isaac answered Esau, "I have made him lord over you and have made all his relatives his servants, and I have sustained him with grain and new wine. So what can I possibly do for you, my son?" {38} Esau said to his father, "Do you have only one blessing, my father? Bless me too, my father!" Then Esau wept aloud. {39} His father Isaac answered him, "Your dwelling will be away from the earth's richness, away from the dew of heaven above. {40} You will live by the sword and you will serve your brother. But when you grow restless, you will throw his yoke from off your neck."

JACOB LEAVES HOME

Gen 27:41-28:9

Esau held a grudge against Jacob because of the blessing his father had given him. He said to himself, "The days of mourning for my father are near; then I will kill my brother Jacob." {42} When Rebekah was told what her older son Esau had said, she sent for her younger son Jacob and said to him, "Your brother Esau is consoling himself with the thought of killing you. {43} Now then, my son, do what I say: Flee at once to my brother Laban in Haran. {44} Stay with him for a while until your brother's fury subsides. {45} When your brother is no longer angry with you and forgets what you did to him, I'll send word for you to come back from there. Why should I lose both of you in one day?"

{46} Then Rebekah said to Isaac, "I'm disgusted with living because of these Hittite women. If Jacob takes a wife from among the women of this land, from Hittite women like these, my life will not be worth living." {28:1} So Isaac called for Jacob and blessed him and commanded him: "Do not marry a Canaanite woman. {2} Go at once to Paddan Aram, to the house of your mother's father Bethuel. Take a wife for yourself there, from among the daughters of Laban, your mother's brother. {3} May God Almighty bless you and make you fruitful and increase your numbers until you become a community of peoples. {4} May he give you and your descendants the blessing given to Abraham, so that you may take possession of the land where you now live as an alien, the land God gave to Abraham." {5} Then Isaac sent Jacob on his way, and he went to Paddan Aram, to Laban son of Bethuel the Aramean, the brother of Rebekah, who was the mother of Jacob and Esau. {6} Now Esau learned that Isaac had blessed Jacob and had sent him to Paddan Aram to take a wife from there, and that when he blessed him he commanded him, "Do not marry a Canaanite woman," {7} and that Jacob had obeyed his father and mother and had gone to Paddan Aram.

{8} Esau then realized how displeasing the Canaanite women were to his father Isaac; {9} so he went to Ishmael and married Mahalath, the sister of Nebaioth and daughter of Ishmael son of Abraham, in addition to the wives he already had.

JACOB HAS A DREAM

Gen 28:10-29:6

Jacob left Beersheba and set out for Haran. {11} When he reached a certain place, he stopped for the night because the sun had set. Taking one of the stones there, he put it under his head and lay down to sleep. {12} He had a dream in which he saw a stairway resting on the earth, with its top reaching to heaven, and the angels of God were ascending and descending on it. {13} There above it stood the LORD, and he said: "I am the LORD, the God of your father Abraham and the God of Isaac. I will give you and your descendants the land on which you are lying. {14} Your descendants will be like the dust of the earth, and you will spread out to the west and to the east, to the north and to the south. All peoples on earth will be blessed through you and your offspring. {15} I am with you and will watch over you wherever you go, and I will bring you back to this land. I will not leave you until I have done what I have promised you." {16} When Jacob awoke from his sleep, he thought, "Surely the LORD is in this place, and I was not aware of it." {17} He was afraid and said, "How awesome is this place! This is none other than the house of God; this is the gate of heaven."

{18} Early the next morning Jacob took the stone he had placed under his head and set it up as a pillar and poured oil on top of it. {19} He called that place Bethel, though the city used to be called Luz. {20} Then Jacob made a vow, saying, "If God will be with me and will watch over me on this journey I am taking and will give me food to eat and clothes to wear {21} so that I return safely to my father's house, then the LORD will be my God {22} and this stone that I have set up as a pillar will be God's house, and of all that you give me I will give you a tenth."

{29:1} Then Jacob continued on his journey and came to the land of the eastern peoples. {2} There he saw a well in the field, with three flocks of sheep lying near it because the flocks were watered from that well. The stone over the mouth of the well was large. {3} When all the flocks were gathered there, the shepherds would roll the stone away from the well's mouth and water the sheep. Then they would return the stone to its place over the mouth of the well. {4} Jacob asked the shepherds, "My brothers, where are you from?" "We're from Haran," they replied. {5} He said to them, "Do you know Laban, Nahor's grandson?" "Yes, we know him," they answered. {6} Then Jacob asked them, "Is he well?" "Yes, he is," they said, "and here comes his daughter Rachel with the sheep."

JACOB MARRIES LEAH AND RACHEL

Gen 29:13-28

As soon as Laban heard the news about Jacob, his sister's son, he hurried to meet him. He embraced him and kissed him and brought him to his home, and there Jacob told him all these things. {14} Then Laban said to him, "You are my own flesh and blood." After Jacob had stayed with him for a whole month, {15} Laban said to him, "Just because you are a relative of mine, should you work for me for nothing? Tell me what your wages should be.

{16} Now Laban had two daughters; the name of the older was Leah, and the name of the younger was Rachel. {17} Leah had weak eyes, but Rachel was lovely in form, and beautiful. {18} Jacob was in love with Rachel and said, "I'll work for you seven years in return for your younger daughter Rachel." {19} Laban said, "It's better that I give her to you than to some other man. Stay here with me." {20} So Jacob served seven years to get Rachel, but they seemed like only a few days to him because of his love for her. {21} Then Jacob said to Laban, "Give me my wife. My time is completed, and I want to lie with her." {22} So Laban brought together all the people of the place and gave a feast. {23} But when evening came, he took his daughter Leah and gave her to Jacob, and Jacob lay with her. {24} And Laban gave his servant girl Zilpah to his daughter as her maidservant. {25} When morning came, there was Leah!

So Jacob said to Laban, "What is this you have done to me? I served you for Rachel, didn't I? Why have you deceived me?" {26} Laban replied, "It is not our custom here to give the younger daughter in marriage before the older one. {27} Finish this daughter's bridal week; then we will give you the younger one also, in return for another seven years of work." {28} And Jacob did so. He finished the week with Leah, and then Laban gave him his daughter Rachel to be his wife.

JACOB LEAVES FOR CANAAN

Gen 31:17-36

Then Jacob put his children and his wives on camels, {18} and he drove all his livestock ahead of him, along with all the goods he had accumulated in Paddan Aram, to go to his father Isaac in the land of Canaan. {19} When Laban had gone to shear his sheep, Rachel stole her father's household gods. {20} Moreover, Jacob deceived Laban the Aramean by not telling him he was running away. {21} So he fled with all he had, and crossing the River, he headed for the hill country of Gilead. {22} On the third day Laban was told that Jacob had fled. {23} Taking his relatives with him, he pursued Jacob for seven days and caught up with him in the hill country of Gilead. {24} Then God came to Laban the Aramean in a dream at night and said to him, "Be careful not to say anything to Jacob, either good or bad."

{25} Jacob had pitched his tent in the hill country of Gilead when Laban overtook him, and Laban and his relatives camped there too. {26} Then Laban said to Jacob, "What have you done? You've deceived me, and you've carried off my daughters like captives in war. {27} Why did you run off secretly and deceive me? Why didn't you tell me, so I could send you away with joy and singing to the music of tambourines and harps? {28} You didn't even let me kiss my grandchildren and my daughters good-by. You have done a foolish thing. {29} I have the power to harm you; but last night the God of your father said to me, 'Be careful not to say anything to Jacob, either good or bad.' {30} Now you have gone off because you longed to return to your father's house. But why did you steal my gods?" {31} Jacob answered Laban, "I was afraid, because I thought you would take your daughters away from me by force. {32} But if you find anyone who has your gods, he shall not live. In the presence of our relatives, see for yourself whether there is anything of yours here with me; and if so, take it." Now Jacob did not know that Rachel had stolen the gods. {33} So Laban went into Jacob's tent and into Leah's tent and into the tent of the two maidservants, but he found nothing. After he came out of Leah's tent, he entered Rachel's tent. {34} Now Rachel had taken the household gods and put them inside her camel's saddle and was sitting on them. Laban searched through everything in the tent but found nothing. {35} Rachel said to her father, "Don't be angry, my lord, that I cannot stand up in your presence; I'm having my period." So he searched but could not find the household gods. {36} Jacob was angry and took Laban to task. "What is my crime?" he asked Laban. "What sin have I committed that you hunt me down?

LABAN AND JACOB SEPARATE IN PEACE

Gen 31:38-55

"I have been with you for twenty years now. Your sheep and goats have not miscarried, nor have I eaten rams from your flocks. {39} I did not bring you animals torn by wild beasts; I bore the loss myself. And you demanded payment from me for whatever was stolen by day or night. {40} This was my situation: The heat consumed me in the daytime and the cold at night, and sleep fled from my eyes. {41} It was like this for the twenty years I was in your household. I worked for you fourteen years for your two daughters and six years for your flocks, and you changed my wages ten times. {42} If the God of my father, the God of Abraham and the Fear of Isaac, had not been with me, you would surely have sent me away empty-handed. But God has seen my hardship and the toil of my hands, and last night he rebuked you."

{43} Laban answered Jacob, "The women are my daughters, the children are my children, and the flocks are my flocks. All you see is mine. Yet what can I do today about these daughters of mine, or about the children they have borne? {44} Come now, let's make a covenant, you and I, and let it serve as a witness between us." {45} So Jacob took a stone and set it up as a pillar. {46} He said to his relatives, "Gather some stones." So they took stones and piled them in a heap, and they ate there by the heap. {47} Laban called it Jegar Sahadutha, and Jacob called it Galeed. {48} Laban said, "This heap is a witness between you and me today." That is why it was called Galeed. {49} It was also called Mizpah, because he said, "May the LORD keep watch between you and me when we are away from each other. {50} If you mistreat my daughters or if you take any wives besides my daughters, even though no one is with us, remember that God is a witness between you and me." {51} Laban also said to Jacob, "Here is this heap, and here is this pillar I have set up between you and me. {52} This heap is a witness, and this pillar is a witness, that I will not go past this heap to your side to harm you and that you will not go past this heap and pillar to my side to harm me. {53} May the God of Abraham and the God of Nahor, the God of their father, judge between us." So Jacob took an oath in the name of the Fear of his father Isaac. {54} He offered a sacrifice there in the hill country and invited his relatives to a meal.

After they had eaten, they spent the night there. {55} Early the next morning Laban kissed his grandchildren and his daughters and blessed them. Then he left and returned home.

JACOB'S NAME CHANGED TO ISRAEL

Gen 32:8-28

He thought, "If Esau comes and attacks one group, the group that is left may escape." {9} Then Jacob prayed, "O God of my father Abraham, God of my father Isaac, O LORD, who said to me, 'Go back to your country and your relatives, and I will make you prosper,' {10} I am unworthy of all the kindness and faithfulness you have shown your servant. I had only my staff when I crossed this Jordan, but now I have become two groups. {11} Save me, I pray, from the hand of my brother Esau, for I am afraid he will come and attack me, and also the mothers with their children. {12} But you have said, 'I will surely make you prosper and will make your descendants like the sand of the sea, which cannot be counted.'"

{13} He spent the night there, and from what he had with him he selected a gift for his brother Esau: {14} two hundred female goats and twenty male goats, two hundred ewes and twenty rams, {15} thirty female camels with their young, forty cows and ten bulls, and twenty female donkeys and ten male donkeys. {16} He put them in the care of his servants, each herd by itself, and said to his servants, "Go ahead of me, and keep some space between the herds." {17} He instructed the one in the lead: "When my brother Esau meets you and asks, 'To whom do you belong, and where are you going, and who owns all these animals in front of you?' {18} then you are to say, 'They belong to your servant Jacob. They are a gift sent to my lord Esau, and he is coming behind us.'" {19} He also instructed the second, the third and all the others who followed the herds: "You are to say the same thing to Esau when you meet him. {20} And be sure to say, 'Your servant Jacob is coming behind us.'" For he thought, "I will pacify him with these gifts I am sending on ahead; later, when I see him, perhaps he will receive me." {21} So Jacob's gifts went on ahead of him, but he himself spent the night in the camp.

{22} That night Jacob got up and took his two wives, his two maidservants and his eleven sons and crossed the ford of the Jabbok. {23} After he had sent them across the stream, he sent over all his possessions. {24} So Jacob was left alone, and a man wrestled with him till daybreak. {25} When the man saw that he could not overpower him, he touched the socket of Jacob's hip so that his hip was wrenched as he wrestled with the man. {26} Then the man said, "Let me go, for it is daybreak." But Jacob replied, "I will not let you go unless you bless me." {27} The man asked him, "What is your name?" "Jacob," he answered. {28} Then the man said, "Your name will no longer be Jacob, but Israel, because you have struggled with God and with men and have overcome."

JACOB AND ESAU MEET IN PEACE

Gen 33:1-18

Jacob looked up and there was Esau, coming with his four hundred men; so he divided the children among Leah, Rachel and the two maidservants. {2} He put the maidservants and their children in front, Leah and her children next, and Rachel and Joseph in the rear. {3} He himself went on ahead and bowed down to the ground seven times as he approached his brother. {4} But Esau ran to meet Jacob and embraced him; he threw his arms around his neck and kissed him. And they wept. {5} Then Esau looked up and saw the women and children. "Who are these with you?" he asked. Jacob answered, "They are the children God has graciously given your servant." {6} Then the maidservants and their children approached and bowed down. {7} Next, Leah and her children came and bowed down. Last of all came Joseph and Rachel, and they too bowed down. {8} Esau asked, "What do you mean by all these droves I met?" "To find favor in your eyes, my lord," he said.

{9} But Esau said, "I already have plenty, my brother. Keep what you have for yourself." {10} "No, please!" said Jacob. "If I have found favor in your eyes, accept this gift from me. For to see your face is like seeing the face of God, now that you have received me favorably. {11} Please accept the present that was brought to you, for God has been gracious to me and I have all I need." And because Jacob insisted, Esau accepted it. {12} Then Esau said, "Let us be on our way; I'll accompany you." {13} But Jacob said to him, "My lord knows that the children are tender and that I must care for the ewes and cows that are nursing their young. If they are driven hard just one day, all the animals will die. {14} So let my lord go on ahead of his servant, while I move along slowly at the pace of the droves before me and that of the children, until I come to my lord in Seir." {15} Esau said, "Then let me leave some of my men with you." "But why do that?" Jacob asked. "Just let me find favor in the eyes of my lord." {16} So that day Esau started on his way back to Seir.

{17} Jacob, however, went to Succoth, where he built a place for himself and made shelters for his livestock. That is why the place is called Succoth. {18} After Jacob came from Paddan Aram, he arrived safely at the city of Shechem in Canaan and camped within sight of the city.

28

RACHEL DIES

Gen 35:9-20

After Jacob returned from Paddan Aram, God appeared to him again and blessed him. {10} God said to him, "Your name is Jacob, but you will no longer be called Jacob; your name will be Israel." So he named him Israel. {11} And God said to him, "I am God Almighty; be fruitful and increase in number. A nation and a community of nations will come from you, and kings will come from your body. {12} The land I gave to Abraham and Isaac I also give to you, and I will give this land to your descendants after you." {13} Then God went up from him at the place where he had talked with him. {14} Jacob set up a stone pillar at the place where God had talked with him, and he poured out a drink offering on it; he also poured oil on it. {15} Jacob called the place where God had talked with him Bethel. {16} Then they moved on from Bethel.

While they were still some distance from Ephrath, Rachel began to give birth and had great difficulty. {17} And as she was having great difficulty in childbirth, the midwife said to her, "Don't be afraid, for you have another son." {18} As she breathed her last—for she was dying—she named her son Ben-Oni. But his father named him Benjamin. {19} So Rachel died and was buried on the way to Ephrath (that is, Bethlehem). {20} Over her tomb Jacob set up a pillar, and to this day that pillar marks Rachel's tomb.

ISAAC DIES AND IS BURIED BY ESAU AND JACOB

Gen 35:22c-29

Jacob had twelve sons: {23} The sons of Leah: Reuben the firstborn of Jacob, Simeon, Levi, Judah, Issachar and Zebulun. {24} The sons of Rachel: Joseph and Benjamin. {25} The sons of Rachel's maidservant Bilhah: Dan and Naphtali. {26} The sons of Leah's maidservant Zilpah: Gad and Asher. These were the sons of Jacob, who were born to him in Paddan Aram. {27} Jacob came home to his father Isaac in Mamre, near Kiriath Arba (that is, Hebron), where Abraham and Isaac had stayed. {28} Isaac lived a hundred and eighty years. {29} Then he breathed his last and died and was gathered to his people, old and full of years. And his sons Esau and Jacob buried him.

ESAU'S DESCENDANTS

Gen 36:2-14

Esau took his wives from the women of Canaan: Adah daughter of Elon the Hittite, and Oholibamah daughter of Anah and granddaughter of Zibeon the Hivite– {3} also Basemath daughter of Ishmael and sister of Nebaioth. {4} Adah bore Eliphaz to Esau, Basemath bore Reuel, {5} and Oholibamah bore Jeush, Jalam and Korah. These were the sons of Esau, who were born to him in Canaan. {6} Esau took his wives and sons and daughters and all the members of his household, as well as his livestock and all his other animals and all the goods he had acquired in Canaan, and moved to a land some distance from his brother Jacob. {7} Their possessions were too great for them to remain together; the land where they were staying could not support them both because of their livestock. {8} So Esau (that is, Edom) settled in the hill country of Seir.

{9} This is the account of Esau the father of the Edomites in the hill country of Seir. {10} These are the names of Esau's sons: Eliphaz, the son of Esau's wife Adah, and Reuel, the son of Esau's wife Basemath. {11} The sons of Eliphaz: Teman, Omar, Zepho, Gatam and Kenaz. {12} Esau's son Eliphaz also had a concubine named Timna, who bore him Amalek. These were grandsons of Esau's wife Adah. {13} The sons of Reuel: Nahath, Zerah, Shammah and Mizzah. These were grandsons of Esau's wife Basemath. {14} The sons of Esau's wife Oholibamah daughter of Anah and granddaughter of Zibeon, whom she bore to Esau: Jeush, Jalam and Korah.

Gen 36:40-43

These were the chiefs descended from Esau, by name, according to their clans and regions: Timna, Alvah, Jetheth, {41} Oholibamah, Elah, Pinon, {42} Kenaz, Teman, Mibzar, {43} Magdiel and Iram. These were the chiefs of Edom, according to their settlements in the land they occupied. This was Esau the father of the Edomites.

YOUNG JOSEPH HAS DREAMS

Gen 37:2b-18

Joseph, a young man of seventeen, was tending the flocks with his brothers, the sons of Bilhah and the sons of Zilpah, his father's wives, and he brought their father a bad report about them. {3} Now Israel loved Joseph more than any of his other sons, because he had been born to him in his old age; and he made a richly ornamented robe for him. {4} When his brothers saw that their father loved him more than any of them, they hated him and could not speak a kind word to him.

{5} Joseph had a dream, and when he told it to his brothers, they hated him all the more. {6} He said to them, "Listen to this dream I had: {7} We were binding sheaves of grain out in the field when suddenly my sheaf rose and stood upright, while your sheaves gathered around mine and bowed down to it." {8} His brothers said to him, "Do you intend to reign over us? Will you actually rule us?" And they hated him all the more because of his dream and what he had said.

{9} Then he had another dream, and he told it to his brothers. "Listen," he said, "I had another dream, and this time the sun and moon and eleven stars were bowing down to me." {10} When he told his father as well as his brothers, his father rebuked him and said, "What is this dream you had? Will your mother and I and your brothers actually come and bow down to the ground before you?" {11} His brothers were jealous of him, but his father kept the matter in mind. {12} Now his brothers had gone to graze their father's flocks near Shechem,

{13} and Israel said to Joseph, "As you know, your brothers are grazing the flocks near Shechem. Come, I am going to send you to them." "Very well," he replied. {14} So he said to him, "Go and see if all is well with your brothers and with the flocks, and bring word back to me." Then he sent him off from the Valley of Hebron. When Joseph arrived at Shechem, {15} a man found him wandering around in the fields and asked him, "What are you looking for?" {16} He replied, "I'm looking for my brothers. Can you tell me where they are grazing their flocks?" {17} "They have moved on from here," the man answered. "I heard them say, 'Let's go to Dothan.'" So Joseph went after his brothers and found them near Dothan. {18} But they saw him in the distance, and before he reached them, they plotted to kill him.

JOSEPH IS SOLD TO TRADERS

Gen 37:19-36

"Here comes that dreamer!" they said to each other. {20} "Come now, let's kill him and throw him into one of these cisterns and say that a ferocious animal devoured him. Then we'll see what comes of his dreams." {21} When Reuben heard this, he tried to rescue him from their hands. "Let's not take his life," he said. {22} "Don't shed any blood. Throw him into this cistern here in the desert, but don't lay a hand on him." Reuben said this to rescue him from them and take him back to his father.

{23} So when Joseph came to his brothers, they stripped him of his robe–the richly ornamented robe he was wearing– {24} and they took him and threw him into the cistern. Now the cistern was empty; there was no water in it. {25} As they sat down to eat their meal, they looked up and saw a caravan of Ishmaelites coming from Gilead. Their camels were loaded with spices, balm and myrrh, and they were on their way to take them down to Egypt. {26} Judah said to his brothers, "What will we gain if we kill our brother and cover up his blood? {27} Come, let's sell him to the Ishmaelites and not lay our hands on him; after all, he is our brother, our own flesh and blood." His brothers agreed.

{28} So when the Midianite merchants came by, his brothers pulled Joseph up out of the cistern and sold him for twenty shekels of silver to the Ishmaelites, who took him to Egypt. {29} When Reuben returned to the cistern and saw that Joseph was not there, he tore his clothes. {30} He went back to his brothers and said, "The boy isn't there! Where can I turn now?" {31} Then they got Joseph's robe, slaughtered a goat and dipped the robe in the blood. {32} They took the ornamented robe back to their father and said, "We found this. Examine it to see whether it is your son's robe." {33} He recognized it and said, "It is my son's robe! Some ferocious animal has devoured him. Joseph has surely been torn to pieces." {34} Then Jacob tore his clothes, put on sackcloth and mourned for his son many days. {35} All his sons and daughters came to comfort him, but he refused to be comforted. "No," he said, "in mourning will I go down to the grave to my son." So his father wept for him. {36} Meanwhile, the Midianites sold Joseph in Egypt to Potiphar, one of Pharaoh's officials, the captain of the guard.

JOSEPH IS BOUGHT BY POTIPHAR

Gen 39:1-21

Potiphar, an Egyptian who was one of Pharaoh's officials, the captain of the guard, bought him from the Ishmaelites who had taken him there. {2} The LORD was with Joseph and he prospered, and he lived in the house of his Egyptian master. {3} When his master saw that the LORD was with him and that the LORD gave him success in everything he did, {4} Joseph found favor in his eyes and became his attendant. Potiphar put him in charge of his household, and he entrusted to his care everything he owned. {5} From the time he put him in charge of his household and of all that he owned, the LORD blessed the household of the Egyptian because of Joseph. The blessing of the LORD was on everything Potiphar had, both in the house and in the field. {6} So he left in Joseph's care everything he had; with Joseph in charge, he did not concern himself with anything except the food he ate. Now Joseph was well-built and handsome, {7} and after a while his master's wife took notice of Joseph and said, "Come to bed with me!" {8} But he refused. "With me in charge," he told her, "my master does not concern himself with anything in the house; everything he owns he has entrusted to my care. {9} No one is greater in this house than I am. My master has withheld nothing from me except you, because you are his wife. How then could I do such a wicked thing and sin against God?" {10} And though she spoke to Joseph day after day, he refused to go to bed with her or even be with her. {11} One day he went into the house to attend to his duties, and none of the household servants was inside. {12} She caught him by his cloak and said, "Come to bed with me!" But he left his cloak in her hand and ran out of the house. {13} When she saw that he had left his cloak in her hand and had run out of the house, {14} she called her household servants. "Look," she said to them, "this Hebrew has been brought to us to make sport of us! He came in here to sleep with me, but I screamed. {15} When he heard me scream for help, he left his cloak beside me and ran out of the house." {16} She kept his cloak beside her until his master came home. {17} Then she told him this story: "That Hebrew slave you brought us came to me to make sport of me. {18} But as soon as I screamed for help, he left his cloak beside me and ran out of the house." {19} When his master heard the story his wife told him, saying, "This is how your slave treated me," he burned with anger. {20} Joseph's master took him and put him in prison, the place where the king's prisoners were confined. But while Joseph was there in the prison, {21} the LORD was with him; he showed him kindness and granted him favor in the eyes of the prison warden.

JOSEPH IN PRISON

Gen 40:1-22a

Some time later, the cupbearer and the baker of the king of Egypt offended their master, the king of Egypt. {2} Pharaoh was angry with his two officials, the chief cupbearer and the chief baker, {3} and put them in custody in the house of the captain of the guard, in the same prison where Joseph was confined. {4} The captain of the guard assigned them to Joseph, and he attended them. After they had been in custody for some time, {5} each of the two men–the cupbearer and the baker of the king of Egypt, who were being held in prison–had a dream the same night, and each dream had a meaning of its own. {6} When Joseph came to them the next morning, he saw that they were dejected. {7} So he asked Pharaoh's officials who were in custody with him in his master's house, "Why are your faces so sad today?" {8} "We both had dreams," they answered, "but there is no one to interpret them." Then Joseph said to them, "Do not interpretations belong to God? Tell me your dreams." {9} So the chief cupbearer told Joseph his dream. He said to him, "In my dream I saw a vine in front of me, {10} and on the vine were three branches. As soon as it budded, it blossomed, and its clusters ripened into grapes. {11} Pharaoh's cup was in my hand, and I took the grapes, squeezed them into Pharaoh's cup and put the cup in his hand." {12} "This is what it means," Joseph said to him. "The three branches are three days. {13} Within three days Pharaoh will lift up your head and restore you to your position, and you will put Pharaoh's cup in his hand, just as you used to do when you were his cupbearer. {14} But when all goes well with you, remember me and show me kindness; mention me to Pharaoh and get me out of this prison. {15} For I was forcibly carried off from the land of the Hebrews, and even here I have done nothing to deserve being put in a dungeon." {16} When the chief baker saw that Joseph had given a favorable interpretation, he said to Joseph, "I too had a dream: On my head were three baskets of bread. {17} In the top basket were all kinds of baked goods for Pharaoh, but the birds were eating them out of the basket on my head." {18} "This is what it means," Joseph said. "The three baskets are three days. {19} Within three days Pharaoh will lift off your head and hang you on a tree. And the birds will eat away your flesh." {20} Now the third day was Pharaoh's birthday, and he gave a feast for all his officials. He lifted up the heads of the chief cupbearer and the chief baker in the presence of his officials: {21} He restored the chief cupbearer to his position, so that he once again put the cup into Pharaoh's hand, {22} but he hanged the chief baker....

PHARAOH HAS A DREAM

Gen 41:1-24

Pharaoh had a dream: He was standing by the Nile, {2} when out of the river there came up seven cows, sleek and fat, and they grazed among the reeds. {3} After them, seven other cows, ugly and gaunt, came up out of the Nile and stood beside those on the riverbank. {4} And the cows that were ugly and gaunt ate up the seven sleek, fat cows. Then Pharaoh woke up. {5} He fell asleep again and had a second dream: Seven heads of grain, healthy and good, were growing on a single stalk. {6} After them, seven other heads of grain sprouted--thin and scorched by the east wind. {7} The thin heads of grain swallowed up the seven healthy, full heads. Then Pharaoh woke up; it had been a dream. {8} In the morning his mind was troubled, so he sent for all the magicians and wise men of Egypt. Pharaoh told them his dreams, but no one could interpret them for him. {9} Then the chief cupbearer said to Pharaoh, "Today I am reminded of my shortcomings. {10} Pharaoh was once angry with his servants, and he imprisoned me and the chief baker in the house of the captain of the guard. {11} Each of us had a dream the same night, and each dream had a meaning of its own. {12} Now a young Hebrew was there with us, a servant of the captain of the guard. We told him our dreams, and he interpreted them for us, giving each man the interpretation of his dream. {13} And things turned out exactly as he interpreted them to us: I was restored to my position, and the other man was hanged." {14} So Pharaoh sent for Joseph, and he was quickly brought from the dungeon. When he had shaved and changed his clothes, he came before Pharaoh. {15} Pharaoh said to Joseph, "I had a dream, and no one can interpret it. But I have heard it said of you that when you hear a dream you can interpret it." {16} "I cannot do it," Joseph replied to Pharaoh, "but God will give Pharaoh the answer he desires." {17} Then Pharaoh said to Joseph, "In my dream I was standing on the bank of the Nile, {18} when out of the river there came up seven cows, fat and sleek, and they grazed among the reeds. {19} After them, seven other cows came up--scrawny and very ugly and lean. I had never seen such ugly cows in all the land of Egypt. {20} The lean, ugly cows ate up the seven fat cows that came up first. {21} But even after they ate them, no one could tell that they had done so; they looked just as ugly as before. Then I woke up. {22} "In my dreams I also saw seven heads of grain, full and good, growing on a single stalk. {23} After them, seven other heads sprouted--withered and thin and scorched by the east wind. {24} The thin heads of grain swallowed up the seven good heads. I told this to the magicians, but none could explain it to me."

JOSEPH BECOMES PRIME MINISTER

Gen 41:26-46

The seven good cows are seven years, and the seven good heads of grain are seven years; it is one and the same dream. {27} The seven lean, ugly cows that came up afterward are seven years, and so are the seven worthless heads of grain scorched by the east wind: They are seven years of famine. {28} "It is just as I said to Pharaoh: God has shown Pharaoh what he is about to do. {29} Seven years of great abundance are coming throughout the land of Egypt, {30} but seven years of famine will follow them. Then all the abundance in Egypt will be forgotten, and the famine will ravage the land. {31} The abundance in the land will not be remembered, because the famine that follows it will be so severe. {32} The reason the dream was given to Pharaoh in two forms is that the matter has been firmly decided by God, and God will do it soon. {33} "And now let Pharaoh look for a discerning and wise man and put him in charge of the land of Egypt. {34} Let Pharaoh appoint commissioners over the land to take a fifth of the harvest of Egypt during the seven years of abundance. {35} They should collect all the food of these good years that are coming and store up the grain under the authority of Pharaoh, to be kept in the cities for food. {36} This food should be held in reserve for the country, to be used during the seven years of famine that will come upon Egypt, so that the country may not be ruined by the famine."

{37} The plan seemed good to Pharaoh and to all his officials. {38} So Pharaoh asked them, "Can we find anyone like this man, one in whom is the spirit of God?" {39} Then Pharaoh said to Joseph, "Since God has made all this known to you, there is no one so discerning and wise as you. {40} You shall be in charge of my palace, and all my people are to submit to your orders. Only with respect to the throne will I be greater than you." {41} So Pharaoh said to Joseph, "I hereby put you in charge of the whole land of Egypt." {42} Then Pharaoh took his signet ring from his finger and put it on Joseph's finger. He dressed him in robes of fine linen and put a gold chain around his neck. {43} He had him ride in a chariot as his second-in-command, and men shouted before him, "Make way!" Thus he put him in charge of the whole land of Egypt. {44} Then Pharaoh said to Joseph, "I am Pharaoh, but without your word no one will lift hand or foot in all Egypt." {45} Pharaoh gave Joseph the name Zaphenath-Paneah and gave him Asenath daughter of Potiphera, priest of On, to be his wife. And Joseph went throughout the land of Egypt. {46} Joseph was thirty years old when he entered the service of Pharaoh king of Egypt.

JOSEPH'S BROTHERS SEEK FOOD IN EGYPT

Gen 42:1-21

When Jacob learned that there was grain in Egypt, he said to his sons, "Why do you just keep looking at each other?" {2} He continued, "I have heard that there is grain in Egypt. Go down there and buy some for us, so that we may live and not die." {3} Then ten of Joseph's brothers went down to buy grain from Egypt. {4} But Jacob did not send Benjamin, Joseph's brother, with the others, because he was afraid that harm might come to him. {5} So Israel's sons were among those who went to buy grain, for the famine was in the land of Canaan also.

{6} Now Joseph was the governor of the land, the one who sold grain to all its people. So when Joseph's brothers arrived, they bowed down to him with their faces to the ground. {7} As soon as Joseph saw his brothers, he recognized them, but he pretended to be a stranger and spoke harshly to them. "Where do you come from?" he asked. "From the land of Canaan," they replied, "to buy food." {8} Although Joseph recognized his brothers, they did not recognize him. {9} Then he remembered his dreams about them and said to them, "You are spies! You have come to see where our land is unprotected." {10} "No, my lord," they answered. "Your servants have come to buy food. {11} We are all the sons of one man. Your servants are honest men, not spies." {12} "No!" he said to them. "You have come to see where our land is unprotected." {13} But they replied, "Your servants were twelve brothers, the sons of one man, who lives in the land of Canaan. The youngest is now with our father, and one is no more." {14} Joseph said to them, "It is just as I told you: You are spies! {15} And this is how you will be tested: As surely as Pharaoh lives, you will not leave this place unless your youngest brother comes here. {16} Send one of your number to get your brother; the rest of you will be kept in prison, so that your words may be tested to see if you are telling the truth. If you are not, then as surely as Pharaoh lives, you are spies!" {17} And he put them all in custody for three days. {18} On the third day, Joseph said to them, "Do this and you will live, for I fear God: {19} If you are honest men, let one of your brothers stay here in prison, while the rest of you go and take grain back for your starving households. {20} But you must bring your youngest brother to me, so that your words may be verified and that you may not die." This they proceeded to do. {21} They said to one another, "Surely we are being punished because of our brother. We saw how distressed he was when he pleaded with us for his life, but we would not listen; that's why this distress has come upon us."

JOSEPH'S BROTHERS PREPARE SECOND TRIP TO EGYPT

Gen 42:35-43:14

As they were emptying their sacks, there in each man's sack was his pouch of silver! When they and their father saw the money pouches, they were frightened. {36} Their father Jacob said to them, "You have deprived me of my children. Joseph is no more and Simeon is no more, and now you want to take Benjamin. Everything is against me!" {37} Then Reuben said to his father, "You may put both of my sons to death if I do not bring him back to you. Entrust him to my care, and I will bring him back." {38} But Jacob said, "My son will not go down there with you; his brother is dead and he is the only one left. If harm comes to him on the journey you are taking, you will bring my gray head down to the grave in sorrow."

{43:1} Now the famine was still severe in the land. {2} So when they had eaten all the grain they had brought from Egypt, their father said to them, "Go back and buy us a little more food." {3} But Judah said to him, "The man warned us solemnly, 'You will not see my face again unless your brother is with you.' {4} If you will send our brother along with us, we will go down and buy food for you. {5} But if you will not send him, we will not go down, because the man said to us, 'You will not see my face again unless your brother is with you.'" {6} Israel asked, "Why did you bring this trouble on me by telling the man you had another brother?" {7} They replied, "The man questioned us closely about ourselves and our family. 'Is your father still living?' he asked us. 'Do you have another brother?' We simply answered his questions. How were we to know he would say, 'Bring your brother down here'?" {8} Then Judah said to Israel his father, "Send the boy along with me and we will go at once, so that we and you and our children may live and not die. {9} I myself will guarantee his safety; you can hold me personally responsible for him. If I do not bring him back to you and set him here before you, I will bear the blame before you all my life. {10} As it is, if we had not delayed, we could have gone and returned twice." {11} Then their father Israel said to them, "If it must be, then do this: Put some of the best products of the land in your bags and take them down to the man as a gift—a little balm and a little honey, some spices and myrrh, some pistachio nuts and almonds. {12} Take double the amount of silver with you, for you must return the silver that was put back into the mouths of your sacks. Perhaps it was a mistake. {13} Take your brother also and go back to the man at once. {14} And may God Almighty grant you mercy before the man so that he will let your other brother and Benjamin come back with you. As for me, if I am bereaved, I am bereaved."

BENJAMIN GOES ALONG TO EGYPT

Gen 43:15-33

So the men took the gifts and double the amount of silver, and Benjamin also. They hurried down to Egypt and presented themselves to Joseph. {16} When Joseph saw Benjamin with them, he said to the steward of his house, "Take these men to my house, slaughter an animal and prepare dinner; they are to eat with me at noon." {17} The man did as Joseph told him and took the men to Joseph's house. {18} Now the men were frightened when they were taken to his house. They thought, "We were brought here because of the silver that was put back into our sacks the first time. He wants to attack us and overpower us and seize us as slaves and take our donkeys." {19} So they went up to Joseph's steward and spoke to him at the entrance to the house. {20} "Please, sir," they said, "we came down here the first time to buy food. {21} But at the place where we stopped for the night we opened our sacks and each of us found his silver–the exact weight–in the mouth of his sack. So we have brought it back with us. {22} We have also brought additional silver with us to buy food. We don't know who put our silver in our sacks." {23} "It's all right," he said. "Don't be afraid. Your God, the God of your father, has given you treasure in your sacks; I received your silver." Then he brought Simeon out to them. {24} The steward took the men into Joseph's house, gave them water to wash their feet and provided fodder for their donkeys. {25} They prepared their gifts for Joseph's arrival at noon, because they had heard that they were to eat there.

{26} When Joseph came home, they presented to him the gifts they had brought into the house, and they bowed down before him to the ground. {27} He asked them how they were, and then he said, "How is your aged father you told me about? Is he still living?" {28} They replied, "Your servant our father is still alive and well." And they bowed low to pay him honor. {29} As he looked about and saw his brother Benjamin, his own mother's son, he asked, "Is this your youngest brother, the one you told me about?" And he said, "God be gracious to you, my son." {30} Deeply moved at the sight of his brother, Joseph hurried out and looked for a place to weep. He went into his private room and wept there. {31} After he had washed his face, he came out and, controlling himself, said, "Serve the food." {32} They served him by himself, the brothers by themselves, and the Egyptians who ate with him by themselves, because Egyptians could not eat with Hebrews, for that is detestable to Egyptians. {33} The men had been seated before him in the order of their ages, from the firstborn to the youngest; and they looked at each other in astonishment.

SILVER CUP FOUND IN BENJAMIN'S BAG

Gen 44:10-31

"Very well, then," he said, "let it be as you say. Whoever is found to have it will become my slave; the rest of you will be free from blame." {11} Each of them quickly lowered his sack to the ground and opened it. {12} Then the steward proceeded to search, beginning with the oldest and ending with the youngest. And the cup was found in Benjamin's sack. {13} At this, they tore their clothes. Then they all loaded their donkeys and returned to the city. {14} Joseph was still in the house when Judah and his brothers came in, and they threw themselves to the ground before him. {15} Joseph said to them, "What is this you have done? Don't you know that a man like me can find things out by divination?" {16} "What can we say to my lord?" Judah replied. "What can we say? How can we prove our innocence? God has uncovered your servants' guilt. We are now my lord's slaves—we ourselves and the one who was found to have the cup." {17} But Joseph said, "Far be it from me to do such a thing! Only the man who was found to have the cup will become my slave. The rest of you, go back to your father in peace." {18} Then Judah went up to him and said: "Please, my lord, let your servant speak a word to my lord. Do not be angry with your servant, though you are equal to Pharaoh himself. {19} My lord asked his servants, 'Do you have a father or a brother?' {20} And we answered, 'We have an aged father, and there is a young son born to him in his old age. His brother is dead, and he is the only one of his mother's sons left, and his father loves him.' {21} "Then you said to your servants, 'Bring him down to me so I can see him for myself.' {22} And we said to my lord, 'The boy cannot leave his father; if he leaves him, his father will die.' {23} But you told your servants, 'Unless your youngest brother comes down with you, you will not see my face again.' {24} When we went back to your servant my father, we told him what my lord had said. {25} "Then our father said, 'Go back and buy a little more food.' {26} But we said, 'We cannot go down. Only if our youngest brother is with us will we go. We cannot see the man's face unless our youngest brother is with us.' {27} "Your servant my father said to us, 'You know that my wife bore me two sons. {28} One of them went away from me, and I said, "He has surely been torn to pieces." And I have not seen him since. {29} If you take this one from me too and harm comes to him, you will bring my gray head down to the grave in misery.' {30} "So now, if the boy is not with us when I go back to your servant my father and if my father, whose life is closely bound up with the boy's life, {31} sees that the boy isn't there, he will die.

JOSEPH REVEALS HIMSELF TO HIS BROTHERS

Gen 45:1-20

Then Joseph could no longer control himself before all his attendants, and he cried out, "Have everyone leave my presence!" So there was no one with Joseph when he made himself known to his brothers. {2} And he wept so loudly that the Egyptians heard him, and Pharaoh's household heard about it. {3} Joseph said to his brothers, "I am Joseph! Is my father still living?" But his brothers were not able to answer him, because they were terrified at his presence. {4} Then Joseph said to his brothers, "Come close to me." When they had done so, he said, "I am your brother Joseph, the one you sold into Egypt! {5} And now, do not be distressed and do not be angry with yourselves for selling me here, because it was to save lives that God sent me ahead of you. {6} For two years now there has been famine in the land, and for the next five years there will not be plowing and reaping. {7} But God sent me ahead of you to preserve for you a remnant on earth and to save your lives by a great deliverance. {8} "So then, it was not you who sent me here, but God. He made me father to Pharaoh, lord of his entire household and ruler of all Egypt.

{9} Now hurry back to my father and say to him, 'This is what your son Joseph says: God has made me lord of all Egypt. Come down to me; don't delay. {10} You shall live in the region of Goshen and be near me—you, your children and grandchildren, your flocks and herds, and all you have. {11} I will provide for you there, because five years of famine are still to come. Otherwise you and your household and all who belong to you will become destitute.' {12} "You can see for yourselves, and so can my brother Benjamin, that it is really I who am speaking to you. {13} Tell my father about all the honor accorded me in Egypt and about everything you have seen. And bring my father down here quickly." {14} Then he threw his arms around his brother Benjamin and wept, and Benjamin embraced him, weeping. {15} And he kissed all his brothers and wept over them. Afterward his brothers talked with him. {16} When the news reached Pharaoh's palace that Joseph's brothers had come, Pharaoh and all his officials were pleased. {17} Pharaoh said to Joseph, "Tell your brothers, 'Do this: Load your animals and return to the land of Canaan, {18} and bring your father and your families back to me. I will give you the best of the land of Egypt and you can enjoy the fat of the land.' {19} "You are also directed to tell them, 'Do this: Take some carts from Egypt for your children and your wives, and get your father and come. {20} Never mind about your belongings, because the best of all Egypt will be yours.'"

JACOB AND HIS DESCENDANTS MOVE TO EGYPT

Gen 46:1-6
So Israel set out with all that was his, and when he reached Beersheba, he offered sacrifices to the God of his father Isaac. {2} And God spoke to Israel in a vision at night and said, "Jacob! Jacob!" "Here I am," he replied. {3} "I am God, the God of your father," he said. "Do not be afraid to go down to Egypt, for I will make you into a great nation there. {4} I will go down to Egypt with you, and I will surely bring you back again. And Joseph's own hand will close your eyes." {5} Then Jacob left Beersheba, and Israel's sons took their father Jacob and their children and their wives in the carts that Pharaoh had sent to transport him. {6} They also took with them their livestock and the possessions they had acquired in Canaan, and Jacob and all his offspring went to Egypt.

Gen 46:26-47:3
All those who went to Egypt with Jacob–those who were his direct descendants, not counting his sons' wives–numbered sixty-six persons. {27} With the two sons who had been born to Joseph in Egypt, the members of Jacob's family, which went to Egypt, were seventy in all. {28} Now Jacob sent Judah ahead of him to Joseph to get directions to Goshen. When they arrived in the region of Goshen, {29} Joseph had his chariot made ready and went to Goshen to meet his father Israel. As soon as Joseph appeared before him, he threw his arms around his father and wept for a long time. {30} Israel said to Joseph, "Now I am ready to die, since I have seen for myself that you are still alive." {31} Then Joseph said to his brothers and to his father's household, "I will go up and speak to Pharaoh and will say to him, 'My brothers and my father's household, who were living in the land of Canaan, have come to me. {32} The men are shepherds; they tend livestock, and they have brought along their flocks and herds and everything they own.' {33} When Pharaoh calls you in and asks, 'What is your occupation?' {34} you should answer, 'Your servants have tended livestock from our boyhood on, just as our fathers did.' Then you will be allowed to settle in the region of Goshen, for all shepherds are detestable to the Egyptians." {47:1} Joseph went and told Pharaoh, "My father and brothers, with their flocks and herds and everything they own, have come from the land of Canaan and are now in Goshen." {2} He chose five of his brothers and presented them before Pharaoh. {3} Pharaoh asked the brothers, "What is your occupation?" "Your servants are shepherds," they replied to Pharaoh, "just as our fathers were."

JACOB DIES

Gen 47:28-48:9

Jacob lived in Egypt seventeen years, and the years of his life were a hundred and forty-seven. {29} When the time drew near for Israel to die, he called for his son Joseph and said to him, "If I have found favor in your eyes, put your hand under my thigh and promise that you will show me kindness and faithfulness. Do not bury me in Egypt, {30} but when I rest with my fathers, carry me out of Egypt and bury me where they are buried." "I will do as you say," he said. {31} "Swear to me," he said. Then Joseph swore to him, and Israel worshiped as he leaned on the top of his staff.

{48:1} Some time later Joseph was told, "Your father is ill." So he took his two sons Manasseh and Ephraim along with him. {2} When Jacob was told, "Your son Joseph has come to you," Israel rallied his strength and sat up on the bed. {3} Jacob said to Joseph, "God Almighty appeared to me at Luz in the land of Canaan, and there he blessed me {4} and said to me, 'I am going to make you fruitful and will increase your numbers. I will make you a community of peoples, and I will give this land as an everlasting possession to your descendants after you.' {5} "Now then, your two sons born to you in Egypt before I came to you here will be reckoned as mine; Ephraim and Manasseh will be mine, just as Reuben and Simeon are mine. {6} Any children born to you after them will be yours; in the territory they inherit they will be reckoned under the names of their brothers. {7} As I was returning from Paddan, to my sorrow Rachel died in the land of Canaan while we were still on the way, a little distance from Ephrath. So I buried her there beside the road to Ephrath" (that is, Bethlehem). {8} When Israel saw the sons of Joseph, he asked, "Who are these?" {9} "They are the sons God has given me here," Joseph said to his father. Then Israel said, "Bring them to me so I may bless them."

Gen 49:29-33

Then he gave them these instructions: "I am about to be gathered to my people. Bury me with my fathers in the cave in the field of Ephron the Hittite, {30} the cave in the field of Machpelah, near Mamre in Canaan, which Abraham bought as a burial place from Ephron the Hittite, along with the field. {31} There Abraham and his wife Sarah were buried, there Isaac and his wife Rebekah were buried, and there I buried Leah. {32} The field and the cave in it were bought from the Hittites." {33} When Jacob had finished giving instructions to his sons, he drew his feet up into the bed, breathed his last and was gathered to his people.

JOSEPH AND HIS BROTHERS BURY JACOB

Gen 50:2-20

Then Joseph directed the physicians in his service to embalm his father Israel. So the physicians embalmed him, {3} taking a full forty days, for that was the time required for embalming. And the Egyptians mourned for him seventy days. {4} When the days of mourning had passed, Joseph said to Pharaoh's court, "If I have found favor in your eyes, speak to Pharaoh for me. Tell him, {5} 'My father made me swear an oath and said, "I am about to die; bury me in the tomb I dug for myself in the land of Canaan." Now let me go up and bury my father; then I will return.'" {6} Pharaoh said, "Go up and bury your father, as he made you swear to do." {7} So Joseph went up to bury his father. All Pharaoh's officials accompanied him–the dignitaries of his court and all the dignitaries of Egypt– {8} besides all the members of Joseph's household and his brothers and those belonging to his father's household. Only their children and their flocks and herds were left in Goshen. {9} Chariots and horsemen also went up with him. It was a very large company. {10} When they reached the threshing floor of Atad, near the Jordan, they lamented loudly and bitterly; and there Joseph observed a seven-day period of mourning for his father. {11} When the Canaanites who lived there saw the mourning at the threshing floor of Atad, they said, "The Egyptians are holding a solemn ceremony of mourning." That is why that place near the Jordan is called Abel Mizraim. {12} So Jacob's sons did as he had commanded them: {13} They carried him to the land of Canaan and buried him in the cave in the field of Machpelah, near Mamre, which Abraham had bought as a burial place from Ephron the Hittite, along with the field. {14} After burying his father, Joseph returned to Egypt, together with his brothers and all the others who had gone with him to bury his father. 15} When Joseph's brothers saw that their father was dead, they said, "What if Joseph holds a grudge against us and pays us back for all the wrongs we did to him?" {16} So they sent word to Joseph, saying, "Your father left these instructions before he died: {17} 'This is what you are to say to Joseph: I ask you to forgive your brothers the sins and the wrongs they committed in treating you so badly.' Now please forgive the sins of the servants of the God of your father." When their message came to him, Joseph wept. {18} His brothers then came and threw themselves down before him. "We are your slaves," they said. {19} But Joseph said to them, "Don't be afraid. Am I in the place of God? {20} You intended to harm me, but God intended it for good to accomplish what is now being done, the saving of many lives.

A NEW KING OPPRESSES THE ISRAELITES

Exo 1:6-22

Now Joseph and all his brothers and all that generation died, {7} but the Israelites were fruitful and multiplied greatly and became exceedingly numerous, so that the land was filled with them. {8} Then a new king, who did not know about Joseph, came to power in Egypt. {9} "Look," he said to his people, "the Israelites have become much too numerous for us. {10} Come, we must deal shrewdly with them or they will become even more numerous and, if war breaks out, will join our enemies, fight against us and leave the country." {11} So they put slave masters over them to oppress them with forced labor, and they built Pithom and Rameses as store cities for Pharaoh. {12} But the more they were oppressed, the more they multiplied and spread; so the Egyptians came to dread the Israelites {13} and worked them ruthlessly. {14} They made their lives bitter with hard labor in brick and mortar and with all kinds of work in the fields; in all their hard labor the Egyptians used them ruthlessly.

{15} The king of Egypt said to the Hebrew midwives, whose names were Shiphrah and Puah, {16} "When you help the Hebrew women in childbirth and observe them on the delivery stool, if it is a boy, kill him; but if it is a girl, let her live." {17} The midwives, however, feared God and did not do what the king of Egypt had told them to do; they let the boys live. {18} Then the king of Egypt summoned the midwives and asked them, "Why have you done this? Why have you let the boys live?" {19} The midwives answered Pharaoh, "Hebrew women are not like Egyptian women; they are vigorous and give birth before the midwives arrive." {20} So God was kind to the midwives and the people increased and became even more numerous. {21} And because the midwives feared God, he gave them families of their own. {22} Then Pharaoh gave this order to all his people: "Every boy that is born you must throw into the Nile, but let every girl live."

MOSES IS BORN; LATER FLEES TO MIDIAN

Exo 2:1-21

Now a man of the house of Levi married a Levite woman, {2} and she became pregnant and gave birth to a son. When she saw that he was a fine child, she hid him for three months. {3} But when she could hide him no longer, she got a papyrus basket for him and coated it with tar and pitch. Then she placed the child in it and put it among the reeds along the bank of the Nile. {4} His sister stood at a distance to see what would happen to him. {5} Then Pharaoh's daughter went down to the Nile to bathe, and her attendants were walking along the river bank. She saw the basket among the reeds and sent her slave girl to get it. {6} She opened it and saw the baby. He was crying, and she felt sorry for him. "This is one of the Hebrew babies," she said. {7} Then his sister asked Pharaoh's daughter, "Shall I go and get one of the Hebrew women to nurse the baby for you?" {8} "Yes, go," she answered. And the girl went and got the baby's mother. {9} Pharaoh's daughter said to her, "Take this baby and nurse him for me, and I will pay you." So the woman took the baby and nursed him. {10} When the child grew older, she took him to Pharaoh's daughter and he became her son. She named him Moses, saying, "I drew him out of the water."

{11} One day, after Moses had grown up, he went out to where his own people were and watched them at their hard labor. He saw an Egyptian beating a Hebrew, one of his own people. {12} Glancing this way and that and seeing no one, he killed the Egyptian and hid him in the sand. {13} The next day he went out and saw two Hebrews fighting. He asked the one in the wrong, "Why are you hitting your fellow Hebrew?" {14} The man said, "Who made you ruler and judge over us? Are you thinking of killing me as you killed the Egyptian?" Then Moses was afraid and thought, "What I did must have become known."

{15} When Pharaoh heard of this, he tried to kill Moses, but Moses fled from Pharaoh and went to live in Midian, where he sat down by a well. {16} Now a priest of Midian had seven daughters, and they came to draw water and fill the troughs to water their father's flock. {17} Some shepherds came along and drove them away, but Moses got up and came to their rescue and watered their flock. {18} When the girls returned to Reuel their father, he asked them, "Why have you returned so early today?" {19} They answered, "An Egyptian rescued us from the shepherds. He even drew water for us and watered the flock." {20} "And where is he?" he asked his daughters. "Why did you leave him? Invite him to have something to eat." {21} Moses agreed to stay with the man, who gave his daughter Zipporah to Moses in marriage.

MOSES IS CALLED TO LEAD ISRAEL OUT OF EGYPT

Exo 3:1-17a

Now Moses was tending the flock of Jethro his father-in-law, the priest of Midian, and he led the flock to the far side of the desert and came to Horeb, the mountain of God. {2} There the angel of the LORD appeared to him in flames of fire from within a bush. Moses saw that though the bush was on fire it did not burn up. {3} So Moses thought, "I will go over and see this strange sight–why the bush does not burn up." {4} When the LORD saw that he had gone over to look, God called to him from within the bush, "Moses! Moses!" And Moses said, "Here I am." {5} "Do not come any closer," God said. "Take off your sandals, for the place where you are standing is holy ground." {6} Then he said, "I am the God of your father, the God of Abraham, the God of Isaac and the God of Jacob." At this, Moses hid his face, because he was afraid to look at God. {7} The LORD said, "I have indeed seen the misery of my people in Egypt. I have heard them crying out because of their slave drivers, and I am concerned about their suffering. {8} So I have come down to rescue them from the hand of the Egyptians and to bring them up out of that land into a good and spacious land, a land flowing with milk and honey– the home of the Canaanites, Hittites, Amorites, Perizzites, Hivites and Jebusites. {9} And now the cry of the Israelites has reached me, and I have seen the way the Egyptians are oppressing them.

{10} So now, go. I am sending you to Pharaoh to bring my people the Israelites out of Egypt." {11} But Moses said to God, "Who am I, that I should go to Pharaoh and bring the Israelites out of Egypt?" {12} And God said, "I will be with you. And this will be the sign to you that it is I who have sent you: When you have brought the people out of Egypt, you will worship God on this mountain."

{13} Moses said to God, "Suppose I go to the Israelites and say to them, 'The God of your fathers has sent me to you,' and they ask me, 'What is his name?' Then what shall I tell them?" {14} God said to Moses, "I AM WHO I AM. This is what you are to say to the Israelites: 'I AM has sent me to you.'" {15} God also said to Moses, "Say to the Israelites, 'The LORD, the God of your fathers–the God of Abraham, the God of Isaac and the God of Jacob–has sent me to you.' This is my name forever, the name by which I am to be remembered from generation to generation. {16} "Go, assemble the elders of Israel and say to them, 'The LORD, the God of your fathers–the God of Abraham, Isaac and Jacob– appeared to me and said: I have watched over you and have seen what has been done to you in Egypt. {17} And I have promised to bring you up out of your misery....

MOSES RETURNS TO EGYPT

Exo 4:1-20

Moses answered, "What if they do not believe me or listen to me and say, 'The LORD did not appear to you'?" {2} Then the LORD said to him, "What is that in your hand?" "A staff," he replied. {3} The LORD said, "Throw it on the ground." Moses threw it on the ground and it became a snake, and he ran from it. {4} Then the LORD said to him, "Reach out your hand and take it by the tail." So Moses reached out and took hold of the snake and it turned back into a staff in his hand. {5} "This," said the LORD, "is so that they may believe that the LORD, the God of their fathers—the God of Abraham, the God of Isaac and the God of Jacob—has appeared to you." {6} Then the LORD said, "Put your hand inside your cloak." So Moses put his hand into his cloak, and when he took it out, it was leprous, like snow. {7} "Now put it back into your cloak," he said. So Moses put his hand back into his cloak, and when he took it out, it was restored, like the rest of his flesh. {8} Then the LORD said, "If they do not believe you or pay attention to the first miraculous sign, they may believe the second. {9} But if they do not believe these two signs or listen to you, take some water from the Nile and pour it on the dry ground. The water you take from the river will become blood on the ground."

{10} Moses said to the LORD, "O Lord, I have never been eloquent, neither in the past nor since you have spoken to your servant. I am slow of speech and tongue." {11} The LORD said to him, "Who gave man his mouth? Who makes him deaf or mute? Who gives him sight or makes him blind? Is it not I, the LORD? {12} Now go; I will help you speak and will teach you what to say." {13} But Moses said, "O Lord, please send someone else to do it." {14} Then the Lord's anger burned against Moses and he said, "What about your brother, Aaron the Levite? I know he can speak well. He is already on his way to meet you, and his heart will be glad when he sees you. {15} You shall speak to him and put words in his mouth; I will help both of you speak and will teach you what to do. {16} He will speak to the people for you, and it will be as if he were your mouth and as if you were God to him. {17} But take this staff in your hand so you can perform miraculous signs with it."

{18} Then Moses went back to Jethro his father-in-law and said to him, "Let me go back to my own people in Egypt to see if any of them are still alive." Jethro said, "Go, and I wish you well." {19} Now the LORD had said to Moses in Midian, "Go back to Egypt, for all the men who wanted to kill you are dead." {20} So Moses took his wife and sons, put them on a donkey and started back to Egypt.

MOSES' APPEAL REJECTED BY PHARAOH

Exo 5:1-21a

Afterward Moses and Aaron went to Pharaoh and said, "This is what the LORD, the God of Israel, says: 'Let my people go, so that they may hold a festival to me in the desert.'" {2} Pharaoh said, "Who is the LORD, that I should obey him and let Israel go? I do not know the LORD and I will not let Israel go." {3} Then they said, "The God of the Hebrews has met with us. Now let us take a three-day journey into the desert to offer sacrifices to the LORD our God, or he may strike us with plagues or with the sword."

{4} But the king of Egypt said, "Moses and Aaron, why are you taking the people away from their labor? Get back to your work!" {5} Then Pharaoh said, "Look, the people of the land are now numerous, and you are stopping them from working." {6} That same day Pharaoh gave this order to the slave drivers and foremen in charge of the people: {7} "You are no longer to supply the people with straw for making bricks; let them go and gather their own straw. {8} But require them to make the same number of bricks as before; don't reduce the quota. They are lazy; that is why they are crying out, 'Let us go and sacrifice to our God.' {9} Make the work harder for the men so that they keep working and pay no attention to lies." {10} Then the slave drivers and the foremen went out and said to the people, "This is what Pharaoh says: 'I will not give you any more straw. {11} Go and get your own straw wherever you can find it, but your work will not be reduced at all.'" {12} So the people scattered all over Egypt to gather stubble to use for straw.

{13} The slave drivers kept pressing them, saying, "Complete the work required of you for each day, just as when you had straw." {14} The Israelite foremen appointed by Pharaoh's slave drivers were beaten and were asked, "Why didn't you meet your quota of bricks yesterday or today, as before?" {15} Then the Israelite foremen went and appealed to Pharaoh: "Why have you treated your servants this way? {16} Your servants are given no straw, yet we are told, 'Make bricks!' Your servants are being beaten, but the fault is with your own people." {17} Pharaoh said, "Lazy, that's what you are–lazy! That is why you keep saying, 'Let us go and sacrifice to the LORD.' {18} Now get to work. You will not be given any straw, yet you must produce your full quota of bricks." {19} The Israelite foremen realized they were in trouble when they were told, "You are not to reduce the number of bricks required of you for each day." {20} When they left Pharaoh, they found Moses and Aaron waiting to meet them, {21} and they said, "May the LORD look upon you and judge you! You have made us a stench to Pharaoh....

AARON HELPS MOSES

Exo 6:28-7:13

Now when the LORD spoke to Moses in Egypt, {29} he said to him, "I am the LORD. Tell Pharaoh king of Egypt everything I tell you." {30} But Moses said to the LORD, "Since I speak with faltering lips, why would Pharaoh listen to me?" {7:1} Then the LORD said to Moses, "See, I have made you like God to Pharaoh, and your brother Aaron will be your prophet. {2} You are to say everything I command you, and your brother Aaron is to tell Pharaoh to let the Israelites go out of his country. {3} But I will harden Pharaoh's heart, and though I multiply my miraculous signs and wonders in Egypt, {4} he will not listen to you. Then I will lay my hand on Egypt and with mighty acts of judgment I will bring out my divisions, my people the Israelites. {5} And the Egyptians will know that I am the LORD when I stretch out my hand against Egypt and bring the Israelites out of it."

{6} Moses and Aaron did just as the LORD commanded them. {7} Moses was eighty years old and Aaron eighty-three when they spoke to Pharaoh. {8} The LORD said to Moses and Aaron, {9} "When Pharaoh says to you, 'Perform a miracle,' then say to Aaron, 'Take your staff and throw it down before Pharaoh,' and it will become a snake." {10} So Moses and Aaron went to Pharaoh and did just as the LORD commanded. Aaron threw his staff down in front of Pharaoh and his officials, and it became a snake. {11} Pharaoh then summoned wise men and sorcerers, and the Egyptian magicians also did the same things by their secret arts: {12} Each one threw down his staff and it became a snake. But Aaron's staff swallowed up their staffs. {13} Yet Pharaoh's heart became hard and he would not listen to them, just as the LORD had said.

Exo 11:1-3

Now the LORD had said to Moses, "I will bring one more plague on Pharaoh and on Egypt. After that, he will let you go from here, and when he does, he will drive you out completely. {2} Tell the people that men and women alike are to ask their neighbors for articles of silver and gold." {3} (The LORD made the Egyptians favorably disposed toward the people, and Moses himself was highly regarded in Egypt by Pharaoh's officials and by the people.)

PASSOVER AND EXODUS

Exo 12:21-36

Then Moses summoned all the elders of Israel and said to them, "Go at once and select the animals for your families and slaughter the Passover lamb. {22} Take a bunch of hyssop, dip it into the blood in the basin and put some of the blood on the top and on both sides of the doorframe. Not one of you shall go out the door of his house until morning. {23} When the LORD goes through the land to strike down the Egyptians, he will see the blood on the top and sides of the doorframe and will pass over that doorway, and he will not permit the destroyer to enter your houses and strike you down. {24} "Obey these instructions as a lasting ordinance for you and your descendants. {25} When you enter the land that the LORD will give you as he promised, observe this ceremony. {26} And when your children ask you, 'What does this ceremony mean to you?' {27} then tell them, 'It is the Passover sacrifice to the LORD, who passed over the houses of the Israelites in Egypt and spared our homes when he struck down the Egyptians.'" Then the people bowed down and worshiped. {28} The Israelites did just what the LORD commanded Moses and Aaron.

{29} At midnight the LORD struck down all the firstborn in Egypt, from the firstborn of Pharaoh, who sat on the throne, to the firstborn of the prisoner, who was in the dungeon, and the firstborn of all the livestock as well. {30} Pharaoh and all his officials and all the Egyptians got up during the night, and there was loud wailing in Egypt, for there was not a house without someone dead.

{31} During the night Pharaoh summoned Moses and Aaron and said, "Up! Leave my people, you and the Israelites! Go, worship the LORD as you have requested. {32} Take your flocks and herds, as you have said, and go. And also bless me." {33} The Egyptians urged the people to hurry and leave the country. "For otherwise," they said, "we will all die!" {34} So the people took their dough before the yeast was added, and carried it on their shoulders in kneading troughs wrapped in clothing. {35} The Israelites did as Moses instructed and asked the Egyptians for articles of silver and gold and for clothing. {36} The LORD had made the Egyptians favorably disposed toward the people, and they gave them what they asked for; so they plundered the Egyptians.

Exo 12:50-51

All the Israelites did just what the LORD had commanded Moses and Aaron. {51} And on that very day the LORD brought the Israelites out of Egypt by their divisions.

PHARAOH PURSUES THE ISRAELITES

Exo 13:17-22

When Pharaoh let the people go, God did not lead them on the road through the Philistine country, though that was shorter. For God said, "If they face war, they might change their minds and return to Egypt." {18} So God led the people around by the desert road toward the Red Sea. The Israelites went up out of Egypt armed for battle. {19} Moses took the bones of Joseph with him because Joseph had made the sons of Israel swear an oath. He had said, "God will surely come to your aid, and then you must carry my bones up with you from this place." {20} After leaving Succoth they camped at Etham on the edge of the desert. {21} By day the LORD went ahead of them in a pillar of cloud to guide them on their way and by night in a pillar of fire to give them light, so that they could travel by day or night. {22} Neither the pillar of cloud by day nor the pillar of fire by night left its place in front of the people.

Exo 14:5-14

When the king of Egypt was told that the people had fled, Pharaoh and his officials changed their minds about them and said, "What have we done? We have let the Israelites go and have lost their services!" {6} So he had his chariot made ready and took his army with him. {7} He took six hundred of the best chariots, along with all the other chariots of Egypt, with officers over all of them. {8} The LORD hardened the heart of Pharaoh king of Egypt, so that he pursued the Israelites, who were marching out boldly. {9} The Egyptians–all Pharaoh's horses and chariots, horsemen and troops–pursued the Israelites and overtook them as they camped by the sea near Pi Hahiroth, opposite Baal Zephon. {10} As Pharaoh approached, the Israelites looked up, and there were the Egyptians, marching after them. They were terrified and cried out to the LORD. {11} They said to Moses, "Was it because there were no graves in Egypt that you brought us to the desert to die? What have you done to us by bringing us out of Egypt? {12} Didn't we say to you in Egypt, 'Leave us alone; let us serve the Egyptians'? It would have been better for us to serve the Egyptians than to die in the desert!"

{13} Moses answered the people, "Do not be afraid. Stand firm and you will see the deliverance the LORD will bring you today. The Egyptians you see today you will never see again. {14} The LORD will fight for you; you need only to be still."

CROSSING THE RED SEA

Exo 14:19-31

Then the angel of God, who had been traveling in front of Israel's army, withdrew and went behind them. The pillar of cloud also moved from in front and stood behind them, {20} coming between the armies of Egypt and Israel. Throughout the night the cloud brought darkness to the one side and light to the other side; so neither went near the other all night long. {21} Then Moses stretched out his hand over the sea, and all that night the LORD drove the sea back with a strong east wind and turned it into dry land. The waters were divided, {22} and the Israelites went through the sea on dry ground, with a wall of water on their right and on their left. {23} The Egyptians pursued them, and all Pharaoh's horses and chariots and horsemen followed them into the sea. {24} During the last watch of the night the LORD looked down from the pillar of fire and cloud at the Egyptian army and threw it into confusion. {25} He made the wheels of their chariots come off so that they had difficulty driving. And the Egyptians said, "Let's get away from the Israelites! The LORD is fighting for them against Egypt."

{26} Then the LORD said to Moses, "Stretch out your hand over the sea so that the waters may flow back over the Egyptians and their chariots and horsemen." {27} Moses stretched out his hand over the sea, and at daybreak the sea went back to its place. The Egyptians were fleeing toward it, and the LORD swept them into the sea. {28} The water flowed back and covered the chariots and horsemen—the entire army of Pharaoh that had followed the Israelites into the sea. Not one of them survived. {29} But the Israelites went through the sea on dry ground, with a wall of water on their right and on their left. {30} That day the LORD saved Israel from the hands of the Egyptians, and Israel saw the Egyptians lying dead on the shore. {31} And when the Israelites saw the great power the LORD displayed against the Egyptians, the people feared the LORD and put their trust in him and in Moses his servant.

Exo 15:19-21

When Pharaoh's horses, chariots and horsemen went into the sea, the LORD brought the waters of the sea back over them, but the Israelites walked through the sea on dry ground. {20} Then Miriam the prophetess, Aaron's sister, took a tambourine in her hand, and all the women followed her, with tambourines and dancing. {21} Miriam sang to them: "Sing to the LORD, for he is highly exalted. The horse and its rider he has hurled into the sea."

WATER AND BREAD

Exo 15:27-16:15

Then they came to Elim, where there were twelve springs and seventy palm trees, and they camped there near the water. {16:1} The whole Israelite community set out from Elim and came to the Desert of Sin, which is between Elim and Sinai, on the fifteenth day of the second month after they had come out of Egypt. {2} In the desert the whole community grumbled against Moses and Aaron. {3} The Israelites said to them, "If only we had died by the Lord's hand in Egypt! There we sat around pots of meat and ate all the food we wanted, but you have brought us out into this desert to starve this entire assembly to death." {4} Then the LORD said to Moses, "I will rain down bread from heaven for you. The people are to go out each day and gather enough for that day. In this way I will test them and see whether they will follow my instructions. {5} On the sixth day they are to prepare what they bring in, and that is to be twice as much as they gather on the other days." {6} So Moses and Aaron said to all the Israelites, "In the evening you will know that it was the LORD who brought you out of Egypt, {7} and in the morning you will see the glory of the LORD, because he has heard your grumbling against him. Who are we, that you should grumble against us?" {8} Moses also said, "You will know that it was the LORD when he gives you meat to eat in the evening and all the bread you want in the morning, because he has heard your grumbling against him. Who are we? You are not grumbling against us, but against the LORD." {9} Then Moses told Aaron, "Say to the entire Israelite community, 'Come before the LORD, for he has heard your grumbling.'" {10} While Aaron was speaking to the whole Israelite community, they looked toward the desert, and there was the glory of the LORD appearing in the cloud. {11} The LORD said to Moses, {12} "I have heard the grumbling of the Israelites. Tell them, 'At twilight you will eat meat, and in the morning you will be filled with bread. Then you will know that I am the LORD your God.'" {13} That evening quail came and covered the camp, and in the morning there was a layer of dew around the camp. {14} When the dew was gone, thin flakes like frost on the ground appeared on the desert floor. {15} When the Israelites saw it, they said to each other, "What is it?" For they did not know what it was. Moses said to them, "It is the bread the LORD has given you to eat.

MOSES STRIKES ROCK FOR WATER, AND RAISES HANDS FOR VICTORY

EXO 17:1-15

The whole Israelite community set out from the Desert of Sin, traveling from place to place as the LORD commanded. They camped at Rephidim, but there was no water for the people to drink. {2} So they quarreled with Moses and said, "Give us water to drink." Moses replied, "Why do you quarrel with me? Why do you put the LORD to the test?" {3} But the people were thirsty for water there, and they grumbled against Moses. They said, "Why did you bring us up out of Egypt to make us and our children and livestock die of thirst?" {4} Then Moses cried out to the LORD, "What am I to do with these people? They are almost ready to stone me." {5} The LORD answered Moses, "Walk on ahead of the people. Take with you some of the elders of Israel and take in your hand the staff with which you struck the Nile, and go. {6} I will stand there before you by the rock at Horeb. Strike the rock, and water will come out of it for the people to drink." So Moses did this in the sight of the elders of Israel. {7} And he called the place Massah and Meribah because the Israelites quarreled and because they tested the LORD saying, "Is the LORD among us or not?"

{8} The Amalekites came and attacked the Israelites at Rephidim. {9} Moses said to Joshua, "Choose some of our men and go out to fight the Amalekites. Tomorrow I will stand on top of the hill with the staff of God in my hands." {10} So Joshua fought the Amalekites as Moses had ordered, and Moses, Aaron and Hur went to the top of the hill. {11} As long as Moses held up his hands, the Israelites were winning, but whenever he lowered his hands, the Amalekites were winning. {12} When Moses' hands grew tired, they took a stone and put it under him and he sat on it. Aaron and Hur held his hands up—one on one side, one on the other—so that his hands remained steady till sunset. {13} So Joshua overcame the Amalekite army with the sword. {14} Then the LORD said to Moses, "Write this on a scroll as something to be remembered and make sure that Joshua hears it, because I will completely blot out the memory of Amalek from under heaven." {15} Moses built an altar and called it The LORD is my Banner.

MOSES ACCEPTS ADVICE FROM HIS FATHER-IN-LAW

Exo 18:6-24

"I, your father-in-law Jethro, am coming to you with your wife and her two sons." {7} So Moses went out to meet his father-in-law and bowed down and kissed him. They greeted each other and then went into the tent. {8} Moses told his father-in-law about everything the LORD had done to Pharaoh and the Egyptians for Israel's sake and about all the hardships they had met along the way and how the LORD had saved them. {9} Jethro was delighted to hear about all the good things the LORD had done for Israel in rescuing them from the hand of the Egyptians. {10} He said, "Praise be to the LORD, who rescued you from the hand of the Egyptians and of Pharaoh, and who rescued the people from the hand of the Egyptians. {11} Now I know that the LORD is greater than all other gods, for he did this to those who had treated Israel arrogantly." {12} Then Jethro, Moses' father-in-law, brought a burnt offering and other sacrifices to God, and Aaron came with all the elders of Israel to eat bread with Moses' father-in-law in the presence of God. {13} The next day Moses took his seat to serve as judge for the people, and they stood around him from morning till evening. {14} When his father-in-law saw all that Moses was doing for the people, he said, "What is this you are doing for the people? Why do you alone sit as judge, while all these people stand around you from morning till evening?" {15} Moses answered him, "Because the people come to me to seek God's will. {16} Whenever they have a dispute, it is brought to me, and I decide between the parties and inform them of God's decrees and laws." {17} Moses' father-in-law replied, "What you are doing is not good. {18} You and these people who come to you will only wear yourselves out. The work is too heavy for you; you cannot handle it alone. {19} Listen now to me and I will give you some advice, and may God be with you. You must be the people's representative before God and bring their disputes to him. {20} Teach them the decrees and laws, and show them the way to live and the duties they are to perform. {21} But select capable men from all the people—men who fear God, trustworthy men who hate dishonest gain—and appoint them as officials over thousands, hundreds, fifties and tens. {22} Have them serve as judges for the people at all times, but have them bring every difficult case to you; the simple cases they can decide themselves. That will make your load lighter, because they will share it with you. {23} If you do this and God so commands, you will be able to stand the strain, and all these people will go home satisfied." {24} Moses listened to his father-in-law and did everything he said.

MOSES MEETS GOD ON MT. SINAI

Exo 19:3-19

Then Moses went up to God, and the LORD called to him from the mountain and said, "This is what you are to say to the house of Jacob and what you are to tell the people of Israel: {4} 'You yourselves have seen what I did to Egypt, and how I carried you on eagles' wings and brought you to myself. {5} Now if you obey me fully and keep my covenant, then out of all nations you will be my treasured possession. Although the whole earth is mine, {6} you will be for me a kingdom of priests and a holy nation.' These are the words you are to speak to the Israelites."

{7} So Moses went back and summoned the elders of the people and set before them all the words the LORD had commanded him to speak. {8} The people all responded together, "We will do everything the LORD has said." So Moses brought their answer back to the LORD. {9} The LORD said to Moses, "I am going to come to you in a dense cloud, so that the people will hear me speaking with you and will always put their trust in you." Then Moses told the LORD what the people had said. {10} And the LORD said to Moses, "Go to the people and consecrate them today and tomorrow. Have them wash their clothes {11} and be ready by the third day, because on that day the LORD will come down on Mount Sinai in the sight of all the people. {12} Put limits for the people around the mountain and tell them, 'Be careful that you do not go up the mountain or touch the foot of it. Whoever touches the mountain shall surely be put to death. {13} He shall surely be stoned or shot with arrows; not a hand is to be laid on him. Whether man or animal, he shall not be permitted to live.' Only when the ram's horn sounds a long blast may they go up to the mountain."

{14} After Moses had gone down the mountain to the people, he consecrated them, and they washed their clothes. {15} Then he said to the people, "Prepare yourselves for the third day. Abstain from sexual relations." {16} On the morning of the third day there was thunder and lightning, with a thick cloud over the mountain, and a very loud trumpet blast. Everyone in the camp trembled. {17} Then Moses led the people out of the camp to meet with God, and they stood at the foot of the mountain. {18} Mount Sinai was covered with smoke, because the LORD descended on it in fire. The smoke billowed up from it like smoke from a furnace, the whole mountain trembled violently, {19} and the sound of the trumpet grew louder and louder. Then Moses spoke and the voice of God answered him.

THE TEN COMMANDMENTS

Exo 20:1-19

And God spoke all these words: {2} "I am the LORD your God, who brought you out of Egypt, out of the land of slavery.

{3} "You shall have no other gods before me.

{4} "You shall not make for yourself an idol in the form of anything in heaven above or on the earth beneath or in the waters below. {5} You shall not bow down to them or worship them; for I, the LORD your God, am a jealous God, punishing the children for the sin of the fathers to the third and fourth generation of those who hate me, {6} but showing love to a thousand <generations> of those who love me and keep my commandments.

{7} "You shall not misuse the name of the LORD your God, for the LORD will not hold anyone guiltless who misuses his name.

{8} "Remember the Sabbath day by keeping it holy. {9} Six days you shall labor and do all your work, {10} but the seventh day is a Sabbath to the LORD your God. On it you shall not do any work, neither you, nor your son or daughter, nor your manservant or maidservant, nor your animals, nor the alien within your gates. {11} For in six days the LORD made the heavens and the earth, the sea, and all that is in them, but he rested on the seventh day. Therefore the LORD blessed the Sabbath day and made it holy.

{12} "Honor your father and your mother, so that you may live long in the land the LORD your God is giving you.

{13} "You shall not murder.

{14} "You shall not commit adultery.

{15} "You shall not steal.

{16} "You shall not give false testimony against your neighbor.

{17} "You shall not covet your neighbor's house. You shall not covet your neighbor's wife, or his manservant or maidservant, his ox or donkey, or anything that belongs to your neighbor."

{18} When the people saw the thunder and lightning and heard the trumpet and saw the mountain in smoke, they trembled with fear. They stayed at a distance {19} and said to Moses, "Speak to us yourself and we will listen. But do not have God speak to us or we will die."

GOD CONFIRMS HIS COVENANT

Exo 24:3-25:2

When Moses went and told the people all the Lord's words and laws, they responded with one voice, "Everything the LORD has said we will do." {4} Moses then wrote down everything the LORD had said. He got up early the next morning and built an altar at the foot of the mountain and set up twelve stone pillars representing the twelve tribes of Israel. {5} Then he sent young Israelite men, and they offered burnt offerings and sacrificed young bulls as fellowship offerings to the LORD. {6} Moses took half of the blood and put it in bowls, and the other half he sprinkled on the altar. {7} Then he took the Book of the Covenant and read it to the people. They responded, "We will do everything the LORD has said; we will obey." {8} Moses then took the blood, sprinkled it on the people and said, "This is the blood of the covenant that the LORD has made with you in accordance with all these words." {9} Moses and Aaron, Nadab and Abihu, and the seventy elders of Israel went up {10} and saw the God of Israel. Under his feet was something like a pavement made of sapphire, clear as the sky itself. {11} But God did not raise his hand against these leaders of the Israelites; they saw God, and they ate and drank.

{12} The LORD said to Moses, "Come up to me on the mountain and stay here, and I will give you the tablets of stone, with the law and commands I have written for their instruction." {13} Then Moses set out with Joshua his aide, and Moses went up on the mountain of God. {14} He said to the elders, "Wait here for us until we come back to you. Aaron and Hur are with you, and anyone involved in a dispute can go to them." {15} When Moses went up on the mountain, the cloud covered it, {16} and the glory of the LORD settled on Mount Sinai. For six days the cloud covered the mountain, and on the seventh day the LORD called to Moses from within the cloud. {17} To the Israelites the glory of the LORD looked like a consuming fire on top of the mountain. {18} Then Moses entered the cloud as he went on up the mountain. And he stayed on the mountain forty days and forty nights.

{25:1} The LORD said to Moses, {2} "Tell the Israelites to bring me an offering. You are to receive the offering for me from each man whose heart prompts him to give.

Exo 25:8-9

"Then have them make a sanctuary for me, and I will dwell among them. {9} Make this tabernacle and all its furnishings exactly like the pattern I will show you.

THE ISRAELITES BUILD THE GOLDEN CALF

Exo 32:1-7

When the people saw that Moses was so long in coming down from the mountain, they gathered around Aaron and said, "Come, make us gods who will go before us. As for this fellow Moses who brought us up out of Egypt, we don't know what has happened to him." {2} Aaron answered them, "Take off the gold earrings that your wives, your sons and your daughters are wearing, and bring them to me." {3} So all the people took off their earrings and brought them to Aaron. {4} He took what they handed him and made it into an idol cast in the shape of a calf, fashioning it with a tool. Then they said, "These are your gods, O Israel, who brought you up out of Egypt." {5} When Aaron saw this, he built an altar in front of the calf and announced, "Tomorrow there will be a festival to the LORD." {6} So the next day the people rose early and sacrificed burnt offerings and presented fellowship offerings. Afterward they sat down to eat and drink and got up to indulge in revelry. {7} Then the LORD said to Moses, "Go down, because your people, whom you brought up out of Egypt, have become corrupt.

Exo 32:15-24

Moses turned and went down the mountain with the two tablets of the Testimony in his hands. They were inscribed on both sides, front and back. {16} The tablets were the work of God; the writing was the writing of God, engraved on the tablets. {17} When Joshua heard the noise of the people shouting, he said to Moses, "There is the sound of war in the camp." {18} Moses replied: "It is not the sound of victory, it is not the sound of defeat; it is the sound of singing that I hear." {19} When Moses approached the camp and saw the calf and the dancing, his anger burned and he threw the tablets out of his hands, breaking them to pieces at the foot of the mountain. {20} And he took the calf they had made and burned it in the fire; then he ground it to powder, scattered it on the water and made the Israelites drink it. {21} He said to Aaron, "What did these people do to you, that you led them into such great sin?" {22} "Do not be angry, my lord," Aaron answered. "You know how prone these people are to evil. {23} They said to me, 'Make us gods who will go before us. As for this fellow Moses who brought us up out of Egypt, we don't know what has happened to him.' {24} So I told them, 'Whoever has any gold jewelry, take it off.' Then they gave me the gold, and I threw it into the fire, and out came this calf!"

MOSES CHISELS TWO STONE TABLETS

Exo 34:1-16

The LORD said to Moses, "Chisel out two stone tablets like the first ones, and I will write on them the words that were on the first tablets, which you broke. {2} Be ready in the morning, and then come up on Mount Sinai. Present yourself to me there on top of the mountain. {3} No one is to come with you or be seen anywhere on the mountain; not even the flocks and herds may graze in front of the mountain." {4} So Moses chiseled out two stone tablets like the first ones and went up Mount Sinai early in the morning, as the LORD had commanded him; and he carried the two stone tablets in his hands. {5} Then the LORD came down in the cloud and stood there with him and proclaimed his name, the LORD. {6} And he passed in front of Moses, proclaiming, "The LORD, the LORD, the compassionate and gracious God, slow to anger, abounding in love and faithfulness, {7} maintaining love to thousands, and forgiving wickedness, rebellion and sin. Yet he does not leave the guilty unpunished; he punishes the children and their children for the sin of the fathers to the third and fourth generation." {8} Moses bowed to the ground at once and worshiped. {9} "O Lord, if I have found favor in your eyes," he said, "then let the Lord go with us. Although this is a stiff-necked people, forgive our wickedness and our sin, and take us as your inheritance."

{10} Then the LORD said: "I am making a covenant with you. Before all your people I will do wonders never before done in any nation in all the world. The people you live among will see how awesome is the work that I, the LORD, will do for you. {11} Obey what I command you today. I will drive out before you the Amorites, Canaanites, Hittites, Perizzites, Hivites and Jebusites. {12} Be careful not to make a treaty with those who live in the land where you are going, or they will be a snare among you. {13} Break down their altars, smash their sacred stones and cut down their Asherah poles. {14} Do not worship any other god, for the LORD, whose name is Jealous, is a jealous God. {15} "Be careful not to make a treaty with those who live in the land; for when they prostitute themselves to their gods and sacrifice to them, they will invite you and you will eat their sacrifices. {16} And when you choose some of their daughters as wives for your sons and those daughters prostitute themselves to their gods, they will lead your sons to do the same.

BUILDING THE TABERNACLE, THE ARK
AND THE ALTAR OF INCENSE

Exo 36:2-6
Then Moses summoned Bezalel and Oholiab and every skilled person to whom the LORD had given ability and who was willing to come and do the work. {3} They received from Moses all the offerings the Israelites had brought to carry out the work of constructing the sanctuary. And the people continued to bring freewill offerings morning after morning. {4} So all the skilled craftsmen who were doing all the work on the sanctuary left their work {5} and said to Moses, "The people are bringing more than enough for doing the work the LORD commanded to be done." {6} Then Moses gave an order and they sent this word throughout the camp: "No man or woman is to make anything else as an offering for the sanctuary." And so the people were restrained from bringing more,

Exo 37:1-9
Bezalel made the ark of acacia wood–two and a half cubits long, a cubit and a half wide, and a cubit and a half high. {2} He overlaid it with pure gold, both inside and out, and made a gold molding around it. {3} He cast four gold rings for it and fastened them to its four feet, with two rings on one side and two rings on the other. {4} Then he made poles of acacia wood and overlaid them with gold. {5} And he inserted the poles into the rings on the sides of the ark to carry it. {6} He made the atonement cover of pure gold–two and a half cubits long and a cubit and a half wide. {7} Then he made two cherubim out of hammered gold at the ends of the cover. {8} He made one cherub on one end and the second cherub on the other; at the two ends he made them of one piece with the cover. {9} The cherubim had their wings spread upward, overshadowing the cover with them. The cherubim faced each other, looking toward the cover.

Exo 37:25-29
They made the altar of incense out of acacia wood. It was square, a cubit long and a cubit wide, and two cubits high –its horns of one piece with it. {26} They overlaid the top and all the sides and the horns with pure gold, and made a gold molding around it. {27} They made two gold rings below the molding–two on opposite sides–to hold the poles used to carry it. {28} They made the poles of acacia wood and overlaid them with gold. {29} They also made the sacred anointing oil and the pure, fragrant incense–the work of a perfumer.

MOSES SETS UP THE TABERNACLE
AND THE TENT OF MEETING

Exo 40:1-17

Then the LORD said to Moses: {2} "Set up the tabernacle, the Tent of Meeting, on the first day of the first month. {3} Place the ark of the Testimony in it and shield the ark with the curtain. {4} Bring in the table and set out what belongs on it. Then bring in the lampstand and set up its lamps. {5} Place the gold altar of incense in front of the ark of the Testimony and put the curtain at the entrance to the tabernacle. {6} "Place the altar of burnt offering in front of the entrance to the tabernacle, the Tent of Meeting; {7} place the basin between the Tent of Meeting and the altar and put water in it. {8} Set up the courtyard around it and put the curtain at the entrance to the courtyard. {9} "Take the anointing oil and anoint the tabernacle and everything in it; consecrate it and all its furnishings, and it will be holy. {10} Then anoint the altar of burnt offering and all its utensils; consecrate the altar, and it will be most holy. {11} Anoint the basin and its stand and consecrate them. {12} "Bring Aaron and his sons to the entrance to the Tent of Meeting and wash them with water. {13} Then dress Aaron in the sacred garments, anoint him and consecrate him so he may serve me as priest. {14} Bring his sons and dress them in tunics. {15} Anoint them just as you anointed their father, so they may serve me as priests. Their anointing will be to a priesthood that will continue for all generations to come." {16} Moses did everything just as the LORD commanded him. {17} So the tabernacle was set up on the first day of the first month in the second year.

Exo 40:34-38

Then the cloud covered the Tent of Meeting, and the glory of the LORD filled the tabernacle. {35} Moses could not enter the Tent of Meeting because the cloud had settled upon it, and the glory of the LORD filled the tabernacle. {36} In all the travels of the Israelites, whenever the cloud lifted from above the tabernacle, they would set out; {37} but if the cloud did not lift, they did not set out—until the day it lifted. {38} So the cloud of the LORD was over the tabernacle by day, and fire was in the cloud by night, in the sight of all the house of Israel during all their travels.

THE SIN OFFERING

Lev 4:5-21

Then the anointed priest shall take some of the bull's blood and carry it into the Tent of Meeting. {6} He is to dip his finger into the blood and sprinkle some of it seven times before the LORD, in front of the curtain of the sanctuary. {7} The priest shall then put some of the blood on the horns of the altar of fragrant incense that is before the LORD in the Tent of Meeting. The rest of the bull's blood he shall pour out at the base of the altar of burnt offering at the entrance to the Tent of Meeting. {8} He shall remove all the fat from the bull of the sin offering–the fat that covers the inner parts or is connected to them, {9} both kidneys with the fat on them near the loins, and the covering of the liver, which he will remove with the kidneys– {10} just as the fat is removed from the ox sacrificed as a fellowship offering. Then the priest shall burn them on the altar of burnt offering. {11} But the hide of the bull and all its flesh, as well as the head and legs, the inner parts and offal– {12} that is, all the rest of the bull–he must take outside the camp to a place ceremonially clean, where the ashes are thrown, and burn it in a wood fire on the ash heap. {13} "If the whole Israelite community sins unintentionally and does what is forbidden in any of the Lord's commands, even though the community is unaware of the matter, they are guilty.

{14} When they become aware of the sin they committed, the assembly must bring a young bull as a sin offering and present it before the Tent of Meeting. {15} The elders of the community are to lay their hands on the bull's head before the LORD, and the bull shall be slaughtered before the LORD. {16} Then the anointed priest is to take some of the bull's blood into the Tent of Meeting. {17} He shall dip his finger into the blood and sprinkle it before the LORD seven times in front of the curtain. {18} He is to put some of the blood on the horns of the altar that is before the LORD in the Tent of Meeting. The rest of the blood he shall pour out at the base of the altar of burnt offering at the entrance to the Tent of Meeting. {19} He shall remove all the fat from it and burn it on the altar, {20} and do with this bull just as he did with the bull for the sin offering. In this way the priest will make atonement for them, and they will be forgiven. {21} Then he shall take the bull outside the camp and burn it as he burned the first bull. This is the sin offering for the community.

AARON AND HIS SONS ANOINTED AS PRIESTS

Lev 8:1-21

The LORD said to Moses, {2} "Bring Aaron and his sons, their garments, the anointing oil, the bull for the sin offering, the two rams and the basket containing bread made without yeast, {3} and gather the entire assembly at the entrance to the Tent of Meeting." {4} Moses did as the LORD commanded him, and the assembly gathered at the entrance to the Tent of Meeting. {5} Moses said to the assembly, "This is what the LORD has commanded to be done." {6} Then Moses brought Aaron and his sons forward and washed them with water. {7} He put the tunic on Aaron, tied the sash around him, clothed him with the robe and put the ephod on him. He also tied the ephod to him by its skillfully woven waistband; so it was fastened on him. {8} He placed the breastpiece on him and put the Urim and Thummim in the breastpiece. {9} Then he placed the turban on Aaron's head and set the gold plate, the sacred diadem, on the front of it, as the LORD commanded Moses.

{10} Then Moses took the anointing oil and anointed the tabernacle and everything in it, and so consecrated them. {11} He sprinkled some of the oil on the altar seven times, anointing the altar and all its utensils and the basin with its stand, to consecrate them. {12} He poured some of the anointing oil on Aaron's head and anointed him to consecrate him. {13} Then he brought Aaron's sons forward, put tunics on them, tied sashes around them and put headbands on them, as the LORD commanded Moses. {14} He then presented the bull for the sin offering, and Aaron and his sons laid their hands on its head. {15} Moses slaughtered the bull and took some of the blood, and with his finger he put it on all the horns of the altar to purify the altar. He poured out the rest of the blood at the base of the altar. So he consecrated it to make atonement for it. {16} Moses also took all the fat around the inner parts, the covering of the liver, and both kidneys and their fat, and burned it on the altar. {17} But the bull with its hide and its flesh and its offal he burned up outside the camp, as the LORD commanded Moses. {18} He then presented the ram for the burnt offering, and Aaron and his sons laid their hands on its head. {19} Then Moses slaughtered the ram and sprinkled the blood against the altar on all sides. {20} He cut the ram into pieces and burned the head, the pieces and the fat. {21} He washed the inner parts and the legs with water and burned the whole ram on the altar as a burnt offering, a pleasing aroma, an offering made to the LORD by fire, as the LORD commanded Moses.

THE PRIESTS BEGIN THEIR MINISTRY

Lev 9:5-23

They took the things Moses commanded to the front of the Tent of Meeting, and the entire assembly came near and stood before the LORD. {6} Then Moses said, "This is what the LORD has commanded you to do, so that the glory of the LORD may appear to you." {7} Moses said to Aaron, "Come to the altar and sacrifice your sin offering and your burnt offering and make atonement for yourself and the people; sacrifice the offering that is for the people and make atonement for them, as the LORD has commanded." {8} So Aaron came to the altar and slaughtered the calf as a sin offering for himself. {9} His sons brought the blood to him, and he dipped his finger into the blood and put it on the horns of the altar; the rest of the blood he poured out at the base of the altar. {10} On the altar he burned the fat, the kidneys and the covering of the liver from the sin offering, as the LORD commanded Moses; {11} the flesh and the hide he burned up outside the camp. {12} Then he slaughtered the burnt offering. His sons handed him the blood, and he sprinkled it against the altar on all sides. {13} They handed him the burnt offering piece by piece, including the head, and he burned them on the altar. {14} He washed the inner parts and the legs and burned them on top of the burnt offering on the altar. {15} Aaron then brought the offering that was for the people. He took the goat for the people's sin offering and slaughtered it and offered it for a sin offering as he did with the first one. {16} He brought the burnt offering and offered it in the prescribed way. {17} He also brought the grain offering, took a handful of it and burned it on the altar in addition to the morning's burnt offering. {18} He slaughtered the ox and the ram as the fellowship offering for the people. His sons handed him the blood, and he sprinkled it against the altar on all sides. {19} But the fat portions of the ox and the ram—the fat tail, the layer of fat, the kidneys and the covering of the liver— {20} these they laid on the breasts, and then Aaron burned the fat on the altar. {21} Aaron waved the breasts and the right thigh before the LORD as a wave offering, as Moses commanded.

{22} Then Aaron lifted his hands toward the people and blessed them. And having sacrificed the sin offering, the burnt offering and the fellowship offering, he stepped down. {23} Moses and Aaron then went into the Tent of Meeting. When they came out, they blessed the people; and the glory of the LORD appeared to all the people.

RULES FOR DAILY LIVING

Lev 19:1-4

The LORD said to Moses, {2} "Speak to the entire assembly of Israel and say to them: 'Be holy because I, the LORD your God, am holy. {3} "'Each of you must respect his mother and father, and you must observe my Sabbaths. I am the LORD your God. {4} "'Do not turn to idols or make gods of cast metal for yourselves. I am the LORD your God.

Lev 19:9-18

"'When you reap the harvest of your land, do not reap to the very edges of your field or gather the gleanings of your harvest. {10} Do not go over your vineyard a second time or pick up the grapes that have fallen. Leave them for the poor and the alien. I am the LORD your God. {11} "'Do not steal. "'Do not lie. "'Do not deceive one another. {12} "'Do not swear falsely by my name and so profane the name of your God. I am the LORD. {13} "'Do not defraud your neighbor or rob him. "'Do not hold back the wages of a hired man overnight. {14} "'Do not curse the deaf or put a stumbling block in front of the blind, but fear your God. I am the LORD. {15} "'Do not pervert justice; do not show partiality to the poor or favoritism to the great, but judge your neighbor fairly. {16} "'Do not go about spreading slander among your people. "'Do not do anything that endangers your neighbor's life. I am the LORD. {17} "'Do not hate your brother in your heart. Rebuke your neighbor frankly so you will not share in his guilt. {18} "'Do not seek revenge or bear a grudge against one of your people, but love your neighbor as yourself. I am the LORD.

Lev 19:30-37

"'Observe my Sabbaths and have reverence for my sanctuary. I am the LORD. {31} "'Do not turn to mediums or seek out spiritists, for you will be defiled by them. I am the LORD your God. {32} "'Rise in the presence of the aged, show respect for the elderly and revere your God. I am the LORD. {33} "'When an alien lives with you in your land, do not mistreat him. {34} The alien living with you must be treated as one of your native-born. Love him as yourself, for you were aliens in Egypt. I am the LORD your God. {35} "'Do not use dishonest standards when measuring length, weight or quantity. {36} Use honest scales and honest weights, an honest ephah and an honest hin. I am the LORD your God, who brought you out of Egypt. {37} "'Keep all my decrees and all my laws and follow them. I am the LORD.'"

THE SABBATICAL YEAR; THE YEAR OF JUBILEE

Lev 25:3-23

For six years sow your fields, and for six years prune your vineyards and gather their crops. {4} But in the seventh year the land is to have a sabbath of rest, a sabbath to the LORD. Do not sow your fields or prune your vineyards. {5} Do not reap what grows of itself or harvest the grapes of your untended vines. The land is to have a year of rest. {6} Whatever the land yields during the sabbath year will be food for you–for yourself, your manservant and maidservant, and the hired worker and temporary resident who live among you, {7} as well as for your livestock and the wild animals in your land. Whatever the land produces may be eaten.

{8} "Count off seven sabbaths of years–seven times seven years– so that the seven sabbaths of years amount to a period of forty-nine years. {9} Then have the trumpet sounded everywhere on the tenth day of the seventh month; on the Day of Atonement sound the trumpet throughout your land. {10} Consecrate the fiftieth year and proclaim liberty throughout the land to all its inhabitants. It shall be a jubilee for you; each one of you is to return to his family property and each to his own clan. {11} The fiftieth year shall be a jubilee for you; do not sow and do not reap what grows of itself or harvest the untended vines. {12} For it is a jubilee and is to be holy for you; eat only what is taken directly from the fields. {13} "In this Year of Jubilee everyone is to return to his own property. {14} "If you sell land to one of your countrymen or buy any from him, do not take advantage of each other. {15} You are to buy from your countryman on the basis of the number of years since the Jubilee. And he is to sell to you on the basis of the number of years left for harvesting crops. {16} When the years are many, you are to increase the price, and when the years are few, you are to decrease the price, because what he is really selling you is the number of crops. {17} Do not take advantage of each other, but fear your God. I am the LORD your God. {18} "Follow my decrees and be careful to obey my laws, and you will live safely in the land. {19} Then the land will yield its fruit, and you will eat your fill and live there in safety. {20} You may ask, "What will we eat in the seventh year if we do not plant or harvest our crops?" {21} I will send you such a blessing in the sixth year that the land will yield enough for three years. {22} While you plant during the eighth year, you will eat from the old crop and will continue to eat from it until the harvest of the ninth year comes in. {23} "The land must not be sold permanently, because the land is mine and you are but aliens and my tenants.

THE REWARDS OF OBEDIENCE,
AND THE PUNISHMENTS FOR DISOBEDIENCE

Lev 26:3-21

"If you follow my decrees and are careful to obey my commands, {4} I will send you rain in its season, and the ground will yield its crops and the trees of the field their fruit. {5} Your threshing will continue until grape harvest and the grape harvest will continue until planting, and you will eat all the food you want and live in safety in your land. {6} "'I will grant peace in the land, and you will lie down and no one will make you afraid. I will remove savage beasts from the land, and the sword will not pass through your country. {7} You will pursue your enemies, and they will fall by the sword before you. {8} Five of you will chase a hundred, and a hundred of you will chase ten thousand, and your enemies will fall by the sword before you. {9} "'I will look on you with favor and make you fruitful and increase your numbers, and I will keep my covenant with you. {10} You will still be eating last year's harvest when you will have to move it out to make room for the new. {11} I will put my dwelling place among you, and I will not abhor you. {12} I will walk among you and be your God, and you will be my people. {13} I am the LORD your God, who brought you out of Egypt so that you would no longer be slaves to the Egyptians; I broke the bars of your yoke and enabled you to walk with heads held high.

{14} "'But if you will not listen to me and carry out all these commands, {15} and if you reject my decrees and abhor my laws and fail to carry out all my commands and so violate my covenant, {16} then I will do this to you: I will bring upon you sudden terror, wasting diseases and fever that will destroy your sight and drain away your life. You will plant seed in vain, because your enemies will eat it. {17} I will set my face against you so that you will be defeated by your enemies; those who hate you will rule over you, and you will flee even when no one is pursuing you. {18} "'If after all this you will not listen to me, I will punish you for your sins seven times over. {19} I will break down your stubborn pride and make the sky above you like iron and the ground beneath you like bronze. {20} Your strength will be spent in vain, because your soil will not yield its crops, nor will the trees of the land yield their fruit. {21} "'If you remain hostile toward me and refuse to listen to me, I will multiply your afflictions seven times over, as your sins deserve.

A TITHE BELONGS TO THE LORD

Lev 27:16-28

"'If a man dedicates to the LORD part of his family land, its value is to be set according to the amount of seed required for it—fifty shekels of silver to a homer of barley seed. {17} If he dedicates his field during the Year of Jubilee, the value that has been set remains. {18} But if he dedicates his field after the Jubilee, the priest will determine the value according to the number of years that remain until the next Year of Jubilee, and its set value will be reduced. {19} If the man who dedicates the field wishes to redeem it, he must add a fifth to its value, and the field will again become his. {20} If, however, he does not redeem the field, or if he has sold it to someone else, it can never be redeemed. {21} When the field is released in the Jubilee, it will become holy, like a field devoted to the LORD; it will become the property of the priests. {22} "'If a man dedicates to the LORD a field he has bought, which is not part of his family land, {23} the priest will determine its value up to the Year of Jubilee, and the man must pay its value on that day as something holy to the LORD. {24} In the Year of Jubilee the field will revert to the person from whom he bought it, the one whose land it was. {25} Every value is to be set according to the sanctuary shekel, twenty gerahs to the shekel. {26} "'No one, however, may dedicate the firstborn of an animal, since the firstborn already belongs to the LORD; whether an ox or a sheep, it is the Lord's. {27} If it is one of the unclean animals, he may buy it back at its set value, adding a fifth of the value to it. If he does not redeem it, it is to be sold at its set value. {28} "'But nothing that a man owns and devotes to the LORD—whether man or animal or family land—may be sold or redeemed; everything so devoted is most holy to the LORD.

Lev 27:30-34

"'A tithe of everything from the land, whether grain from the soil or fruit from the trees, belongs to the LORD; it is holy to the LORD. {31} If a man redeems any of his tithe, he must add a fifth of the value to it. {32} The entire tithe of the herd and flock—every tenth animal that passes under the shepherd's rod—will be holy to the LORD. {33} He must not pick out the good from the bad or make any substitution. If he does make a substitution, both the animal and its substitute become holy and cannot be redeemed.'" {34} These are the commands the LORD gave Moses on Mount Sinai for the Israelites.

A CENSUS OF ISRAEL

Num 1:20 From the descendants of Reuben the firstborn son of Israel: All the men twenty years old or more who were able to serve in the army were listed by name, one by one, according to the records of their clans and families.

Num 1:21
The number from the tribe of Reuben was 46,500.

Num 1:23
The number from the tribe of Simeon was 59,300.

Num 1:25
The number from the tribe of Gad was 45,650.

Num 1:27
The number from the tribe of Judah was 74,600.

Num 1:29
The number from the tribe of Issachar was 54,400.

Num 1:31
The number from the tribe of Zebulun was 57,400.

Num 1:33
The number from the tribe of Ephraim was 40,500.

Num 1:35
The number from the tribe of Manasseh was 32,200.

Num 1:37
The number from the tribe of Benjamin was 35,400.

Num 1:39
The number from the tribe of Dan was 62,700.

Num 1:41
The number from the tribe of Asher was 41,500.

Num 1:43
The number from the tribe of Naphtali was 53,400.

Num 1:45-50 All the Israelites twenty years old or more who were able to serve in Israel's army were counted according to their families. {46} The total number was 603,550. {47} The families of the tribe of Levi, however, were not counted along with the others. {48} The LORD had said to Moses: {49} "You must not count the tribe of Levi or include them in the census of the other Israelites. {50} Instead, appoint the Levites to be in charge of the tabernacle of the Testimony—over all its furnishings and everything belonging to it. They are to carry the tabernacle and all its furnishings; they are to take care of it and encamp around it.

AARON AND SONS APPOINTED AS PRIESTS

Num 3:1-16

This is the account of the family of Aaron and Moses at the time the LORD talked with Moses on Mount Sinai. {2} The names of the sons of Aaron were Nadab the firstborn and Abihu, Eleazar and Ithamar. {3} Those were the names of Aaron's sons, the anointed priests, who were ordained to serve as priests. {4} Nadab and Abihu, however, fell dead before the LORD when they made an offering with unauthorized fire before him in the Desert of Sinai. They had no sons; so only Eleazar and Ithamar served as priests during the lifetime of their father Aaron. {5} The LORD said to Moses, {6} "Bring the tribe of Levi and present them to Aaron the priest to assist him. {7} They are to perform duties for him and for the whole community at the Tent of Meeting by doing the work of the tabernacle. {8} They are to take care of all the furnishings of the Tent of Meeting, fulfilling the obligations of the Israelites by doing the work of the tabernacle. {9} Give the Levites to Aaron and his sons; they are the Israelites who are to be given wholly to him.

{10} Appoint Aaron and his sons to serve as priests; anyone else who approaches the sanctuary must be put to death." {11} The LORD also said to Moses, {12} "I have taken the Levites from among the Israelites in place of the first male offspring of every Israelite woman. The Levites are mine, {13} for all the firstborn are mine. When I struck down all the firstborn in Egypt, I set apart for myself every firstborn in Israel, whether man or animal. They are to be mine. I am the LORD." {14} The LORD said to Moses in the Desert of Sinai, {15} "Count the Levites by their families and clans. Count every male a month old or more." {16} So Moses counted them, as he was commanded by the word of the LORD.

Num 3:39-43

The total number of Levites counted at the Lord's command by Moses and Aaron according to their clans, including every male a month old or more, was 22,000. {40} The LORD said to Moses, "Count all the firstborn Israelite males who are a month old or more and make a list of their names. {41} Take the Levites for me in place of all the firstborn of the Israelites, and the livestock of the Levites in place of all the firstborn of the livestock of the Israelites. I am the LORD." {42} So Moses counted all the firstborn of the Israelites, as the LORD commanded him. {43} The total number of firstborn males a month old or more, listed by name, was 22,273.

LEVITES SET APART

Num 8:5-25

The LORD said to Moses: {6} "Take the Levites from among the other Israelites and make them ceremonially clean. {7} To purify them, do this: Sprinkle the water of cleansing on them; then have them shave their whole bodies and wash their clothes, and so purify themselves. {8} Have them take a young bull with its grain offering of fine flour mixed with oil; then you are to take a second young bull for a sin offering. {9} Bring the Levites to the front of the Tent of Meeting and assemble the whole Israelite community. {10} You are to bring the Levites before the LORD, and the Israelites are to lay their hands on them. {11} Aaron is to present the Levites before the LORD as a wave offering from the Israelites, so that they may be ready to do the work of the LORD. {12} "After the Levites lay their hands on the heads of the bulls, use the one for a sin offering to the LORD and the other for a burnt offering, to make atonement for the Levites. {13} Have the Levites stand in front of Aaron and his sons and then present them as a wave offering to the LORD. {14} In this way you are to set the Levites apart from the other Israelites, and the Levites will be mine. {15} "After you have purified the Levites and presented them as a wave offering, they are to come to do their work at the Tent of Meeting. {16} They are the Israelites who are to be given wholly to me. I have taken them as my own in place of the firstborn, the first male offspring from every Israelite woman.

{17} Every firstborn male in Israel, whether man or animal, is mine. When I struck down all the firstborn in Egypt, I set them apart for myself. {18} And I have taken the Levites in place of all the firstborn sons in Israel. {19} Of all the Israelites, I have given the Levites as gifts to Aaron and his sons to do the work at the Tent of Meeting on behalf of the Israelites and to make atonement for them so that no plague will strike the Israelites when they go near the sanctuary." {20} Moses, Aaron and the whole Israelite community did with the Levites just as the LORD commanded Moses. {21} The Levites purified themselves and washed their clothes. Then Aaron presented them as a wave offering before the LORD and made atonement for them to purify them. {22} After that, the Levites came to do their work at the Tent of Meeting under the supervision of Aaron and his sons. They did with the Levites just as the LORD commanded Moses. {23} The LORD said to Moses, {24} "This applies to the Levites: Men twenty-five years old or more shall come to take part in the work at the Tent of Meeting, {25} but at the age of fifty, they must retire from their regular service and work no longer.

ISRAELITES LEAVE SINAI

Num 10:11-17

On the twentieth day of the second month of the second year, the cloud lifted from above the tabernacle of the Testimony. {12} Then the Israelites set out from the Desert of Sinai and traveled from place to place until the cloud came to rest in the Desert of Paran. {13} They set out, this first time, at the Lord's command through Moses. {14} The divisions of the camp of Judah went first, under their standard. Nahshon son of Amminadab was in command. {15} Nethanel son of Zuar was over the division of the tribe of Issachar, {16} and Eliab son of Helon was over the division of the tribe of Zebulun. {17} Then the tabernacle was taken down, and the Gershonites and Merarites, who carried it, set out.

Num 10:29-36

Now Moses said to Hobab son of Reuel the Midianite, Moses' father-in-law, "We are setting out for the place about which the LORD said, 'I will give it to you.' Come with us and we will treat you well, for the LORD has promised good things to Israel." {30} He answered, "No, I will not go; I am going back to my own land and my own people." {31} But Moses said, "Please do not leave us. You know where we should camp in the desert, and you can be our eyes. {32} If you come with us, we will share with you whatever good things the LORD gives us." {33} So they set out from the mountain of the LORD and traveled for three days. The ark of the covenant of the LORD went before them during those three days to find them a place to rest. {34} The cloud of the LORD was over them by day when they set out from the camp. {35} Whenever the ark set out, Moses said, "Rise up, O LORD! May your enemies be scattered; may your foes flee before you." {36} Whenever it came to rest, he said, "Return, O LORD, to the countless thousands of Israel."

SEVENTY ELDERS APPOINTED

Num 11:11-17

He asked the LORD, "Why have you brought this trouble on your servant? What have I done to displease you that you put the burden of all these people on me? {12} Did I conceive all these people? Did I give them birth? Why do you tell me to carry them in my arms, as a nurse carries an infant, to the land you promised on oath to their forefathers? {13} Where can I get meat for all these people? They keep wailing to me, 'Give us meat to eat!' {14} I cannot carry all these people by myself; the burden is too heavy for me. {15} If this is how you are going to treat me, put me to death right now—if I have found favor in your eyes—and do not let me face my own ruin." {16} The LORD said to Moses: "Bring me seventy of Israel's elders who are known to you as leaders and officials among the people. Have them come to the Tent of Meeting, that they may stand there with you. {17} I will come down and speak with you there, and I will take of the Spirit that is on you and put the Spirit on them. They will help you carry the burden of the people so that you will not have to carry it alone.

THE PEOPLE COMPLAIN AND GET QUAIL

Num 11:31-34

Now a wind went out from the LORD and drove quail in from the sea. It brought them down all around the camp to about three feet above the ground, as far as a day's walk in any direction. {32} All that day and night and all the next day the people went out and gathered quail. No one gathered less than ten homers. Then they spread them out all around the camp. {33} But while the meat was still between their teeth and before it could be consumed, the anger of the LORD burned against the people, and he struck them with a severe plague. {34} Therefore the place was named Kibroth Hattaavah, because there they buried the people who had craved other food.

MIRIAM AND AARON TALK AGAINST MOSES

Num 12:1-15

Miriam and Aaron began to talk against Moses because of his Cushite wife, for he had married a Cushite. {2} "Has the LORD spoken only through Moses?" they asked. "Hasn't he also spoken through us?" And the LORD heard this. {3} (Now Moses was a very humble man, more humble than anyone else on the face of the earth.) {4} At once the LORD said to Moses, Aaron and Miriam, "Come out to the Tent of Meeting, all three of you." So the three of them came out. {5} Then the LORD came down in a pillar of cloud; he stood at the entrance to the Tent and summoned Aaron and Miriam. When both of them stepped forward, {6} he said, "Listen to my words: "When a prophet of the LORD is among you, I reveal myself to him in visions, I speak to him in dreams. {7} But this is not true of my servant Moses; he is faithful in all my house. {8} With him I speak face to face, clearly and not in riddles; he sees the form of the LORD. Why then were you not afraid to speak against my servant Moses?"

{9} The anger of the LORD burned against them, and he left them. {10} When the cloud lifted from above the Tent, there stood Miriam—leprous, like snow. Aaron turned toward her and saw that she had leprosy; {11} and he said to Moses, "Please, my lord, do not hold against us the sin we have so foolishly committed. {12} Do not let her be like a stillborn infant coming from its mother's womb with its flesh half eaten away." {13} So Moses cried out to the LORD, "O God, please heal her!" {14} The LORD replied to Moses, "If her father had spit in her face, would she not have been in disgrace for seven days? Confine her outside the camp for seven days; after that she can be brought back." {15} So Miriam was confined outside the camp for seven days, and the people did not move on till she was brought back.

SCOUTS LOOK AT CANAAN

Num 13:1-2

The LORD said to Moses, {2} "Send some men to explore the land of Canaan, which I am giving to the Israelites. From each ancestral tribe send one of its leaders."

Num 13:17-33

When Moses sent them to explore Canaan, he said, "Go up through the Negev and on into the hill country. {18} See what the land is like and whether the people who live there are strong or weak, few or many. {19} What kind of land do they live in? Is it good or bad? What kind of towns do they live in? Are they unwalled or fortified? {20} How is the soil? Is it fertile or poor? Are there trees on it or not? Do your best to bring back some of the fruit of the land." (It was the season for the first ripe grapes.) {21} So they went up and explored the land from the Desert of Zin as far as Rehob, toward Lebo Hamath. {22} They went up through the Negev and came to Hebron, where Ahiman, Sheshai and Talmai, the descendants of Anak, lived. (Hebron had been built seven years before Zoan in Egypt.) {23} When they reached the Valley of Eshcol, they cut off a branch bearing a single cluster of grapes. Two of them carried it on a pole between them, along with some pomegranates and figs. {24} That place was called the Valley of Eshcol because of the cluster of grapes the Israelites cut off there. {25} At the end of forty days they returned from exploring the land. {26} They came back to Moses and Aaron and the whole Israelite community at Kadesh in the Desert of Paran. There they reported to them and to the whole assembly and showed them the fruit of the land. {27} They gave Moses this account: "We went into the land to which you sent us, and it does flow with milk and honey! Here is its fruit. {28} But the people who live there are powerful, and the cities are fortified and very large. We even saw descendants of Anak there. {29} The Amalekites live in the Negev; the Hittites, Jebusites and Amorites live in the hill country; and the Canaanites live near the sea and along the Jordan." {30} Then Caleb silenced the people before Moses and said, "We should go up and take possession of the land, for we can certainly do it." {31} But the men who had gone up with him said, "We can't attack those people; they are stronger than we are." {32} And they spread among the Israelites a bad report about the land they had explored. They said, "The land we explored devours those living in it. All the people we saw there are of great size. {33} We saw the Nephilim there (the descendants of Anak come from the Nephilim). We seemed like grasshoppers in our own eyes, and we looked the same to them."

AGAIN THE PEOPLE GRUMBLE

Num 14:7-24
"The land we passed through and explored is exceedingly good. {8} If the LORD is pleased with us, he will lead us into that land, a land flowing with milk and honey, and will give it to us. {9} Only do not rebel against the LORD. And do not be afraid of the people of the land, because we will swallow them up. Their protection is gone, but the LORD is with us. Do not be afraid of them." {10} But the whole assembly talked about stoning them. Then the glory of the LORD appeared at the Tent of Meeting to all the Israelites.

{11} The LORD said to Moses, "How long will these people treat me with contempt? How long will they refuse to believe in me, in spite of all the miraculous signs I have performed among them? {12} I will strike them down with a plague and destroy them, but I will make you into a nation greater and stronger than they."

{13} Moses said to the LORD, "Then the Egyptians will hear about it! By your power you brought these people up from among them. {14} And they will tell the inhabitants of this land about it. They have already heard that you, O LORD, are with these people and that you, O LORD, have been seen face to face, that your cloud stays over them, and that you go before them in a pillar of cloud by day and a pillar of fire by night. {15} If you put these people to death all at one time, the nations who have heard this report about you will say, {16} 'The LORD was not able to bring these people into the land he promised them on oath; so he slaughtered them in the desert.' {17} "Now may the Lord's strength be displayed, just as you have declared: {18} 'The LORD is slow to anger, abounding in love and forgiving sin and rebellion. Yet he does not leave the guilty unpunished; he punishes the children for the sin of the fathers to the third and fourth generation.' {19} In accordance with your great love, forgive the sin of these people, just as you have pardoned them from the time they left Egypt until now."

{20} The LORD replied, "I have forgiven them, as you asked. {21} Nevertheless, as surely as I live and as surely as the glory of the LORD fills the whole earth, {22} not one of the men who saw my glory and the miraculous signs I performed in Egypt and in the desert but who disobeyed me and tested me ten times– {23} not one of them will ever see the land I promised on oath to their forefathers. No one who has treated me with contempt will ever see it. {24} But because my servant Caleb has a different spirit and follows me wholeheartedly, I will bring him into the land he went to, and his descendants will inherit it.

78

MOSES STRIKES ROCK FOR WATER

Num 20:2-12

Now there was no water for the community, and the people gathered in opposition to Moses and Aaron. {3} They quarreled with Moses and said, "If only we had died when our brothers fell dead before the LORD! {4} Why did you bring the Lord's community into this desert, that we and our livestock should die here? {5} Why did you bring us up out of Egypt to this terrible place? It has no grain or figs, grapevines or pomegranates. And there is no water to drink!" {6} Moses and Aaron went from the assembly to the entrance to the Tent of Meeting and fell facedown, and the glory of the LORD appeared to them. {7} The LORD said to Moses, {8} "Take the staff, and you and your brother Aaron gather the assembly together. Speak to that rock before their eyes and it will pour out its water. You will bring water out of the rock for the community so they and their livestock can drink." {9} So Moses took the staff from the Lord's presence, just as he commanded him. {10} He and Aaron gathered the assembly together in front of the rock and Moses said to them, "Listen, you rebels, must we bring you water out of this rock?" {11} Then Moses raised his arm and struck the rock twice with his staff. Water gushed out, and the community and their livestock drank. {12} But the LORD said to Moses and Aaron, "Because you did not trust in me enough to honor me as holy in the sight of the Israelites, you will not bring this community into the land I give them."

EDOM REFUSES PASSAGE TO ISRAEL

Num 20:15-21

"Our forefathers went down into Egypt, and we lived there many years. The Egyptians mistreated us and our fathers, {16} but when we cried out to the LORD, he heard our cry and sent an angel and brought us out of Egypt. "Now we are here at Kadesh, a town on the edge of your territory. {17} Please let us pass through your country. We will not go through any field or vineyard, or drink water from any well. We will travel along the king's highway and not turn to the right or to the left until we have passed through your territory." {18} But Edom answered: "You may not pass through here; if you try, we will march out and attack you with the sword." {19} The Israelites replied: "We will go along the main road, and if we or our livestock drink any of your water, we will pay for it. We only want to pass through on foot—nothing else." {20} Again they answered: "You may not pass through." Then Edom came out against them with a large and powerful army. {21} Since Edom refused to let them go through their territory, Israel turned away from them.

AARON DIES

Num 20:22-29

The whole Israelite community set out from Kadesh and came to Mount Hor. {23} At Mount Hor, near the border of Edom, the LORD said to Moses and Aaron, {24} "Aaron will be gathered to his people. He will not enter the land I give the Israelites, because both of you rebelled against my command at the waters of Meribah. {25} Get Aaron and his son Eleazar and take them up Mount Hor. {26} Remove Aaron's garments and put them on his son Eleazar, for Aaron will be gathered to his people; he will die there." {27} Moses did as the LORD commanded: They went up Mount Hor in the sight of the whole community. {28} Moses removed Aaron's garments and put them on his son Eleazar. And Aaron died there on top of the mountain. Then Moses and Eleazar came down from the mountain, {29} and when the whole community learned that Aaron had died, the entire house of Israel mourned for him thirty days.

BRONZE SNAKE ON A POLE

Num 21:4-9

They traveled from Mount Hor along the route to the Red Sea, to go around Edom. But the people grew impatient on the way; {5} they spoke against God and against Moses, and said, "Why have you brought us up out of Egypt to die in the desert? There is no bread! There is no water! And we detest this miserable food!" {6} Then the LORD sent venomous snakes among them; they bit the people and many Israelites died. {7} The people came to Moses and said, "We sinned when we spoke against the LORD and against you. Pray that the LORD will take the snakes away from us." So Moses prayed for the people. {8} The LORD said to Moses, "Make a snake and put it up on a pole; anyone who is bitten can look at it and live." {9} So Moses made a bronze snake and put it up on a pole. Then when anyone was bitten by a snake and looked at the bronze snake, he lived.

BALAAM IS ASKED TO PROPHECY

Num 22:21-38

Balaam got up in the morning, saddled his donkey and went with the princes of Moab. {22} But God was very angry when he went, and the angel of the LORD stood in the road to oppose him. Balaam was riding on his donkey, and his two servants were with him. {23} When the donkey saw the angel of the LORD standing in the road with a drawn sword in his hand, she turned off the road into a field. Balaam beat her to get her back on the road. {24} Then the angel of the LORD stood in a narrow path between two vineyards, with walls on both sides. {25} When the donkey saw the angel of the LORD, she pressed close to the wall, crushing Balaam's foot against it. So he beat her again. {26} Then the angel of the LORD moved on ahead and stood in a narrow place where there was no room to turn, either to the right or to the left. {27} When the donkey saw the angel of the LORD, she lay down under Balaam, and he was angry and beat her with his staff. {28} Then the LORD opened the donkey's mouth, and she said to Balaam, "What have I done to you to make you beat me these three times?" {29} Balaam answered the donkey, "You have made a fool of me! If I had a sword in my hand, I would kill you right now." {30} The donkey said to Balaam, "Am I not your own donkey, which you have always ridden, to this day? Have I been in the habit of doing this to you?" "No," he said. {31} Then the LORD opened Balaam's eyes, and he saw the angel of the LORD standing in the road with his sword drawn. So he bowed low and fell facedown. {32} The angel of the LORD asked him, "Why have you beaten your donkey these three times? I have come here to oppose you because your path is a reckless one before me. {33} The donkey saw me and turned away from me these three times. If she had not turned away, I would certainly have killed you by now, but I would have spared her." {34} Balaam said to the angel of the LORD, "I have sinned. I did not realize you were standing in the road to oppose me. Now if you are displeased, I will go back." {35} The angel of the LORD said to Balaam, "Go with the men, but speak only what I tell you." So Balaam went with the princes of Balak. {36} When Balak heard that Balaam was coming, he went out to meet him at the Moabite town on the Arnon border, at the edge of his territory. {37} Balak said to Balaam, "Did I not send you an urgent summons? Why didn't you come to me? Am I really not able to reward you?" {38} "Well, I have come to you now," Balaam replied. "But can I say just anything? I must speak only what God puts in my mouth."

BALAAM BLESSES ISRAEL

Num 23:7-12

Then Balaam uttered his oracle: "Balak brought me from Aram, the king of Moab from the eastern mountains. 'Come,' he said, 'curse Jacob for me; come, denounce Israel.' {8} How can I curse those whom God has not cursed? How can I denounce those whom the LORD has not denounced? {9} From the rocky peaks I see them, from the heights I view them. I see a people who live apart and do not consider themselves one of the nations. {10} Who can count the dust of Jacob or number the fourth part of Israel? Let me die the death of the righteous, and may my end be like theirs!" {11} Balak said to Balaam, "What have you done to me? I brought you to curse my enemies, but you have done nothing but bless them!" {12} He answered, "Must I not speak what the LORD puts in my mouth?"

Num 24:1-9

Now when Balaam saw that it pleased the LORD to bless Israel, he did not resort to sorcery as at other times, but turned his face toward the desert. {2} When Balaam looked out and saw Israel encamped tribe by tribe, the Spirit of God came upon him {3} and he uttered his oracle: "The oracle of Balaam son of Beor, the oracle of one whose eye sees clearly, {4} the oracle of one who hears the words of God, who sees a vision from the Almighty, who falls prostrate, and whose eyes are opened: {5} "How beautiful are your tents, O Jacob, your dwelling places, O Israel! {6} "Like valleys they spread out, like gardens beside a river, like aloes planted by the LORD, like cedars beside the waters. {7} Water will flow from their buckets; their seed will have abundant water. "Their king will be greater than Agag; their kingdom will be exalted. {8} "God brought them out of Egypt; they have the strength of a wild ox. They devour hostile nations and break their bones in pieces; with their arrows they pierce them. {9} Like a lion they crouch and lie down, like a lioness–who dares to rouse them? "May those who bless you be blessed and those who curse you be cursed!"

ANOTHER CENSUS BEFORE ENTERING CANAAN

Num 26:1-4

After the plague the LORD said to Moses and Eleazar son of Aaron, the priest, {2} "Take a census of the whole Israelite community by families—all those twenty years old or more who are able to serve in the army of Israel." {3} So on the plains of Moab by the Jordan across from Jericho, Moses and Eleazar the priest spoke with them and said, {4} "Take a census of the men twenty years old or more, as the LORD commanded Moses." These were the Israelites who came out of Egypt:

Num 26:51-56

The total number of the men of Israel was 601,730. {52} The LORD said to Moses, {53} "The land is to be allotted to them as an inheritance based on the number of names. {54} To a larger group give a larger inheritance, and to a smaller group a smaller one; each is to receive its inheritance according to the number of those listed. {55} Be sure that the land is distributed by lot. What each group inherits will be according to the names for its ancestral tribe. {56} Each inheritance is to be distributed by lot among the larger and smaller groups."

Num 26:62-65

All the male Levites a month old or more numbered 23,000. They were not counted along with the other Israelites because they received no inheritance among them. {63} These are the ones counted by Moses and Eleazar the priest when they counted the Israelites on the plains of Moab by the Jordan across from Jericho. {64} Not one of them was among those counted by Moses and Aaron the priest when they counted the Israelites in the Desert of Sinai. {65} For the LORD had told those Israelites they would surely die in the desert, and not one of them was left except Caleb son of Jephunneh and Joshua son of Nun.

JOSHUA SUCCEEDS MOSES AS LEADER

Num 27:18-23
So the LORD said to Moses, "Take Joshua son of Nun, a man in whom is the spirit, and lay your hand on him. {19} Have him stand before Eleazar the priest and the entire assembly and commission him in their presence. {20} Give him some of your authority so the whole Israelite community will obey him. {21} He is to stand before Eleazar the priest, who will obtain decisions for him by inquiring of the Urim before the LORD. At his command he and the entire community of the Israelites will go out, and at his command they will come in." {22} Moses did as the LORD commanded him. He took Joshua and had him stand before Eleazar the priest and the whole assembly. {23} Then he laid his hands on him and commissioned him, as the LORD instructed through Moses.

REUBEN AND GAD STAY EAST OF JORDAN

Num 32:6-17
Moses said to the Gadites and Reubenites, "Shall your countrymen go to war while you sit here? {7} Why do you discourage the Israelites from going over into the land the LORD has given them? {8} This is what your fathers did when I sent them from Kadesh Barnea to look over the land. {9} After they went up to the Valley of Eshcol and viewed the land, they discouraged the Israelites from entering the land the LORD had given them. {10} The Lord's anger was aroused that day and he swore this oath: {11} 'Because they have not followed me wholeheartedly, not one of the men twenty years old or more who came up out of Egypt will see the land I promised on oath to Abraham, Isaac and Jacob– {12} not one except Caleb son of Jephunneh the Kenizzite and Joshua son of Nun, for they followed the LORD wholeheartedly.' {13} The Lord's anger burned against Israel and he made them wander in the desert forty years, until the whole generation of those who had done evil in his sight was gone. {14} "And here you are, a brood of sinners, standing in the place of your fathers and making the LORD even more angry with Israel. {15} If you turn away from following him, he will again leave all this people in the desert, and you will be the cause of their destruction." {16} Then they came up to him and said, "We would like to build pens here for our livestock and cities for our women and children. {17} But we are ready to arm ourselves and go ahead of the Israelites until we have brought them to their place. Meanwhile our women and children will live in fortified cities, for protection from the inhabitants of the land.

84

INSTRUCTIONS ON HOW TO TAKE CANAAN

Num 33:51b-56

'When you cross the Jordan into Canaan, {52} drive out all the inhabitants of the land before you. Destroy all their carved images and their cast idols, and demolish all their high places. {53} Take possession of the land and settle in it, for I have given you the land to possess. {54} Distribute the land by lot, according to your clans. To a larger group give a larger inheritance, and to a smaller group a smaller one. Whatever falls to them by lot will be theirs. Distribute it according to your ancestral tribes. {55} "'But if you do not drive out the inhabitants of the land, those you allow to remain will become barbs in your eyes and thorns in your sides. They will give you trouble in the land where you will live. {56} And then I will do to you what I plan to do to them.'"

TOWNS FOR LEVITES AND CITIES OF REFUGE

Num 35:2-14

"Command the Israelites to give the Levites towns to live in from the inheritance the Israelites will possess. And give them pasturelands around the towns. {3} Then they will have towns to live in and pasturelands for their cattle, flocks and all their other livestock. {4} "The pasturelands around the towns that you give the Levites will extend out fifteen hundred feet from the town wall. {5} Outside the town, measure three thousand feet on the east side, three thousand on the south side, three thousand on the west and three thousand on the north, with the town in the center. They will have this area as pastureland for the towns. {6} "Six of the towns you give the Levites will be cities of refuge, to which a person who has killed someone may flee. In addition, give them forty-two other towns. {7} In all you must give the Levites forty-eight towns, together with their pasturelands. {8} The towns you give the Levites from the land the Israelites possess are to be given in proportion to the inheritance of each tribe: Take many towns from a tribe that has many, but few from one that has few." {9} Then the LORD said to Moses: {10} "Speak to the Israelites and say to them: 'When you cross the Jordan into Canaan, {11} select some towns to be your cities of refuge, to which a person who has killed someone accidentally may flee. {12} They will be places of refuge from the avenger, so that a person accused of murder may not die before he stands trial before the assembly. {13} These six towns you give will be your cities of refuge. {14} Give three on this side of the Jordan and three in Canaan as cities of refuge.

GOD MAKES FOR HIMSELF ONE NATION

Deu 4:23-38

Be careful not to forget the covenant of the LORD your God that he made with you; do not make for yourselves an idol in the form of anything the LORD your God has forbidden. {24} For the LORD your God is a consuming fire, a jealous God. {25} After you have had children and grandchildren and have lived in the land a long time–if you then become corrupt and make any kind of idol, doing evil in the eyes of the LORD your God and provoking him to anger, {26} I call heaven and earth as witnesses against you this day that you will quickly perish from the land that you are crossing the Jordan to possess. You will not live there long but will certainly be destroyed. {27} The LORD will scatter you among the peoples, and only a few of you will survive among the nations to which the LORD will drive you. {28} There you will worship man-made gods of wood and stone, which cannot see or hear or eat or smell. {29} But if from there you seek the LORD your God, you will find him if you look for him with all your heart and with all your soul. {30} When you are in distress and all these things have happened to you, then in later days you will return to the LORD your God and obey him. {31} For the LORD your God is a merciful God; he will not abandon or destroy you or forget the covenant with your forefathers, which he confirmed to them by oath. {32} Ask now about the former days, long before your time, from the day God created man on the earth; ask from one end of the heavens to the other. Has anything so great as this ever happened, or has anything like it ever been heard of? {33} Has any other people heard the voice of God speaking out of fire, as you have, and lived? {34} Has any god ever tried to take for himself one nation out of another nation, by testings, by miraculous signs and wonders, by war, by a mighty hand and an outstretched arm, or by great and awesome deeds, like all the things the LORD your God did for you in Egypt before your very eyes? {35} You were shown these things so that you might know that the LORD is God; besides him there is no other. {36} From heaven he made you hear his voice to discipline you. On earth he showed you his great fire, and you heard his words from out of the fire. {37} Because he loved your forefathers and chose their descendants after them, he brought you out of Egypt by his Presence and his great strength, {38} to drive out before you nations greater and stronger than you and to bring you into their land to give it to you for your inheritance, as it is today.

86

THE TEN COMMANDMENTS

Deu 5:4-22

The LORD spoke to you face to face out of the fire on the mountain. {5} (At that time I stood between the LORD and you to declare to you the word of the LORD, because you were afraid of the fire and did not go up the mountain.) And he said: {6} "I am the LORD your God, who brought you out of Egypt, out of the land of slavery.

{7} "You shall have no other gods before me.

{8} "You shall not make for yourself an idol in the form of anything in heaven above or on the earth beneath or in the waters below. {9} You shall not bow down to them or worship them; for I, the LORD your God, am a jealous God, punishing the children for the sin of the fathers to the third and fourth generation of those who hate me, {10} but showing love to a thousand <generations> of those who love me and keep my commandments.

{11} "You shall not misuse the name of the LORD your God, for the LORD will not hold anyone guiltless who misuses his name.

{12} "Observe the Sabbath day by keeping it holy, as the LORD your God has commanded you. {13} Six days you shall labor and do all your work, {14} but the seventh day is a Sabbath to the LORD your God. On it you shall not do any work, neither you, nor your son or daughter, nor your manservant or maidservant, nor your ox, your donkey or any of your animals, nor the alien within your gates, so that your manservant and maidservant may rest, as you do. {15} Remember that you were slaves in Egypt and that the LORD your God brought you out of there with a mighty hand and an outstretched arm. Therefore the LORD your God has commanded you to observe the Sabbath day.

{16} "Honor your father and your mother, as the LORD your God has commanded you, so that you may live long and that it may go well with you in the land the LORD your God is giving you.

{17} "You shall not murder.

{18} "You shall not commit adultery.

{19} "You shall not steal.

{20} "You shall not give false testimony against your neighbor.

{21} "You shall not covet your neighbor's wife. You shall not set your desire on your neighbor's house or land, his manservant or maidservant, his ox or donkey, or anything that belongs to your neighbor."

{22} These are the commandments the LORD proclaimed in a loud voice to your whole assembly there on the mountain from out of the fire, the cloud and the deep darkness; and he added nothing more. Then he wrote them on two stone tablets and gave them to me.

FEAR THE LORD AND SERVE HIM ONLY

Deu 6:3-25

Hear, O Israel, and be careful to obey so that it may go well with you and that you may increase greatly in a land flowing with milk and honey, just as the LORD, the God of your fathers, promised you. {4} Hear, O Israel: The LORD our God, the LORD is one. {5} Love the LORD your God with all your heart and with all your soul and with all your strength. {6} These commandments that I give you today are to be upon your hearts. {7} Impress them on your children. Talk about them when you sit at home and when you walk along the road, when you lie down and when you get up. {8} Tie them as symbols on your hands and bind them on your foreheads. {9} Write them on the doorframes of your houses and on your gates. {10} When the LORD your God brings you into the land he swore to your fathers, to Abraham, Isaac and Jacob, to give you–a land with large, flourishing cities you did not build, {11} houses filled with all kinds of good things you did not provide, wells you did not dig, and vineyards and olive groves you did not plant–then when you eat and are satisfied, {12} be careful that you do not forget the LORD, who brought you out of Egypt, out of the land of slavery. {13} Fear the LORD your God, serve him only and take your oaths in his name. {14} Do not follow other gods, the gods of the peoples around you; {15} for the LORD your God, who is among you, is a jealous God and his anger will burn against you, and he will destroy you from the face of the land. {16} Do not test the LORD your God as you did at Massah. {17} Be sure to keep the commands of the LORD your God and the stipulations and decrees he has given you. {18} Do what is right and good in the Lord's sight, so that it may go well with you and you may go in and take over the good land that the LORD promised on oath to your forefathers, {19} thrusting out all your enemies before you, as the LORD said.

{20} In the future, when your son asks you, "What is the meaning of the stipulations, decrees and laws the LORD our God has commanded you?" {21} tell him: "We were slaves of Pharaoh in Egypt, but the LORD brought us out of Egypt with a mighty hand. {22} Before our eyes the LORD sent miraculous signs and wonders–great and terrible–upon Egypt and Pharaoh and his whole household. {23} But he brought us out from there to bring us in and give us the land that he promised on oath to our forefathers. {24} The LORD commanded us to obey all these decrees and to fear the LORD our God, so that we might always prosper and be kept alive, as is the case today. {25} And if we are careful to obey all this law before the LORD our God, as he has commanded us, that will be our righteousness."

A SPECIAL PEOPLE LOVED OF GOD

Deu 7:7-19

The LORD did not set his affection on you and choose you because you were more numerous than other peoples, for you were the fewest of all peoples. {8} But it was because the LORD loved you and kept the oath he swore to your forefathers that he brought you out with a mighty hand and redeemed you from the land of slavery, from the power of Pharaoh king of Egypt. {9} Know therefore that the LORD your God is God; he is the faithful God, keeping his covenant of love to a thousand generations of those who love him and keep his commands. {10} But those who hate him he will repay to their face by destruction; he will not be slow to repay to their face those who hate him. {11} Therefore, take care to follow the commands, decrees and laws I give you today. {12} If you pay attention to these laws and are careful to follow them, then the LORD your God will keep his covenant of love with you, as he swore to your forefathers. {13} He will love you and bless you and increase your numbers. He will bless the fruit of your womb, the crops of your land–your grain, new wine and oil–the calves of your herds and the lambs of your flocks in the land that he swore to your forefathers to give you. {14} You will be blessed more than any other people; none of your men or women will be childless, nor any of your livestock without young. {15} The LORD will keep you free from every disease. He will not inflict on you the horrible diseases you knew in Egypt, but he will inflict them on all who hate you. {16} You must destroy all the peoples the LORD your God gives over to you. Do not look on them with pity and do not serve their gods, for that will be a snare to you. {17} You may say to yourselves, "These nations are stronger than we are. How can we drive them out?" {18} But do not be afraid of them; remember well what the LORD your God did to Pharaoh and to all Egypt. {19} You saw with your own eyes the great trials, the miraculous signs and wonders, the mighty hand and outstretched arm, with which the LORD your God brought you out. The LORD your God will do the same to all the peoples you now fear.

Deu 7:25-26

The images of their gods you are to burn in the fire. Do not covet the silver and gold on them, and do not take it for yourselves, or you will be ensnared by it, for it is detestable to the LORD your God. {26} Do not bring a detestable thing into your house or you, like it, will be set apart for destruction. Utterly abhor and detest it, for it is set apart for destruction.

GIVE A TITHE; HELP THE POOR

Deu 14:22-23

Be sure to set aside a tenth of all that your fields produce each year. {23} Eat the tithe of your grain, new wine and oil, and the firstborn of your herds and flocks in the presence of the LORD your God at the place he will choose as a dwelling for his Name, so that you may learn to revere the LORD your God always.

Deu 14:27-29

And do not neglect the Levites living in your towns, for they have no allotment or inheritance of their own. {28} At the end of every three years, bring all the tithes of that year's produce and store it in your towns, {29} so that the Levites (who have no allotment or inheritance of their own) and the aliens, the fatherless and the widows who live in your towns may come and eat and be satisfied, and so that the LORD your God may bless you in all the work of your hands.

Deu 15:1-11

At the end of every seven years you must cancel debts. {2} This is how it is to be done: Every creditor shall cancel the loan he has made to his fellow Israelite. He shall not require payment from his fellow Israelite or brother, because the Lord's time for canceling debts has been proclaimed. {3} You may require payment from a foreigner, but you must cancel any debt your brother owes you. {4} However, there should be no poor among you, for in the land the LORD your God is giving you to possess as your inheritance, he will richly bless you, {5} if only you fully obey the LORD your God and are careful to follow all these commands I am giving you today. {6} For the LORD your God will bless you as he has promised, and you will lend to many nations but will borrow from none. You will rule over many nations but none will rule over you. {7} If there is a poor man among your brothers in any of the towns of the land that the LORD your God is giving you, do not be hardhearted or tightfisted toward your poor brother. {8} Rather be openhanded and freely lend him whatever he needs. {9} Be careful not to harbor this wicked thought: "The seventh year, the year for canceling debts, is near," so that you do not show ill will toward your needy brother and give him nothing. He may then appeal to the LORD against you, and you will be found guilty of sin. {10} Give generously to him and do so without a grudging heart; then because of this the LORD your God will bless you in all your work and in everything you put your hand to. {11} There will always be poor people in the land. Therefore I command you to be openhanded toward your brothers and toward the poor and needy in your land.

RESPECT EDOMITES AND EGYPTIANS

Deu 23:7-8

Do not abhor an Edomite, for he is your brother. Do not abhor an Egyptian, because you lived as an alien in his country. {8} The third generation of children born to them may enter the assembly of the LORD.

NEWLY-MARRIEDS SHOULD STAY AT HOME

Deu 24:5

If a man has recently married, he must not be sent to war or have any other duty laid on him. For one year he is to be free to stay at home and bring happiness to the wife he has married.

LOANS, WEIGHTS, MEASURES

Deu 24:10-15

When you make a loan of any kind to your neighbor, do not go into his house to get what he is offering as a pledge. {11} Stay outside and let the man to whom you are making the loan bring the pledge out to you. {12} If the man is poor, do not go to sleep with his pledge in your possession. {13} Return his cloak to him by sunset so that he may sleep in it. Then he will thank you, and it will be regarded as a righteous act in the sight of the LORD your God. {14} Do not take advantage of a hired man who is poor and needy, whether he is a brother Israelite or an alien living in one of your towns. {15} Pay him his wages each day before sunset, because he is poor and is counting on it. Otherwise he may cry to the LORD against you, and you will be guilty of sin.

Deu 24:19-22

When you are harvesting in your field and you overlook a sheaf, do not go back to get it. Leave it for the alien, the fatherless and the widow, so that the LORD your God may bless you in all the work of your hands. {20} When you beat the olives from your trees, do not go over the branches a second time. Leave what remains for the alien, the fatherless and the widow. {21} When you harvest the grapes in your vineyard, do not go over the vines again. Leave what remains for the alien, the fatherless and the widow. {22} Remember that you were slaves in Egypt. That is why I command you to do this.

Deu 25:13-16

Do not have two differing weights in your bag—one heavy, one light. {14} Do not have two differing measures in your house—one large, one small. {15} You must have accurate and honest weights and measures, so that you may live long in the land the LORD your God is giving you. {16} For the LORD your God detests anyone who does these things, anyone who deals dishonestly.

BLESSINGS AND CURSES

Deu 28:1-14

If you fully obey the LORD your God and carefully follow all his commands I give you today, the LORD your God will set you high above all the nations on earth. {2} All these blessings will come upon you and accompany you if you obey the LORD your God: {3} You will be blessed in the city and blessed in the country. {4} The fruit of your womb will be blessed, and the crops of your land and the young of your livestock–the calves of your herds and the lambs of your flocks. {5} Your basket and your kneading trough will be blessed. {6} You will be blessed when you come in and blessed when you go out. {7} The LORD will grant that the enemies who rise up against you will be defeated before you. They will come at you from one direction but flee from you in seven. {8} The LORD will send a blessing on your barns and on everything you put your hand to. The LORD your God will bless you in the land he is giving you. {9} The LORD will establish you as his holy people, as he promised you on oath, if you keep the commands of the LORD your God and walk in his ways. {10} Then all the peoples on earth will see that you are called by the name of the LORD, and they will fear you. {11} The LORD will grant you abundant prosperity–in the fruit of your womb, the young of your livestock and the crops of your ground–in the land he swore to your forefathers to give you. {12} The LORD will open the heavens, the storehouse of his bounty, to send rain on your land in season and to bless all the work of your hands. You will lend to many nations but will borrow from none. {13} The LORD will make you the head, not the tail. If you pay attention to the commands of the LORD your God that I give you this day and carefully follow them, you will always be at the top, never at the bottom. {14} Do not turn aside from any of the commands I give you today, to the right or to the left....

Deu 28:20-24

The LORD will send on you curses, confusion and rebuke in everything you put your hand to, until you are destroyed and come to sudden ruin because of the evil you have done in forsaking him. {21} The LORD will plague you with diseases until he has destroyed you from the land you are entering to possess. {22} The LORD will strike you with wasting disease, with fever and inflammation, with scorching heat and drought, with blight and mildew, which will plague you until you perish. {23} The sky over your head will be bronze, the ground beneath you iron. {24} The LORD will turn the rain of your country into dust and powder; it will come down from the skies until you are destroyed.

PROSPERITY WHEN YOU OBEY THE LORD

Deu 30:1-18a

When all these blessings and curses I have set before you come upon you and you take them to heart wherever the LORD your God disperses you among the nations, {2} and when you and your children return to the LORD your God and obey him with all your heart and with all your soul according to everything I command you today, {3} then the LORD your God will restore your fortunes and have compassion on you and gather you again from all the nations where he scattered you. {4} Even if you have been banished to the most distant land under the heavens, from there the LORD your God will gather you and bring you back. {5} He will bring you to the land that belonged to your fathers, and you will take possession of it. He will make you more prosperous and numerous than your fathers. {6} The LORD your God will circumcise your hearts and the hearts of your descendants, so that you may love him with all your heart and with all your soul, and live. {7} The LORD your God will put all these curses on your enemies who hate and persecute you. {8} You will again obey the LORD and follow all his commands I am giving you today. {9} Then the LORD your God will make you most prosperous in all the work of your hands and in the fruit of your womb, the young of your livestock and the crops of your land. The LORD will again delight in you and make you prosperous, just as he delighted in your fathers, {10} if you obey the LORD your God and keep his commands and decrees that are written in this Book of the Law and turn to the LORD your God with all your heart and with all your soul. {11} Now what I am commanding you today is not too difficult for you or beyond your reach. {12} It is not up in heaven, so that you have to ask, "Who will ascend into heaven to get it and proclaim it to us so we may obey it?" {13} Nor is it beyond the sea, so that you have to ask, "Who will cross the sea to get it and proclaim it to us so we may obey it?" {14} No, the word is very near you; it is in your mouth and in your heart so you may obey it. {15} See, I set before you today life and prosperity, death and destruction. {16} For I command you today to love the LORD your God, to walk in his ways, and to keep his commands, decrees and laws; then you will live and increase, and the LORD your God will bless you in the land you are entering to possess. {17} But if your heart turns away and you are not obedient, and if you are drawn away to bow down to other gods and worship them, {18} I declare to you this day that you will certainly be destroyed.

JOSHUA SUCCEEDS MOSES

Deu 31:1-8

Then Moses went out and spoke these words to all Israel: {2} "I am now a hundred and twenty years old and I am no longer able to lead you. The LORD has said to me, 'You shall not cross the Jordan.' {3} The LORD your God himself will cross over ahead of you. He will destroy these nations before you, and you will take possession of their land. Joshua also will cross over ahead of you, as the LORD said. {4} And the LORD will do to them what he did to Sihon and Og, the kings of the Amorites, whom he destroyed along with their land. {5} The LORD will deliver them to you, and you must do to them all that I have commanded you. {6} Be strong and courageous. Do not be afraid or terrified because of them, for the LORD your God goes with you; he will never leave you nor forsake you." {7} Then Moses summoned Joshua and said to him in the presence of all Israel, "Be strong and courageous, for you must go with this people into the land that the LORD swore to their forefathers to give them, and you must divide it among them as their inheritance. {8} The LORD himself goes before you and will be with you; he will never leave you nor forsake you. Do not be afraid; do not be discouraged."

Deu 31:19-26a

"Now write down for yourselves this song and teach it to the Israelites and have them sing it, so that it may be a witness for me against them. {20} When I have brought them into the land flowing with milk and honey, the land I promised on oath to their forefathers, and when they eat their fill and thrive, they will turn to other gods and worship them, rejecting me and breaking my covenant. {21} And when many disasters and difficulties come upon them, this song will testify against them, because it will not be forgotten by their descendants. I know what they are disposed to do, even before I bring them into the land I promised them on oath." {22} So Moses wrote down this song that day and taught it to the Israelites. {23} The LORD gave this command to Joshua son of Nun: "Be strong and courageous, for you will bring the Israelites into the land I promised them on oath, and I myself will be with you." {24} After Moses finished writing in a book the words of this law from beginning to end, {25} he gave this command to the Levites who carried the ark of the covenant of the LORD: {26} "Take this Book of the Law and place it beside the ark of the covenant of the LORD your God.

MOSES DIES

Deu 32:48-52

On that same day the LORD told Moses, {49} "Go up into the Abarim Range to Mount Nebo in Moab, across from Jericho, and view Canaan, the land I am giving the Israelites as their own possession. {50} There on the mountain that you have climbed you will die and be gathered to your people, just as your brother Aaron died on Mount Hor and was gathered to his people. {51} This is because both of you broke faith with me in the presence of the Israelites at the waters of Meribah Kadesh in the Desert of Zin and because you did not uphold my holiness among the Israelites. {52} Therefore, you will see the land only from a distance; you will not enter the land I am giving to the people of Israel."

Deu 34:1-12

Then Moses climbed Mount Nebo from the plains of Moab to the top of Pisgah, across from Jericho. There the LORD showed him the whole land—from Gilead to Dan, {2} all of Naphtali, the territory of Ephraim and Manasseh, all the land of Judah as far as the western sea, {3} the Negev and the whole region from the Valley of Jericho, the City of Palms, as far as Zoar. {4} Then the LORD said to him, "This is the land I promised on oath to Abraham, Isaac and Jacob when I said, 'I will give it to your descendants.' I have let you see it with your eyes, but you will not cross over into it." {5} And Moses the servant of the LORD died there in Moab, as the LORD had said. {6} He buried him in Moab, in the valley opposite Beth Peor, but to this day no one knows where his grave is. {7} Moses was a hundred and twenty years old when he died, yet his eyes were not weak nor his strength gone. {8} The Israelites grieved for Moses in the plains of Moab thirty days, until the time of weeping and mourning was over. {9} Now Joshua son of Nun was filled with the spirit of wisdom because Moses had laid his hands on him. So the Israelites listened to him and did what the LORD had commanded Moses. {10} Since then, no prophet has risen in Israel like Moses, whom the LORD knew face to face, {11} who did all those miraculous signs and wonders the LORD sent him to do in Egypt—to Pharaoh and to all his officials and to his whole land. {12} For no one has ever shown the mighty power or performed the awesome deeds that Moses did in the sight of all Israel.

INSTRUCTIONS TO JOSHUA

Josh 1:1-18

After the death of Moses the servant of the LORD, the LORD said to Joshua son of Nun, Moses' aide: {2} "Moses my servant is dead. Now then, you and all these people, get ready to cross the Jordan River into the land I am about to give to them—to the Israelites. {3} I will give you every place where you set your foot, as I promised Moses. {4} Your territory will extend from the desert to Lebanon, and from the great river, the Euphrates—all the Hittite country—to the Great Sea on the west. {5} No one will be able to stand up against you all the days of your life. As I was with Moses, so I will be with you; I will never leave you nor forsake you. {6} "Be strong and courageous, because you will lead these people to inherit the land I swore to their forefathers to give them. {7} Be strong and very courageous. Be careful to obey all the law my servant Moses gave you; do not turn from it to the right or to the left, that you may be successful wherever you go. {8} Do not let this Book of the Law depart from your mouth; meditate on it day and night, so that you may be careful to do everything written in it. Then you will be prosperous and successful. {9} Have I not commanded you? Be strong and courageous. Do not be terrified; do not be discouraged, for the LORD your God will be with you wherever you go." {10} So Joshua ordered the officers of the people: {11} "Go through the camp and tell the people, 'Get your supplies ready. Three days from now you will cross the Jordan here to go in and take possession of the land the LORD your God is giving you for your own.'" {12} But to the Reubenites, the Gadites and the half-tribe of Manasseh, Joshua said, {13} "Remember the command that Moses the servant of the LORD gave you: 'The LORD your God is giving you rest and has granted you this land.' {14} Your wives, your children and your livestock may stay in the land that Moses gave you east of the Jordan, but all your fighting men, fully armed, must cross over ahead of your brothers. You are to help your brothers {15} until the LORD gives them rest, as he has done for you, and until they too have taken possession of the land that the LORD your God is giving them. After that, you may go back and occupy your own land, which Moses the servant of the LORD gave you east of the Jordan toward the sunrise." {16} Then they answered Joshua, "Whatever you have commanded us we will do, and wherever you send us we will go. {17} Just as we fully obeyed Moses, so we will obey you. Only may the LORD your God be with you as he was with Moses. {18} Whoever rebels against your word and does not obey your words, whatever you may command them, will be put to death. Only be strong and courageous!"

SPIES MAKE A DEAL WITH RAHAB

Josh 2:1-18

Then Joshua son of Nun secretly sent two spies from Shittim. "Go, look over the land," he said, "especially Jericho." So they went and entered the house of a prostitute named Rahab and stayed there. {2} The king of Jericho was told, "Look! Some of the Israelites have come here tonight to spy out the land." {3} So the king of Jericho sent this message to Rahab: "Bring out the men who came to you and entered your house, because they have come to spy out the whole land." {4} But the woman had taken the two men and hidden them. She said, "Yes, the men came to me, but I did not know where they had come from. {5} At dusk, when it was time to close the city gate, the men left. I don't know which way they went. Go after them quickly. You may catch up with them." {6} (But she had taken them up to the roof and hidden them under the stalks of flax she had laid out on the roof.) {7} So the men set out in pursuit of the spies on the road that leads to the fords of the Jordan, and as soon as the pursuers had gone out, the gate was shut. {8} Before the spies lay down for the night, she went up on the roof {9} and said to them, "I know that the LORD has given this land to you and that a great fear of you has fallen on us, so that all who live in this country are melting in fear because of you. {10} We have heard how the LORD dried up the water of the Red Sea for you when you came out of Egypt, and what you did to Sihon and Og, the two kings of the Amorites east of the Jordan, whom you completely destroyed. {11} When we heard of it, our hearts melted and everyone's courage failed because of you, for the LORD your God is God in heaven above and on the earth below. {12} Now then, please swear to me by the LORD that you will show kindness to my family, because I have shown kindness to you. Give me a sure sign {13} that you will spare the lives of my father and mother, my brothers and sisters, and all who belong to them, and that you will save us from death." {14} "Our lives for your lives!" the men assured her. "If you don't tell what we are doing, we will treat you kindly and faithfully when the LORD gives us the land." {15} So she let them down by a rope through the window, for the house she lived in was part of the city wall. {16} Now she had said to them, "Go to the hills so the pursuers will not find you. Hide yourselves there three days until they return, and then go on your way." {17} The men said to her, "This oath you made us swear will not be binding on us {18} unless, when we enter the land, you have tied this scarlet cord in the window through which you let us down, and unless you have brought your father and mother, your brothers and all your family into your house.

ISRAELITES CROSS THE JORDAN INTO CANAAN

Josh 3:1-17

Early in the morning Joshua and all the Israelites set out from Shittim and went to the Jordan, where they camped before crossing over. {2} After three days the officers went throughout the camp, {3} giving orders to the people: "When you see the ark of the covenant of the LORD your God, and the priests, who are Levites, carrying it, you are to move out from your positions and follow it. {4} Then you will know which way to go, since you have never been this way before. But keep a distance of about a thousand yards between you and the ark; do not go near it." {5} Joshua told the people, "Consecrate yourselves, for tomorrow the LORD will do amazing things among you." {6} Joshua said to the priests, "Take up the ark of the covenant and pass on ahead of the people." So they took it up and went ahead of them. {7} And the LORD said to Joshua, "Today I will begin to exalt you in the eyes of all Israel, so they may know that I am with you as I was with Moses. {8} Tell the priests who carry the ark of the covenant: 'When you reach the edge of the Jordan's waters, go and stand in the river.'"

{9} Joshua said to the Israelites, "Come here and listen to the words of the LORD your God. {10} This is how you will know that the living God is among you and that he will certainly drive out before you the Canaanites, Hittites, Hivites, Perizzites, Girgashites, Amorites and Jebusites. {11} See, the ark of the covenant of the Lord of all the earth will go into the Jordan ahead of you. {12} Now then, choose twelve men from the tribes of Israel, one from each tribe. {13} And as soon as the priests who carry the ark of the LORD–the Lord of all the earth–set foot in the Jordan, its waters flowing downstream will be cut off and stand up in a heap." {14} So when the people broke camp to cross the Jordan, the priests carrying the ark of the covenant went ahead of them. {15} Now the Jordan is at flood stage all during harvest. Yet as soon as the priests who carried the ark reached the Jordan and their feet touched the water's edge, {16} the water from upstream stopped flowing. It piled up in a heap a great distance away, at a town called Adam in the vicinity of Zarethan, while the water flowing down to the Sea of the Arabah (the Salt Sea) was completely cut off. So the people crossed over opposite Jericho. {17} The priests who carried the ark of the covenant of the LORD stood firm on dry ground in the middle of the Jordan, while all Israel passed by until the whole nation had completed the crossing on dry ground.

THE FALL OF JERICHO

Josh 6:10-23

But Joshua had commanded the people, "Do not give a war cry, do not raise your voices, do not say a word until the day I tell you to shout. Then shout!" {11} So he had the ark of the LORD carried around the city, circling it once. Then the people returned to camp and spent the night there. {12} Joshua got up early the next morning and the priests took up the ark of the LORD. {13} The seven priests carrying the seven trumpets went forward, marching before the ark of the LORD and blowing the trumpets. The armed men went ahead of them and the rear guard followed the ark of the LORD, while the trumpets kept sounding. {14} So on the second day they marched around the city once and returned to the camp. They did this for six days.

{15} On the seventh day, they got up at daybreak and marched around the city seven times in the same manner, except that on that day they circled the city seven times. {16} The seventh time around, when the priests sounded the trumpet blast, Joshua commanded the people, "Shout! For the LORD has given you the city! {17} The city and all that is in it are to be devoted to the LORD. Only Rahab the prostitute and all who are with her in her house shall be spared, because she hid the spies we sent. {18} But keep away from the devoted things, so that you will not bring about your own destruction by taking any of them. Otherwise you will make the camp of Israel liable to destruction and bring trouble on it. {19} All the silver and gold and the articles of bronze and iron are sacred to the LORD and must go into his treasury." {20} When the trumpets sounded, the people shouted, and at the sound of the trumpet, when the people gave a loud shout, the wall collapsed; so every man charged straight in, and they took the city. {21} They devoted the city to the LORD and destroyed with the sword every living thing in it—men and women, young and old, cattle, sheep and donkeys. {22} Joshua said to the two men who had spied out the land, "Go into the prostitute's house and bring her out and all who belong to her, in accordance with your oath to her." {23} So the young men who had done the spying went in and brought out Rahab, her father and mother and brothers and all who belonged to her. They brought out her entire family and put them in a place outside the camp of Israel.

THE GIBEONITES DECEIVE THE ISRAELITES

Josh 9:3-21

However, when the people of Gibeon heard what Joshua had done to Jericho and Ai, {4} they resorted to a ruse: They went as a delegation whose donkeys were loaded with worn-out sacks and old wineskins, cracked and mended. {5} The men put worn and patched sandals on their feet and wore old clothes. All the bread of their food supply was dry and moldy. {6} Then they went to Joshua in the camp at Gilgal and said to him and the men of Israel, "We have come from a distant country; make a treaty with us." {7} The men of Israel said to the Hivites, "But perhaps you live near us. How then can we make a treaty with you?" {8} "We are your servants," they said to Joshua. But Joshua asked, "Who are you and where do you come from?"

{9} They answered: "Your servants have come from a very distant country because of the fame of the LORD your God. For we have heard reports of him: all that he did in Egypt, {10} and all that he did to the two kings of the Amorites east of the Jordan–Sihon king of Heshbon, and Og king of Bashan, who reigned in Ashtaroth. {11} And our elders and all those living in our country said to us, 'Take provisions for your journey; go and meet them and say to them, "We are your servants; make a treaty with us."' {12} This bread of ours was warm when we packed it at home on the day we left to come to you. But now see how dry and moldy it is. {13} And these wineskins that we filled were new, but see how cracked they are. And our clothes and sandals are worn out by the very long journey." {14} The men of Israel sampled their provisions but did not inquire of the LORD. {15} Then Joshua made a treaty of peace with them to let them live, and the leaders of the assembly ratified it by oath. {16} Three days after they made the treaty with the Gibeonites, the Israelites heard that they were neighbors, living near them. {17} So the Israelites set out and on the third day came to their cities: Gibeon, Kephirah, Beeroth and Kiriath Jearim. {18} But the Israelites did not attack them, because the leaders of the assembly had sworn an oath to them by the LORD, the God of Israel. The whole assembly grumbled against the leaders, {19} but all the leaders answered, "We have given them our oath by the LORD, the God of Israel, and we cannot touch them now. {20} This is what we will do to them: We will let them live, so that wrath will not fall on us for breaking the oath we swore to them." {21} They continued, "Let them live, but let them be woodcutters and water carriers for the entire community." So the leaders' promise to them was kept.

THE SUN STANDS STILL AT GIBEON

Josh 10:1-15

Now Adoni-Zedek king of Jerusalem heard that Joshua had taken Ai and totally destroyed it, doing to Ai and its king as he had done to Jericho and its king, and that the people of Gibeon had made a treaty of peace with Israel and were living near them. {2} He and his people were very much alarmed at this, because Gibeon was an important city, like one of the royal cities; it was larger than Ai, and all its men were good fighters. {3} So Adoni-Zedek king of Jerusalem appealed to Hoham king of Hebron, Piram king of Jarmuth, Japhia king of Lachish and Debir king of Eglon. {4} "Come up and help me attack Gibeon," he said, "because it has made peace with Joshua and the Israelites." {5} Then the five kings of the Amorites–the kings of Jerusalem, Hebron, Jarmuth, Lachish and Eglon–joined forces. They moved up with all their troops and took up positions against Gibeon and attacked it. {6} The Gibeonites then sent word to Joshua in the camp at Gilgal: "Do not abandon your servants. Come up to us quickly and save us! Help us, because all the Amorite kings from the hill country have joined forces against us." {7} So Joshua marched up from Gilgal with his entire army, including all the best fighting men. {8} The LORD said to Joshua, "Do not be afraid of them; I have given them into your hand. Not one of them will be able to withstand you." {9} After an all-night march from Gilgal, Joshua took them by surprise. {10} The LORD threw them into confusion before Israel, who defeated them in a great victory at Gibeon. Israel pursued them along the road going up to Beth Horon and cut them down all the way to Azekah and Makkedah. {11} As they fled before Israel on the road down from Beth Horon to Azekah, the LORD hurled large hailstones down on them from the sky, and more of them died from the hailstones than were killed by the swords of the Israelites. {12} On the day the LORD gave the Amorites over to Israel, Joshua said to the LORD in the presence of Israel: "O sun, stand still over Gibeon, O moon, over the Valley of Aijalon." {13} So the sun stood still, and the moon stopped, till the nation avenged itself on its enemies, as it is written in the Book of Jashar. The sun stopped in the middle of the sky and delayed going down about a full day. {14} There has never been a day like it before or since, a day when the LORD listened to a man. Surely the LORD was fighting for Israel! {15} Then Joshua returned with all Israel to the camp at Gilgal.

ALL OF CANAAN GIVEN TO ISRAELITES

Josh 21:43-45
So the LORD gave Israel all the land he had sworn to give their forefathers, and they took possession of it and settled there. {44} The LORD gave them rest on every side, just as he had sworn to their forefathers. Not one of their enemies withstood them; the LORD handed all their enemies over to them. {45} Not one of all the Lord's good promises to the house of Israel failed; every one was fulfilled.

REUBEN, GAD AND MANASSEH RETURN TO EAST OF JORDAN

Josh 22:1-9
Then Joshua summoned the Reubenites, the Gadites and the half-tribe of Manasseh {2} and said to them, "You have done all that Moses the servant of the LORD commanded, and you have obeyed me in everything I commanded. {3} For a long time now–to this very day–you have not deserted your brothers but have carried out the mission the LORD your God gave you. {4} Now that the LORD your God has given your brothers rest as he promised, return to your homes in the land that Moses the servant of the LORD gave you on the other side of the Jordan. {5} But be very careful to keep the commandment and the law that Moses the servant of the LORD gave you: to love the LORD your God, to walk in all his ways, to obey his commands, to hold fast to him and to serve him with all your heart and all your soul." {6} Then Joshua blessed them and sent them away, and they went to their homes. {7} (To the half-tribe of Manasseh Moses had given land in Bashan, and to the other half of the tribe Joshua gave land on the west side of the Jordan with their brothers.) When Joshua sent them home, he blessed them, {8} saying, "Return to your homes with your great wealth–with large herds of livestock, with silver, gold, bronze and iron, and a great quantity of clothing–and divide with your brothers the plunder from your enemies." {9} So the Reubenites, the Gadites and the half-tribe of Manasseh left the Israelites at Shiloh in Canaan to return to Gilead, their own land, which they had acquired in accordance with the command of the LORD through Moses.

DEATH OF JOSHUA AND OF ELEAZAR

Josh 24:19-24

Joshua said to the people, "You are not able to serve the LORD. He is a holy God; he is a jealous God. He will not forgive your rebellion and your sins. {20} If you forsake the LORD and serve foreign gods, he will turn and bring disaster on you and make an end of you, after he has been good to you." {21} But the people said to Joshua, "No! We will serve the LORD." {22} Then Joshua said, "You are witnesses against yourselves that you have chosen to serve the LORD." "Yes, we are witnesses," they replied. {23} "Now then," said Joshua, "throw away the foreign gods that are among you and yield your hearts to the LORD, the God of Israel." {24} And the people said to Joshua, "We will serve the LORD our God and obey him."

Josh 24:29-33

After these things, Joshua son of Nun, the servant of the LORD, died at the age of a hundred and ten. {30} And they buried him in the land of his inheritance, at Timnath Serah in the hill country of Ephraim, north of Mount Gaash. {31} Israel served the LORD throughout the lifetime of Joshua and of the elders who outlived him and who had experienced everything the LORD had done for Israel. {32} And Joseph's bones, which the Israelites had brought up from Egypt, were buried at Shechem in the tract of land that Jacob bought for a hundred pieces of silver from the sons of Hamor, the father of Shechem. This became the inheritance of Joseph's descendants. {33} And Eleazar son of Aaron died and was buried at Gibeah, which had been allotted to his son Phinehas in the hill country of Ephraim.

ISRAEL FIGHTS THE CANAANITE TRIBES

Judg 1:1-3
After the death of Joshua, the Israelites asked the LORD, "Who will be the first to go up and fight for us against the Canaanites?" {2} The LORD answered, "Judah is to go; I have given the land into their hands." {3} Then the men of Judah said to the Simeonites their brothers, "Come up with us into the territory allotted to us, to fight against the Canaanites. We in turn will go with you into yours." So the Simeonites went with them.

Judg 1:8-18
The men of Judah attacked Jerusalem also and took it. They put the city to the sword and set it on fire. {9} After that, the men of Judah went down to fight against the Canaanites living in the hill country, the Negev and the western foothills. {10} They advanced against the Canaanites living in Hebron (formerly called Kiriath Arba) and defeated Sheshai, Ahiman and Talmai. {11} From there they advanced against the people living in Debir (formerly called Kiriath Sepher). {12} And Caleb said, "I will give my daughter Acsah in marriage to the man who attacks and captures Kiriath Sepher." {13} Othniel son of Kenaz, Caleb's younger brother, took it; so Caleb gave his daughter Acsah to him in marriage. {14} One day when she came to Othniel, she urged him to ask her father for a field. When she got off her donkey, Caleb asked her, "What can I do for you?" {15} She replied, "Do me a special favor. Since you have given me land in the Negev, give me also springs of water." Then Caleb gave her the upper and lower springs. {16} The descendants of Moses' father-in-law, the Kenite, went up from the City of Palms with the men of Judah to live among the people of the Desert of Judah in the Negev near Arad. {17} Then the men of Judah went with the Simeonites their brothers and attacked the Canaanites living in Zephath, and they totally destroyed the city. Therefore it was called Hormah. {18} The men of Judah also took Gaza, Ashkelon and Ekron—each city with its territory.

Judg 1:27-29
But Manasseh did not drive out the people of Beth Shan or Taanach or Dor or Ibleam or Megiddo and their surrounding settlements, for the Canaanites were determined to live in that land. {28} When Israel became strong, they pressed the Canaanites into forced labor but never drove them out completely. {29} Nor did Ephraim drive out the Canaanites living in Gezer, but the Canaanites continued to live there among them.

ISRAEL LIVES WITH THE CANAANITES

Judg 2:1-3

The angel of the LORD went up from Gilgal to Bokim and said, "I brought you up out of Egypt and led you into the land that I swore to give to your forefathers. I said, 'I will never break my covenant with you, {2} and you shall not make a covenant with the people of this land, but you shall break down their altars.' Yet you have disobeyed me. Why have you done this? {3} Now therefore I tell you that I will not drive them out before you; they will be <thorns> in your sides and their gods will be a snare to you."

Judg 2:14-23

In his anger against Israel the LORD handed them over to raiders who plundered them. He sold them to their enemies all around, whom they were no longer able to resist. {15} Whenever Israel went out to fight, the hand of the LORD was against them to defeat them, just as he had sworn to them. They were in great distress. {16} Then the LORD raised up judges, who saved them out of the hands of these raiders. {17} Yet they would not listen to their judges but prostituted themselves to other gods and worshiped them. Unlike their fathers, they quickly turned from the way in which their fathers had walked, the way of obedience to the Lord's commands. {18} Whenever the LORD raised up a judge for them, he was with the judge and saved them out of the hands of their enemies as long as the judge lived; for the LORD had compassion on them as they groaned under those who oppressed and afflicted them. {19} But when the judge died, the people returned to ways even more corrupt than those of their fathers, following other gods and serving and worshiping them. They refused to give up their evil practices and stubborn ways. {20} Therefore the LORD was very angry with Israel and said, "Because this nation has violated the covenant that I laid down for their forefathers and has not listened to me, {21} I will no longer drive out before them any of the nations Joshua left when he died. {22} I will use them to test Israel and see whether they will keep the way of the LORD and walk in it as their forefathers did." {23} The LORD had allowed those nations to remain; he did not drive them out at once by giving them into the hands of Joshua.

Judg 3:5-6

The Israelites lived among the Canaanites, Hittites, Amorites, Perizzites, Hivites and Jebusites. {6} They took their daughters in marriage and gave their own daughters to their sons, and served their gods.

DEBORAH LEADS ISRAEL

Judg 4:1-16

After Ehud died, the Israelites once again did evil in the eyes of the LORD. {2} So the LORD sold them into the hands of Jabin, a king of Canaan, who reigned in Hazor. The commander of his army was Sisera, who lived in Harosheth Haggoyim. {3} Because he had nine hundred iron chariots and had cruelly oppressed the Israelites for twenty years, they cried to the LORD for help. {4} Deborah, a prophetess, the wife of Lappidoth, was leading Israel at that time. {5} She held court under the Palm of Deborah between Ramah and Bethel in the hill country of Ephraim, and the Israelites came to her to have their disputes decided. {6} She sent for Barak son of Abinoam from Kedesh in Naphtali and said to him, "The LORD, the God of Israel, commands you: 'Go, take with you ten thousand men of Naphtali and Zebulun and lead the way to Mount Tabor. {7} I will lure Sisera, the commander of Jabin's army, with his chariots and his troops to the Kishon River and give him into your hands.'" {8} Barak said to her, "If you go with me, I will go; but if you don't go with me, I won't go." {9} "Very well," Deborah said, "I will go with you. But because of the way you are going about this, the honor will not be yours, for the LORD will hand Sisera over to a woman." So Deborah went with Barak to Kedesh, {10} where he summoned Zebulun and Naphtali. Ten thousand men followed him, and Deborah also went with him. {11} Now Heber the Kenite had left the other Kenites, the descendants of Hobab, Moses' brother-in-law, and pitched his tent by the great tree in Zaanannim near Kedesh. {12} When they told Sisera that Barak son of Abinoam had gone up to Mount Tabor, {13} Sisera gathered together his nine hundred iron chariots and all the men with him, from Harosheth Haggoyim to the Kishon River. {14} Then Deborah said to Barak, "Go! This is the day the LORD has given Sisera into your hands. Has not the LORD gone ahead of you?" So Barak went down Mount Tabor, followed by ten thousand men. {15} At Barak's advance, the LORD routed Sisera and all his chariots and army by the sword, and Sisera abandoned his chariot and fled on foot. {16} But Barak pursued the chariots and army as far as Harosheth Haggoyim. All the troops of Sisera fell by the sword; not a man was left.

Judg 5:1-3

On that day Deborah and Barak son of Abinoam sang this song: {2} "When the princes in Israel take the lead, when the people willingly offer themselves– praise the LORD! {3} "Hear this, you kings! Listen, you rulers! I will sing to the LORD, I will sing; I will make music to the LORD, the God of Israel.

GIDEON PUTS OUT A FLEECE

Judg 6:14-23

The LORD turned to him and said, "Go in the strength you have and save Israel out of Midian's hand. Am I not sending you?" {15} "But Lord, " Gideon asked, "how can I save Israel? My clan is the weakest in Manasseh, and I am the least in my family." {16} The LORD answered, "I will be with you, and you will strike down all the Midianites together." {17} Gideon replied, "If now I have found favor in your eyes, give me a sign that it is really you talking to me. {18} Please do not go away until I come back and bring my offering and set it before you." And the LORD said, "I will wait until you return." {19} Gideon went in, prepared a young goat, and from an ephah of flour he made bread without yeast. Putting the meat in a basket and its broth in a pot, he brought them out and offered them to him under the oak. {20} The angel of God said to him, "Take the meat and the unleavened bread, place them on this rock, and pour out the broth." And Gideon did so. {21} With the tip of the staff that was in his hand, the angel of the LORD touched the meat and the unleavened bread. Fire flared from the rock, consuming the meat and the bread. And the angel of the LORD disappeared. {22} When Gideon realized that it was the angel of the LORD, he exclaimed, "Ah, Sovereign LORD! I have seen the angel of the LORD face to face!" {23} But the LORD said to him, "Peace! Do not be afraid. You are not going to die."

Judg 6:33-40

Now all the Midianites, Amalekites and other eastern peoples joined forces and crossed over the Jordan and camped in the Valley of Jezreel. {34} Then the Spirit of the LORD came upon Gideon, and he blew a trumpet, summoning the Abiezrites to follow him. {35} He sent messengers throughout Manasseh, calling them to arms, and also into Asher, Zebulun and Naphtali, so that they too went up to meet them. {36} Gideon said to God, "If you will save Israel by my hand as you have promised– {37} look, I will place a wool fleece on the threshing floor. If there is dew only on the fleece and all the ground is dry, then I will know that you will save Israel by my hand, as you said." {38} And that is what happened. Gideon rose early the next day; he squeezed the fleece and wrung out the dew–a bowlful of water. {39} Then Gideon said to God, "Do not be angry with me. Let me make just one more request. Allow me one more test with the fleece. This time make the fleece dry and the ground covered with dew." {40} That night God did so. Only the fleece was dry; all the ground was covered with dew.

GIDEON'S THREE HUNDRED FIGHT MIDIAN

Judg 7:5b-20
There the LORD told him, "Separate those who lap the water with their tongues like a dog from those who kneel down to drink." {6} Three hundred men lapped with their hands to their mouths. All the rest got down on their knees to drink. {7} The LORD said to Gideon, "With the three hundred men that lapped I will save you and give the Midianites into your hands. Let all the other men go, each to his own place." {8} So Gideon sent the rest of the Israelites to their tents but kept the three hundred, who took over the provisions and trumpets of the others. Now the camp of Midian lay below him in the valley. {9} During that night the LORD said to Gideon, "Get up, go down against the camp, because I am going to give it into your hands. {10} If you are afraid to attack, go down to the camp with your servant Purah {11} and listen to what they are saying. Afterward, you will be encouraged to attack the camp." So he and Purah his servant went down to the outposts of the camp. {12} The Midianites, the Amalekites and all the other eastern peoples had settled in the valley, thick as locusts. Their camels could no more be counted than the sand on the seashore. {13} Gideon arrived just as a man was telling a friend his dream. "I had a dream," he was saying. "A round loaf of barley bread came tumbling into the Midianite camp. It struck the tent with such force that the tent overturned and collapsed." {14} His friend responded, "This can be nothing other than the sword of Gideon son of Joash, the Israelite. God has given the Midianites and the whole camp into his hands." {15} When Gideon heard the dream and its interpretation, he worshiped God. He returned to the camp of Israel and called out, "Get up! The LORD has given the Midianite camp into your hands." {16} Dividing the three hundred men into three companies, he placed trumpets and empty jars in the hands of all of them, with torches inside. {17} "Watch me," he told them. "Follow my lead. When I get to the edge of the camp, do exactly as I do. {18} When I and all who are with me blow our trumpets, then from all around the camp blow yours and shout, 'For the LORD and for Gideon.'" {19} Gideon and the hundred men with him reached the edge of the camp at the beginning of the middle watch, just after they had changed the guard. They blew their trumpets and broke the jars that were in their hands. {20} The three companies blew the trumpets and smashed the jars. Grasping the torches in their left hands and holding in their right hands the trumpets they were to blow, they shouted, "A sword for the LORD and for Gideon!"

Judg 8:22-35

The Israelites   –you, your son and
your grandson–becau   the hand of Midian."
{23} But Gideon told   nor will my son rule
over you. The LORD w   said, "I do have one
request, that each o   n your share of the
plunder." (It was the   wear gold earrings.)
{25} They answered, "We'll be glad to give them." So they spread out a
garment, and each man threw a ring from his plunder onto it. {26} The
weight of the gold rings he asked for came to seventeen hundred
shekels, not counting the ornaments, the pendants and the purple
garments worn by the kings of Midian or the chains that were on their
camels' necks. {27} Gideon made the gold into an ephod, which he
placed in Ophrah, his town. All Israel prostituted themselves by
worshiping it there, and it became a snare to Gideon and his family. {28}
Thus Midian was subdued before the Israelites and did not raise its head
again. During Gideon's lifetime, the land enjoyed peace forty years. {29}
Jerub-Baal son of Joash went back home to live. {30} He had seventy
sons of his own, for he had many wives. {31} His concubine, who lived in
Shechem, also bore him a son, whom he named Abimelech. {32} Gideon
son of Joash died at a good old age and was buried in the tomb of his
father Joash in Ophrah of the Abiezrites. {33} No sooner had Gideon died
than the Israelites again prostituted themselves to the Baals. They set up
Baal-Berith as their god and {34} did not remember the LORD their God,
who had rescued them from the hands of all their enemies on every side.
{35} They also failed to show kindness to the family of Jerub-Baal (that is,
Gideon) for all the good things he had done for them.

JEPHTHAH SACRIFICES HIS DAUGHTER

Judg 11:1-6

Jephthah the Gileadite was a mighty warrior. His father was Gilead; his mother was a prostitute. {2} Gilead's wife also bore him sons, and when they were grown up, they drove Jephthah away. "You are not going to get any inheritance in our family," they said, "because you are the son of another woman." {3} So Jephthah fled from his brothers and settled in the land of Tob, where a group of adventurers gathered around him and followed him. {4} Some time later, when the Ammonites made war on Israel, {5} the elders of Gilead went to get Jephthah from the land of Tob. {6} "Come," they said, "be our commander, so we can fight the Ammonites."

Judg 11:9-10

Jephthah answered, "Suppose you take me back to fight the Ammonites and the LORD gives them to me–will I really be your head?" {10} The elders of Gilead replied, "The LORD is our witness; we will certainly do as you say."

Judg 11:29-39a

Then the Spirit of the LORD came upon Jephthah. He crossed Gilead and Manasseh, passed through Mizpah of Gilead, and from there he advanced against the Ammonites. {30} And Jephthah made a vow to the LORD: "If you give the Ammonites into my hands, {31} whatever comes out of the door of my house to meet me when I return in triumph from the Ammonites will be the Lord's, and I will sacrifice it as a burnt offering." {32} Then Jephthah went over to fight the Ammonites, and the LORD gave them into his hands. {33} He devastated twenty towns from Aroer to the vicinity of Minnith, as far as Abel Keramim. Thus Israel subdued Ammon. {34} When Jephthah returned to his home in Mizpah, who should come out to meet him but his daughter, dancing to the sound of tambourines! She was an only child. Except for her he had neither son nor daughter. {35} When he saw her, he tore his clothes and cried, "Oh! My daughter! You have made me miserable and wretched, because I have made a vow to the LORD that I cannot break." {36} "My father," she replied, "you have given your word to the LORD. Do to me just as you promised, now that the LORD has avenged you of your enemies, the Ammonites. {37} But grant me this one request," she said. "Give me two months to roam the hills and weep with my friends, because I will never marry." {38} "You may go," he said. And he let her go for two months. She and the girls went into the hills and wept because she would never marry. {39} After the two months, she returned to her father and he did to her as he had vowed.

SAMSON IS BORN

Judg 13:6-24

Then the woman went to her husband and told him, "A man of God came to me. He looked like an angel of God, very awesome. I didn't ask him where he came from, and he didn't tell me his name. {7} But he said to me, 'You will conceive and give birth to a son. Now then, drink no wine or other fermented drink and do not eat anything unclean, because the boy will be a Nazirite of God from birth until the day of his death.'" {8} Then Manoah prayed to the LORD: "O Lord, I beg you, let the man of God you sent to us come again to teach us how to bring up the boy who is to be born." {9} God heard Manoah, and the angel of God came again to the woman while she was out in the field; but her husband Manoah was not with her. {10} The woman hurried to tell her husband, "He's here! The man who appeared to me the other day!" {11} Manoah got up and followed his wife. When he came to the man, he said, "Are you the one who talked to my wife?" "I am," he said. {12} So Manoah asked him, "When your words are fulfilled, what is to be the rule for the boy's life and work?" {13} The angel of the LORD answered, "Your wife must do all that I have told her. {14} She must not eat anything that comes from the grapevine, nor drink any wine or other fermented drink nor eat anything unclean. She must do everything I have commanded her." {15} Manoah said to the angel of the LORD, "We would like you to stay until we prepare a young goat for you." {16} The angel of the LORD replied, "Even though you detain me, I will not eat any of your food. But if you prepare a burnt offering, offer it to the LORD." (Manoah did not realize that it was the angel of the LORD.) {17} Then Manoah inquired of the angel of the LORD, "What is your name, so that we may honor you when your word comes true?" {18} He replied, "Why do you ask my name? It is beyond understanding. " {19} Then Manoah took a young goat, together with the grain offering, and sacrificed it on a rock to the LORD. And the LORD did an amazing thing while Manoah and his wife watched: {20} As the flame blazed up from the altar toward heaven, the angel of the LORD ascended in the flame. Seeing this, Manoah and his wife fell with their faces to the ground. {21} When the angel of the LORD did not show himself again to Manoah and his wife, Manoah realized that it was the angel of the LORD. {22} "We are doomed to die!" he said to his wife. "We have seen God!" {23} But his wife answered, "If the LORD had meant to kill us, he would not have accepted a burnt offering and grain offering from our hands, nor shown us all these things or now told us this." {24} The woman gave birth to a boy and named him Samson. He grew and the LORD blessed him,

SAMSON MARRIES A PHILISTINE WOMAN

Judg 14:1-3

Samson went down to Timnah and saw there a young Philistine woman. {2} When he returned, he said to his father and mother, "I have seen a Philistine woman in Timnah; now get her for me as my wife." {3} His father and mother replied, "Isn't there an acceptable woman among your relatives or among all our people? Must you go to the uncircumcised Philistines to get a wife?" But Samson said to his father, "Get her for me. She's the right one for me."

Judg 14:10-20

Now his father went down to see the woman. And Samson made a feast there, as was customary for bridegrooms. {11} When he appeared, he was given thirty companions. {12} "Let me tell you a riddle," Samson said to them. "If you can give me the answer within the seven days of the feast, I will give you thirty linen garments and thirty sets of clothes. {13} If you can't tell me the answer, you must give me thirty linen garments and thirty sets of clothes." "Tell us your riddle," they said. "Let's hear it." {14} He replied, "Out of the eater, something to eat; out of the strong, something sweet." For three days they could not give the answer. {15} On the fourth day, they said to Samson's wife, "Coax your husband into explaining the riddle for us, or we will burn you and your father's household to death. Did you invite us here to rob us?" {16} Then Samson's wife threw herself on him, sobbing, "You hate me! You don't really love me. You've given my people a riddle, but you haven't told me the answer." "I haven't even explained it to my father or mother," he replied, "so why should I explain it to you?" {17} She cried the whole seven days of the feast. So on the seventh day he finally told her, because she continued to press him. She in turn explained the riddle to her people. {18} Before sunset on the seventh day the men of the town said to him, "What is sweeter than honey? What is stronger than a lion?" Samson said to them, "If you had not plowed with my heifer, you would not have solved my riddle." {19} Then the Spirit of the LORD came upon him in power. He went down to Ashkelon, struck down thirty of their men, stripped them of their belongings and gave their clothes to those who had explained the riddle. Burning with anger, he went up to his father's house. {20} And Samson's wife was given to the friend who had attended him at his wedding.

DELILAH BETRAYS SAMSON

Judg 16:8-22

Then the rulers of the Philistines brought her seven fresh thongs that had not been dried, and she tied him with them. {9} With men hidden in the room, she called to him, "Samson, the Philistines are upon you!" But he snapped the thongs as easily as a piece of string snaps when it comes close to a flame. So the secret of his strength was not discovered. {10} Then Delilah said to Samson, "You have made a fool of me; you lied to me. Come now, tell me how you can be tied." {11} He said, "If anyone ties me securely with new ropes that have never been used, I'll become as weak as any other man." {12} So Delilah took new ropes and tied him with them. Then, with men hidden in the room, she called to him, "Samson, the Philistines are upon you!" But he snapped the ropes off his arms as if they were threads. {13} Delilah then said to Samson, "Until now, you have been making a fool of me and lying to me. Tell me how you can be tied." He replied, "If you weave the seven braids of my head into the fabric <on the loom> and tighten it with the pin, I'll become as weak as any other man." So while he was sleeping, Delilah took the seven braids of his head, wove them into the fabric {14} and tightened it with the pin. Again she called to him, "Samson, the Philistines are upon you!" He awoke from his sleep and pulled up the pin and the loom, with the fabric. {15} Then she said to him, "How can you say, 'I love you,' when you won't confide in me? This is the third time you have made a fool of me and haven't told me the secret of your great strength." {16} With such nagging she prodded him day after day until he was tired to death. {17} So he told her everything. "No razor has ever been used on my head," he said, "because I have been a Nazirite set apart to God since birth. If my head were shaved, my strength would leave me, and I would become as weak as any other man." {18} When Delilah saw that he had told her everything, she sent word to the rulers of the Philistines, "Come back once more; he has told me everything." So the rulers of the Philistines returned with the silver in their hands. {19} Having put him to sleep on her lap, she called a man to shave off the seven braids of his hair, and so began to subdue him. And his strength left him. {20} Then she called, "Samson, the Philistines are upon you!" He awoke from his sleep and thought, "I'll go out as before and shake myself free." But he did not know that the LORD had left him. {21} Then the Philistines seized him, gouged out his eyes and took him down to Gaza. Binding him with bronze shackles, they set him to grinding in the prison. {22} But the hair on his head began to grow again after it had been shaved.

DEATH OF SAMSON

Judg 16:23-31

Now the rulers of the Philistines assembled to offer a great sacrifice to Dagon their god and to celebrate, saying, "Our god has delivered Samson, our enemy, into our hands." {24} When the people saw him, they praised their god, saying, "Our god has delivered our enemy into our hands, the one who laid waste our land and multiplied our slain." {25} While they were in high spirits, they shouted, "Bring out Samson to entertain us." So they called Samson out of the prison, and he performed for them. When they stood him among the pillars, {26} Samson said to the servant who held his hand, "Put me where I can feel the pillars that support the temple, so that I may lean against them." {27} Now the temple was crowded with men and women; all the rulers of the Philistines were there, and on the roof were about three thousand men and women watching Samson perform. {28} Then Samson prayed to the LORD, "O Sovereign LORD, remember me. O God, please strengthen me just once more, and let me with one blow get revenge on the Philistines for my two eyes." {29} Then Samson reached toward the two central pillars on which the temple stood. Bracing himself against them, his right hand on the one and his left hand on the other, {30} Samson said, "Let me die with the Philistines!" Then he pushed with all his might, and down came the temple on the rulers and all the people in it. Thus he killed many more when he died than while he lived. {31} Then his brothers and his father's whole family went down to get him. They brought him back and buried him between Zorah and Eshtaol in the tomb of Manoah his father. He had led Israel twenty years.

RUTH MIGRATES WITH NAOMI

Ruth 1:1-19

In the days when the judges ruled, there was a famine in the land, and a man from Bethlehem in Judah, together with his wife and two sons, went to live for a while in the country of Moab. {2} The man's name was Elimelech, his wife's name Naomi, and the names of his two sons were Mahlon and Kilion. They were Ephrathites from Bethlehem, Judah. And they went to Moab and lived there. {3} Now Elimelech, Naomi's husband, died, and she was left with her two sons. {4} They married Moabite women, one named Orpah and the other Ruth. After they had lived there about ten years, {5} both Mahlon and Kilion also died, and Naomi was left without her two sons and her husband. {6} When she heard in Moab that the LORD had come to the aid of his people by providing food for them, Naomi and her daughters-in-law prepared to return home from there. {7} With her two daughters-in-law she left the place where she had been living and set out on the road that would take them back to the land of Judah. {8} Then Naomi said to her two daughters-in-law, "Go back, each of you, to your mother's home. May the LORD show kindness to you, as you have shown to your dead and to me. {9} May the LORD grant that each of you will find rest in the home of another husband." Then she kissed them and they wept aloud {10} and said to her, "We will go back with you to your people." {11} But Naomi said, "Return home, my daughters. Why would you come with me? Am I going to have any more sons, who could become your husbands? {12} Return home, my daughters; I am too old to have another husband. Even if I thought there was still hope for me—even if I had a husband tonight and then gave birth to sons– {13} would you wait until they grew up? Would you remain unmarried for them? No, my daughters. It is more bitter for me than for you, because the Lord's hand has gone out against me!" {14} At this they wept again. Then Orpah kissed her mother-in-law good-by, but Ruth clung to her. {15} "Look," said Naomi, "your sister-in-law is going back to her people and her gods. Go back with her." {16} But Ruth replied, "Don't urge me to leave you or to turn back from you. Where you go I will go, and where you stay I will stay. Your people will be my people and your God my God. {17} Where you die I will die, and there I will be buried. May the LORD deal with me, be it ever so severely, if anything but death separates you and me." {18} When Naomi realized that Ruth was determined to go with her, she stopped urging her. {19} So the two women went on until they came to Bethlehem. When they arrived in Bethlehem, the whole town was stirred because of them, and the women exclaimed, "Can this be Naomi?"

RUTH MEETS BOAZ

Ruth 2:8-20a

So Boaz said to Ruth, "My daughter, listen to me. Don't go and glean in another field and don't go away from here. Stay here with my servant girls. {9} Watch the field where the men are harvesting, and follow along after the girls. I have told the men not to touch you. And whenever you are thirsty, go and get a drink from the water jars the men have filled." {10} At this, she bowed down with her face to the ground. She exclaimed, "Why have I found such favor in your eyes that you notice me–a foreigner?" {11} Boaz replied, "I've been told all about what you have done for your mother-in-law since the death of your husband–how you left your father and mother and your homeland and came to live with a people you did not know before. {12} May the LORD repay you for what you have done. May you be richly rewarded by the LORD, the God of Israel, under whose wings you have come to take refuge." {13} "May I continue to find favor in your eyes, my lord," she said. "You have given me comfort and have spoken kindly to your servant–though I do not have the standing of one of your servant girls." {14} At mealtime Boaz said to her, "Come over here. Have some bread and dip it in the wine vinegar." When she sat down with the harvesters, he offered her some roasted grain. She ate all she wanted and had some left over. {15} As she got up to glean, Boaz gave orders to his men, "Even if she gathers among the sheaves, don't embarrass her. {16} Rather, pull out some stalks for her from the bundles and leave them for her to pick up, and don't rebuke her." {17} So Ruth gleaned in the field until evening. Then she threshed the barley she had gathered, and it amounted to about an ephah. {18} She carried it back to town, and her mother-in-law saw how much she had gathered. Ruth also brought out and gave her what she had left over after she had eaten enough. {19} Her mother-in-law asked her, "Where did you glean today? Where did you work? Blessed be the man who took notice of you!" Then Ruth told her mother-in-law about the one at whose place she had been working. "The name of the man I worked with today is Boaz," she said. {20} "The LORD bless him!" Naomi said to her daughter-in-law. "He has not stopped showing his kindness to the living and the dead."

BOAZ PROMISES TO FIND A HUSBAND FOR RUTH

Ruth 3:1-18

One day Naomi her mother-in-law said to her, "My daughter, should I not try to find a home for you, where you will be well provided for? {2} Is not Boaz, with whose servant girls you have been, a kinsman of ours? Tonight he will be winnowing barley on the threshing floor. {3} Wash and perfume yourself, and put on your best clothes. Then go down to the threshing floor, but don't let him know you are there until he has finished eating and drinking. {4} When he lies down, note the place where he is lying. Then go and uncover his feet and lie down. He will tell you what to do." {5} "I will do whatever you say," Ruth answered. {6} So she went down to the threshing floor and did everything her mother-in-law told her to do. {7} When Boaz had finished eating and drinking and was in good spirits, he went over to lie down at the far end of the grain pile. Ruth approached quietly, uncovered his feet and lay down. {8} In the middle of the night something startled the man, and he turned and discovered a woman lying at his feet. {9} "Who are you?" he asked. "I am your servant Ruth," she said. "Spread the corner of your garment over me, since you are a kinsman-redeemer." {10} "The LORD bless you, my daughter," he replied. "This kindness is greater than that which you showed earlier: You have not run after the younger men, whether rich or poor. {11} And now, my daughter, don't be afraid. I will do for you all you ask. All my fellow townsmen know that you are a woman of noble character. {12} Although it is true that I am near of kin, there is a kinsman-redeemer nearer than I. {13} Stay here for the night, and in the morning if he wants to redeem, good; let him redeem. But if he is not willing, as surely as the LORD lives I will do it. Lie here until morning." {14} So she lay at his feet until morning, but got up before anyone could be recognized; and he said, "Don't let it be known that a woman came to the threshing floor." {15} He also said, "Bring me the shawl you are wearing and hold it out." When she did so, he poured into it six measures of barley and put it on her. Then he went back to town. {16} When Ruth came to her mother-in-law, Naomi asked, "How did it go, my daughter?" Then she told her everything Boaz had done for her {17} and added, "He gave me these six measures of barley, saying, 'Don't go back to your mother-in-law empty-handed.'" {18} Then Naomi said, "Wait, my daughter, until you find out what happens. For the man will not rest until the matter is settled today."

BOAZ MARRIES RUTH

Ruth 4:2-17

Boaz took ten of the elders of the town and said, "Sit here," and they did so. {3} Then he said to the kinsman-redeemer, "Naomi, who has come back from Moab, is selling the piece of land that belonged to our brother Elimelech. {4} I thought I should bring the matter to your attention and suggest that you buy it in the presence of these seated here and in the presence of the elders of my people. If you will redeem it, do so. But if you will not, tell me, so I will know. For no one has the right to do it except you, and I am next in line." "I will redeem it," he said. {5} Then Boaz said, "On the day you buy the land from Naomi and from Ruth the Moabitess, you acquire the dead man's widow, in order to maintain the name of the dead with his property." {6} At this, the kinsman-redeemer said, "Then I cannot redeem it because I might endanger my own estate. You redeem it yourself. I cannot do it." {7} (Now in earlier times in Israel, for the redemption and transfer of property to become final, one party took off his sandal and gave it to the other. This was the method of legalizing transactions in Israel.) {8} So the kinsman-redeemer said to Boaz, "Buy it yourself." And he removed his sandal. {9} Then Boaz announced to the elders and all the people, "Today you are witnesses that I have bought from Naomi all the property of Elimelech, Kilion and Mahlon. {10} I have also acquired Ruth the Moabitess, Mahlon's widow, as my wife, in order to maintain the name of the dead with his property, so that his name will not disappear from among his family or from the town records. Today you are witnesses!" {11} Then the elders and all those at the gate said, "We are witnesses. May the LORD make the woman who is coming into your home like Rachel and Leah, who together built up the house of Israel. May you have standing in Ephrathah and be famous in Bethlehem. {12} Through the offspring the LORD gives you by this young woman, may your family be like that of Perez, whom Tamar bore to Judah." {13} So Boaz took Ruth and she became his wife. Then he went to her, and the LORD enabled her to conceive, and she gave birth to a son. {14} The women said to Naomi: "Praise be to the LORD, who this day has not left you without a kinsman-redeemer. May he become famous throughout Israel! {15} He will renew your life and sustain you in your old age. For your daughter-in-law, who loves you and who is better to you than seven sons, has given him birth." {16} Then Naomi took the child, laid him in her lap and cared for him. {17} The women living there said, "Naomi has a son." And they named him Obed. He was the father of Jesse, the father of David.

BIRTH OF SAMUEL

1 Sam 1:3-20

Year after year this man went up from his town to worship and sacrifice to the LORD Almighty at Shiloh, where Hophni and Phinehas, the two sons of Eli, were priests of the LORD. {4} Whenever the day came for Elkanah to sacrifice, he would give portions of the meat to his wife Peninnah and to all her sons and daughters. {5} But to Hannah he gave a double portion because he loved her, and the LORD had closed her womb. {6} And because the LORD had closed her womb, her rival kept provoking her in order to irritate her. {7} This went on year after year. Whenever Hannah went up to the house of the LORD, her rival provoked her till she wept and would not eat. {8} Elkanah her husband would say to her, "Hannah, why are you weeping? Why don't you eat? Why are you downhearted? Don't I mean more to you than ten sons?" {9} Once when they had finished eating and drinking in Shiloh, Hannah stood up. Now Eli the priest was sitting on a chair by the doorpost of the Lord's temple. {10} In bitterness of soul Hannah wept much and prayed to the LORD. {11} And she made a vow, saying, "O LORD Almighty, if you will only look upon your servant's misery and remember me, and not forget your servant but give her a son, then I will give him to the LORD for all the days of his life, and no razor will ever be used on his head." {12} As she kept on praying to the LORD, Eli observed her mouth. {13} Hannah was praying in her heart, and her lips were moving but her voice was not heard. Eli thought she was drunk {14} and said to her, "How long will you keep on getting drunk? Get rid of your wine." {15} "Not so, my lord," Hannah replied, "I am a woman who is deeply troubled. I have not been drinking wine or beer; I was pouring out my soul to the LORD. {16} Do not take your servant for a wicked woman; I have been praying here out of my great anguish and grief." {17} Eli answered, "Go in peace, and may the God of Israel grant you what you have asked of him." {18} She said, "May your servant find favor in your eyes." Then she went her way and ate something, and her face was no longer downcast. {19} Early the next morning they arose and worshiped before the LORD and then went back to their home at Ramah. Elkanah lay with Hannah his wife, and the LORD remembered her. {20} So in the course of time Hannah conceived and gave birth to a son. She named him Samuel, saying, "Because I asked the LORD for him."

SAMUEL IS DEDICATED TO THE LORD

1 Sam 1:21-28

When the man Elkanah went up with all his family to offer the annual sacrifice to the LORD and to fulfill his vow, {22} Hannah did not go. She said to her husband, "After the boy is weaned, I will take him and present him before the LORD, and he will live there always." {23} "Do what seems best to you," Elkanah her husband told her. "Stay here until you have weaned him; only may the LORD make good his word." So the woman stayed at home and nursed her son until she had weaned him. {24} After he was weaned, she took the boy with her, young as he was, along with a three-year-old bull, an ephah of flour and a skin of wine, and brought him to the house of the LORD at Shiloh. {25} When they had slaughtered the bull, they brought the boy to Eli, {26} and she said to him, "As surely as you live, my lord, I am the woman who stood here beside you praying to the LORD. {27} I prayed for this child, and the LORD has granted me what I asked of him. {28} So now I give him to the LORD. For his whole life he will be given over to the LORD." And he worshiped the LORD there.

1 Sam 2:19-21

Each year his mother made him a little robe and took it to him when she went up with her husband to offer the annual sacrifice. {20} Eli would bless Elkanah and his wife, saying, "May the LORD give you children by this woman to take the place of the one she prayed for and gave to the LORD." Then they would go home. {21} And the LORD was gracious to Hannah; she conceived and gave birth to three sons and two daughters. Meanwhile, the boy Samuel grew up in the presence of the LORD.

1 Sam 2:26

And the boy Samuel continued to grow in stature and in favor with the LORD and with men.

THE SONS OF ELI ARE WICKED

1 Sam 2:22-36

Now Eli, who was very old, heard about everything his sons were doing to all Israel and how they slept with the women who served at the entrance to the Tent of Meeting. {23} So he said to them, "Why do you do such things? I hear from all the people about these wicked deeds of yours. {24} No, my sons; it is not a good report that I hear spreading among the Lord's people. {25} If a man sins against another man, God may mediate for him; but if a man sins against the LORD, who will intercede for him?" His sons, however, did not listen to their father's rebuke, for it was the Lord's will to put them to death. {26} And the boy Samuel continued to grow in stature and in favor with the LORD and with men. {27} Now a man of God came to Eli and said to him, "This is what the LORD says: 'Did I not clearly reveal myself to your father's house when they were in Egypt under Pharaoh? {28} I chose your father out of all the tribes of Israel to be my priest, to go up to my altar, to burn incense, and to wear an ephod in my presence. I also gave your father's house all the offerings made with fire by the Israelites. {29} Why do you scorn my sacrifice and offering that I prescribed for my dwelling? Why do you honor your sons more than me by fattening yourselves on the choice parts of every offering made by my people Israel?' {30} "Therefore the LORD, the God of Israel, declares: 'I promised that your house and your father's house would minister before me forever.' But now the LORD declares: 'Far be it from me! Those who honor me I will honor, but those who despise me will be disdained. {31} The time is coming when I will cut short your strength and the strength of your father's house, so that there will not be an old man in your family line {32} and you will see distress in my dwelling. Although good will be done to Israel, in your family line there will never be an old man. {33} Every one of you that I do not cut off from my altar will be spared only to blind your eyes with tears and to grieve your heart, and all your descendants will die in the prime of life. {34} "'And what happens to your two sons, Hophni and Phinehas, will be a sign to you–they will both die on the same day. {35} I will raise up for myself a faithful priest, who will do according to what is in my heart and mind. I will firmly establish his house, and he will minister before my anointed one always. {36} Then everyone left in your family line will come and bow down before him for a piece of silver and a crust of bread and plead, "Appoint me to some priestly office so I can have food to eat."'"

THE LORD CALLS SAMUEL

1 Sam 3:1-21

The boy Samuel ministered before the LORD under Eli. In those days the word of the LORD was rare; there were not many visions. {2} One night Eli, whose eyes were becoming so weak that he could barely see, was lying down in his usual place. {3} The lamp of God had not yet gone out, and Samuel was lying down in the temple of the LORD, where the ark of God was. {4} Then the LORD called Samuel. Samuel answered, "Here I am." {5} And he ran to Eli and said, "Here I am; you called me." But Eli said, "I did not call; go back and lie down." So he went and lay down. {6} Again the LORD called, "Samuel!" And Samuel got up and went to Eli and said, "Here I am; you called me." "My son," Eli said, "I did not call; go back and lie down." {7} Now Samuel did not yet know the LORD: The word of the LORD had not yet been revealed to him. {8} The LORD called Samuel a third time, and Samuel got up and went to Eli and said, "Here I am; you called me." Then Eli realized that the LORD was calling the boy. {9} So Eli told Samuel, "Go and lie down, and if he calls you, say, 'Speak, LORD, for your servant is listening.'" So Samuel went and lay down in his place. {10} The LORD came and stood there, calling as at the other times, "Samuel! Samuel!" Then Samuel said, "Speak, for your servant is listening." {11} And the LORD said to Samuel: "See, I am about to do something in Israel that will make the ears of everyone who hears of it tingle. {12} At that time I will carry out against Eli everything I spoke against his family–from beginning to end. {13} For I told him that I would judge his family forever because of the sin he knew about; his sons made themselves contemptible, and he failed to restrain them. {14} Therefore, I swore to the house of Eli, 'The guilt of Eli's house will never be atoned for by sacrifice or offering.'" {15} Samuel lay down until morning and then opened the doors of the house of the LORD. He was afraid to tell Eli the vision, {16} but Eli called him and said, "Samuel, my son." Samuel answered, "Here I am." {17} "What was it he said to you?" Eli asked. "Do not hide it from me. May God deal with you, be it ever so severely, if you hide from me anything he told you." {18} So Samuel told him everything, hiding nothing from him. Then Eli said, "He is the LORD; let him do what is good in his eyes." {19} The LORD was with Samuel as he grew up, and he let none of his words fall to the ground. {20} And all Israel from Dan to Beersheba recognized that Samuel was attested as a prophet of the LORD. {21} The LORD continued to appear at Shiloh, and there he revealed himself to Samuel through his word.

ELI'S SONS ARE KILLED AND ELI DIES

1 Sam 4:5-21

When the ark of the Lord's covenant came into the camp, all Israel raised such a great shout that the ground shook. {6} Hearing the uproar, the Philistines asked, "What's all this shouting in the Hebrew camp?" When they learned that the ark of the LORD had come into the camp, {7} the Philistines were afraid. "A god has come into the camp," they said. "We're in trouble! Nothing like this has happened before. {8} Woe to us! Who will deliver us from the hand of these mighty gods? They are the gods who struck the Egyptians with all kinds of plagues in the desert. {9} Be strong, Philistines! Be men, or you will be subject to the Hebrews, as they have been to you. Be men, and fight!" {10} So the Philistines fought, and the Israelites were defeated and every man fled to his tent. The slaughter was very great; Israel lost thirty thousand foot soldiers. {11} The ark of God was captured, and Eli's two sons, Hophni and Phinehas, died. {12} That same day a Benjamite ran from the battle line and went to Shiloh, his clothes torn and dust on his head. {13} When he arrived, there was Eli sitting on his chair by the side of the road, watching, because his heart feared for the ark of God. When the man entered the town and told what had happened, the whole town sent up a cry. {14} Eli heard the outcry and asked, "What is the meaning of this uproar?" The man hurried over to Eli, {15} who was ninety-eight years old and whose eyes were set so that he could not see. {16} He told Eli, "I have just come from the battle line; I fled from it this very day." Eli asked, "What happened, my son?" {17} The man who brought the news replied, "Israel fled before the Philistines, and the army has suffered heavy losses. Also your two sons, Hophni and Phinehas, are dead, and the ark of God has been captured." {18} When he mentioned the ark of God, Eli fell backward off his chair by the side of the gate. His neck was broken and he died, for he was an old man and heavy. He had led Israel forty years. {19} His daughter-in-law, the wife of Phinehas, was pregnant and near the time of delivery. When she heard the news that the ark of God had been captured and that her father-in-law and her husband were dead, she went into labor and gave birth, but was overcome by her labor pains. {20} As she was dying, the women attending her said, "Don't despair; you have given birth to a son." But she did not respond or pay any attention. {21} She named the boy Ichabod, saying, "The glory has departed from Israel"–because of the capture of the ark of God and the deaths of her father-in-law and her husband.

PHILISTINES RETURN THE ARK OF THE COVENANT

1 Sam 5:10b-6:12

As the ark of God was entering Ekron, the people of Ekron cried out, "They have brought the ark of the god of Israel around to us to kill us and our people." {11} So they called together all the rulers of the Philistines and said, "Send the ark of the god of Israel away; let it go back to its own place, or it will kill us and our people." For death had filled the city with panic; God's hand was very heavy upon it. {12} Those who did not die were afflicted with tumors, and the outcry of the city went up to heaven. {6:1} When the ark of the LORD had been in Philistine territory seven months, {2} the Philistines called for the priests and the diviners and said, "What shall we do with the ark of the LORD? Tell us how we should send it back to its place." {3} They answered, "If you return the ark of the god of Israel, do not send it away empty, but by all means send a guilt offering to him. Then you will be healed, and you will know why his hand has not been lifted from you." {4} The Philistines asked, "What guilt offering should we send to him?" They replied, "Five gold tumors and five gold rats, according to the number of the Philistine rulers, because the same plague has struck both you and your rulers. {5} Make models of the tumors and of the rats that are destroying the country, and pay honor to Israel's god. Perhaps he will lift his hand from you and your gods and your land. {6} Why do you harden your hearts as the Egyptians and Pharaoh did? When he treated them harshly, did they not send the Israelites out so they could go on their way? {7} "Now then, get a new cart ready, with two cows that have calved and have never been yoked. Hitch the cows to the cart, but take their calves away and pen them up. {8} Take the ark of the LORD and put it on the cart, and in a chest beside it put the gold objects you are sending back to him as a guilt offering. Send it on its way, {9} but keep watching it. If it goes up to its own territory, toward Beth Shemesh, then the LORD has brought this great disaster on us. But if it does not, then we will know that it was not his hand that struck us and that it happened to us by chance." {10} So they did this. They took two such cows and hitched them to the cart and penned up their calves. {11} They placed the ark of the LORD on the cart and along with it the chest containing the gold rats and the models of the tumors. {12} Then the cows went straight up toward Beth Shemesh, keeping on the road and lowing all the way; they did not turn to the right or to the left. The rulers of the Philistines followed them as far as the border of Beth Shemesh.

124

PEACE IN ISRAEL WHILE SAMUEL IS JUDGE

1 Sam 7:2-17

It was a long time, twenty years in all, that the ark remained at Kiriath Jearim, and all the people of Israel mourned and sought after the LORD. {3} And Samuel said to the whole house of Israel, "If you are returning to the LORD with all your hearts, then rid yourselves of the foreign gods and the Ashtoreths and commit yourselves to the LORD and serve him only, and he will deliver you out of the hand of the Philistines." {4} So the Israelites put away their Baals and Ashtoreths, and served the LORD only. {5} Then Samuel said, "Assemble all Israel at Mizpah and I will intercede with the LORD for you." {6} When they had assembled at Mizpah, they drew water and poured it out before the LORD. On that day they fasted and there they confessed, "We have sinned against the LORD." And Samuel was leader of Israel at Mizpah. {7} When the Philistines heard that Israel had assembled at Mizpah, the rulers of the Philistines came up to attack them. And when the Israelites heard of it, they were afraid because of the Philistines. {8} They said to Samuel, "Do not stop crying out to the LORD our God for us, that he may rescue us from the hand of the Philistines." {9} Then Samuel took a suckling lamb and offered it up as a whole burnt offering to the LORD. He cried out to the LORD on Israel's behalf, and the LORD answered him. {10} While Samuel was sacrificing the burnt offering, the Philistines drew near to engage Israel in battle. But that day the LORD thundered with loud thunder against the Philistines and threw them into such a panic that they were routed before the Israelites. {11} The men of Israel rushed out of Mizpah and pursued the Philistines, slaughtering them along the way to a point below Beth Car. {12} Then Samuel took a stone and set it up between Mizpah and Shen. He named it Ebenezer, saying, "Thus far has the LORD helped us." {13} So the Philistines were subdued and did not invade Israelite territory again. Throughout Samuel's lifetime, the hand of the LORD was against the Philistines. {14} The towns from Ekron to Gath that the Philistines had captured from Israel were restored to her, and Israel delivered the neighboring territory from the power of the Philistines. And there was peace between Israel and the Amorites. {15} Samuel continued as judge over Israel all the days of his life. {16} From year to year he went on a circuit from Bethel to Gilgal to Mizpah, judging Israel in all those places. {17} But he always went back to Ramah, where his home was, and there he also judged Israel. And he built an altar there to the LORD.

ISRAEL ASKS FOR A KING

1 Sam 8:1-22

When Samuel grew old, he appointed his sons as judges for Israel. {2} The name of his firstborn was Joel and the name of his second was Abijah, and they served at Beersheba. {3} But his sons did not walk in his ways. They turned aside after dishonest gain and accepted bribes and perverted justice. {4} So all the elders of Israel gathered together and came to Samuel at Ramah. {5} They said to him, "You are old, and your sons do not walk in your ways; now appoint a king to lead us, such as all the other nations have." {6} But when they said, "Give us a king to lead us," this displeased Samuel; so he prayed to the LORD. {7} And the LORD told him: "Listen to all that the people are saying to you; it is not you they have rejected, but they have rejected me as their king. {8} As they have done from the day I brought them up out of Egypt until this day, forsaking me and serving other gods, so they are doing to you. {9} Now listen to them; but warn them solemnly and let them know what the king who will reign over them will do." {10} Samuel told all the words of the LORD to the people who were asking him for a king. {11} He said, "This is what the king who will reign over you will do: He will take your sons and make them serve with his chariots and horses, and they will run in front of his chariots. {12} Some he will assign to be commanders of thousands and commanders of fifties, and others to plow his ground and reap his harvest, and still others to make weapons of war and equipment for his chariots. {13} He will take your daughters to be perfumers and cooks and bakers. {14} He will take the best of your fields and vineyards and olive groves and give them to his attendants. {15} He will take a tenth of your grain and of your vintage and give it to his officials and attendants. {16} Your menservants and maidservants and the best of your cattle and donkeys he will take for his own use. {17} He will take a tenth of your flocks, and you yourselves will become his slaves. {18} When that day comes, you will cry out for relief from the king you have chosen, and the LORD will not answer you in that day." {19} But the people refused to listen to Samuel. "No!" they said. "We want a king over us. {20} Then we will be like all the other nations, with a king to lead us and to go out before us and fight our battles." {21} When Samuel heard all that the people said, he repeated it before the LORD. {22} The LORD answered, "Listen to them and give them a king." Then Samuel said to the men of Israel, "Everyone go back to his town."

SAMUEL LOOKS FOR A KING

1 Sam 9:1-17

There was a Benjamite, a man of standing, whose name was Kish.... {2} He had a son named Saul, an impressive young man without equal among the Israelites–a head taller than any of the others. {3} Now the donkeys belonging to Saul's father Kish were lost, and Kish said to his son Saul, "Take one of the servants with you and go and look for the donkeys." {4} So he passed through the hill country of Ephraim and through the area around Shalisha, but they did not find them. They went on into the district of Shaalim, but the donkeys were not there. Then he passed through the territory of Benjamin, but they did not find them. {5} When they reached the district of Zuph, Saul said to the servant who was with him, "Come, let's go back, or my father will stop thinking about the donkeys and start worrying about us." {6} But the servant replied, "Look, in this town there is a man of God; he is highly respected, and everything he says comes true. Let's go there now. Perhaps he will tell us what way to take." {7} Saul said to his servant, "If we go, what can we give the man? The food in our sacks is gone. We have no gift to take to the man of God. What do we have?" {8} The servant answered him again. "Look," he said, "I have a quarter of a shekel of silver. I will give it to the man of God so that he will tell us what way to take." {9} (Formerly in Israel, if a man went to inquire of God, he would say, "Come, let us go to the seer," because the prophet of today used to be called a seer.) {10} "Good," Saul said to his servant. "Come, let's go." So they set out for the town where the man of God was. {11} As they were going up the hill to the town, they met some girls coming out to draw water, and they asked them, "Is the seer here?" {12} "He is," they answered. "He's ahead of you. Hurry now; he has just come to our town today, for the people have a sacrifice at the high place. {13} As soon as you enter the town, you will find him before he goes up to the high place to eat. The people will not begin eating until he comes, because he must bless the sacrifice; afterward, those who are invited will eat. Go up now; you should find him about this time." {14} They went up to the town, and as they were entering it, there was Samuel, coming toward them on his way up to the high place. {15} Now the day before Saul came, the LORD had revealed this to Samuel: {16} "About this time tomorrow I will send you a man from the land of Benjamin. Anoint him leader over my people Israel; he will deliver my people from the hand of the Philistines. I have looked upon my people, for their cry has reached me." {17} When Samuel caught sight of Saul, the LORD said to him, "This is the man I spoke to you about; he will govern my people."

SAMUEL ANOINTS SAUL AS KING

1 Sam 9:22-10:8

Then Samuel brought Saul and his servant into the hall and seated them at the head of those who were invited–about thirty in number. {23} Samuel said to the cook, "Bring the piece of meat I gave you, the one I told you to lay aside." {24} So the cook took up the leg with what was on it and set it in front of Saul. Samuel said, "Here is what has been kept for you. Eat, because it was set aside for you for this occasion, from the time I said, 'I have invited guests.'" And Saul dined with Samuel that day. {25} After they came down from the high place to the town, Samuel talked with Saul on the roof of his house. {26} They rose about daybreak and Samuel called to Saul on the roof, "Get ready, and I will send you on your way." When Saul got ready, he and Samuel went outside together. {27} As they were going down to the edge of the town, Samuel said to Saul, "Tell the servant to go on ahead of us"–and the servant did so–"but you stay here awhile, so that I may give you a message from God." {10:1} Then Samuel took a flask of oil and poured it on Saul's head and kissed him, saying, "Has not the LORD anointed you leader over his inheritance? {2} When you leave me today, you will meet two men near Rachel's tomb, at Zelzah on the border of Benjamin. They will say to you, 'The donkeys you set out to look for have been found. And now your father has stopped thinking about them and is worried about you. He is asking, "What shall I do about my son?"' {3} "Then you will go on from there until you reach the great tree of Tabor. Three men going up to God at Bethel will meet you there. One will be carrying three young goats, another three loaves of bread, and another a skin of wine. {4} They will greet you and offer you two loaves of bread, which you will accept from them. {5} "After that you will go to Gibeah of God, where there is a Philistine outpost. As you approach the town, you will meet a procession of prophets coming down from the high place with lyres, tambourines, flutes and harps being played before them, and they will be prophesying. {6} The Spirit of the LORD will come upon you in power, and you will prophesy with them; and you will be changed into a different person. {7} Once these signs are fulfilled, do whatever your hand finds to do, for God is with you. {8} "Go down ahead of me to Gilgal. I will surely come down to you to sacrifice burnt offerings and fellowship offerings, but you must wait seven days until I come to you and tell you what you are to do."

SAUL BECOMES KING OF ISRAEL

1 Sam 10:11-27

When all those who had formerly known him saw him prophesying with the prophets, they asked each other, "What is this that has happened to the son of Kish? Is Saul also among the prophets?" {12} A man who lived there answered, "And who is their father?" So it became a saying: "Is Saul also among the prophets?" {13} After Saul stopped prophesying, he went to the high place. {14} Now Saul's uncle asked him and his servant, "Where have you been?" "Looking for the donkeys," he said. "But when we saw they were not to be found, we went to Samuel." {15} Saul's uncle said, "Tell me what Samuel said to you." {16} Saul replied, "He assured us that the donkeys had been found." But he did not tell his uncle what Samuel had said about the kingship. {17} Samuel summoned the people of Israel to the LORD at Mizpah {18} and said to them, "This is what the LORD, the God of Israel, says: 'I brought Israel up out of Egypt, and I delivered you from the power of Egypt and all the kingdoms that oppressed you.' {19} But you have now rejected your God, who saves you out of all your calamities and distresses. And you have said, 'No, set a king over us.' So now present yourselves before the LORD by your tribes and clans." {20} When Samuel brought all the tribes of Israel near, the tribe of Benjamin was chosen. {21} Then he brought forward the tribe of Benjamin, clan by clan, and Matri's clan was chosen. Finally Saul son of Kish was chosen. But when they looked for him, he was not to be found. {22} So they inquired further of the LORD, "Has the man come here yet?" And the LORD said, "Yes, he has hidden himself among the baggage." {23} They ran and brought him out, and as he stood among the people he was a head taller than any of the others. {24} Samuel said to all the people, "Do you see the man the LORD has chosen? There is no one like him among all the people." Then the people shouted, "Long live the king!" {25} Samuel explained to the people the regulations of the kingship. He wrote them down on a scroll and deposited it before the LORD. Then Samuel dismissed the people, each to his own home. {26} Saul also went to his home in Gibeah, accompanied by valiant men whose hearts God had touched. {27} But some troublemakers said, "How can this fellow save us?" They despised him and brought him no gifts. But Saul kept silent.

1 Sam 13:1

Saul was <thirty> years old when he became king, and he reigned over Israel <forty>-two years.

JONATHAN ATTACKS THE PHILISTINES

1 Sam 14:4-15

On each side of the pass that Jonathan intended to cross to reach the Philistine outpost was a cliff; one was called Bozez, and the other Seneh. {5} One cliff stood to the north toward Micmash, the other to the south toward Geba. {6} Jonathan said to his young armor-bearer, "Come, let's go over to the outpost of those uncircumcised fellows. Perhaps the LORD will act in our behalf. Nothing can hinder the LORD from saving, whether by many or by few." {7} "Do all that you have in mind," his armor-bearer said. "Go ahead; I am with you heart and soul." {8} Jonathan said, "Come, then; we will cross over toward the men and let them see us. {9} If they say to us, 'Wait there until we come to you,' we will stay where we are and not go up to them. {10} But if they say, 'Come up to us,' we will climb up, because that will be our sign that the LORD has given them into our hands." {11} So both of them showed themselves to the Philistine outpost. "Look!" said the Philistines. "The Hebrews are crawling out of the holes they were hiding in." {12} The men of the outpost shouted to Jonathan and his armor-bearer, "Come up to us and we'll teach you a lesson." So Jonathan said to his armor-bearer, "Climb up after me; the LORD has given them into the hand of Israel." {13} Jonathan climbed up, using his hands and feet, with his armor-bearer right behind him. The Philistines fell before Jonathan, and his armor-bearer followed and killed behind him. {14} In that first attack Jonathan and his armor-bearer killed some twenty men in an area of about half an acre. {15} Then panic struck the whole army–those in the camp and field, and those in the outposts and raiding parties–and the ground shook. It was a panic sent by God.

1 Sam 14:20-23

Then Saul and all his men assembled and went to the battle. They found the Philistines in total confusion, striking each other with their swords. {21} Those Hebrews who had previously been with the Philistines and had gone up with them to their camp went over to the Israelites who were with Saul and Jonathan. {22} When all the Israelites who had hidden in the hill country of Ephraim heard that the Philistines were on the run, they joined the battle in hot pursuit. {23} So the LORD rescued Israel that day, and the battle moved on beyond Beth Aven.

SAUL REJECTED AS KING

1 Sam 15:10-26

Then the word of the LORD came to Samuel: {11} "I am grieved that I have made Saul king, because he has turned away from me and has not carried out my instructions." Samuel was troubled, and he cried out to the LORD all that night. {12} Early in the morning Samuel got up and went to meet Saul, but he was told, "Saul has gone to Carmel. There he has set up a monument in his own honor and has turned and gone on down to Gilgal." {13} When Samuel reached him, Saul said, "The LORD bless you! I have carried out the Lord's instructions." {14} But Samuel said, "What then is this bleating of sheep in my ears? What is this lowing of cattle that I hear?" {15} Saul answered, "The soldiers brought them from the Amalekites; they spared the best of the sheep and cattle to sacrifice to the LORD your God, but we totally destroyed the rest." {16} "Stop!" Samuel said to Saul. "Let me tell you what the LORD said to me last night." "Tell me," Saul replied. {17} Samuel said, "Although you were once small in your own eyes, did you not become the head of the tribes of Israel? The LORD anointed you king over Israel. {18} And he sent you on a mission, saying, 'Go and completely destroy those wicked people, the Amalekites; make war on them until you have wiped them out.' {19} Why did you not obey the LORD? Why did you pounce on the plunder and do evil in the eyes of the LORD?" {20} "But I did obey the LORD," Saul said. "I went on the mission the LORD assigned me. I completely destroyed the Amalekites and brought back Agag their king. {21} The soldiers took sheep and cattle from the plunder, the best of what was devoted to God, in order to sacrifice them to the LORD your God at Gilgal." {22} But Samuel replied: "Does the LORD delight in burnt offerings and sacrifices as much as in obeying the voice of the LORD? To obey is better than sacrifice, and to heed is better than the fat of rams. {23} For rebellion is like the sin of divination, and arrogance like the evil of idolatry. Because you have rejected the word of the LORD, he has rejected you as king." {24} Then Saul said to Samuel, "I have sinned. I violated the Lord's command and your instructions. I was afraid of the people and so I gave in to them. {25} Now I beg you, forgive my sin and come back with me, so that I may worship the LORD." {26} But Samuel said to him, "I will not go back with you. You have rejected the word of the LORD, and the LORD has rejected you as king over Israel!"

SAMUEL ANOINTS DAVID AS THE NEW KING
YET DAVID SERVES SAUL

1 Sam 16:5b-23

Then he consecrated Jesse and his sons and invited them to the sacrifice. {6} When they arrived, Samuel saw Eliab and thought, "Surely the Lord's anointed stands here before the LORD." {7} But the LORD said to Samuel, "Do not consider his appearance or his height, for I have rejected him. The LORD does not look at the things man looks at. Man looks at the outward appearance, but the LORD looks at the heart." {8} Then Jesse called Abinadab and had him pass in front of Samuel. But Samuel said, "The LORD has not chosen this one either." {9} Jesse then had Shammah pass by, but Samuel said, "Nor has the LORD chosen this one." {10} Jesse had seven of his sons pass before Samuel, but Samuel said to him, "The LORD has not chosen these." {11} So he asked Jesse, "Are these all the sons you have?" "There is still the youngest," Jesse answered, "but he is tending the sheep." Samuel said, "Send for him; we will not sit down until he arrives." {12} So he sent and had him brought in. He was ruddy, with a fine appearance and handsome features. Then the LORD said, "Rise and anoint him; he is the one." {13} So Samuel took the horn of oil and anointed him in the presence of his brothers, and from that day on the Spirit of the LORD came upon David in power. Samuel then went to Ramah. {14} Now the Spirit of the LORD had departed from Saul, and an evil spirit from the LORD tormented him. {15} Saul's attendants said to him, "See, an evil spirit from God is tormenting you. {16} Let our lord command his servants here to search for someone who can play the harp. He will play when the evil spirit from God comes upon you, and you will feel better." {17} So Saul said to his attendants, "Find someone who plays well and bring him to me." {18} One of the servants answered, "I have seen a son of Jesse of Bethlehem who knows how to play the harp. He is a brave man and a warrior. He speaks well and is a fine-looking man. And the LORD is with him." {19} Then Saul sent messengers to Jesse and said, "Send me your son David, who is with the sheep." {20} So Jesse took a donkey loaded with bread, a skin of wine and a young goat and sent them with his son David to Saul. {21} David came to Saul and entered his service. Saul liked him very much, and David became one of his armor-bearers. {22} Then Saul sent word to Jesse, saying, "Allow David to remain in my service, for I am pleased with him." {23} Whenever the spirit from God came upon Saul, David would take his harp and play. Then relief would come to Saul; he would feel better, and the evil spirit would leave him.

DAVID AND GOLIATH

1 Sam 17:4-10

A champion named Goliath, who was from Gath, came out of the Philistine camp. He was over nine feet tall. {5} He had a bronze helmet on his head and wore a coat of scale armor of bronze weighing five thousand shekels ; {6} on his legs he wore bronze greaves, and a bronze javelin was slung on his back. {7} His spear shaft was like a weaver's rod, and its iron point weighed six hundred shekels. His shield bearer went ahead of him. {8} Goliath stood and shouted to the ranks of Israel, "Why do you come out and line up for battle? Am I not a Philistine, and are you not the servants of Saul? Choose a man and have him come down to me. {9} If he is able to fight and kill me, we will become your subjects; but if I overcome him and kill him, you will become our subjects and serve us." {10} Then the Philistine said, "This day I defy the ranks of Israel! Give me a man and let us fight each other."

1 Sam 17:32

David said to Saul, "Let no one lose heart on account of this Philistine; your servant will go and fight him."

1 Sam 17:41-50

Meanwhile, the Philistine, with his shield bearer in front of him, kept coming closer to David. {42} He looked David over and saw that he was only a boy, ruddy and handsome, and he despised him. {43} He said to David, "Am I a dog, that you come at me with sticks?" And the Philistine cursed David by his gods. {44} "Come here," he said, "and I'll give your flesh to the birds of the air and the beasts of the field!" {45} David said to the Philistine, "You come against me with sword and spear and javelin, but I come against you in the name of the LORD Almighty, the God of the armies of Israel, whom you have defied. {46} This day the LORD will hand you over to me, and I'll strike you down and cut off your head. Today I will give the carcasses of the Philistine army to the birds of the air and the beasts of the earth, and the whole world will know that there is a God in Israel. {47} All those gathered here will know that it is not by sword or spear that the LORD saves; for the battle is the Lord's, and he will give all of you into our hands." {48} As the Philistine moved closer to attack him, David ran quickly toward the battle line to meet him. {49} Reaching into his bag and taking out a stone, he slung it and struck the Philistine on the forehead. The stone sank into his forehead, and he fell facedown on the ground. {50} So David triumphed over the Philistine with a sling and a stone; without a sword in his hand he struck down the Philistine and killed him.

DAVID MARRIES SAUL'S DAUGHTER

1 Sam 18:9-16

And from that time on Saul kept a jealous eye on David. {10} The next day an evil spirit from God came forcefully upon Saul. He was prophesying in his house, while David was playing the harp, as he usually did. Saul had a spear in his hand {11} and he hurled it, saying to himself, "I'll pin David to the wall." But David eluded him twice. {12} Saul was afraid of David, because the LORD was with David but had left Saul. {13} So he sent David away from him and gave him command over a thousand men, and David led the troops in their campaigns. {14} In everything he did he had great success, because the LORD was with him. {15} When Saul saw how successful he was, he was afraid of him. {16} But all Israel and Judah loved David, because he led them in their campaigns.

1 Sam 18:20-30

Now Saul's daughter Michal was in love with David, and when they told Saul about it, he was pleased. {21} "I will give her to him," he thought, "so that she may be a snare to him and so that the hand of the Philistines may be against him." So Saul said to David, "Now you have a second opportunity to become my son-in-law." {22} Then Saul ordered his attendants: "Speak to David privately and say, 'Look, the king is pleased with you, and his attendants all like you; now become his son-in-law.'" {23} They repeated these words to David. But David said, "Do you think it is a small matter to become the king's son-in-law? I'm only a poor man and little known." {24} When Saul's servants told him what David had said, {25} Saul replied, "Say to David, 'The king wants no other price for the bride than a hundred Philistine foreskins, to take revenge on his enemies.'" Saul's plan was to have David fall by the hands of the Philistines. {26} When the attendants told David these things, he was pleased to become the king's son-in-law. So before the allotted time elapsed, {27} David and his men went out and killed two hundred Philistines. He brought their foreskins and presented the full number to the king so that he might become the king's son-in-law. Then Saul gave him his daughter Michal in marriage. {28} When Saul realized that the LORD was with David and that his daughter Michal loved David, {29} Saul became still more afraid of him, and he remained his enemy the rest of his days. {30} The Philistine commanders continued to go out to battle, and as often as they did, David met with more success than the rest of Saul's officers, and his name became well known.

SAUL PURSUES DAVID

1 Sam 19:1b-20

But Jonathan was very fond of David {2} and warned him, "My father Saul is looking for a chance to kill you. Be on your guard tomorrow morning; go into hiding and stay there. {3} I will go out and stand with my father in the field where you are. I'll speak to him about you and will tell you what I find out." {4} Jonathan spoke well of David to Saul his father and said to him, "Let not the king do wrong to his servant David; he has not wronged you, and what he has done has benefited you greatly. {5} He took his life in his hands when he killed the Philistine. The LORD won a great victory for all Israel, and you saw it and were glad. Why then would you do wrong to an innocent man like David by killing him for no reason?" {6} Saul listened to Jonathan and took this oath: "As surely as the LORD lives, David will not be put to death." {7} So Jonathan called David and told him the whole conversation. He brought him to Saul, and David was with Saul as before. {8} Once more war broke out, and David went out and fought the Philistines. He struck them with such force that they fled before him. {9} But an evil spirit from the LORD came upon Saul as he was sitting in his house with his spear in his hand. While David was playing the harp, {10} Saul tried to pin him to the wall with his spear, but David eluded him as Saul drove the spear into the wall. That night David made good his escape. {11} Saul sent men to David's house to watch it and to kill him in the morning. But Michal, David's wife, warned him, "If you don't run for your life tonight, tomorrow you'll be killed." {12} So Michal let David down through a window, and he fled and escaped. {13} Then Michal took an idol and laid it on the bed, covering it with a garment and putting some goats' hair at the head. {14} When Saul sent the men to capture David, Michal said, "He is ill." {15} Then Saul sent the men back to see David and told them, "Bring him up to me in his bed so that I may kill him." {16} But when the men entered, there was the idol in the bed, and at the head was some goats' hair. {17} Saul said to Michal, "Why did you deceive me like this and send my enemy away so that he escaped?" Michal told him, "He said to me, 'Let me get away. Why should I kill you?'" {18} When David had fled and made his escape, he went to Samuel at Ramah and told him all that Saul had done to him. Then he and Samuel went to Naioth and stayed there. {19} Word came to Saul: "David is in Naioth at Ramah"; {20} so he sent men to capture him. But when they saw a group of prophets prophesying, with Samuel standing there as their leader, the Spirit of God came upon Saul's men and they also prophesied.

DAVID AND JONATHAN

1 Sam 20:24-42a

So David hid in the field, and when the New Moon festival came, the king sat down to eat. {25} He sat in his customary place by the wall, opposite Jonathan, and Abner sat next to Saul, but David's place was empty. {26} Saul said nothing that day, for he thought, "Something must have happened to David to make him ceremonially unclean—surely he is unclean." {27} But the next day, the second day of the month, David's place was empty again. Then Saul said to his son Jonathan, "Why hasn't the son of Jesse come to the meal, either yesterday or today?" {28} Jonathan answered, "David earnestly asked me for permission to go to Bethlehem. {29} He said, 'Let me go, because our family is observing a sacrifice in the town and my brother has ordered me to be there. If I have found favor in your eyes, let me get away to see my brothers.' That is why he has not come to the king's table." {30} Saul's anger flared up at Jonathan and he said to him, "You son of a perverse and rebellious woman! Don't I know that you have sided with the son of Jesse to your own shame and to the shame of the mother who bore you? {31} As long as the son of Jesse lives on this earth, neither you nor your kingdom will be established. Now send and bring him to me, for he must die!" {32} "Why should he be put to death? What has he done?" Jonathan asked his father. {33} But Saul hurled his spear at him to kill him. Then Jonathan knew that his father intended to kill David. {34} Jonathan got up from the table in fierce anger; on that second day of the month he did not eat, because he was grieved at his father's shameful treatment of David. {35} In the morning Jonathan went out to the field for his meeting with David. He had a small boy with him, {36} and he said to the boy, "Run and find the arrows I shoot." As the boy ran, he shot an arrow beyond him. {37} When the boy came to the place where Jonathan's arrow had fallen, Jonathan called out after him, "Isn't the arrow beyond you?" {38} Then he shouted, "Hurry! Go quickly! Don't stop!" The boy picked up the arrow and returned to his master. {39} (The boy knew nothing of all this; only Jonathan and David knew.) {40} Then Jonathan gave his weapons to the boy and said, "Go, carry them back to town." {41} After the boy had gone, David got up from the south side <of the stone> and bowed down before Jonathan three times, with his face to the ground. Then they kissed each other and wept together—but David wept the most. {42} Jonathan said to David, "Go in peace, for we have sworn friendship with each other in the name of the LORD, saying, 'The LORD is witness between you and me, and between your descendants and my descendants forever.'"

DAVID COULD HAVE KILLED SAUL

1 Sam 24:7-22

With these words David rebuked his men and did not allow them to attack Saul. And Saul left the cave and went his way. {8} Then David went out of the cave and called out to Saul, "My lord the king!" When Saul looked behind him, David bowed down and prostrated himself with his face to the ground. {9} He said to Saul, "Why do you listen when men say, 'David is bent on harming you'? {10} This day you have seen with your own eyes how the LORD delivered you into my hands in the cave. Some urged me to kill you, but I spared you; I said, 'I will not lift my hand against my master, because he is the Lord's anointed.' {11} See, my father, look at this piece of your robe in my hand! I cut off the corner of your robe but did not kill you. Now understand and recognize that I am not guilty of wrongdoing or rebellion. I have not wronged you, but you are hunting me down to take my life. {12} May the LORD judge between you and me. And may the LORD avenge the wrongs you have done to me, but my hand will not touch you. {13} As the old saying goes, 'From evildoers come evil deeds,' so my hand will not touch you. {14} "Against whom has the king of Israel come out? Whom are you pursuing? A dead dog? A flea? {15} May the LORD be our judge and decide between us. May he consider my cause and uphold it; may he vindicate me by delivering me from your hand." {16} When David finished saying this, Saul asked, "Is that your voice, David my son?" And he wept aloud. {17} "You are more righteous than I," he said. "You have treated me well, but I have treated you badly. {18} You have just now told me of the good you did to me; the LORD delivered me into your hands, but you did not kill me. {19} When a man finds his enemy, does he let him get away unharmed? May the LORD reward you well for the way you treated me today. {20} I know that you will surely be king and that the kingdom of Israel will be established in your hands. {21} Now swear to me by the LORD that you will not cut off my descendants or wipe out my name from my father's family." {22} So David gave his oath to Saul. Then Saul returned home, but David and his men went up to the stronghold.

SAMUEL DIES

1 Sam 25:1

Now Samuel died, and all Israel assembled and mourned for him; and they buried him at his home in Ramah. Then David moved down into the Desert of Maon.

SAUL CONSULTS A WITCH

1 Sam 28:3-20

Now Samuel was dead, and all Israel had mourned for him and buried him in his own town of Ramah. Saul had expelled the mediums and spiritists from the land. {4} The Philistines assembled and came and set up camp at Shunem, while Saul gathered all the Israelites and set up camp at Gilboa. {5} When Saul saw the Philistine army, he was afraid; terror filled his heart. {6} He inquired of the LORD, but the LORD did not answer him by dreams or Urim or prophets. {7} Saul then said to his attendants, "Find me a woman who is a medium, so I may go and inquire of her." "There is one in Endor," they said. {8} So Saul disguised himself, putting on other clothes, and at night he and two men went to the woman. "Consult a spirit for me," he said, "and bring up for me the one I name." {9} But the woman said to him, "Surely you know what Saul has done. He has cut off the mediums and spiritists from the land. Why have you set a trap for my life to bring about my death?" {10} Saul swore to her by the LORD, "As surely as the LORD lives, you will not be punished for this." {11} Then the woman asked, "Whom shall I bring up for you?" "Bring up Samuel," he said. {12} When the woman saw Samuel, she cried out at the top of her voice and said to Saul, "Why have you deceived me? You are Saul!" {13} The king said to her, "Don't be afraid. What do you see?" The woman said, "I see a spirit coming up out of the ground." {14} "What does he look like?" he asked. "An old man wearing a robe is coming up," she said. Then Saul knew it was Samuel, and he bowed down and prostrated himself with his face to the ground. {15} Samuel said to Saul, "Why have you disturbed me by bringing me up?" "I am in great distress," Saul said. "The Philistines are fighting against me, and God has turned away from me. He no longer answers me, either by prophets or by dreams. So I have called on you to tell me what to do." {16} Samuel said, "Why do you consult me, now that the LORD has turned away from you and become your enemy? {17} The LORD has done what he predicted through me. The LORD has torn the kingdom out of your hands and given it to one of your neighbors–to David. {18} Because you did not obey the LORD or carry out his fierce wrath against the Amalekites, the LORD has done this to you today. {19} The LORD will hand over both Israel and you to the Philistines, and tomorrow you and your sons will be with me. The LORD will also hand over the army of Israel to the Philistines." {20} Immediately Saul fell full length on the ground, filled with fear because of Samuel's words. His strength was gone, for he had eaten nothing all that day and night.

SAUL TAKES HIS OWN LIFE

1 Sam 31:1-13

Now the Philistines fought against Israel; the Israelites fled before them, and many fell slain on Mount Gilboa. {2} The Philistines pressed hard after Saul and his sons, and they killed his sons Jonathan, Abinadab and Malki-Shua. {3} The fighting grew fierce around Saul, and when the archers overtook him, they wounded him critically. {4} Saul said to his armor-bearer, "Draw your sword and run me through, or these uncircumcised fellows will come and run me through and abuse me." But his armor-bearer was terrified and would not do it; so Saul took his own sword and fell on it. {5} When the armor-bearer saw that Saul was dead, he too fell on his sword and died with him. {6} So Saul and his three sons and his armor-bearer and all his men died together that same day. {7} When the Israelites along the valley and those across the Jordan saw that the Israelite army had fled and that Saul and his sons had died, they abandoned their towns and fled. And the Philistines came and occupied them. {8} The next day, when the Philistines came to strip the dead, they found Saul and his three sons fallen on Mount Gilboa. {9} They cut off his head and stripped off his armor, and they sent messengers throughout the land of the Philistines to proclaim the news in the temple of their idols and among their people. {10} They put his armor in the temple of the Ashtoreths and fastened his body to the wall of Beth Shan. {11} When the people of Jabesh Gilead heard of what the Philistines had done to Saul, {12} all their valiant men journeyed through the night to Beth Shan. They took down the bodies of Saul and his sons from the wall of Beth Shan and went to Jabesh, where they burned them. {13} Then they took their bones and buried them under a tamarisk tree at Jabesh, and they fasted seven days.

DAVID BECOMES KING OF JUDAH

2 Sam 2:1-17

In the course of time, David inquired of the LORD. "Shall I go up to one of the towns of Judah?" he asked. The LORD said, "Go up." David asked, "Where shall I go?" "To Hebron," the LORD answered. {2} So David went up there with his two wives, Ahinoam of Jezreel and Abigail, the widow of Nabal of Carmel. {3} David also took the men who were with him, each with his family, and they settled in Hebron and its towns. {4} Then the men of Judah came to Hebron and there they anointed David king over the house of Judah. When David was told that it was the men of Jabesh Gilead who had buried Saul, {5} he sent messengers to the men of Jabesh Gilead to say to them, "The LORD bless you for showing this kindness to Saul your master by burying him. {6} May the LORD now show you kindness and faithfulness, and I too will show you the same favor because you have done this. {7} Now then, be strong and brave, for Saul your master is dead, and the house of Judah has anointed me king over them." {8} Meanwhile, Abner son of Ner, the commander of Saul's army, had taken Ish-Bosheth son of Saul and brought him over to Mahanaim. {9} He made him king over Gilead, Ashuri and Jezreel, and also over Ephraim, Benjamin and all Israel. {10} Ish-Bosheth son of Saul was forty years old when he became king over Israel, and he reigned two years. The house of Judah, however, followed David. {11} The length of time David was king in Hebron over the house of Judah was seven years and six months. {12} Abner son of Ner, together with the men of Ish-Bosheth son of Saul, left Mahanaim and went to Gibeon. {13} Joab son of Zeruiah and David's men went out and met them at the pool of Gibeon. One group sat down on one side of the pool and one group on the other side. {14} Then Abner said to Joab, "Let's have some of the young men get up and fight hand to hand in front of us." "All right, let them do it," Joab said. {15} So they stood up and were counted off– twelve men for Benjamin and Ish-Bosheth son of Saul, and twelve for David. {16} Then each man grabbed his opponent by the head and thrust his dagger into his opponent's side, and they fell down together. So that place in Gibeon was called Helkath Hazzurim. {17} The battle that day was very fierce, and Abner and the men of Israel were defeated by David's men.

ABNER JOINS DAVID AND IS MURDERED BY JOAB

2 Sam 3:12-27

Then Abner sent messengers on his behalf to say to David, "Whose land is it? Make an agreement with me, and I will help you bring all Israel over to you." {13} "Good," said David. "I will make an agreement with you. But I demand one thing of you: Do not come into my presence unless you bring Michal daughter of Saul when you come to see me." {14} Then David sent messengers to Ish-Bosheth son of Saul, demanding, "Give me my wife Michal, whom I betrothed to myself for the price of a hundred Philistine foreskins." {15} So Ish-Bosheth gave orders and had her taken away from her husband Paltiel son of Laish. {16} Her husband, however, went with her, weeping behind her all the way to Bahurim. Then Abner said to him, "Go back home!" So he went back. {17} Abner conferred with the elders of Israel and said, "For some time you have wanted to make David your king. {18} Now do it! For the LORD promised David, 'By my servant David I will rescue my people Israel from the hand of the Philistines and from the hand of all their enemies.'" {19} Abner also spoke to the Benjamites in person. Then he went to Hebron to tell David everything that Israel and the whole house of Benjamin wanted to do. {20} When Abner, who had twenty men with him, came to David at Hebron, David prepared a feast for him and his men. {21} Then Abner said to David, "Let me go at once and assemble all Israel for my lord the king, so that they may make a compact with you, and that you may rule over all that your heart desires." So David sent Abner away, and he went in peace. {22} Just then David's men and Joab returned from a raid and brought with them a great deal of plunder. But Abner was no longer with David in Hebron, because David had sent him away, and he had gone in peace. {23} When Joab and all the soldiers with him arrived, he was told that Abner son of Ner had come to the king and that the king had sent him away and that he had gone in peace. {24} So Joab went to the king and said, "What have you done? Look, Abner came to you. Why did you let him go? Now he is gone! {25} You know Abner son of Ner; he came to deceive you and observe your movements and find out everything you are doing." {26} Joab then left David and sent messengers after Abner, and they brought him back from the well of Sirah. But David did not know it. {27} Now when Abner returned to Hebron, Joab took him aside into the gateway, as though to speak with him privately. And there, to avenge the blood of his brother Asahel, Joab stabbed him in the stomach, and he died.

DAVID BECOMES KING OF ISRAEL

2 Sam 4:5-5:5

Now Recab and Baanah, the sons of Rimmon the Beerothite, set out for the house of Ish-Bosheth, and they arrived there in the heat of the day while he was taking his noonday rest. {6} They went into the inner part of the house as if to get some wheat, and they stabbed him in the stomach. Then Recab and his brother Baanah slipped away. {7} They had gone into the house while he was lying on the bed in his bedroom. After they stabbed and killed him, they cut off his head. Taking it with them, they traveled all night by way of the Arabah. {8} They brought the head of Ish-Bosheth to David at Hebron and said to the king, "Here is the head of Ish-Bosheth son of Saul, your enemy, who tried to take your life. This day the LORD has avenged my lord the king against Saul and his offspring." {9} David answered Recab and his brother Baanah, the sons of Rimmon the Beerothite, "As surely as the LORD lives, who has delivered me out of all trouble, {10} when a man told me, 'Saul is dead,' and thought he was bringing good news, I seized him and put him to death in Ziklag. That was the reward I gave him for his news! {11} How much more–when wicked men have killed an innocent man in his own house and on his own bed–should I not now demand his blood from your hand and rid the earth of you!" {12} So David gave an order to his men, and they killed them. They cut off their hands and feet and hung the bodies by the pool in Hebron. But they took the head of Ish-Bosheth and buried it in Abner's tomb at Hebron. {5:1} All the tribes of Israel came to David at Hebron and said, "We are your own flesh and blood. {2} In the past, while Saul was king over us, you were the one who led Israel on their military campaigns. And the LORD said to you, 'You will shepherd my people Israel, and you will become their ruler.'" {3} When all the elders of Israel had come to King David at Hebron, the king made a compact with them at Hebron before the LORD, and they anointed David king over Israel. {4} David was thirty years old when he became king, and he reigned forty years. {5} In Hebron he reigned over Judah seven years and six months, and in Jerusalem he reigned over all Israel and Judah thirty-three years.

JERUSALEM BECOMES CITY OF DAVID

2 Sam 5:6-12

The king and his men marched to Jerusalem to attack the Jebusites, who lived there. The Jebusites said to David, "You will not get in here; even the blind and the lame can ward you off." They thought, "David cannot get in here." {7} Nevertheless, David captured the fortress of Zion, the City of David. {8} On that day, David said, "Anyone who conquers the Jebusites will have to use the water shaft to reach those 'lame and blind' who are David's enemies. " That is why they say, "The 'blind and lame' will not enter the palace." {9} David then took up residence in the fortress and called it the City of David. He built up the area around it, from the supporting terraces inward. {10} And he became more and more powerful, because the LORD God Almighty was with him. {11} Now Hiram king of Tyre sent messengers to David, along with cedar logs and carpenters and stonemasons, and they built a palace for David. {12} And David knew that the LORD had established him as king over Israel and had exalted his kingdom for the sake of his people Israel.

2 Sam 5:17-25

When the Philistines heard that David had been anointed king over Israel, they went up in full force to search for him, but David heard about it and went down to the stronghold. {18} Now the Philistines had come and spread out in the Valley of Rephaim; {19} so David inquired of the LORD, "Shall I go and attack the Philistines? Will you hand them over to me?" The LORD answered him, "Go, for I will surely hand the Philistines over to you." {20} So David went to Baal Perazim, and there he defeated them. He said, "As waters break out, the LORD has broken out against my enemies before me." So that place was called Baal Perazim. {21} The Philistines abandoned their idols there, and David and his men carried them off. {22} Once more the Philistines came up and spread out in the Valley of Rephaim; {23} so David inquired of the LORD, and he answered, "Do not go straight up, but circle around behind them and attack them in front of the balsam trees. {24} As soon as you hear the sound of marching in the tops of the balsam trees, move quickly, because that will mean the LORD has gone out in front of you to strike the Philistine army." {25} So David did as the LORD commanded him, and he struck down the Philistines all the way from Gibeon to Gezer.

DAVID RETURNS ARK OF THE COVENANT TO JERUSALEM

2 Sam 6:2-19

He and all his men set out from Baalah of Judah to bring up from there the ark of God, which is called by the Name, the name of the LORD Almighty, who is enthroned between the cherubim that are on the ark. {3} They set the ark of God on a new cart and brought it from the house of Abinadab, which was on the hill. Uzzah and Ahio, sons of Abinadab, were guiding the new cart {4} with the ark of God on it, and Ahio was walking in front of it. {5} David and the whole house of Israel were celebrating with all their might before the LORD, with songs and with harps, lyres, tambourines, sistrums and cymbals. {6} When they came to the threshing floor of Nacon, Uzzah reached out and took hold of the ark of God, because the oxen stumbled. {7} The Lord's anger burned against Uzzah because of his irreverent act; therefore God struck him down and he died there beside the ark of God. {8} Then David was angry because the Lord's wrath had broken out against Uzzah, and to this day that place is called Perez Uzzah. {9} David was afraid of the LORD that day and said, "How can the ark of the LORD ever come to me?" {10} He was not willing to take the ark of the LORD to be with him in the City of David. Instead, he took it aside to the house of Obed-Edom the Gittite. {11} The ark of the LORD remained in the house of Obed-Edom the Gittite for three months, and the LORD blessed him and his entire household. {12} Now King David was told, "The LORD has blessed the household of Obed-Edom and everything he has, because of the ark of God." So David went down and brought up the ark of God from the house of Obed-Edom to the City of David with rejoicing. {13} When those who were carrying the ark of the LORD had taken six steps, he sacrificed a bull and a fattened calf. {14} David, wearing a linen ephod, danced before the LORD with all his might, {15} while he and the entire house of Israel brought up the ark of the LORD with shouts and the sound of trumpets. {16} As the ark of the LORD was entering the City of David, Michal daughter of Saul watched from a window. And when she saw King David leaping and dancing before the LORD, she despised him in her heart. {17} They brought the ark of the LORD and set it in its place inside the tent that David had pitched for it, and David sacrificed burnt offerings and fellowship offerings before the LORD. {18} After he had finished sacrificing the burnt offerings and fellowship offerings, he blessed the people in the name of the LORD Almighty. {19} Then he gave a loaf of bread, a cake of dates and a cake of raisins to each person in the whole crowd of Israelites, both men and women. And all the people went to their homes.

DAVID'S SON TO BUILD A HOUSE FOR THE LORD

2 Sam 7:1-17

After the king was settled in his palace and the LORD had given him rest from all his enemies around him, {2} he said to Nathan the prophet, "Here I am, living in a palace of cedar, while the ark of God remains in a tent." {3} Nathan replied to the king, "Whatever you have in mind, go ahead and do it, for the LORD is with you." {4} That night the word of the LORD came to Nathan, saying: {5} "Go and tell my servant David, 'This is what the LORD says: Are you the one to build me a house to dwell in? {6} I have not dwelt in a house from the day I brought the Israelites up out of Egypt to this day. I have been moving from place to place with a tent as my dwelling. {7} Wherever I have moved with all the Israelites, did I ever say to any of their rulers whom I commanded to shepherd my people Israel, "Why have you not built me a house of cedar?" ' {8} "Now then, tell my servant David, 'This is what the LORD Almighty says: I took you from the pasture and from following the flock to be ruler over my people Israel. {9} I have been with you wherever you have gone, and I have cut off all your enemies from before you. Now I will make your name great, like the names of the greatest men of the earth. {10} And I will provide a place for my people Israel and will plant them so that they can have a home of their own and no longer be disturbed. Wicked people will not oppress them anymore, as they did at the beginning {11} and have done ever since the time I appointed leaders over my people Israel. I will also give you rest from all your enemies. "'The LORD declares to you that the LORD himself will establish a house for you: {12} When your days are over and you rest with your fathers, I will raise up your offspring to succeed you, who will come from your own body, and I will establish his kingdom. {13} He is the one who will build a house for my Name, and I will establish the throne of his kingdom forever. {14} I will be his father, and he will be my son. When he does wrong, I will punish him with the rod of men, with floggings inflicted by men. {15} But my love will never be taken away from him, as I took it away from Saul, whom I removed from before you. {16} Your house and your kingdom will endure forever before me ; your throne will be established forever.'" {17} Nathan reported to David all the words of this entire revelation.

DAVID SHOWS KINDNESS TO JONATHAN'S SON

2 Sam 9:1-13

David asked, "Is there anyone still left of the house of Saul to whom I can show kindness for Jonathan's sake?" {2} Now there was a servant of Saul's household named Ziba. They called him to appear before David, and the king said to him, "Are you Ziba?" "Your servant," he replied. {3} The king asked, "Is there no one still left of the house of Saul to whom I can show God's kindness?" Ziba answered the king, "There is still a son of Jonathan; he is crippled in both feet." {4} "Where is he?" the king asked. Ziba answered, "He is at the house of Makir son of Ammiel in Lo Debar." {5} So King David had him brought from Lo Debar, from the house of Makir son of Ammiel. {6} When Mephibosheth son of Jonathan, the son of Saul, came to David, he bowed down to pay him honor. David said, "Mephibosheth!" "Your servant," he replied. {7} "Don't be afraid," David said to him, "for I will surely show you kindness for the sake of your father Jonathan. I will restore to you all the land that belonged to your grandfather Saul, and you will always eat at my table." {8} Mephibosheth bowed down and said, "What is your servant, that you should notice a dead dog like me?" {9} Then the king summoned Ziba, Saul's servant, and said to him, "I have given your master's grandson everything that belonged to Saul and his family. {10} You and your sons and your servants are to farm the land for him and bring in the crops, so that your master's grandson may be provided for. And Mephibosheth, grandson of your master, will always eat at my table." (Now Ziba had fifteen sons and twenty servants.) {11} Then Ziba said to the king, "Your servant will do whatever my lord the king commands his servant to do." So Mephibosheth ate at David's table like one of the king's sons. {12} Mephibosheth had a young son named Mica, and all the members of Ziba's household were servants of Mephibosheth. {13} And Mephibosheth lived in Jerusalem, because he always ate at the king's table, and he was crippled in both feet.

DAVID, BATHSHEBA AND URIAH

2 Sam 11:2b-21

From the roof he saw a woman bathing. The woman was very beautiful, {3} and David sent someone to find out about her. The man said, "Isn't this Bathsheba, the daughter of Eliam and the wife of Uriah the Hittite?" {4} Then David sent messengers to get her. She came to him, and he slept with her. (She had purified herself from her uncleanness.) Then she went back home. {5} The woman conceived and sent word to David, saying, "I am pregnant." {6} So David sent this word to Joab: "Send me Uriah the Hittite." And Joab sent him to David. {7} When Uriah came to him, David asked him how Joab was, how the soldiers were and how the war was going. {8} Then David said to Uriah, "Go down to your house and wash your feet." So Uriah left the palace, and a gift from the king was sent after him. {9} But Uriah slept at the entrance to the palace with all his master's servants and did not go down to his house. {10} When David was told, "Uriah did not go home," he asked him, "Haven't you just come from a distance? Why didn't you go home?" {11} Uriah said to David, "The ark and Israel and Judah are staying in tents, and my master Joab and my lord's men are camped in the open fields. How could I go to my house to eat and drink and lie with my wife? As surely as you live, I will not do such a thing!" {12} Then David said to him, "Stay here one more day, and tomorrow I will send you back." So Uriah remained in Jerusalem that day and the next. {13} At David's invitation, he ate and drank with him, and David made him drunk. But in the evening Uriah went out to sleep on his mat among his master's servants; he did not go home. {14} In the morning David wrote a letter to Joab and sent it with Uriah. {15} In it he wrote, "Put Uriah in the front line where the fighting is fiercest. Then withdraw from him so he will be struck down and die." {16} So while Joab had the city under siege, he put Uriah at a place where he knew the strongest defenders were. {17} When the men of the city came out and fought against Joab, some of the men in David's army fell; moreover, Uriah the Hittite died. {18} Joab sent David a full account of the battle. {19} He instructed the messenger: "When you have finished giving the king this account of the battle, {20} the king's anger may flare up, and he may ask you, 'Why did you get so close to the city to fight? Didn't you know they would shoot arrows from the wall? {21} Who killed Abimelech son of Jerub-Besheth ? Didn't a woman throw an upper millstone on him from the wall, so that he died in Thebez? Why did you get so close to the wall?' If he asks you this, then say to him, 'Also, your servant Uriah the Hittite is dead.'"

DAVID REPENTS

2 Sam 12:1-18a

The LORD sent Nathan to David. When he came to him, he said, "There were two men in a certain town, one rich and the other poor. {2} The rich man had a very large number of sheep and cattle, {3} but the poor man had nothing except one little ewe lamb he had bought. He raised it, and it grew up with him and his children. It shared his food, drank from his cup and even slept in his arms. It was like a daughter to him. {4} "Now a traveler came to the rich man, but the rich man refrained from taking one of his own sheep or cattle to prepare a meal for the traveler who had come to him. Instead, he took the ewe lamb that belonged to the poor man and prepared it for the one who had come to him." {5} David burned with anger against the man and said to Nathan, "As surely as the LORD lives, the man who did this deserves to die! {6} He must pay for that lamb four times over, because he did such a thing and had no pity." {7} Then Nathan said to David, "You are the man! This is what the LORD, the God of Israel, says: 'I anointed you king over Israel, and I delivered you from the hand of Saul. {8} I gave your master's house to you, and your master's wives into your arms. I gave you the house of Israel and Judah. And if all this had been too little, I would have given you even more. {9} Why did you despise the word of the LORD by doing what is evil in his eyes? You struck down Uriah the Hittite with the sword and took his wife to be your own. You killed him with the sword of the Ammonites. {10} Now, therefore, the sword will never depart from your house, because you despised me and took the wife of Uriah the Hittite to be your own.' {11} "This is what the LORD says: 'Out of your own household I am going to bring calamity upon you. Before your very eyes I will take your wives and give them to one who is close to you, and he will lie with your wives in broad daylight. {12} You did it in secret, but I will do this thing in broad daylight before all Israel.'" {13} Then David said to Nathan, "I have sinned against the LORD." Nathan replied, "The LORD has taken away your sin. You are not going to die. {14} But because by doing this you have made the enemies of the LORD show utter contempt, the son born to you will die." {15} After Nathan had gone home, the LORD struck the child that Uriah's wife had borne to David, and he became ill. {16} David pleaded with God for the child. He fasted and went into his house and spent the nights lying on the ground. {17} The elders of his household stood beside him to get him up from the ground, but he refused, and he would not eat any food with them. {18} On the seventh day the child died.

ABSALOM LEADS A REBELLION AND DAVID FLEES

2 Sam 15:1-17a

In the course of time, Absalom provided himself with a chariot and horses and with fifty men to run ahead of him. {2} He would get up early and stand by the side of the road leading to the city gate. Whenever anyone came with a complaint to be placed before the king for a decision, Absalom would call out to him, "What town are you from?" He would answer, "Your servant is from one of the tribes of Israel." {3} Then Absalom would say to him, "Look, your claims are valid and proper, but there is no representative of the king to hear you." {4} And Absalom would add, "If only I were appointed judge in the land! Then everyone who has a complaint or case could come to me and I would see that he gets justice." {5} Also, whenever anyone approached him to bow down before him, Absalom would reach out his hand, take hold of him and kiss him. {6} Absalom behaved in this way toward all the Israelites who came to the king asking for justice, and so he stole the hearts of the men of Israel. {7} At the end of four years, Absalom said to the king, "Let me go to Hebron and fulfill a vow I made to the LORD. {8} While your servant was living at Geshur in Aram, I made this vow: 'If the LORD takes me back to Jerusalem, I will worship the LORD in Hebron. '" {9} The king said to him, "Go in peace." So he went to Hebron. {10} Then Absalom sent secret messengers throughout the tribes of Israel to say, "As soon as you hear the sound of the trumpets, then say, 'Absalom is king in Hebron.'" {11} Two hundred men from Jerusalem had accompanied Absalom. They had been invited as guests and went quite innocently, knowing nothing about the matter. {12} While Absalom was offering sacrifices, he also sent for Ahithophel the Gilonite, David's counselor, to come from Giloh, his hometown. And so the conspiracy gained strength, and Absalom's following kept on increasing. {13} A messenger came and told David, "The hearts of the men of Israel are with Absalom." {14} Then David said to all his officials who were with him in Jerusalem, "Come! We must flee, or none of us will escape from Absalom. We must leave immediately, or he will move quickly to overtake us and bring ruin upon us and put the city to the sword." {15} The king's officials answered him, "Your servants are ready to do whatever our lord the king chooses." {16} The king set out, with his entire household following him; but he left ten concubines to take care of the palace. {17} So the king set out, with all the people following him....

AHITOPHEL AND HUSHAI ADVISE ABSALOM

2 Sam 17:1-16

Ahithophel said to Absalom, "I would choose twelve thousand men and set out tonight in pursuit of David. {2} I would attack him while he is weary and weak. I would strike him with terror, and then all the people with him will flee. I would strike down only the king {3} and bring all the people back to you. The death of the man you seek will mean the return of all; all the people will be unharmed." {4} This plan seemed good to Absalom and to all the elders of Israel. {5} But Absalom said, "Summon also Hushai the Arkite, so we can hear what he has to say." {6} When Hushai came to him, Absalom said, "Ahithophel has given this advice. Should we do what he says? If not, give us your opinion." {7} Hushai replied to Absalom, "The advice Ahithophel has given is not good this time. {8} You know your father and his men; they are fighters, and as fierce as a wild bear robbed of her cubs. Besides, your father is an experienced fighter; he will not spend the night with the troops. {9} Even now, he is hidden in a cave or some other place. If he should attack your troops first, whoever hears about it will say, 'There has been a slaughter among the troops who follow Absalom.' {10} Then even the bravest soldier, whose heart is like the heart of a lion, will melt with fear, for all Israel knows that your father is a fighter and that those with him are brave. {11} "So I advise you: Let all Israel, from Dan to Beersheba–as numerous as the sand on the seashore–be gathered to you, with you yourself leading them into battle. {12} Then we will attack him wherever he may be found, and we will fall on him as dew settles on the ground. Neither he nor any of his men will be left alive. {13} If he withdraws into a city, then all Israel will bring ropes to that city, and we will drag it down to the valley until not even a piece of it can be found." {14} Absalom and all the men of Israel said, "The advice of Hushai the Arkite is better than that of Ahithophel." For the LORD had determined to frustrate the good advice of Ahithophel in order to bring disaster on Absalom. {15} Hushai told Zadok and Abiathar, the priests, "Ahithophel has advised Absalom and the elders of Israel to do such and such, but I have advised them to do so and so. {16} Now send a message immediately and tell David, 'Do not spend the night at the fords in the desert; cross over without fail, or the king and all the people with him will be swallowed up.'"

ABSALOM DIES

2 Sam 18:1-17

David mustered the men who were with him and appointed over them commanders of thousands and commanders of hundreds. {2} David sent the troops out–a third under the command of Joab, a third under Joab's brother Abishai son of Zeruiah, and a third under Ittai the Gittite. The king told the troops, "I myself will surely march out with you." {3} But the men said, "You must not go out; if we are forced to flee, they won't care about us. Even if half of us die, they won't care; but you are worth ten thousand of us. It would be better now for you to give us support from the city." {4} The king answered, "I will do whatever seems best to you." So the king stood beside the gate while all the men marched out in units of hundreds and of thousands. {5} The king commanded Joab, Abishai and Ittai, "Be gentle with the young man Absalom for my sake." And all the troops heard the king giving orders concerning Absalom to each of the commanders. {6} The army marched into the field to fight Israel, and the battle took place in the forest of Ephraim. {7} There the army of Israel was defeated by David's men, and the casualties that day were great–twenty thousand men. {8} The battle spread out over the whole countryside, and the forest claimed more lives that day than the sword. {9} Now Absalom happened to meet David's men. He was riding his mule, and as the mule went under the thick branches of a large oak, Absalom's head got caught in the tree. He was left hanging in midair, while the mule he was riding kept on going. {10} When one of the men saw this, he told Joab, "I just saw Absalom hanging in an oak tree." {11} Joab said to the man who had told him this, "What! You saw him? Why didn't you strike him to the ground right there? Then I would have had to give you ten shekels of silver and a warrior's belt." {12} But the man replied, "Even if a thousand shekels were weighed out into my hands, I would not lift my hand against the king's son. In our hearing the king commanded you and Abishai and Ittai, 'Protect the young man Absalom for my sake. ' {13} And if I had put my life in jeopardy –and nothing is hidden from the king–you would have kept your distance from me." {14} Joab said, "I'm not going to wait like this for you." So he took three javelins in his hand and plunged them into Absalom's heart while Absalom was still alive in the oak tree. {15} And ten of Joab's armor-bearers surrounded Absalom, struck him and killed him. {16} Then Joab sounded the trumpet, and the troops stopped pursuing Israel, for Joab halted them. {17} They took Absalom, threw him into a big pit in the forest and piled up a large heap of rocks over him. Meanwhile, all the Israelites fled to their homes.

DAVID RETURNS TO JERUSALEM

2 Sam 18:32b-19:14

"Is the young man Absalom safe?" The Cushite replied, "May the enemies of my lord the king and all who rise up to harm you be like that young man." {33} The king was shaken. He went up to the room over the gateway and wept. As he went, he said: "O my son Absalom! My son, my son Absalom! If only I had died instead of you—O Absalom, my son, my son!" {19:1} Joab was told, "The king is weeping and mourning for Absalom." {2} And for the whole army the victory that day was turned into mourning, because on that day the troops heard it said, "The king is grieving for his son." {3} The men stole into the city that day as men steal in who are ashamed when they flee from battle. {4} The king covered his face and cried aloud, "O my son Absalom! O Absalom, my son, my son!" {5} Then Joab went into the house to the king and said, "Today you have humiliated all your men, who have just saved your life and the lives of your sons and daughters and the lives of your wives and concubines. {6} You love those who hate you and hate those who love you. You have made it clear today that the commanders and their men mean nothing to you. I see that you would be pleased if Absalom were alive today and all of us were dead. {7} Now go out and encourage your men. I swear by the LORD that if you don't go out, not a man will be left with you by nightfall. This will be worse for you than all the calamities that have come upon you from your youth till now." {8} So the king got up and took his seat in the gateway. When the men were told, "The king is sitting in the gateway," they all came before him. Meanwhile, the Israelites had fled to their homes. {9} Throughout the tribes of Israel, the people were all arguing with each other, saying, "The king delivered us from the hand of our enemies; he is the one who rescued us from the hand of the Philistines. But now he has fled the country because of Absalom; {10} and Absalom, whom we anointed to rule over us, has died in battle. So why do you say nothing about bringing the king back?" {11} King David sent this message to Zadok and Abiathar, the priests: "Ask the elders of Judah, 'Why should you be the last to bring the king back to his palace, since what is being said throughout Israel has reached the king at his quarters? {12} You are my brothers, my own flesh and blood. So why should you be the last to bring back the king?' {13} And say to Amasa, 'Are you not my own flesh and blood? May God deal with me, be it ever so severely, if from now on you are not the commander of my army in place of Joab.'" {14} He won over the hearts of all the men of Judah as though they were one man. They sent word to the king, "Return, you and all your men."

SHEBA LEADS A REBELLION

2 Sam 20:1-15a

Now a troublemaker named Sheba son of Bicri, a Benjamite, happened to be there. He sounded the trumpet and shouted, "We have no share in David, no part in Jesse's son! Every man to his tent, O Israel!" {2} So all the men of Israel deserted David to follow Sheba son of Bicri. But the men of Judah stayed by their king all the way from the Jordan to Jerusalem. {3} When David returned to his palace in Jerusalem, he took the ten concubines he had left to take care of the palace and put them in a house under guard. He provided for them, but did not lie with them. They were kept in confinement till the day of their death, living as widows. {4} Then the king said to Amasa, "Summon the men of Judah to come to me within three days, and be here yourself." {5} But when Amasa went to summon Judah, he took longer than the time the king had set for him. {6} David said to Abishai, "Now Sheba son of Bicri will do us more harm than Absalom did. Take your master's men and pursue him, or he will find fortified cities and escape from us." {7} So Joab's men and the Kerethites and Pelethites and all the mighty warriors went out under the command of Abishai. They marched out from Jerusalem to pursue Sheba son of Bicri. {8} While they were at the great rock in Gibeon, Amasa came to meet them. Joab was wearing his military tunic, and strapped over it at his waist was a belt with a dagger in its sheath. As he stepped forward, it dropped out of its sheath. {9} Joab said to Amasa, "How are you, my brother?" Then Joab took Amasa by the beard with his right hand to kiss him. {10} Amasa was not on his guard against the dagger in Joab's hand, and Joab plunged it into his belly, and his intestines spilled out on the ground. Without being stabbed again, Amasa died. Then Joab and his brother Abishai pursued Sheba son of Bicri. {11} One of Joab's men stood beside Amasa and said, "Whoever favors Joab, and whoever is for David, let him follow Joab!" {12} Amasa lay wallowing in his blood in the middle of the road, and the man saw that all the troops came to a halt there. When he realized that everyone who came up to Amasa stopped, he dragged him from the road into a field and threw a garment over him. {13} After Amasa had been removed from the road, all the men went on with Joab to pursue Sheba son of Bicri. {14} Sheba passed through all the tribes of Israel to Abel Beth Maacah and through the entire region of the Berites, who gathered together and followed him. {15} All the troops with Joab came and besieged Sheba in Abel Beth Maacah. They built a siege ramp up to the city....

DAVID'S SONG OF PRAISE

2 Sam 22:31-51

"As for God, his way is perfect; the word of the LORD is flawless. He is a shield for all who take refuge in him. {32} For who is God besides the LORD? And who is the Rock except our God? {33} It is God who arms me with strength and makes my way perfect. {34} He makes my feet like the feet of a deer; he enables me to stand on the heights. {35} He trains my hands for battle; my arms can bend a bow of bronze. {36} You give me your shield of victory; you stoop down to make me great. {37} You broaden the path beneath me, so that my ankles do not turn. {38} "I pursued my enemies and crushed them; I did not turn back till they were destroyed. {39} I crushed them completely, and they could not rise; they fell beneath my feet. {40} You armed me with strength for battle; you made my adversaries bow at my feet. {41} You made my enemies turn their backs in flight, and I destroyed my foes. {42} They cried for help, but there was no one to save them– to the LORD, but he did not answer. {43} I beat them as fine as the dust of the earth; I pounded and trampled them like mud in the streets. {44} "You have delivered me from the attacks of my people; you have preserved me as the head of nations. People I did not know are subject to me, {45} and foreigners come cringing to me; as soon as they hear me, they obey me. {46} They all lose heart; they come trembling from their strongholds. {47} "The LORD lives! Praise be to my Rock! Exalted be God, the Rock, my Savior! {48} He is the God who avenges me, who puts the nations under me, {49} who sets me free from my enemies. You exalted me above my foes; from violent men you rescued me. {50} Therefore I will praise you, O LORD, among the nations; I will sing praises to your name. {51} He gives his king great victories; he shows unfailing kindness to his anointed, to David and his descendants forever."

GOD PUNISHES DAVID FOR COUNTING HIS FORCES

2 Sam 24:1-4

Again the anger of the LORD burned against Israel, and he incited David against them, saying, "Go and take a census of Israel and Judah." {2} So the king said to Joab and the army commanders with him, "Go throughout the tribes of Israel from Dan to Beersheba and enroll the fighting men, so that I may know how many there are." {3} But Joab replied to the king, "May the LORD your God multiply the troops a hundred times over, and may the eyes of my lord the king see it. But why does my lord the king want to do such a thing?" {4} The king's word, however, overruled Joab and the army commanders; so they left the presence of the king to enroll the fighting men of Israel.

2 Sam 24:8-17

After they had gone through the entire land, they came back to Jerusalem at the end of nine months and twenty days. {9} Joab reported the number of the fighting men to the king: In Israel there were eight hundred thousand able-bodied men who could handle a sword, and in Judah five hundred thousand. {10} David was conscience-stricken after he had counted the fighting men, and he said to the LORD, "I have sinned greatly in what I have done. Now, O LORD, I beg you, take away the guilt of your servant. I have done a very foolish thing." {11} Before David got up the next morning, the word of the LORD had come to Gad the prophet, David's seer: {12} "Go and tell David, 'This is what the LORD says: I am giving you three options. Choose one of them for me to carry out against you.'" {13} So Gad went to David and said to him, "Shall there come upon you three years of famine in your land? Or three months of fleeing from your enemies while they pursue you? Or three days of plague in your land? Now then, think it over and decide how I should answer the one who sent me." {14} David said to Gad, "I am in deep distress. Let us fall into the hands of the LORD, for his mercy is great; but do not let me fall into the hands of men." {15} So the LORD sent a plague on Israel from that morning until the end of the time designated, and seventy thousand of the people from Dan to Beersheba died. {16} When the angel stretched out his hand to destroy Jerusalem, the LORD was grieved because of the calamity and said to the angel who was afflicting the people, "Enough! Withdraw your hand." The angel of the LORD was then at the threshing floor of Araunah the Jebusite. {17} When David saw the angel who was striking down the people, he said to the LORD, "I am the one who has sinned and done wrong. These are but sheep. What have they done? Let your hand fall upon me and my family."

ADONIJAH USURPS THE THRONE

1 Ki 1:11-30a

Then Nathan asked Bathsheba, Solomon's mother, "Have you not heard that Adonijah, the son of Haggith, has become king without our lord David's knowing it? {12} Now then, let me advise you how you can save your own life and the life of your son Solomon. {13} Go in to King David and say to him, 'My lord the king, did you not swear to me your servant: "Surely Solomon your son shall be king after me, and he will sit on my throne"? Why then has Adonijah become king?' {14} While you are still there talking to the king, I will come in and confirm what you have said." {15} So Bathsheba went to see the aged king in his room, where Abishag the Shunammite was attending him. {16} Bathsheba bowed low and knelt before the king. "What is it you want?" the king asked. {17} She said to him, "My lord, you yourself swore to me your servant by the LORD your God: 'Solomon your son shall be king after me, and he will sit on my throne.' {18} But now Adonijah has become king, and you, my lord the king, do not know about it. {19} He has sacrificed great numbers of cattle, fattened calves, and sheep, and has invited all the king's sons, Abiathar the priest and Joab the commander of the army, but he has not invited Solomon your servant. {20} My lord the king, the eyes of all Israel are on you, to learn from you who will sit on the throne of my lord the king after him. {21} Otherwise, as soon as my lord the king is laid to rest with his fathers, I and my son Solomon will be treated as criminals." {22} While she was still speaking with the king, Nathan the prophet arrived. {23} And they told the king, "Nathan the prophet is here." So he went before the king and bowed with his face to the ground. {24} Nathan said, "Have you, my lord the king, declared that Adonijah shall be king after you, and that he will sit on your throne? {25} Today he has gone down and sacrificed great numbers of cattle, fattened calves, and sheep. He has invited all the king's sons, the commanders of the army and Abiathar the priest. Right now they are eating and drinking with him and saying, 'Long live King Adonijah!' {26} But me your servant, and Zadok the priest, and Benaiah son of Jehoiada, and your servant Solomon he did not invite. {27} Is this something my lord the king has done without letting his servants know who should sit on the throne of my lord the king after him?" {28} Then King David said, "Call in Bathsheba." So she came into the king's presence and stood before him. {29} The king then took an oath: "As surely as the LORD lives, who has delivered me out of every trouble, {30} I will surely carry out today what I swore to you by the LORD, the God of Israel: Solomon your son shall be king after me...."

SOLOMON IS ANOINTED KING

1 Ki 1:36-53

Benaiah son of Jehoiada answered the king, "Amen! May the LORD, the God of my lord the king, so declare it. {37} As the LORD was with my lord the king, so may he be with Solomon to make his throne even greater than the throne of my lord King David!" {38} So Zadok the priest, Nathan the prophet, Benaiah son of Jehoiada, the Kerethites and the Pelethites went down and put Solomon on King David's mule and escorted him to Gihon. ok the priest took the horn of oil from the sacred tent and anointed Solomon. Then they sounded the trumpet and all the people shouted, "Long live King Solomon!" {40} And all the people went up after him, playing flutes and rejoicing greatly, so that the ground shook with the sound. {41} Adonijah and all the guests who were with him heard it as they were finishing their feast. On hearing the sound of the trumpet, Joab asked, "What's the meaning of all the noise in the city?" {42} Even as he was speaking, Jonathan son of Abiathar the priest arrived. Adonijah said, "Come in. A worthy man like you must be bringing good news." {43} "Not at all!" Jonathan answered. "Our lord King David has made Solomon king. {44} The king has sent with him Zadok the priest, Nathan the prophet, Benaiah son of Jehoiada, the Kerethites and the Pelethites, and they have put him on the king's mule, {45} and Zadok the priest and Nathan the prophet have anointed him king at Gihon. From there they have gone up cheering, and the city resounds with it. That's the noise you hear. {46} Moreover, Solomon has taken his seat on the royal throne. {47} Also, the royal officials have come to congratulate our lord King David, saying, 'May your God make Solomon's name more famous than yours and his throne greater than yours!' And the king bowed in worship on his bed {48} and said, 'Praise be to the LORD, the God of Israel, who has allowed my eyes to see a successor on my throne today.'" {49} At this, all Adonijah's guests rose in alarm and dispersed. {50} But Adonijah, in fear of Solomon, went and took hold of the horns of the altar. {51} Then Solomon was told, "Adonijah is afraid of King Solomon and is clinging to the horns of the altar. He says, 'Let King Solomon swear to me today that he will not put his servant to death with the sword.'" {52} Solomon replied, "If he shows himself to be a worthy man, not a hair of his head will fall to the ground; but if evil is found in him, he will die." {53} Then King Solomon sent men, and they brought him down from the altar. And Adonijah came and bowed down to King Solomon, and Solomon said, "Go to your home."

DAVID'S FINAL INSTRUCTIONS TO SOLOMON

1 Ki 2:1-11

When the time drew near for David to die, he gave a charge to Solomon his son. {2} "I am about to go the way of all the earth," he said. "So be strong, show yourself a man, {3} and observe what the LORD your God requires: Walk in his ways, and keep his decrees and commands, his laws and requirements, as written in the Law of Moses, so that you may prosper in all you do and wherever you go, {4} and that the LORD may keep his promise to me: 'If your descendants watch how they live, and if they walk faithfully before me with all their heart and soul, you will never fail to have a man on the throne of Israel.' {5} "Now you yourself know what Joab son of Zeruiah did to me–what he did to the two commanders of Israel's armies, Abner son of Ner and Amasa son of Jether. He killed them, shedding their blood in peacetime as if in battle, and with that blood stained the belt around his waist and the sandals on his feet. {6} Deal with him according to your wisdom, but do not let his gray head go down to the grave in peace. {7} "But show kindness to the sons of Barzillai of Gilead and let them be among those who eat at your table. They stood by me when I fled from your brother Absalom. {8} "And remember, you have with you Shimei son of Gera, the Benjamite from Bahurim, who called down bitter curses on me the day I went to Mahanaim. When he came down to meet me at the Jordan, I swore to him by the LORD: 'I will not put you to death by the sword.' {9} But now, do not consider him innocent. You are a man of wisdom; you will know what to do to him. Bring his gray head down to the grave in blood." {10} Then David rested with his fathers and was buried in the City of David. {11} He had reigned forty years over Israel–seven years in Hebron and thirty-three in Jerusalem.

158

SOLOMON ESTABLISHES HIS OWN ADMINISTRATION

1 Ki 2:30-46

So Benaiah entered the tent of the LORD and said to Joab, "The king says, 'Come out!'" But he answered, "No, I will die here." Benaiah reported to the king, "This is how Joab answered me." {31} Then the king commanded Benaiah, "Do as he says. Strike him down and bury him, and so clear me and my father's house of the guilt of the innocent blood that Joab shed. {32} The LORD will repay him for the blood he shed, because without the knowledge of my father David he attacked two men and killed them with the sword. Both of them—Abner son of Ner, commander of Israel's army, and Amasa son of Jether, commander of Judah's army— were better men and more upright than he. {33} May the guilt of their blood rest on the head of Joab and his descendants forever. But on David and his descendants, his house and his throne, may there be the Lord's peace forever." {34} So Benaiah son of Jehoiada went up and struck down Joab and killed him, and he was buried on his own land in the desert. {35} The king put Benaiah son of Jehoiada over the army in Joab's position and replaced Abiathar with Zadok the priest. {36} Then the king sent for Shimei and said to him, "Build yourself a house in Jerusalem and live there, but do not go anywhere else. {37} The day you leave and cross the Kidron Valley, you can be sure you will die; your blood will be on your own head." {38} Shimei answered the king, "What you say is good. Your servant will do as my lord the king has said." And Shimei stayed in Jerusalem for a long time. {39} But three years later, two of Shimei's slaves ran off to Achish son of Maacah, king of Gath, and Shimei was told, "Your slaves are in Gath." {40} At this, he saddled his donkey and went to Achish at Gath in search of his slaves. So Shimei went away and brought the slaves back from Gath. {41} When Solomon was told that Shimei had gone from Jerusalem to Gath and had returned, {42} the king summoned Shimei and said to him, "Did I not make you swear by the LORD and warn you, 'On the day you leave to go anywhere else, you can be sure you will die'? At that time you said to me, 'What you say is good. I will obey.' {43} Why then did you not keep your oath to the LORD and obey the command I gave you?" {44} The king also said to Shimei, "You know in your heart all the wrong you did to my father David. Now the LORD will repay you for your wrongdoing. {45} But King Solomon will be blessed, and David's throne will remain secure before the LORD forever." {46} Then the king gave the order to Benaiah son of Jehoiada, and he went out and struck Shimei down and killed him. The kingdom was now firmly established in Solomon's hands.

SOLOMON THE WISE

1 Ki 3:11-28

So God said to him, "Since you have asked for this and not for long life or wealth for yourself, nor have asked for the death of your enemies but for discernment in administering justice, {12} I will do what you have asked. I will give you a wise and discerning heart, so that there will never have been anyone like you, nor will there ever be. {13} Moreover, I will give you what you have not asked for—both riches and honor—so that in your lifetime you will have no equal among kings. {14} And if you walk in my ways and obey my statutes and commands as David your father did, I will give you a long life." {15} Then Solomon awoke—and he realized it had been a dream. He returned to Jerusalem, stood before the ark of the Lord's covenant and sacrificed burnt offerings and fellowship offerings. Then he gave a feast for all his court. {16} Now two prostitutes came to the king and stood before him. {17} One of them said, "My lord, this woman and I live in the same house. I had a baby while she was there with me. {18} The third day after my child was born, this woman also had a baby. We were alone; there was no one in the house but the two of us. {19} "During the night this woman's son died because she lay on him. {20} So she got up in the middle of the night and took my son from my side while I your servant was asleep. She put him by her breast and put her dead son by my breast. {21} The next morning, I got up to nurse my son—and he was dead! But when I looked at him closely in the morning light, I saw that it wasn't the son I had borne." {22} The other woman said, "No! The living one is my son; the dead one is yours." But the first one insisted, "No! The dead one is yours; the living one is mine." And so they argued before the king. {23} The king said, "This one says, 'My son is alive and your son is dead,' while that one says, 'No! Your son is dead and mine is alive.'" {24} Then the king said, "Bring me a sword." So they brought a sword for the king. {25} He then gave an order: "Cut the living child in two and give half to one and half to the other." {26} The woman whose son was alive was filled with compassion for her son and said to the king, "Please, my lord, give her the living baby! Don't kill him!" But the other said, "Neither I nor you shall have him. Cut him in two!" {27} Then the king gave his ruling: "Give the living baby to the first woman. Do not kill him; she is his mother." {28} When all Israel heard the verdict the king had given, they held the king in awe, because they saw that he had wisdom from God to administer justice.

SOLOMON PREPARES TO BUILD THE TEMPLE

1 Ki 5:1-18

When Hiram king of Tyre heard that Solomon had been anointed king to succeed his father David, he sent his envoys to Solomon, because he had always been on friendly terms with David. {2} Solomon sent back this message to Hiram: {3} "You know that because of the wars waged against my father David from all sides, he could not build a temple for the Name of the LORD his God until the LORD put his enemies under his feet. {4} But now the LORD my God has given me rest on every side, and there is no adversary or disaster. {5} I intend, therefore, to build a temple for the Name of the LORD my God, as the LORD told my father David, when he said, 'Your son whom I will put on the throne in your place will build the temple for my Name.' {6} "So give orders that cedars of Lebanon be cut for me. My men will work with yours, and I will pay you for your men whatever wages you set. You know that we have no one so skilled in felling timber as the Sidonians." {7} When Hiram heard Solomon's message, he was greatly pleased and said, "Praise be to the LORD today, for he has given David a wise son to rule over this great nation." {8} So Hiram sent word to Solomon: "I have received the message you sent me and will do all you want in providing the cedar and pine logs. {9} My men will haul them down from Lebanon to the sea, and I will float them in rafts by sea to the place you specify. There I will separate them and you can take them away. And you are to grant my wish by providing food for my royal household." {10} In this way Hiram kept Solomon supplied with all the cedar and pine logs he wanted, {11} and Solomon gave Hiram twenty thousand cors of wheat as food for his household, in addition to twenty thousand baths of pressed olive oil. Solomon continued to do this for Hiram year after year. {12} The LORD gave Solomon wisdom, just as he had promised him. There were peaceful relations between Hiram and Solomon, and the two of them made a treaty. {13} King Solomon conscripted laborers from all Israel—thirty thousand men. {14} He sent them off to Lebanon in shifts of ten thousand a month, so that they spent one month in Lebanon and two months at home. Adoniram was in charge of the forced labor. {15} Solomon had seventy thousand carriers and eighty thousand stonecutters in the hills, {16} as well as thirty-three hundred foremen who supervised the project and directed the workmen. {17} At the king's command they removed from the quarry large blocks of quality stone to provide a foundation of dressed stone for the temple. {18} The craftsmen of Solomon and Hiram and the men of Gebal cut and prepared the timber and stone for the building of the temple.

SOLOMON BUILDS THE TEMPLE

1 Ki 6:11-18

The word of the LORD came to Solomon: {12} "As for this temple you are building, if you follow my decrees, carry out my regulations and keep all my commands and obey them, I will fulfill through you the promise I gave to David your father. {13} And I will live among the Israelites and will not abandon my people Israel." {14} So Solomon built the temple and completed it. {15} He lined its interior walls with cedar boards, paneling them from the floor of the temple to the ceiling, and covered the floor of the temple with planks of pine. {16} He partitioned off twenty cubits at the rear of the temple with cedar boards from floor to ceiling to form within the temple an inner sanctuary, the Most Holy Place. {17} The main hall in front of this room was forty cubits long. {18} The inside of the temple was cedar, carved with gourds and open flowers. Everything was cedar; no stone was to be seen.

SOLOMON BUILDS HIS PALACE

1 Ki 7:1-11

It took Solomon thirteen years, however, to complete the contruction of his palace. {2} He built the Palace of the Forest of Lebanon a hundred cubits long, fifty wide and thirty high, with four rows of cedar columns supporting trimmed cedar beams. {3} It was roofed with cedar above the beams that rested on the columns–forty-five beams, fifteen to a row. {4} Its windows were placed high in sets of three, facing each other. {5} All the doorways had rectangular frames; they were in the front part in sets of three, facing each other. {6} He made a colonnade fifty cubits long and thirty wide. In front of it was a portico, and in front of that were pillars and an overhanging roof. {7} He built the throne hall, the Hall of Justice, where he was to judge, and he covered it with cedar from floor to ceiling. {8} And the palace in which he was to live, set farther back, was similar in design. Solomon also made a palace like this hall for Pharaoh's daughter, whom he had married. {9} All these structures, from the outside to the great courtyard and from foundation to eaves, were made of blocks of high-grade stone cut to size and trimmed with a saw on their inner and outer faces. {10} The foundations were laid with large stones of good quality, some measuring ten cubits and some eight. {11} Above were high-grade stones, cut to size, and cedar beams.

DEDICATION OF THE TEMPLE

1 Ki 8:15-30

"Praise be to the LORD, the God of Israel, who with his own hand has fulfilled what he promised with his own mouth to my father David. For he said, {16} 'Since the day I brought my people Israel out of Egypt, I have not chosen a city in any tribe of Israel to have a temple built for my Name to be there, but I have chosen David to rule my people Israel.' {17} "My father David had it in his heart to build a temple for the Name of the LORD, the God of Israel. {18} But the LORD said to my father David, 'Because it was in your heart to build a temple for my Name, you did well to have this in your heart. {19} Nevertheless, you are not the one to build the temple, but your son, who is your own flesh and blood–he is the one who will build the temple for my Name.' {20} "The LORD has kept the promise he made: I have succeeded David my father and now I sit on the throne of Israel, just as the LORD promised, and I have built the temple for the Name of the LORD, the God of Israel. {21} I have provided a place there for the ark, in which is the covenant of the LORD that he made with our fathers when he brought them out of Egypt." {22} Then Solomon stood before the altar of the LORD in front of the whole assembly of Israel, spread out his hands toward heaven {23} and said: "O LORD, God of Israel, there is no God like you in heaven above or on earth below–you who keep your covenant of love with your servants who continue wholeheartedly in your way. {24} You have kept your promise to your servant David my father; with your mouth you have promised and with your hand you have fulfilled it–as it is today. {25} "Now LORD, God of Israel, keep for your servant David my father the promises you made to him when you said, 'You shall never fail to have a man to sit before me on the throne of Israel, if only your sons are careful in all they do to walk before me as you have done.' {26} And now, O God of Israel, let your word that you promised your servant David my father come true. {27} "But will God really dwell on earth? The heavens, even the highest heaven, cannot contain you. How much less this temple I have built! {28} Yet give attention to your servant's prayer and his plea for mercy, O LORD my God. Hear the cry and the prayer that your servant is praying in your presence this day. {29} May your eyes be open toward this temple night and day, this place of which you said, 'My Name shall be there,' so that you will hear the prayer your servant prays toward this place. {30} Hear the supplication of your servant and of your people Israel when they pray toward this place. Hear from heaven, your dwelling place, and when you hear, forgive.

GOD'S PROMISE TO SOLOMON

1 Ki 9:1-14

When Solomon had finished building the temple of the LORD and the royal palace, and had achieved all he had desired to do, {2} the LORD appeared to him a second time, as he had appeared to him at Gibeon. {3} The LORD said to him: "I have heard the prayer and plea you have made before me; I have consecrated this temple, which you have built, by putting my Name there forever. My eyes and my heart will always be there. {4} "As for you, if you walk before me in integrity of heart and uprightness, as David your father did, and do all I command and observe my decrees and laws, {5} I will establish your royal throne over Israel forever, as I promised David your father when I said, 'You shall never fail to have a man on the throne of Israel.' {6} "But if you or your sons turn away from me and do not observe the commands and decrees I have given you and go off to serve other gods and worship them, {7} then I will cut off Israel from the land I have given them and will reject this temple I have consecrated for my Name. Israel will then become a byword and an object of ridicule among all peoples. {8} And though this temple is now imposing, all who pass by will be appalled and will scoff and say, 'Why has the LORD done such a thing to this land and to this temple?' {9} People will answer, 'Because they have forsaken the LORD their God, who brought their fathers out of Egypt, and have embraced other gods, worshiping and serving them–that is why the LORD brought all this disaster on them.'" {10} At the end of twenty years, during which Solomon built these two buildings–the temple of the LORD and the royal palace– {11} King Solomon gave twenty towns in Galilee to Hiram king of Tyre, because Hiram had supplied him with all the cedar and pine and gold he wanted. {12} But when Hiram went from Tyre to see the towns that Solomon had given him, he was not pleased with them. {13} "What kind of towns are these you have given me, my brother?" he asked. And he called them the Land of Cabul, a name they have to this day. {14} Now Hiram had sent to the king 120 talents of gold.

1 Ki 9:24-25

After Pharaoh's daughter had come up from the City of David to the palace Solomon had built for her, he constructed the supporting terraces. {25} Three times a year Solomon sacrificed burnt offerings and fellowship offerings on the altar he had built for the LORD, burning incense before the LORD along with them, and so fulfilled the temple obligations.

SOLOMON IS RICH, VISITED BY THE QUEEN OF SHEBA

1 Ki 10:1-10
	When the queen of Sheba heard about the fame of Solomon and his relation to the name of the LORD, she came to test him with hard questions. {2} Arriving at Jerusalem with a very great caravan–with camels carrying spices, large quantities of gold, and precious stones–she came to Solomon and talked with him about all that she had on her mind. {3} Solomon answered all her questions; nothing was too hard for the king to explain to her. {4} When the queen of Sheba saw all the wisdom of Solomon and the palace he had built, {5} the food on his table, the seating of his officials, the attending servants in their robes, his cupbearers, and the burnt offerings he made at the temple of the LORD, she was overwhelmed. {6} She said to the king, "The report I heard in my own country about your achievements and your wisdom is true. {7} But I did not believe these things until I came and saw with my own eyes. Indeed, not even half was told me; in wisdom and wealth you have far exceeded the report I heard. {8} How happy your men must be! How happy your officials, who continually stand before you and hear your wisdom! {9} Praise be to the LORD your God, who has delighted in you and placed you on the throne of Israel. Because of the Lord's eternal love for Israel, he has made you king, to maintain justice and righteousness." {10} And she gave the king 120 talents of gold, large quantities of spices, and precious stones. Never again were so many spices brought in as those the queen of Sheba gave to King Solomon.

1 Ki 10:23-29
	King Solomon was greater in riches and wisdom than all the other kings of the earth. {24} The whole world sought audience with Solomon to hear the wisdom God had put in his heart. {25} Year after year, everyone who came brought a gift–articles of silver and gold, robes, weapons and spices, and horses and mules. {26} Solomon accumulated chariots and horses; he had fourteen hundred chariots and twelve thousand horses, which he kept in the chariot cities and also with him in Jerusalem. {27} The king made silver as common in Jerusalem as stones, and cedar as plentiful as sycamore-fig trees in the foothills. {28} Solomon's horses were imported from Egypt and from Kue –the royal merchants purchased them from Kue. {29} They imported a chariot from Egypt for six hundred shekels of silver, and a horse for a hundred and fifty. They also exported them to all the kings of the Hittites and of the Arameans.

SOLOMON'S MANY WIVES INCREASE HIS DIFFICULTIES

1 Ki 11:1-18

King Solomon, however, loved many foreign women besides Pharaoh's daughter—Moabites, Ammonites, Edomites, Sidonians and Hittites. {2} They were from nations about which the LORD had told the Israelites, "You must not intermarry with them, because they will surely turn your hearts after their gods." Nevertheless, Solomon held fast to them in love. {3} He had seven hundred wives of royal birth and three hundred concubines, and his wives led him astray. {4} As Solomon grew old, his wives turned his heart after other gods, and his heart was not fully devoted to the LORD his God, as the heart of David his father had been. {5} He followed Ashtoreth the goddess of the Sidonians, and Molech the detestable god of the Ammonites. {6} So Solomon did evil in the eyes of the LORD; he did not follow the LORD completely, as David his father had done. {7} On a hill east of Jerusalem, Solomon built a high place for Chemosh the detestable god of Moab, and for Molech the detestable god of the Ammonites. {8} He did the same for all his foreign wives, who burned incense and offered sacrifices to their gods. {9} The LORD became angry with Solomon because his heart had turned away from the LORD, the God of Israel, who had appeared to him twice. {10} Although he had forbidden Solomon to follow other gods, Solomon did not keep the Lord's command. {11} So the LORD said to Solomon, "Since this is your attitude and you have not kept my covenant and my decrees, which I commanded you, I will most certainly tear the kingdom away from you and give it to one of your subordinates. {12} Nevertheless, for the sake of David your father, I will not do it during your lifetime. I will tear it out of the hand of your son. {13} Yet I will not tear the whole kingdom from him, but will give him one tribe for the sake of David my servant and for the sake of Jerusalem, which I have chosen." {14} Then the LORD raised up against Solomon an adversary, Hadad the Edomite, from the royal line of Edom. {15} Earlier when David was fighting with Edom, Joab the commander of the army, who had gone up to bury the dead, had struck down all the men in Edom. {16} Joab and all the Israelites stayed there for six months, until they had destroyed all the men in Edom. {17} But Hadad, still only a boy, fled to Egypt with some Edomite officials who had served his father. {18} They set out from Midian and went to Paran. Then taking men from Paran with them, they went to Egypt, to Pharaoh king of Egypt, who gave Hadad a house and land and provided him with food.

REBELLION OF JEROBOAM; DEATH OF SOLOMON

1 Ki 11:27-43

Here is the account of how [Jeroboam] rebelled against the king: Solomon had built the supporting terraces and had filled in the gap in the wall of the city of David his father. {28} Now Jeroboam was a man of standing, and when Solomon saw how well the young man did his work, he put him in charge of the whole labor force of the house of Joseph. {29} About that time Jeroboam was going out of Jerusalem, and Ahijah the prophet of Shiloh met him on the way, wearing a new cloak. The two of them were alone out in the country, {30} and Ahijah took hold of the new cloak he was wearing and tore it into twelve pieces. {31} Then he said to Jeroboam, "Take ten pieces for yourself, for this is what the LORD, the God of Israel, says: 'See, I am going to tear the kingdom out of Solomon's hand and give you ten tribes. {32} But for the sake of my servant David and the city of Jerusalem, which I have chosen out of all the tribes of Israel, he will have one tribe. {33} I will do this because they have forsaken me and worshiped Ashtoreth the goddess of the Sidonians, Chemosh the god of the Moabites, and Molech the god of the Ammonites, and have not walked in my ways, nor done what is right in my eyes, nor kept my statutes and laws as David, Solomon's father, did. {34} " 'But I will not take the whole kingdom out of Solomon's hand; I have made him ruler all the days of his life for the sake of David my servant, whom I chose and who observed my commands and statutes. {35} I will take the kingdom from his son's hands and give you ten tribes. {36} I will give one tribe to his son so that David my servant may always have a lamp before me in Jerusalem, the city where I chose to put my Name. {37} However, as for you, I will take you, and you will rule over all that your heart desires; you will be king over Israel. {38} If you do whatever I command you and walk in my ways and do what is right in my eyes by keeping my statutes and commands, as David my servant did, I will be with you. I will build you a dynasty as enduring as the one I built for David and will give Israel to you. {39} I will humble David's descendants because of this, but not forever.'" {40} Solomon tried to kill Jeroboam, but Jeroboam fled to Egypt, to Shishak the king, and stayed there until Solomon's death.

{41} As for the other events of Solomon's reign—all he did and the wisdom he displayed—are they not written in the book of the annals of Solomon? {42} Solomon reigned in Jerusalem over all Israel forty years. {43} Then he rested with his fathers and was buried in the city of David his father. And Rehoboam his son succeeded him as king.

ISRAEL REBELS AGAINST REHOBOAM

1 Ki 12:3-20

So they sent for Jeroboam, and he and the whole assembly of Israel went to Rehoboam and said to him: {4} "Your father put a heavy yoke on us, but now lighten the harsh labor and the heavy yoke he put on us, and we will serve you." {5} Rehoboam answered, "Go away for three days and then come back to me." So the people went away. {6} Then King Rehoboam consulted the elders who had served his father Solomon during his lifetime. "How would you advise me to answer these people?" he asked. {7} They replied, "If today you will be a servant to these people and serve them and give them a favorable answer, they will always be your servants." {8} But Rehoboam rejected the advice the elders gave him and consulted the young men who had grown up with him and were serving him. {9} He asked them, "What is your advice? How should we answer these people who say to me, 'Lighten the yoke your father put on us'?" {10} The young men who had grown up with him replied, "Tell these people who have said to you, 'Your father put a heavy yoke on us, but make our yoke lighter'–tell them, 'My little finger is thicker than my father's waist. {11} My father laid on you a heavy yoke; I will make it even heavier. My father scourged you with whips; I will scourge you with scorpions.'" {12} Three days later Jeroboam and all the people returned to Rehoboam, as the king had said, "Come back to me in three days." {13} The king answered the people harshly. Rejecting the advice given him by the elders, {14} he followed the advice of the young men and said, "My father made your yoke heavy; I will make it even heavier. My father scourged you with whips; I will scourge you with scorpions." {15} So the king did not listen to the people, for this turn of events was from the LORD, to fulfill the word the LORD had spoken to Jeroboam son of Nebat through Ahijah the Shilonite. {16} When all Israel saw that the king refused to listen to them, they answered the king: "What share do we have in David, what part in Jesse's son? To your tents, O Israel! Look after your own house, O David!" So the Israelites went home. {17} But as for the Israelites who were living in the towns of Judah, Rehoboam still ruled over them. {18} King Rehoboam sent out Adoniram, who was in charge of forced labor, but all Israel stoned him to death. King Rehoboam, however, managed to get into his chariot and escape to Jerusalem. {19} So Israel has been in rebellion against the house of David to this day. {20} When all the Israelites heard that Jeroboam had returned, they sent and called him to the assembly and made him king over all Israel. Only the tribe of Judah remained loyal to the house of David.

JEROBOAM KING OF ISRAEL; REHOBOAM KING OF JUDAH

1 Ki 14:7-9
Go, tell Jeroboam that this is what the LORD, the God of Israel, says: 'I raised you up from among the people and made you a leader over my people Israel. {8} I tore the kingdom away from the house of David and gave it to you, but you have not been like my servant David, who kept my commands and followed me with all his heart, doing only what was right in my eyes. {9} You have done more evil than all who lived before you. You have made for yourself other gods, idols made of metal; you have provoked me to anger and thrust me behind your back.

1 Ki 14:19-20
The other events of Jeroboam's reign, his wars and how he ruled, are written in the book of the annals of the kings of Israel. {20} He reigned for twenty-two years and then rested with his fathers. And Nadab his son succeeded him as king.

1 Ki 14:21-31a
Rehoboam son of Solomon was king in Judah. He was forty-one years old when he became king, and he reigned seventeen years in Jerusalem, the city the LORD had chosen out of all the tribes of Israel in which to put his Name. His mother's name was Naamah; she was an Ammonite. {22} Judah did evil in the eyes of the LORD. By the sins they committed they stirred up his jealous anger more than their fathers had done. {23} They also set up for themselves high places, sacred stones and Asherah poles on every high hill and under every spreading tree. {24} There were even male shrine prostitutes in the land; the people engaged in all the detestable practices of the nations the LORD had driven out before the Israelites. {25} In the fifth year of King Rehoboam, Shishak king of Egypt attacked Jerusalem. {26} He carried off the treasures of the temple of the LORD and the treasures of the royal palace. He took everything, including all the gold shields Solomon had made. {27} So King Rehoboam made bronze shields to replace them and assigned these to the commanders of the guard on duty at the entrance to the royal palace. {28} Whenever the king went to the Lord's temple, the guards bore the shields, and afterward they returned them to the guardroom. {29} As for the other events of Rehoboam's reign, and all he did, are they not written in the book of the annals of the kings of Judah? {30} There was continual warfare between Rehoboam and Jeroboam. {31} And Rehoboam rested with his fathers and was buried with them in the City of David.

ELIJAH IS FED BY RAVENS; A WIDOW HAS FLOUR AND OIL

1 Ki 17:5-24

So he did what the LORD had told him. He went to the Kerith Ravine, east of the Jordan, and stayed there. {6} The ravens brought him bread and meat in the morning and bread and meat in the evening, and he drank from the brook. {7} Some time later the brook dried up because there had been no rain in the land. {8} Then the word of the LORD came to him: {9} "Go at once to Zarephath of Sidon and stay there. I have commanded a widow in that place to supply you with food." {10} So he went to Zarephath. When he came to the town gate, a widow was there gathering sticks. He called to her and asked, "Would you bring me a little water in a jar so I may have a drink?" {11} As she was going to get it, he called, "And bring me, please, a piece of bread." {12} "As surely as the LORD your God lives," she replied, "I don't have any bread–only a handful of flour in a jar and a little oil in a jug. I am gathering a few sticks to take home and make a meal for myself and my son, that we may eat it–and die." {13} Elijah said to her, "Don't be afraid. Go home and do as you have said. But first make a small cake of bread for me from what you have and bring it to me, and then make something for yourself and your son. {14} For this is what the LORD, the God of Israel, says: 'The jar of flour will not be used up and the jug of oil will not run dry until the day the LORD gives rain on the land.'" {15} She went away and did as Elijah had told her. So there was food every day for Elijah and for the woman and her family. {16} For the jar of flour was not used up and the jug of oil did not run dry, in keeping with the word of the LORD spoken by Elijah. {17} Some time later the son of the woman who owned the house became ill. He grew worse and worse, and finally stopped breathing. {18} She said to Elijah, "What do you have against me, man of God? Did you come to remind me of my sin and kill my son?" {19} "Give me your son," Elijah replied. He took him from her arms, carried him to the upper room where he was staying, and laid him on his bed. {20} Then he cried out to the LORD, "O LORD my God, have you brought tragedy also upon this widow I am staying with, by causing her son to die?" {21} Then he stretched himself out on the boy three times and cried to the LORD, "O LORD my God, let this boy's life return to him!" {22} The LORD heard Elijah's cry, and the boy's life returned to him, and he lived. {23} Elijah picked up the child and carried him down from the room into the house. He gave him to his mother and said, "Look, your son is alive!" {24} Then the woman said to Elijah, "Now I know that you are a man of God and that the word of the LORD from your mouth is the truth."

ELIJAH AND OBADIAH, MEN OF GOD

1 Ki 18:1-20

After a long time, in the third year, the word of the LORD came to Elijah: "Go and present yourself to Ahab, and I will send rain on the land." {2} So Elijah went to present himself to Ahab. Now the famine was severe in Samaria, {3} and Ahab had summoned Obadiah, who was in charge of his palace. (Obadiah was a devout believer in the LORD. {4} While Jezebel was killing off the Lord's prophets, Obadiah had taken a hundred prophets and hidden them in two caves, fifty in each, and had supplied them with food and water.) {5} Ahab had said to Obadiah, "Go through the land to all the springs and valleys. Maybe we can find some grass to keep the horses and mules alive so we will not have to kill any of our animals." {6} So they divided the land they were to cover, Ahab going in one direction and Obadiah in another. {7} As Obadiah was walking along, Elijah met him. Obadiah recognized him, bowed down to the ground, and said, "Is it really you, my lord Elijah?" {8} "Yes," he replied. "Go tell your master, 'Elijah is here.'" {9} "What have I done wrong," asked Obadiah, "that you are handing your servant over to Ahab to be put to death? {10} As surely as the LORD your God lives, there is not a nation or kingdom where my master has not sent someone to look for you. And whenever a nation or kingdom claimed you were not there, he made them swear they could not find you. {11} But now you tell me to go to my master and say, 'Elijah is here.' {12} I don't know where the Spirit of the LORD may carry you when I leave you. If I go and tell Ahab and he doesn't find you, he will kill me. Yet I your servant have worshiped the LORD since my youth. {13} Haven't you heard, my lord, what I did while Jezebel was killing the prophets of the LORD? I hid a hundred of the Lord's prophets in two caves, fifty in each, and supplied them with food and water. {14} And now you tell me to go to my master and say, 'Elijah is here.' He will kill me!" {15} Elijah said, "As the LORD Almighty lives, whom I serve, I will surely present myself to Ahab today." {16} So Obadiah went to meet Ahab and told him, and Ahab went to meet Elijah. {17} When he saw Elijah, he said to him, "Is that you, you troubler of Israel?" {18} "I have not made trouble for Israel," Elijah replied. "But you and your father's family have. You have abandoned the Lord's commands and have followed the Baals. {19} Now summon the people from all over Israel to meet me on Mount Carmel. And bring the four hundred and fifty prophets of Baal and the four hundred prophets of Asherah, who eat at Jezebel's table." {20} So Ahab sent word throughout all Israel and assembled the prophets on Mount Carmel.

ELIJAH SACRIFICES TO GOD AND ENDS THE DROUGHT

1 Ki 18:30-46

Then Elijah said to all the people, "Come here to me." They came to him, and he repaired the altar of the LORD, which was in ruins. {31} Elijah took twelve stones, one for each of the tribes descended from Jacob, to whom the word of the LORD had come, saying, "Your name shall be Israel." {32} With the stones he built an altar in the name of the LORD, and he dug a trench around it large enough to hold two seahs of seed. {33} He arranged the wood, cut the bull into pieces and laid it on the wood. Then he said to them, "Fill four large jars with water and pour it on the offering and on the wood." {34} "Do it again," he said, and they did it again. "Do it a third time," he ordered, and they did it the third time. {35} The water ran down around the altar and even filled the trench. {36} At the time of sacrifice, the prophet Elijah stepped forward and prayed: "O LORD, God of Abraham, Isaac and Israel, let it be known today that you are God in Israel and that I am your servant and have done all these things at your command. {37} Answer me, O LORD, answer me, so these people will know that you, O LORD, are God, and that you are turning their hearts back again." {38} Then the fire of the LORD fell and burned up the sacrifice, the wood, the stones and the soil, and also licked up the water in the trench. {39} When all the people saw this, they fell prostrate and cried, "The LORD–he is God! The LORD–he is God!" {40} Then Elijah commanded them, "Seize the prophets of Baal. Don't let anyone get away!" They seized them, and Elijah had them brought down to the Kishon Valley and slaughtered there. {41} And Elijah said to Ahab, "Go, eat and drink, for there is the sound of a heavy rain." {42} So Ahab went off to eat and drink, but Elijah climbed to the top of Carmel, bent down to the ground and put his face between his knees. {43} "Go and look toward the sea," he told his servant. And he went up and looked. "There is nothing there," he said. Seven times Elijah said, "Go back." {44} The seventh time the servant reported, "A cloud as small as a man's hand is rising from the sea." So Elijah said, "Go and tell Ahab, 'Hitch up your chariot and go down before the rain stops you.'" {45} Meanwhile, the sky grew black with clouds, the wind rose, a heavy rain came on and Ahab rode off to Jezreel. {46} The power of the LORD came upon Elijah and, tucking his cloak into his belt, he ran ahead of Ahab all the way to Jezreel.

ELIJAH FLEES AND CALLS ELISHA

1 Ki 19:7-21

The angel of the LORD came back a second time and touched him and said, "Get up and eat, for the journey is too much for you." {8} So he got up and ate and drank. Strengthened by that food, he traveled forty days and forty nights until he reached Horeb, the mountain of God. {9} There he went into a cave and spent the night. And the word of the LORD came to him: "What are you doing here, Elijah?" {10} He replied, "I have been very zealous for the LORD God Almighty. The Israelites have rejected your covenant, broken down your altars, and put your prophets to death with the sword. I am the only one left, and now they are trying to kill me too." {11} The LORD said, "Go out and stand on the mountain in the presence of the LORD, for the LORD is about to pass by." Then a great and powerful wind tore the mountains apart and shattered the rocks before the LORD, but the LORD was not in the wind. After the wind there was an earthquake, but the LORD was not in the earthquake. {12} After the earthquake came a fire, but the LORD was not in the fire. And after the fire came a gentle whisper. {13} When Elijah heard it, he pulled his cloak over his face and went out and stood at the mouth of the cave. Then a voice said to him, "What are you doing here, Elijah?" {14} He replied, "I have been very zealous for the LORD God Almighty. The Israelites have rejected your covenant, broken down your altars, and put your prophets to death with the sword. I am the only one left, and now they are trying to kill me too." {15} The LORD said to him, "Go back the way you came, and go to the Desert of Damascus. When you get there, anoint Hazael king over Aram. {16} Also, anoint Jehu son of Nimshi king over Israel, and anoint Elisha son of Shaphat from Abel Meholah to succeed you as prophet. {17} Jehu will put to death any who escape the sword of Hazael, and Elisha will put to death any who escape the sword of Jehu. {18} Yet I reserve seven thousand in Israel–all whose knees have not bowed down to Baal and all whose mouths have not kissed him." {19} So Elijah went from there and found Elisha son of Shaphat. He was plowing with twelve yoke of oxen, and he himself was driving the twelfth pair. Elijah went up to him and threw his cloak around him. {20} Elisha then left his oxen and ran after Elijah. "Let me kiss my father and mother good-by," he said, "and then I will come with you." "Go back," Elijah replied. "What have I done to you?" {21} So Elisha left him and went back. He took his yoke of oxen and slaughtered them. He burned the plowing equipment to cook the meat and gave it to the people, and they ate. Then he set out to follow Elijah and became his attendant.

JEZEBEL GETS VINEYARD FOR AHAB

1 Ki 21:5-23

His wife Jezebel came in and asked him, "Why are you so sullen? Why won't you eat?" {6} He answered her, "Because I said to Naboth the Jezreelite, 'Sell me your vineyard; or if you prefer, I will give you another vineyard in its place.' But he said, 'I will not give you my vineyard.'" {7} Jezebel his wife said, "Is this how you act as king over Israel? Get up and eat! Cheer up. I'll get you the vineyard of Naboth the Jezreelite." {8} So she wrote letters in Ahab's name, placed his seal on them, and sent them to the elders and nobles who lived in Naboth's city with him. {9} In those letters she wrote: "Proclaim a day of fasting and seat Naboth in a prominent place among the people. {10} But seat two scoundrels opposite him and have them testify that he has cursed both God and the king. Then take him out and stone him to death." {11} So the elders and nobles who lived in Naboth's city did as Jezebel directed in the letters she had written to them. {12} They proclaimed a fast and seated Naboth in a prominent place among the people. {13} Then two scoundrels came and sat opposite him and brought charges against Naboth before the people, saying, "Naboth has cursed both God and the king." So they took him outside the city and stoned him to death. {14} Then they sent word to Jezebel: "Naboth has been stoned and is dead." {15} As soon as Jezebel heard that Naboth had been stoned to death, she said to Ahab, "Get up and take possession of the vineyard of Naboth the Jezreelite that he refused to sell you. He is no longer alive, but dead." {16} When Ahab heard that Naboth was dead, he got up and went down to take possession of Naboth's vineyard. {17} Then the word of the LORD came to Elijah the Tishbite: {18} "Go down to meet Ahab king of Israel, who rules in Samaria. He is now in Naboth's vineyard, where he has gone to take possession of it. {19} Say to him, 'This is what the LORD says: Have you not murdered a man and seized his property?' Then say to him, 'This is what the LORD says: In the place where dogs licked up Naboth's blood, dogs will lick up your blood–yes, yours!'" {20} Ahab said to Elijah, "So you have found me, my enemy!" "I have found you," he answered, "because you have sold yourself to do evil in the eyes of the LORD. {21} 'I am going to bring disaster on you. I will consume your descendants and cut off from Ahab every last male in Israel–slave or free. {22} I will make your house like that of Jeroboam son of Nebat and that of Baasha son of Ahijah, because you have provoked me to anger and have caused Israel to sin.' {23} "And also concerning Jezebel the LORD says: 'Dogs will devour Jezebel by the wall of Jezreel.'

MICAIAH, A PROPHET OF GOD; AHAB DIES

1 Ki 22:7-9
   "Is there not a prophet of the LORD here whom we can inquire of?" {8} The king of Israel answered Jehoshaphat, "There is still one man through whom we can inquire of the LORD, but I hate him because he never prophesies anything good about me, but always bad. He is Micaiah son of Imlah." "The king should not say that," Jehoshaphat replied. {9} So the king of Israel called one of his officials and said, "Bring Micaiah son of Imlah at once."

1 Ki 22:17-28
   Then Micaiah answered, "I saw all Israel scattered on the hills like sheep without a shepherd, and the LORD said, 'These people have no master. Let each one go home in peace.'" {18} The king of Israel said to Jehoshaphat, "Didn't I tell you that he never prophesies anything good about me, but only bad?" {19} Micaiah continued, "Therefore hear the word of the LORD: I saw the LORD sitting on his throne with all the host of heaven standing around him on his right and on his left. {20} And the LORD said, 'Who will entice Ahab into attacking Ramoth Gilead and going to his death there?' "One suggested this, and another that. {21} Finally, a spirit came forward, stood before the LORD and said, 'I will entice him.' {22} " 'By what means?' the LORD asked. " 'I will go out and be a lying spirit in the mouths of all his prophets,' he said." 'You will succeed in enticing him,' said the LORD. 'Go and do it.' {23} "So now the LORD has put a lying spirit in the mouths of all these prophets of yours. The LORD has decreed disaster for you." {24} Then Zedekiah son of Kenaanah went up and slapped Micaiah in the face. "Which way did the spirit from the LORD go when he went from me to speak to you?" he asked. {25} Micaiah replied, "You will find out on the day you go to hide in an inner room." {26} The king of Israel then ordered, "Take Micaiah and send him back to Amon the ruler of the city and to Joash the king's son {27} and say, 'This is what the king says: Put this fellow in prison and give him nothing but bread and water until I return safely.'" {28} Micaiah declared, "If you ever return safely, the LORD has not spoken through me." Then he added, "Mark my words, all you people!"

1 Ki 22:34a
   But someone drew his bow at random and hit the king of Israel between the sections of his armor.
1 Ki 22:37
   So the king died and was brought to Samaria, and they buried him there.

ELIJAH IS TAKEN TO HEAVEN

2 Ki 2:1-15

When the LORD was about to take Elijah up to heaven in a whirlwind, Elijah and Elisha were on their way from Gilgal. {2} Elijah said to Elisha, "Stay here; the LORD has sent me to Bethel." But Elisha said, "As surely as the LORD lives and as you live, I will not leave you." So they went down to Bethel. {3} The company of the prophets at Bethel came out to Elisha and asked, "Do you know that the LORD is going to take your master from you today?" "Yes, I know," Elisha replied, "but do not speak of it." {4} Then Elijah said to him, "Stay here, Elisha; the LORD has sent me to Jericho." And he replied, "As surely as the LORD lives and as you live, I will not leave you." So they went to Jericho. {5} The company of the prophets at Jericho went up to Elisha and asked him, "Do you know that the LORD is going to take your master from you today?" "Yes, I know," he replied, "but do not speak of it." {6} Then Elijah said to him, "Stay here; the LORD has sent me to the Jordan." And he replied, "As surely as the LORD lives and as you live, I will not leave you." So the two of them walked on. {7} Fifty men of the company of the prophets went and stood at a distance, facing the place where Elijah and Elisha had stopped at the Jordan. {8} Elijah took his cloak, rolled it up and struck the water with it. The water divided to the right and to the left, and the two of them crossed over on dry ground. {9} When they had crossed, Elijah said to Elisha, "Tell me, what can I do for you before I am taken from you?" "Let me inherit a double portion of your spirit," Elisha replied. {10} "You have asked a difficult thing," Elijah said, "yet if you see me when I am taken from you, it will be yours—otherwise not." {11} As they were walking along and talking together, suddenly a chariot of fire and horses of fire appeared and separated the two of them, and Elijah went up to heaven in a whirlwind. {12} Elisha saw this and cried out, "My father! My father! The chariots and horsemen of Israel!" And Elisha saw him no more. Then he took hold of his own clothes and tore them apart. {13} He picked up the cloak that had fallen from Elijah and went back and stood on the bank of the Jordan. {14} Then he took the cloak that had fallen from him and struck the water with it. "Where now is the LORD, the God of Elijah?" he asked. When he struck the water, it divided to the right and to the left, and he crossed over. {15} The company of the prophets from Jericho, who were watching, said, "The spirit of Elijah is resting on Elisha." And they went to meet him and bowed to the ground before him.

ELISHA RAISES A BOY FROM THE DEAD

2 Ki 4:14-21

"What can be done for her?" Elisha asked. Gehazi said, "Well, she has no son and her husband is old." {15} Then Elisha said, "Call her." So he called her, and she stood in the doorway. {16} "About this time next year," Elisha said, "you will hold a son in your arms." "No, my lord," she objected. "Don't mislead your servant, O man of God!" {17} But the woman became pregnant, and the next year about that same time she gave birth to a son, just as Elisha had told her. {18} The child grew, and one day he went out to his father, who was with the reapers. {19} "My head! My head!" he said to his father. His father told a servant, "Carry him to his mother." {20} After the servant had lifted him up and carried him to his mother, the boy sat on her lap until noon, and then he died. {21} She went up and laid him on the bed of the man of God, then shut the door and went out.

2 Ki 4:27-37

When she reached the man of God at the mountain, she took hold of his feet. Gehazi came over to push her away, but the man of God said, "Leave her alone! She is in bitter distress, but the LORD has hidden it from me and has not told me why." {28} "Did I ask you for a son, my lord?" she said. "Didn't I tell you, 'Don't raise my hopes'?" {29} Elisha said to Gehazi, "Tuck your cloak into your belt, take my staff in your hand and run. If you meet anyone, do not greet him, and if anyone greets you, do not answer. Lay my staff on the boy's face." {30} But the child's mother said, "As surely as the LORD lives and as you live, I will not leave you." So he got up and followed her. {31} Gehazi went on ahead and laid the staff on the boy's face, but there was no sound or response. So Gehazi went back to meet Elisha and told him, "The boy has not awakened." {32} When Elisha reached the house, there was the boy lying dead on his couch. {33} He went in, shut the door on the two of them and prayed to the LORD. {34} Then he got on the bed and lay upon the boy, mouth to mouth, eyes to eyes, hands to hands. As he stretched himself out upon him, the boy's body grew warm. {35} Elisha turned away and walked back and forth in the room and then got on the bed and stretched out upon him once more. The boy sneezed seven times and opened his eyes. {36} Elisha summoned Gehazi and said, "Call the Shunammite." And he did. When she came, he said, "Take your son." {37} She came in, fell at his feet and bowed to the ground. Then she took her son and went out.

NAAMAN IS HEALED

2 Ki 5:1-16

Now Naaman was commander of the army of the king of Aram. He was a great man in the sight of his master and highly regarded, because through him the LORD had given victory to Aram. He was a valiant soldier, but he had leprosy. {2} Now bands from Aram had gone out and had taken captive a young girl from Israel, and she served Naaman's wife. {3} She said to her mistress, "If only my master would see the prophet who is in Samaria! He would cure him of his leprosy." {4} Naaman went to his master and told him what the girl from Israel had said. {5} "By all means, go," the king of Aram replied. "I will send a letter to the king of Israel." So Naaman left, taking with him ten talents of silver, six thousand shekels of gold and ten sets of clothing. {6} The letter that he took to the king of Israel read: "With this letter I am sending my servant Naaman to you so that you may cure him of his leprosy." {7} As soon as the king of Israel read the letter, he tore his robes and said, "Am I God? Can I kill and bring back to life? Why does this fellow send someone to me to be cured of his leprosy? See how he is trying to pick a quarrel with me!" {8} When Elisha the man of God heard that the king of Israel had torn his robes, he sent him this message: "Why have you torn your robes? Have the man come to me and he will know that there is a prophet in Israel." {9} So Naaman went with his horses and chariots and stopped at the door of Elisha's house. {10} Elisha sent a messenger to say to him, "Go, wash yourself seven times in the Jordan, and your flesh will be restored and you will be cleansed." {11} But Naaman went away angry and said, "I thought that he would surely come out to me and stand and call on the name of the LORD his God, wave his hand over the spot and cure me of my leprosy. {12} Are not Abana and Pharpar, the rivers of Damascus, better than any of the waters of Israel? Couldn't I wash in them and be cleansed?" So he turned and went off in a rage. {13} Naaman's servants went to him and said, "My father, if the prophet had told you to do some great thing, would you not have done it? How much more, then, when he tells you, 'Wash and be cleansed'!" {14} So he went down and dipped himself in the Jordan seven times, as the man of God had told him, and his flesh was restored and became clean like that of a young boy. {15} Then Naaman and all his attendants went back to the man of God. He stood before him and said, "Now I know that there is no God in all the world except in Israel. Please accept now a gift from your servant." {16} The prophet answered, "As surely as the LORD lives, whom I serve, I will not accept a thing." And even though Naaman urged him, he refused.

ISRAEL IS TAKEN IN EXILE TO ASSYRIA

2 Ki 17:6-20

In the ninth year of Hoshea, the king of Assyria captured Samaria and deported the Israelites to Assyria. He settled them in Halah, in Gozan on the Habor River and in the towns of the Medes. {7} All this took place because the Israelites had sinned against the LORD their God, who had brought them up out of Egypt from under the power of Pharaoh king of Egypt. They worshiped other gods {8} and followed the practices of the nations the LORD had driven out before them, as well as the practices that the kings of Israel had introduced. {9} The Israelites secretly did things against the LORD their God that were not right. From watchtower to fortified city they built themselves high places in all their towns. {10} They set up sacred stones and Asherah poles on every high hill and under every spreading tree. {11} At every high place they burned incense, as the nations whom the LORD had driven out before them had done. They did wicked things that provoked the LORD to anger. {12} They worshiped idols, though the LORD had said, "You shall not do this." {13} The LORD warned Israel and Judah through all his prophets and seers: "Turn from your evil ways. Observe my commands and decrees, in accordance with the entire Law that I commanded your fathers to obey and that I delivered to you through my servants the prophets." {14} But they would not listen and were as stiff-necked as their fathers, who did not trust in the LORD their God. {15} They rejected his decrees and the covenant he had made with their fathers and the warnings he had given them. They followed worthless idols and themselves became worthless. They imitated the nations around them although the LORD had ordered them, "Do not do as they do," and they did the things the LORD had forbidden them to do. {16} They forsook all the commands of the LORD their God and made for themselves two idols cast in the shape of calves, and an Asherah pole. They bowed down to all the starry hosts, and they worshiped Baal. {17} They sacrificed their sons and daughters in the fire. They practiced divination and sorcery and sold themselves to do evil in the eyes of the LORD, provoking him to anger. {18} So the LORD was very angry with Israel and removed them from his presence. Only the tribe of Judah was left, {19} and even Judah did not keep the commands of the LORD their God. They followed the practices Israel had introduced. {20} Therefore the LORD rejected all the people of Israel; he afflicted them and gave them into the hands of plunderers, until he thrust them from his presence.

SENNECHARIB OF ASSYRIA THREATENS JUDAH

2 Ki 18:13-25

In the fourteenth year of King Hezekiah's reign, Sennacherib king of Assyria attacked all the fortified cities of Judah and captured them. {14} So Hezekiah king of Judah sent this message to the king of Assyria at Lachish: "I have done wrong. Withdraw from me, and I will pay whatever you demand of me." The king of Assyria exacted from Hezekiah king of Judah three hundred talents of silver and thirty talents of gold. {15} So Hezekiah gave him all the silver that was found in the temple of the LORD and in the treasuries of the royal palace. {16} At this time Hezekiah king of Judah stripped off the gold with which he had covered the doors and doorposts of the temple of the LORD, and gave it to the king of Assyria. {17} The king of Assyria sent his supreme commander, his chief officer and his field commander with a large army, from Lachish to King Hezekiah at Jerusalem. They came up to Jerusalem and stopped at the aqueduct of the Upper Pool, on the road to the Washerman's Field. {18} They called for the king; and Eliakim son of Hilkiah the palace administrator, Shebna the secretary, and Joah son of Asaph the recorder went out to them. {19} The field commander said to them, "Tell Hezekiah: "'This is what the great king, the king of Assyria, says: On what are you basing this confidence of yours? {20} You say you have strategy and military strength—but you speak only empty words. On whom are you depending, that you rebel against me? {21} Look now, you are depending on Egypt, that splintered reed of a staff, which pierces a man's hand and wounds him if he leans on it! Such is Pharaoh king of Egypt to all who depend on him. {22} And if you say to me, "We are depending on the LORD our God"—isn't he the one whose high places and altars Hezekiah removed, saying to Judah and Jerusalem, "You must worship before this altar in Jerusalem"? {23} "'Come now, make a bargain with my master, the king of Assyria: I will give you two thousand horses—if you can put riders on them! {24} How can you repulse one officer of the least of my master's officials, even though you are depending on Egypt for chariots and horsemen ? {25} Furthermore, have I come to attack and destroy this place without word from the LORD? The LORD himself told me to march against this country and destroy it.'"

ISAIAH FORESEES THE WITHDRAWAL OF SENNECHARIB

2 Ki 19:5-19

When King Hezekiah's officials came to Isaiah, {6} Isaiah said to them, "Tell your master, 'This is what the LORD says: Do not be afraid of what you have heard–those words with which the underlings of the king of Assyria have blasphemed me. {7} Listen! I am going to put such a spirit in him that when he hears a certain report, he will return to his own country, and there I will have him cut down with the sword.'" {8} When the field commander heard that the king of Assyria had left Lachish, he withdrew and found the king fighting against Libnah. {9} Now Sennacherib received a report that Tirhakah, the Cushite king <of Egypt>, was marching out to fight against him. So he again sent messengers to Hezekiah with this word: {10} "Say to Hezekiah king of Judah: Do not let the god you depend on deceive you when he says, 'Jerusalem will not be handed over to the king of Assyria.' {11} Surely you have heard what the kings of Assyria have done to all the countries, destroying them completely. And will you be delivered? {12} Did the gods of the nations that were destroyed by my forefathers deliver them: the gods of Gozan, Haran, Rezeph and the people of Eden who were in Tel Assar? {13} Where is the king of Hamath, the king of Arpad, the king of the city of Sepharvaim, or of Hena or Ivvah?" {14} Hezekiah received the letter from the messengers and read it. Then he went up to the temple of the LORD and spread it out before the LORD. {15} And Hezekiah prayed to the LORD: "O LORD, God of Israel, enthroned between the cherubim, you alone are God over all the kingdoms of the earth. You have made heaven and earth. {16} Give ear, O LORD, and hear; open your eyes, O LORD, and see; listen to the words Sennacherib has sent to insult the living God. {17} "It is true, O LORD, that the Assyrian kings have laid waste these nations and their lands. {18} They have thrown their gods into the fire and destroyed them, for they were not gods but only wood and stone, fashioned by men's hands. {19} Now, O LORD our God, deliver us from his hand, so that all kingdoms on earth may know that you alone, O LORD, are God."

2 Ki 19:35-36

That night the angel of the LORD went out and put to death a hundred and eighty-five thousand men in the Assyrian camp. When the people got up the next morning–there were all the dead bodies! {36} So Sennacherib king of Assyria broke camp and withdrew. He returned to Nineveh and stayed there.

ISAIAH FORESEES JUDAH'S CAPTIVITY IN BABYLON

2 Ki 20:1-17

In those days Hezekiah became ill and was at the point of death. The prophet Isaiah son of Amoz went to him and said, "This is what the LORD says: Put your house in order, because you are going to die; you will not recover." {2} Hezekiah turned his face to the wall and prayed to the LORD, {3} "Remember, O LORD, how I have walked before you faithfully and with wholehearted devotion and have done what is good in your eyes." And Hezekiah wept bitterly. {4} Before Isaiah had left the middle court, the word of the LORD came to him: {5} "Go back and tell Hezekiah, the leader of my people, 'This is what the LORD, the God of your father David, says: I have heard your prayer and seen your tears; I will heal you. On the third day from now you will go up to the temple of the LORD. {6} I will add fifteen years to your life. And I will deliver you and this city from the hand of the king of Assyria. I will defend this city for my sake and for the sake of my servant David.'" {7} Then Isaiah said, "Prepare a poultice of figs." They did so and applied it to the boil, and he recovered. {8} Hezekiah had asked Isaiah, "What will be the sign that the LORD will heal me and that I will go up to the temple of the LORD on the third day from now?" {9} Isaiah answered, "This is the Lord's sign to you that the LORD will do what he has promised: Shall the shadow go forward ten steps, or shall it go back ten steps?" {10} "It is a simple matter for the shadow to go forward ten steps," said Hezekiah. "Rather, have it go back ten steps." {11} Then the prophet Isaiah called upon the LORD, and the LORD made the shadow go back the ten steps it had gone down on the stairway of Ahaz. {12} At that time Merodach-Baladan son of Baladan king of Babylon sent Hezekiah letters and a gift, because he had heard of Hezekiah's illness. {13} Hezekiah received the messengers and showed them all that was in his storehouses–the silver, the gold, the spices and the fine oil–his armory and everything found among his treasures. There was nothing in his palace or in all his kingdom that Hezekiah did not show them. {14} Then Isaiah the prophet went to King Hezekiah and asked, "What did those men say, and where did they come from?" "From a distant land," Hezekiah replied. "They came from Babylon." {15} The prophet asked, "What did they see in your palace?" "They saw everything in my palace," Hezekiah said. "There is nothing among my treasures that I did not show them." {16} Then Isaiah said to Hezekiah, "Hear the word of the LORD: {17} The time will surely come when everything in your palace, and all that your fathers have stored up until this day, will be carried off to Babylon.

NEBUCHADNEZZAR OF BABYLON CAPTURES JERUSALEM

2 Ki 25:5-21

The Babylonian army pursued the king and overtook him in the plains of Jericho. All his soldiers were separated from him and scattered, {6} and he was captured. He was taken to the king of Babylon at Riblah, where sentence was pronounced on him. {7} They killed the sons of Zedekiah before his eyes. Then they put out his eyes, bound him with bronze shackles and took him to Babylon. {8} On the seventh day of the fifth month, in the nineteenth year of Nebuchadnezzar king of Babylon, Nebuzaradan commander of the imperial guard, an official of the king of Babylon, came to Jerusalem. {9} He set fire to the temple of the LORD, the royal palace and all the houses of Jerusalem. Every important building he burned down. {10} The whole Babylonian army, under the commander of the imperial guard, broke down the walls around Jerusalem. {11} Nebuzaradan the commander of the guard carried into exile the people who remained in the city, along with the rest of the populace and those who had gone over to the king of Babylon. {12} But the commander left behind some of the poorest people of the land to work the vineyards and fields. {13} The Babylonians broke up the bronze pillars, the movable stands and the bronze Sea that were at the temple of the LORD and they carried the bronze to Babylon. {14} They also took away the pots, shovels, wick trimmers, dishes and all the bronze articles used in the temple service. {15} The commander of the imperial guard took away the censers and sprinkling bowls–all that were made of pure gold or silver. {16} The bronze from the two pillars, the Sea and the movable stands, which Solomon had made for the temple of the LORD, was more than could be weighed. {17} Each pillar was twenty-seven feet high. The bronze capital on top of one pillar was four and a half feet high and was decorated with a network and pomegranates of bronze all around. The other pillar, with its network, was similar. {18} The commander of the guard took as prisoners Seraiah the chief priest, Zephaniah the priest next in rank and the three doorkeepers. {19} Of those still in the city, he took the officer in charge of the fighting men and five royal advisers. He also took the secretary who was chief officer in charge of conscripting the people of the land and sixty of his men who were found in the city. {20} Nebuzaradan the commander took them all and brought them to the king of Babylon at Riblah. {21} There at Riblah, in the land of Hamath, the king had them executed. So Judah went into captivity, away from her land.

EXILES RETURN TO JERUSALEM

Ezra 1:1-8

In the first year of Cyrus king of Persia, in order to fulfill the word of the LORD spoken by Jeremiah, the LORD moved the heart of Cyrus king of Persia to make a proclamation throughout his realm and to put it in writing: {2} "This is what Cyrus king of Persia says: "'The LORD, the God of heaven, has given me all the kingdoms of the earth and he has appointed me to build a temple for him at Jerusalem in Judah. {3} Anyone of his people among you—may his God be with him, and let him go up to Jerusalem in Judah and build the temple of the LORD, the God of Israel, the God who is in Jerusalem. {4} And the people of any place where survivors may now be living are to provide him with silver and gold, with goods and livestock, and with freewill offerings for the temple of God in Jerusalem.'" {5} Then the family heads of Judah and Benjamin, and the priests and Levites—everyone whose heart God had moved—prepared to go up and build the house of the LORD in Jerusalem. {6} All their neighbors assisted them with articles of silver and gold, with goods and livestock, and with valuable gifts, in addition to all the freewill offerings. {7} Moreover, King Cyrus brought out the articles belonging to the temple of the LORD, which Nebuchadnezzar had carried away from Jerusalem and had placed in the temple of his god. {8} Cyrus king of Persia had them brought by Mithredath the treasurer, who counted them out to Sheshbazzar the prince of Judah.

Ezra 2:64-70

The whole company numbered 42,360, {65} besides their 7,337 menservants and maidservants; and they also had 200 men and women singers. {66} They had 736 horses, 245 mules, {67} 435 camels and 6,720 donkeys. {68} When they arrived at the house of the LORD in Jerusalem, some of the heads of the families gave freewill offerings toward the rebuilding of the house of God on its site. {69} According to their ability they gave to the treasury for this work 61,000 drachmas of gold, 5,000 minas of silver and 100 priestly garments. {70} The priests, the Levites, the singers, the gatekeepers and the temple servants settled in their own towns, along with some of the other people, and the rest of the Israelites settled in their towns.

Ezra 3:1

When the seventh month came and the Israelites had settled in their towns, the people assembled as one man in Jerusalem.

THE JEWS START TO REBUILD THE TEMPLE

Ezra 3:7-4:5

Then they gave money to the masons and carpenters, and gave food and drink and oil to the people of Sidon and Tyre, so that they would bring cedar logs by sea from Lebanon to Joppa, as authorized by Cyrus king of Persia. {8} In the second month of the second year after their arrival at the house of God in Jerusalem, Zerubbabel son of Shealtiel, Jeshua son of Jozadak and the rest of their brothers (the priests and the Levites and all who had returned from the captivity to Jerusalem) began the work, appointing Levites twenty years of age and older to supervise the building of the house of the LORD. {9} Jeshua and his sons and brothers and Kadmiel and his sons (descendants of Hodaviah) and the sons of Henadad and their sons and brothers–all Levites–joined together in supervising those working on the house of God. {10} When the builders laid the foundation of the temple of the LORD, the priests in their vestments and with trumpets, and the Levites (the sons of Asaph) with cymbals, took their places to praise the LORD, as prescribed by David king of Israel. {11} With praise and thanksgiving they sang to the LORD: "He is good; his love to Israel endures forever." And all the people gave a great shout of praise to the LORD, because the foundation of the house of the LORD was laid. {12} But many of the older priests and Levites and family heads, who had seen the former temple, wept aloud when they saw the foundation of this temple being laid, while many others shouted for joy. {13} No one could distinguish the sound of the shouts of joy from the sound of weeping, because the people made so much noise. And the sound was heard far away. {4:1} When the enemies of Judah and Benjamin heard that the exiles were building a temple for the LORD, the God of Israel, {2} they came to Zerubbabel and to the heads of the families and said, "Let us help you build because, like you, we seek your God and have been sacrificing to him since the time of Esarhaddon king of Assyria, who brought us here." {3} But Zerubbabel, Jeshua and the rest of the heads of the families of Israel answered, "You have no part with us in building a temple to our God. We alone will build it for the LORD, the God of Israel, as King Cyrus, the king of Persia, commanded us." {4} Then the peoples around them set out to discourage the people of Judah and make them afraid to go on building. {5} They hired counselors to work against them and frustrate their plans during the entire reign of Cyrus king of Persia and down to the reign of Darius king of Persia.

THE JEWS APPEAL TO CYRUS' EARLIER DECREE

Ezra 5:3-17

At that time Tattenai, governor of Trans-Euphrates, and Shethar-Bozenai and their associates went to them and asked, "Who authorized you to rebuild this temple and restore this structure?" {4} They also asked, "What are the names of the men constructing this building?" {5} But the eye of their God was watching over the elders of the Jews, and they were not stopped until a report could go to Darius and his written reply be received. {6} This is a copy of the letter that Tattenai, governor of Trans-Euphrates, and Shethar-Bozenai and their associates, the officials of Trans-Euphrates, sent to King Darius. {7} The report they sent him read as follows: To King Darius: Cordial greetings. {8} The king should know that we went to the district of Judah, to the temple of the great God. The people are building it with large stones and placing the timbers in the walls. The work is being carried on with diligence and is making rapid progress under their direction. {9} We questioned the elders and asked them, "Who authorized you to rebuild this temple and restore this structure?" {10} We also asked them their names, so that we could write down the names of their leaders for your information. {11} This is the answer they gave us: "We are the servants of the God of heaven and earth, and we are rebuilding the temple that was built many years ago, one that a great king of Israel built and finished. {12} But because our fathers angered the God of heaven, he handed them over to Nebuchadnezzar the Chaldean, king of Babylon, who destroyed this temple and deported the people to Babylon. {13} "However, in the first year of Cyrus king of Babylon, King Cyrus issued a decree to rebuild this house of God. {14} He even removed from the temple of Babylon the gold and silver articles of the house of God, which Nebuchadnezzar had taken from the temple in Jerusalem and brought to the temple in Babylon. "Then King Cyrus gave them to a man named Sheshbazzar, whom he had appointed governor, {15} and he told him, 'Take these articles and go and deposit them in the temple in Jerusalem. And rebuild the house of God on its site.' {16} So this Sheshbazzar came and laid the foundations of the house of God in Jerusalem. From that day to the present it has been under construction but is not yet finished." {17} Now if it pleases the king, let a search be made in the royal archives of Babylon to see if King Cyrus did in fact issue a decree to rebuild this house of God in Jerusalem. Then let the king send us his decision in this matter.

CYRUS' DECREE IS CONFIRMED BY DARIUS; THE TEMPLE IS REBUILT

Ezra 6:2-16

A scroll was found ... and this was written on it: Memorandum: {3} In the first year of King Cyrus, the king issued a decree concerning the temple of God in Jerusalem: Let the temple be rebuilt as a place to present sacrifices, and let its foundations be laid. It is to be ninety feet high and ninety feet wide, {4} with three courses of large stones and one of timbers. The costs are to be paid by the royal treasury. {5} Also, the gold and silver articles of the house of God, which Nebuchadnezzar took from the temple in Jerusalem and brought to Babylon, are to be returned to their places in the temple in Jerusalem; they are to be deposited in the house of God. {6} Now then, Tattenai, governor of Trans-Euphrates, and Shethar-Bozenai and you, their fellow officials of that province, stay away from there. {7} Do not interfere with the work on this temple of God. Let the governor of the Jews and the Jewish elders rebuild this house of God on its site. {8} Moreover, I hereby decree what you are to do for these elders of the Jews in the construction of this house of God: The expenses of these men are to be fully paid out of the royal treasury, from the revenues of Trans-Euphrates, so that the work will not stop. {9} Whatever is needed—young bulls, rams, male lambs for burnt offerings to the God of heaven, and wheat, salt, wine and oil, as requested by the priests in Jerusalem—must be given them daily without fail, {10} so that they may offer sacrifices pleasing to the God of heaven and pray for the well-being of the king and his sons. {11} Furthermore, I decree that if anyone changes this edict, a beam is to be pulled from his house and he is to be lifted up and impaled on it. And for this crime his house is to be made a pile of rubble. {12} May God, who has caused his Name to dwell there, overthrow any king or people who lifts a hand to change this decree or to destroy this temple in Jerusalem. I Darius have decreed it. Let it be carried out with diligence. {13} Then, because of the decree King Darius had sent, Tattenai, governor of Trans-Euphrates, and Shethar-Bozenai and their associates carried it out with diligence. {14} So the elders of the Jews continued to build and prosper under the preaching of Haggai the prophet and Zechariah, a descendant of Iddo. They finished building the temple according to the command of the God of Israel and the decrees of Cyrus, Darius and Artaxerxes, kings of Persia. {15} The temple was completed on the third day of the month Adar, in the sixth year of the reign of King Darius. {16} Then the people of Israel—the priests, the Levites and the rest of the exiles—celebrated the dedication of the house of God with joy.

EZRA RETURNS TO JERUSALEM

Ezra 7:8-23a

Ezra arrived in Jerusalem in the fifth month of the seventh year of the king. {9} He had begun his journey from Babylon on the first day of the first month, and he arrived in Jerusalem on the first day of the fifth month, for the gracious hand of his God was on him. {10} For Ezra had devoted himself to the study and observance of the Law of the LORD, and to teaching its decrees and laws in Israel. {11} This is a copy of the letter King Artaxerxes had given to Ezra the priest and teacher, a man learned in matters concerning the commands and decrees of the LORD for Israel: {12} Artaxerxes, king of kings, To Ezra the priest, a teacher of the Law of the God of heaven: Greetings. {13} Now I decree that any of the Israelites in my kingdom, including priests and Levites, who wish to go to Jerusalem with you, may go. {14} You are sent by the king and his seven advisers to inquire about Judah and Jerusalem with regard to the Law of your God, which is in your hand. {15} Moreover, you are to take with you the silver and gold that the king and his advisers have freely given to the God of Israel, whose dwelling is in Jerusalem, {16} together with all the silver and gold you may obtain from the province of Babylon, as well as the freewill offerings of the people and priests for the temple of their God in Jerusalem. {17} With this money be sure to buy bulls, rams and male lambs, together with their grain offerings and drink offerings, and sacrifice them on the altar of the temple of your God in Jerusalem. {18} You and your brother Jews may then do whatever seems best with the rest of the silver and gold, in accordance with the will of your God. {19} Deliver to the God of Jerusalem all the articles entrusted to you for worship in the temple of your God. {20} And anything else needed for the temple of your God that you may have occasion to supply, you may provide from the royal treasury. {21} Now I, King Artaxerxes, order all the treasurers of Trans-Euphrates to provide with diligence whatever Ezra the priest, a teacher of the Law of the God of heaven, may ask of you– {22} up to a hundred talents of silver, a hundred cors of wheat, a hundred baths of wine, a hundred baths of olive oil, and salt without limit. {23} Whatever the God of heaven has prescribed, let it be done with diligence for the temple of the God of heaven.

EZRA DISTURBED ABOUT MIXED MARRIAGES

Ezra 9:1-12

After these things had been done, the leaders came to me and said, "The people of Israel, including the priests and the Levites, have not kept themselves separate from the neighboring peoples with their detestable practices, like those of the Canaanites, Hittites, Perizzites, Jebusites, Ammonites, Moabites, Egyptians and Amorites. {2} They have taken some of their daughters as wives for themselves and their sons, and have mingled the holy race with the peoples around them. And the leaders and officials have led the way in this unfaithfulness." {3} When I heard this, I tore my tunic and cloak, pulled hair from my head and beard and sat down appalled. {4} Then everyone who trembled at the words of the God of Israel gathered around me because of this unfaithfulness of the exiles. And I sat there appalled until the evening sacrifice. {5} Then, at the evening sacrifice, I rose from my self-abasement, with my tunic and cloak torn, and fell on my knees with my hands spread out to the LORD my God {6} and prayed: "O my God, I am too ashamed and disgraced to lift up my face to you, my God, because our sins are higher than our heads and our guilt has reached to the heavens. {7} From the days of our forefathers until now, our guilt has been great. Because of our sins, we and our kings and our priests have been subjected to the sword and captivity, to pillage and humiliation at the hand of foreign kings, as it is today. {8} "But now, for a brief moment, the LORD our God has been gracious in leaving us a remnant and giving us a firm place in his sanctuary, and so our God gives light to our eyes and a little relief in our bondage. {9} Though we are slaves, our God has not deserted us in our bondage. He has shown us kindness in the sight of the kings of Persia: He has granted us new life to rebuild the house of our God and repair its ruins, and he has given us a wall of protection in Judah and Jerusalem. {10} "But now, O our God, what can we say after this? For we have disregarded the commands {11} you gave through your servants the prophets when you said: 'The land you are entering to possess is a land polluted by the corruption of its peoples. By their detestable practices they have filled it with their impurity from one end to the other. {12} Therefore, do not give your daughters in marriage to their sons or take their daughters for your sons. Do not seek a treaty of friendship with them at any time, that you may be strong and eat the good things of the land and leave it to your children as an everlasting inheritance.'

NEHEMIAH GOES TO JERUSALEM

Neh 2:6-20

Then the king, with the queen sitting beside him, asked me, "How long will your journey take, and when will you get back?" It pleased the king to send me; so I set a time. {7} I also said to him, "If it pleases the king, may I have letters to the governors of Trans-Euphrates, so that they will provide me safe-conduct until I arrive in Judah? {8} And may I have a letter to Asaph, keeper of the king's forest, so he will give me timber to make beams for the gates of the citadel by the temple and for the city wall and for the residence I will occupy?" And because the gracious hand of my God was upon me, the king granted my requests. {9} So I went to the governors of Trans-Euphrates and gave them the king's letters. The king had also sent army officers and cavalry with me. {10} When Sanballat the Horonite and Tobiah the Ammonite official heard about this, they were very much disturbed that someone had come to promote the welfare of the Israelites. {11} I went to Jerusalem, and after staying there three days {12} I set out during the night with a few men. I had not told anyone what my God had put in my heart to do for Jerusalem. There were no mounts with me except the one I was riding on. {13} By night I went out through the Valley Gate toward the Jackal Well and the Dung Gate, examining the walls of Jerusalem, which had been broken down, and its gates, which had been destroyed by fire. {14} Then I moved on toward the Fountain Gate and the King's Pool, but there was not enough room for my mount to get through; {15} so I went up the valley by night, examining the wall. Finally, I turned back and reentered through the Valley Gate. {16} The officials did not know where I had gone or what I was doing, because as yet I had said nothing to the Jews or the priests or nobles or officials or any others who would be doing the work. {17} Then I said to them, "You see the trouble we are in: Jerusalem lies in ruins, and its gates have been burned with fire. Come, let us rebuild the wall of Jerusalem, and we will no longer be in disgrace." {18} I also told them about the gracious hand of my God upon me and what the king had said to me. They replied, "Let us start rebuilding." So they began this good work. {19} But when Sanballat the Horonite, Tobiah the Ammonite official and Geshem the Arab heard about it, they mocked and ridiculed us. "What is this you are doing?" they asked. "Are you rebelling against the king?" {20} I answered them by saying, "The God of heaven will give us success. We his servants will start rebuilding, but as for you, you have no share in Jerusalem or any claim or historic right to it."

JEWS REBUILD THE WALL WHILE UNDER ATTACK

Neh 4:1-18a

When Sanballat heard that we were rebuilding the wall, he became angry and was greatly incensed. He ridiculed the Jews, {2} and in the presence of his associates and the army of Samaria, he said, "What are those feeble Jews doing? Will they restore their wall? Will they offer sacrifices? Will they finish in a day? Can they bring the stones back to life from those heaps of rubble–burned as they are?" {3} Tobiah the Ammonite, who was at his side, said, "What they are building–if even a fox climbed up on it, he would break down their wall of stones!" {4} Hear us, O our God, for we are despised. Turn their insults back on their own heads. Give them over as plunder in a land of captivity. {5} Do not cover up their guilt or blot out their sins from your sight, for they have thrown insults in the face of the builders. {6} So we rebuilt the wall till all of it reached half its height, for the people worked with all their heart. {7} But when Sanballat, Tobiah, the Arabs, the Ammonites and the men of Ashdod heard that the repairs to Jerusalem's walls had gone ahead and that the gaps were being closed, they were very angry. {8} They all plotted together to come and fight against Jerusalem and stir up trouble against it. {9} But we prayed to our God and posted a guard day and night to meet this threat. {10} Meanwhile, the people in Judah said, "The strength of the laborers is giving out, and there is so much rubble that we cannot rebuild the wall." {11} Also our enemies said, "Before they know it or see us, we will be right there among them and will kill them and put an end to the work." {12} Then the Jews who lived near them came and told us ten times over, "Wherever you turn, they will attack us." {13} Therefore I stationed some of the people behind the lowest points of the wall at the exposed places, posting them by families, with their swords, spears and bows. {14} After I looked things over, I stood up and said to the nobles, the officials and the rest of the people, "Don't be afraid of them. Remember the Lord, who is great and awesome, and fight for your brothers, your sons and your daughters, your wives and your homes." {15} When our enemies heard that we were aware of their plot and that God had frustrated it, we all returned to the wall, each to his own work. {16} From that day on, half of my men did the work, while the other half were equipped with spears, shields, bows and armor. The officers posted themselves behind all the people of Judah {17} who were building the wall. Those who carried materials did their work with one hand and held a weapon in the other, {18} and each of the builders wore his sword at his side as he worked.

NEHEMIAH HELPS THE POOR

Neh 5:1-15

Now the men and their wives raised a great outcry against their Jewish brothers. {2} Some were saying, "We and our sons and daughters are numerous; in order for us to eat and stay alive, we must get grain." {3} Others were saying, "We are mortgaging our fields, our vineyards and our homes to get grain during the famine." {4} Still others were saying, "We have had to borrow money to pay the king's tax on our fields and vineyards. {5} Although we are of the same flesh and blood as our countrymen and though our sons are as good as theirs, yet we have to subject our sons and daughters to slavery. Some of our daughters have already been enslaved, but we are powerless, because our fields and our vineyards belong to others." {6} When I heard their outcry and these charges, I was very angry. {7} I pondered them in my mind and then accused the nobles and officials. I told them, "You are exacting usury from your own countrymen!" So I called together a large meeting to deal with them {8} and said: "As far as possible, we have bought back our Jewish brothers who were sold to the Gentiles. Now you are selling your brothers, only for them to be sold back to us!" They kept quiet, because they could find nothing to say. {9} So I continued, "What you are doing is not right. Shouldn't you walk in the fear of our God to avoid the reproach of our Gentile enemies? {10} I and my brothers and my men are also lending the people money and grain. But let the exacting of usury stop! {11} Give back to them immediately their fields, vineyards, olive groves and houses, and also the usury you are charging them—the hundredth part of the money, grain, new wine and oil." {12} "We will give it back," they said. "And we will not demand anything more from them. We will do as you say." Then I summoned the priests and made the nobles and officials take an oath to do what they had promised. {13} I also shook out the folds of my robe and said, "In this way may God shake out of his house and possessions every man who does not keep this promise. So may such a man be shaken out and emptied!" At this the whole assembly said, "Amen," and praised the LORD. And the people did as they had promised. {14} Moreover, from the twentieth year of King Artaxerxes, when I was appointed to be their governor in the land of Judah, until his thirty-second year—twelve years—neither I nor my brothers ate the food allotted to the governor. {15} But the earlier governors—those preceding me—placed a heavy burden on the people and took forty shekels of silver from them in addition to food and wine. Their assistants also lorded it over the people. But out of reverence for God I did not act like that.

THE WALL OF JERUSALEM IS REBUILT

Neh 6:1-16

When word came to Sanballat, Tobiah, Geshem the Arab and the rest of our enemies that I had rebuilt the wall and not a gap was left in it–though up to that time I had not set the doors in the gates– {2} Sanballat and Geshem sent me this message: "Come, let us meet together in one of the villages on the plain of Ono." But they were scheming to harm me; {3} so I sent messengers to them with this reply: "I am carrying on a great project and cannot go down. Why should the work stop while I leave it and go down to you?" {4} Four times they sent me the same message, and each time I gave them the same answer. {5} Then, the fifth time, Sanballat sent his aide to me with the same message, and in his hand was an unsealed letter {6} in which was written: "It is reported among the nations–and Geshem says it is true– that you and the Jews are plotting to revolt, and therefore you are building the wall. Moreover, according to these reports you are about to become their king {7} and have even appointed prophets to make this proclamation about you in Jerusalem: 'There is a king in Judah!' Now this report will get back to the king; so come, let us confer together." {8} I sent him this reply: "Nothing like what you are saying is happening; you are just making it up out of your head." {9} They were all trying to frighten us, thinking, "Their hands will get too weak for the work, and it will not be completed." <But I prayed>, "Now strengthen my hands." {10} One day I went to the house of Shemaiah son of Delaiah, the son of Mehetabel, who was shut in at his home. He said, "Let us meet in the house of God, inside the temple, and let us close the temple doors, because men are coming to kill you–by night they are coming to kill you." {11} But I said, "Should a man like me run away? Or should one like me go into the temple to save his life? I will not go!" {12} I realized that God had not sent him, but that he had prophesied against me because Tobiah and Sanballat had hired him. {13} He had been hired to intimidate me so that I would commit a sin by doing this, and then they would give me a bad name to discredit me. {14} Remember Tobiah and Sanballat, O my God, because of what they have done; remember also the prophetess Noadiah and the rest of the prophets who have been trying to intimidate me. {15} So the wall was completed on the twenty-fifth of Elul, in fifty-two days. {16} When all our enemies heard about this, all the surrounding nations were afraid and lost their self-confidence, because they realized that this work had been done with the help of our God.

EZRA, NEHEMIAH AND THE LEVITES INSTRUCT THE PEOPLE

Neh 8:1b-3

All the people assembled as one man in the square before the Water Gate. They told Ezra the scribe to bring out the Book of the Law of Moses, which the LORD had commanded for Israel. {2} So on the first day of the seventh month Ezra the priest brought the Law before the assembly, which was made up of men and women and all who were able to understand. {3} He read it aloud from daybreak till noon as he faced the square before the Water Gate in the presence of the men, women and others who could understand. And all the people listened attentively to the Book of the Law.

Neh 8:15-18

And that they should proclaim this word and spread it throughout their towns and in Jerusalem: "Go out into the hill country and bring back branches from olive and wild olive trees, and from myrtles, palms and shade trees, to make booths"–as it is written. {16} So the people went out and brought back branches and built themselves booths on their own roofs, in their courtyards, in the courts of the house of God and in the square by the Water Gate and the one by the Gate of Ephraim. {17} The whole company that had returned from exile built booths and lived in them. From the days of Joshua son of Nun until that day, the Israelites had not celebrated it like this. And their joy was very great. {18} Day after day, from the first day to the last, Ezra read from the Book of the Law of God. They celebrated the feast for seven days, and on the eighth day, in accordance with the regulation, there was an assembly.

NEHEMIAH'S FINAL INSTRUCTIONS

Neh 13:1-13

On that day the Book of Moses was read aloud in the hearing of the people and there it was found written that no Ammonite or Moabite should ever be admitted into the assembly of God, {2} because they had not met the Israelites with food and water but had hired Balaam to call a curse down on them. (Our God, however, turned the curse into a blessing.) {3} When the people heard this law, they excluded from Israel all who were of foreign descent. {4} Before this, Eliashib the priest had been put in charge of the storerooms of the house of our God. He was closely associated with Tobiah, {5} and he had provided him with a large room formerly used to store the grain offerings and incense and temple articles, and also the tithes of grain, new wine and oil prescribed for the Levites, singers and gatekeepers, as well as the contributions for the priests. {6} But while all this was going on, I was not in Jerusalem, for in the thirty-second year of Artaxerxes king of Babylon I had returned to the king. Some time later I asked his permission {7} and came back to Jerusalem. Here I learned about the evil thing Eliashib had done in providing Tobiah a room in the courts of the house of God. {8} I was greatly displeased and threw all Tobiah's household goods out of the room. {9} I gave orders to purify the rooms, and then I put back into them the equipment of the house of God, with the grain offerings and the incense. {10} I also learned that the portions assigned to the Levites had not been given to them, and that all the Levites and singers responsible for the service had gone back to their own fields. {11} So I rebuked the officials and asked them, "Why is the house of God neglected?" Then I called them together and stationed them at their posts. {12} All Judah brought the tithes of grain, new wine and oil into the storerooms. {13} I put Shelemiah the priest, Zadok the scribe, and a Levite named Pedaiah in charge of the storerooms and made Hanan son of Zaccur, the son of Mattaniah, their assistant, because these men were considered trustworthy. They were made responsible for distributing the supplies to their brothers.

Neh 13:15

In those days I saw men in Judah treading winepresses on the Sabbath and bringing in grain and loading it on donkeys, together with wine, grapes, figs and all other kinds of loads. And they were bringing all this into Jerusalem on the Sabbath. Therefore I warned them against selling food on that day.

QUEEN VASHTI IS BANISHED

Est 1:9-22

Queen Vashti also gave a banquet for the women in the royal palace of King Xerxes. {10} On the seventh day, when King Xerxes was in high spirits from wine, he commanded the seven eunuchs who served him–Mehuman, Biztha, Harbona, Bigtha, Abagtha, Zethar and Carcas–{11} to bring before him Queen Vashti, wearing her royal crown, in order to display her beauty to the people and nobles, for she was lovely to look at. {12} But when the attendants delivered the king's command, Queen Vashti refused to come. Then the king became furious and burned with anger. {13} Since it was customary for the king to consult experts in matters of law and justice, he spoke with the wise men who understood the times {14} and were closest to the king–Carshena, Shethar, Admatha, Tarshish, Meres, Marsena and Memucan, the seven nobles of Persia and Media who had special access to the king and were highest in the kingdom. {15} "According to law, what must be done to Queen Vashti?" he asked. "She has not obeyed the command of King Xerxes that the eunuchs have taken to her." {16} Then Memucan replied in the presence of the king and the nobles, "Queen Vashti has done wrong, not only against the king but also against all the nobles and the peoples of all the provinces of King Xerxes. {17} For the queen's conduct will become known to all the women, and so they will despise their husbands and say, 'King Xerxes commanded Queen Vashti to be brought before him, but she would not come.' {18} This very day the Persian and Median women of the nobility who have heard about the queen's conduct will respond to all the king's nobles in the same way. There will be no end of disrespect and discord. {19} "Therefore, if it pleases the king, let him issue a royal decree and let it be written in the laws of Persia and Media, which cannot be repealed, that Vashti is never again to enter the presence of King Xerxes. Also let the king give her royal position to someone else who is better than she. {20} Then when the king's edict is proclaimed throughout all his vast realm, all the women will respect their husbands, from the least to the greatest." {21} The king and his nobles were pleased with this advice, so the king did as Memucan proposed. {22} He sent dispatches to all parts of the kingdom, to each province in its own script and to each people in its own language, proclaiming in each people's tongue that every man should be ruler over his own household.

ESTHER BECOMES QUEEN

Est 2:5-18

Now there was in the citadel of Susa a Jew of the tribe of Benjamin, named Mordecai son of Jair, the son of Shimei, the son of Kish, {6} who had been carried into exile from Jerusalem by Nebuchadnezzar king of Babylon, among those taken captive with Jehoiachin king of Judah. {7} Mordecai had a cousin named Hadassah, whom he had brought up because she had neither father nor mother. This girl, who was also known as Esther, was lovely in form and features, and Mordecai had taken her as his own daughter when her father and mother died. {8} When the king's order and edict had been proclaimed, many girls were brought to the citadel of Susa and put under the care of Hegai. Esther also was taken to the king's palace and entrusted to Hegai, who had charge of the harem. {9} The girl pleased him and won his favor. Immediately he provided her with her beauty treatments and special food. He assigned to her seven maids selected from the king's palace and moved her and her maids into the best place in the harem. {10} Esther had not revealed her nationality and family background, because Mordecai had forbidden her to do so. {11} Every day he walked back and forth near the courtyard of the harem to find out how Esther was and what was happening to her. {12} Before a girl's turn came to go in to King Xerxes, she had to complete twelve months of beauty treatments prescribed for the women, six months with oil of myrrh and six with perfumes and cosmetics. {13} And this is how she would go to the king: Anything she wanted was given her to take with her from the harem to the king's palace. {14} In the evening she would go there and in the morning return to another part of the harem to the care of Shaashgaz, the king's eunuch who was in charge of the concubines. She would not return to the king unless he was pleased with her and summoned her by name. {15} When the turn came for Esther (the girl Mordecai had adopted, the daughter of his uncle Abihail) to go to the king, she asked for nothing other than what Hegai, the king's eunuch who was in charge of the harem, suggested. And Esther won the favor of everyone who saw her. {16} She was taken to King Xerxes in the royal residence in the tenth month, the month of Tebeth, in the seventh year of his reign. {17} Now the king was attracted to Esther more than to any of the other women, and she won his favor and approval more than any of the other virgins. So he set a royal crown on her head and made her queen instead of Vashti. {18} And the king gave a great banquet, Esther's banquet, for all his nobles and officials. He proclaimed a holiday throughout the provinces and distributed gifts with royal liberality.

MORDECAI DISCOVERS HAMAN'S PLOT

Est 3:2-15

All the royal officials at the king's gate knelt down and paid honor to Haman, for the king had commanded this concerning him. But Mordecai would not kneel down or pay him honor. {3} Then the royal officials at the king's gate asked Mordecai, "Why do you disobey the king's command?" {4} Day after day they spoke to him but he refused to comply. Therefore they told Haman about it to see whether Mordecai's behavior would be tolerated, for he had told them he was a Jew. {5} When Haman saw that Mordecai would not kneel down or pay him honor, he was enraged. {6} Yet having learned who Mordecai's people were, he scorned the idea of killing only Mordecai. Instead Haman looked for a way to destroy all Mordecai's people, the Jews, throughout the whole kingdom of Xerxes. {7} In the twelfth year of King Xerxes, in the first month, the month of Nisan, they cast the <pur> (that is, the lot) in the presence of Haman to select a day and month. And the lot fell on the twelfth month, the month of Adar. {8} Then Haman said to King Xerxes, "There is a certain people dispersed and scattered among the peoples in all the provinces of your kingdom whose customs are different from those of all other people and who do not obey the king's laws; it is not in the king's best interest to tolerate them. {9} If it pleases the king, let a decree be issued to destroy them, and I will put ten thousand talents of silver into the royal treasury for the men who carry out this business." {10} So the king took his signet ring from his finger and gave it to Haman son of Hammedatha, the Agagite, the enemy of the Jews. {11} "Keep the money," the king said to Haman, "and do with the people as you please." {12} Then on the thirteenth day of the first month the royal secretaries were summoned. They wrote out in the script of each province and in the language of each people all Haman's orders to the king's satraps, the governors of the various provinces and the nobles of the various peoples. These were written in the name of King Xerxes himself and sealed with his own ring. {13} Dispatches were sent by couriers to all the king's provinces with the order to destroy, kill and annihilate all the Jews–young and old, women and little children–on a single day, the thirteenth day of the twelfth month, the month of Adar, and to plunder their goods. {14} A copy of the text of the edict was to be issued as law in every

ESTHER PREPARES A BANQUET

Est 4:7-5:6

Mordecai told him everything that had happened to him, including the exact amount of money Haman had promised to pay into the royal treasury for the destruction of the Jews. {8} He also gave him a copy of the text of the edict for their annihilation, which had been published in Susa, to show to Esther and explain it to her, and he told him to urge her to go into the king's presence to beg for mercy and plead with him for her people. {9} Hathach went back and reported to Esther what Mordecai had said. {10} Then she instructed him to say to Mordecai, {11} "All the king's officials and the people of the royal provinces know that for any man or woman who approaches the king in the inner court without being summoned the king has but one law: that he be put to death. The only exception to this is for the king to extend the gold scepter to him and spare his life. But thirty days have passed since I was called to go to the king." {12} When Esther's words were reported to Mordecai, {13} he sent back this answer: "Do not think that because you are in the king's house you alone of all the Jews will escape. {14} For if you remain silent at this time, relief and deliverance for the Jews will arise from another place, but you and your father's family will perish. And who knows but that you have come to royal position for such a time as this?" {15} Then Esther sent this reply to Mordecai: {16} "Go, gather together all the Jews who are in Susa, and fast for me. Do not eat or drink for three days, night or day. I and my maids will fast as you do. When this is done, I will go to the king, even though it is against the law. And if I perish, I perish." {17} So Mordecai went away and carried out all of Esther's instructions. {5:1} On the third day Esther put on her royal robes and stood in the inner court of the palace, in front of the king's hall. The king was sitting on his royal throne in the hall, facing the entrance. {2} When he saw Queen Esther standing in the court, he was pleased with her and held out to her the gold scepter that was in his hand. So Esther approached and touched the tip of the scepter. {3} Then the king asked, "What is it, Queen Esther? What is your request? Even up to half the kingdom, it will be given you." {4} "If it pleases the king," replied Esther, "let the king, together with Haman, come today to a banquet I have prepared for him." {5} "Bring Haman at once," the king said, "so that we may do what Esther asks." So the king and Haman went to the banquet Esther had prepared. {6} As they were drinking wine, the king again asked Esther, "Now what is your petition? It will be given you. And what is your request? Even up to half the kingdom, it will be granted."

MORDECAI IS HONORED BY THE KING

Est 5:9-6:10

Haman went out that day happy and in high spirits. But when he saw Mordecai at the king's gate and observed that he neither rose nor showed fear in his presence, he was filled with rage against Mordecai. {10} Nevertheless, Haman restrained himself and went home. Calling together his friends and Zeresh, his wife, {11} Haman boasted to them about his vast wealth, his many sons, and all the ways the king had honored him and how he had elevated him above the other nobles and officials. {12} "And that's not all," Haman added. "I'm the only person Queen Esther invited to accompany the king to the banquet she gave. And she has invited me along with the king tomorrow. {13} But all this gives me no satisfaction as long as I see that Jew Mordecai sitting at the king's gate." {14} His wife Zeresh and all his friends said to him, "Have a gallows built, seventy-five feet high, and ask the king in the morning to have Mordecai hanged on it. Then go with the king to the dinner and be happy." This suggestion delighted Haman, and he had the gallows built. {6:1} That night the king could not sleep; so he ordered the book of the chronicles, the record of his reign, to be brought in and read to him. {2} It was found recorded there that Mordecai had exposed Bigthana and Teresh, two of the king's officers who guarded the doorway, who had conspired to assassinate King Xerxes. {3} "What honor and recognition has Mordecai received for this?" the king asked. "Nothing has been done for him," his attendants answered. {4} The king said, "Who is in the court?" Now Haman had just entered the outer court of the palace to speak to the king about hanging Mordecai on the gallows he had erected for him. {5} His attendants answered, "Haman is standing in the court." "Bring him in," the king ordered. {6} When Haman entered, the king asked him, "What should be done for the man the king delights to honor?" Now Haman thought to himself, "Who is there that the king would rather honor than me?" {7} So he answered the king, "For the man the king delights to honor, {8} have them bring a royal robe the king has worn and a horse the king has ridden, one with a royal crest placed on its head. {9} Then let the robe and horse be entrusted to one of the king's most noble princes. Let them robe the man the king delights to honor, and lead him on the horse through the city streets, proclaiming before him, 'This is what is done for the man the king delights to honor!'" {10} "Go at once," the king commanded Haman. "Get the robe and the horse and do just as you have suggested for Mordecai the Jew, who sits at the king's gate. Do not neglect anything you have recommended."

HAMAN IS HANGED, AND THE JEWS PROTECTED

Est 7:3-8:8a

Then Queen Esther answered, "If I have found favor with you, O king, and if it pleases your majesty, grant me my life–this is my petition. And spare my people–this is my request. {4} For I and my people have been sold for destruction and slaughter and annihilation. If we had merely been sold as male and female slaves, I would have kept quiet, because no such distress would justify disturbing the king." {5} King Xerxes asked Queen Esther, "Who is he? Where is the man who has dared to do such a thing?" {6} Esther said, "The adversary and enemy is this vile Haman." Then Haman was terrified before the king and queen. {7} The king got up in a rage, left his wine and went out into the palace garden. But Haman, realizing that the king had already decided his fate, stayed behind to beg Queen Esther for his life. {8} Just as the king returned from the palace garden to the banquet hall, Haman was falling on the couch where Esther was reclining. The king exclaimed, "Will he even molest the queen while she is with me in the house?" As soon as the word left the king's mouth, they covered Haman's face. {9} Then Harbona, one of the eunuchs attending the king, said, "A gallows seventy-five feet high stands by Haman's house. He had it made for Mordecai, who spoke up to help the king." The king said, "Hang him on it!" {10} So they hanged Haman on the gallows he had prepared for Mordecai. Then the king's fury subsided. {8:1} That same day King Xerxes gave Queen Esther the estate of Haman, the enemy of the Jews. And Mordecai came into the presence of the king, for Esther had told how he was related to her. {2} The king took off his signet ring, which he had reclaimed from Haman, and presented it to Mordecai. And Esther appointed him over Haman's estate. {3} Esther again pleaded with the king, falling at his feet and weeping. She begged him to put an end to the evil plan of Haman the Agagite, which he had devised against the Jews. {4} Then the king extended the gold scepter to Esther and she arose and stood before him. {5} "If it pleases the king," she said, "and if he regards me with favor and thinks it the right thing to do, and if he is pleased with me, let an order be written overruling the dispatches that Haman son of Hammedatha, the Agagite, devised and wrote to destroy the Jews in all the king's provinces. {6} For how can I bear to see disaster fall on my people? How can I bear to see the destruction of my family?" {7} King Xerxes replied to Queen Esther and to Mordecai the Jew, "Because Haman attacked the Jews, I have given his estate to Esther, and they have hanged him on the gallows. {8} Now write another decree in the king's name in behalf of the Jews as seems best to you...."

THE JEWS OBSERVE PURIM

Est 9:18-32

The Jews in Susa, however, had assembled on the thirteenth and fourteenth, and then on the fifteenth they rested and made it a day of feasting and joy. {19} That is why rural Jews–those living in villages–observe the fourteenth of the month of Adar as a day of joy and feasting, a day for giving presents to each other. {20} Mordecai recorded these events, and he sent letters to all the Jews throughout the provinces of King Xerxes, near and far, {21} to have them celebrate annually the fourteenth and fifteenth days of the month of Adar {22} as the time when the Jews got relief from their enemies, and as the month when their sorrow was turned into joy and their mourning into a day of celebration. He wrote them to observe the days as days of feasting and joy and giving presents of food to one another and gifts to the poor. {23} So the Jews agreed to continue the celebration they had begun, doing what Mordecai had written to them. {24} For Haman son of Hammedatha, the Agagite, the enemy of all the Jews, had plotted against the Jews to destroy them and had cast the <pur> (that is, the lot) for their ruin and destruction. {25} But when the plot came to the king's attention, he issued written orders that the evil scheme Haman had devised against the Jews should come back onto his own head, and that he and his sons should be hanged on the gallows. {26} (Therefore these days were called Purim, from the word <pur>.) Because of everything written in this letter and because of what they had seen and what had happened to them, {27} the Jews took it upon themselves to establish the custom that they and their descendants and all who join them should without fail observe these two days every year, in the way prescribed and at the time appointed. {28} These days should be remembered and observed in every generation by every family, and in every province and in every city. And these days of Purim should never cease to be celebrated by the Jews, nor should the memory of them die out among their descendants. {29} So Queen Esther, daughter of Abihail, along with Mordecai the Jew, wrote with full authority to confirm this second letter concerning Purim. {30} And Mordecai sent letters to all the Jews in the 127 provinces of the kingdom of Xerxes–words of goodwill and assurance– {31} to establish these days of Purim at their designated times, as Mordecai the Jew and Queen Esther had decreed for them, and as they had established for themselves and their descendants in regard to their times of fasting and lamentation. {32} Esther's decree confirmed these regulations about Purim, and it was written down in the records.

Psa 4

For the director of music. With stringed instruments. A psalm of David. Answer me when I call to you, O my righteous God. Give me relief from my distress; be merciful to me and hear my prayer. {2} How long, O men, will you turn my glory into shame ? How long will you love delusions and seek false gods ? <Selah> {3} Know that the LORD has set apart the godly for himself; the LORD will hear when I call to him. {4} In your anger do not sin; when you are on your beds, search your hearts and be silent. <Selah> {5} Offer right sacrifices and trust in the LORD. {6} Many are asking, "Who can show us any good?" Let the light of your face shine upon us, O LORD. {7} You have filled my heart with greater joy than when their grain and new wine abound. {8} I will lie down and sleep in peace, for you alone, O LORD, make me dwell in safety.

Psa 5:1-8

For the director of music. For flutes. A psalm of David. Give ear to my words, O LORD, consider my sighing. {2} Listen to my cry for help, my King and my God, for to you I pray. {3} In the morning, O LORD, you hear my voice; in the morning I lay my requests before you and wait in expectation. {4} You are not a God who takes pleasure in evil; with you the wicked cannot dwell. {5} The arrogant cannot stand in your presence; you hate all who do wrong. {6} You destroy those who tell lies; bloodthirsty and deceitful men the LORD abhors. {7} But I, by your great mercy, will come into your house; in reverence will I bow down toward your holy temple. {8} Lead me, O LORD, in your righteousness because of my enemies– make straight your way before me.

Psa 37:21-40

The wicked borrow and do not repay, but the righteous give generously; {22} those the LORD blesses will inherit the land, but those he curses will be cut off. {23} If the LORD delights in a man's way, he makes his steps firm; {24} though he stumble, he will not fall, for the LORD upholds him with his hand. {25} I was young and now I am old, yet I have never seen the righteous forsaken or their children begging bread. {26} They are always generous and lend freely; their children will be blessed. {27} Turn from evil and do good; then you will dwell in the land forever. {28} For the LORD loves the just and will not forsake his faithful ones. They will be protected forever, but the offspring of the wicked will be cut off; {29} the righteous will inherit the land and dwell in it forever. {30} The mouth of the righteous man utters wisdom, and his tongue speaks what is just. {31} The law of his God is in his heart; his feet do not slip. {32} The wicked lie in wait for the righteous, seeking their very lives; {33} but the LORD will not leave them in their power or let them be condemned when brought to trial. {34} Wait for the LORD and keep his way. He will exalt you to inherit the land; when the wicked are cut off, you will see it. {35} I have seen a wicked and ruthless man flourishing like a green tree in its native soil, {36} but he soon passed away and was no more; though I looked for him, he could not be found. {37} Consider the blameless, observe the upright; there is a future for the man of peace. {38} But all sinners will be destroyed; the future of the wicked will be cut off. {39} The salvation of the righteous comes from the LORD; he is their stronghold in time of trouble. {40} The LORD helps them and delivers them; he delivers them from the wicked and saves them, because they take refuge in him.

Psa 53

For the director of music. According to <mahalath>.A <maskil> of David. The fool says in his heart, "There is no God." They are corrupt, and their ways are vile; there is no one who does good. {2} God looks down from heaven on the sons of men to see if there are any who understand, any who seek God. {3} Everyone has turned away, they have together become corrupt; there is no one who does good, not even one. {4} Will the evildoers never learn– those who devour my people as men eat bread and who do not call on God? {5} There they were, overwhelmed with dread, where there was nothing to dread. God scattered the bones of those who attacked you; you put them to shame, for God despised them. {6} Oh, that salvation for Israel would come out of Zion! When God restores the fortunes of his people, let Jacob rejoice and Israel be glad!

Psa 54

For the director of music. With stringed instruments. A <maskil> of David. When the Ziphites had gone to Saul and said, "Is not David hiding among us?" Save me, O God, by your name; vindicate me by your might. {2} Hear my prayer, O God; listen to the words of my mouth. {3} Strangers are attacking me; ruthless men seek my life– men without regard for God. <Selah> {4} Surely God is my help; the Lord is the one who sustains me. {5} Let evil recoil on those who slander me; in your faithfulness destroy them. {6} I will sacrifice a freewill offering to you; I will praise your name, O LORD, for it is good. {7} For he has delivered me from all my troubles, and my eyes have looked in triumph on my foes.

Psa 90

A prayer of Moses the man of God. Lord, you have been our dwelling place throughout all generations. {2} Before the mountains were born or you brought forth the earth and the world, from everlasting to everlasting you are God. {3} You turn men back to dust, saying, "Return to dust, O sons of men." {4} For a thousand years in your sight are like a day that has just gone by, or like a watch in the night. {5} You sweep men away in the sleep of death; they are like the new grass of the morning– {6} though in the morning it springs up new, by evening it is dry and withered. {7} We are consumed by your anger and terrified by your indignation. {8} You have set our iniquities before you, our secret sins in the light of your presence. {9} All our days pass away under your wrath; we finish our years with a moan. {10} The length of our days is seventy years– or eighty, if we have the strength; yet their span is but trouble and sorrow, for they quickly pass, and we fly away. {11} Who knows the power of your anger? For your wrath is as great as the fear that is due you. {12} Teach us to number our days aright, that we may gain a heart of wisdom. {13} Relent, O LORD! How long will it be? Have compassion on your servants. {14} Satisfy us in the morning with your unfailing love, that we may sing for joy and be glad all our days. {15} Make us glad for as many days as you have afflicted us, for as many years as we have seen trouble. {16} May your deeds be shown to your servants, your splendor to their children. {17} May the favor of the Lord our God rest upon us; establish the work of our hands for us– yes, establish the work of our hands.

Prov 3:1-14

My son, do not forget my teaching, but keep my commands in your heart, {2} for they will prolong your life many years and bring you prosperity. {3} Let love and faithfulness never leave you; bind them around your neck, write them on the tablet of your heart. {4} Then you will win favor and a good name in the sight of God and man. {5} Trust in the LORD with all your heart and lean not on your own understanding; {6} in all your ways acknowledge him, and he will make your paths straight. {7} Do not be wise in your own eyes; fear the LORD and shun evil. {8} This will bring health to your body and nourishment to your bones. {9} Honor the LORD with your wealth, with the firstfruits of all your crops; {10} then your barns will be filled to overflowing, and your vats will brim over with new wine. {11} My son, do not despise the Lord's discipline and do not resent his rebuke, {12} because the LORD disciplines those he loves, as a father the son he delights in. {13} Blessed is the man who finds wisdom, the man who gains understanding, {14} for she is more profitable than silver and yields better returns than gold.

Prov 3:27-29

Do not withhold good from those who deserve it, when it is in your power to act. {28} Do not say to your neighbor, "Come back later; I'll give it tomorrow"– when you now have it with you. {29} Do not plot harm against your neighbor, who lives trustfully near you.

Prov 17:1

Better a dry crust with peace and quiet than a house full of feasting, with strife.

Prov 17:5-6

He who mocks the poor shows contempt for their Maker; whoever gloats over disaster will not go unpunished. {6} Children's children are a crown to the aged, and parents are the pride of their children.

Prov 17:9-10

He who covers over an offense promotes love, but whoever repeats the matter separates close friends. {10} A rebuke impresses a man of discernment more than a hundred lashes a fool.

Prov 17:12-16

Better to meet a bear robbed of her cubs than a fool in his folly. {13} If a man pays back evil for good, evil will never leave his house. {14} Starting a quarrel is like breaching a dam; so drop the matter before a dispute breaks out. {15} Acquitting the guilty and condemning the innocent– the LORD detests them both. {16} Of what use is money in the hand of a fool, since he has no desire to get wisdom?

GOD COMMISSIONS ISAIAH

Isa 6:1-12

In the year that King Uzziah died, I saw the Lord seated on a throne, high and exalted, and the train of his robe filled the temple. {2} Above him were seraphs, each with six wings: With two wings they covered their faces, with two they covered their feet, and with two they were flying. {3} And they were calling to one another: "Holy, holy, holy is the LORD Almighty; the whole earth is full of his glory." {4} At the sound of their voices the doorposts and thresholds shook and the temple was filled with smoke. {5} "Woe to me!" I cried. "I am ruined! For I am a man of unclean lips, and I live among a people of unclean lips, and my eyes have seen the King, the LORD Almighty." {6} Then one of the seraphs flew to me with a live coal in his hand, which he had taken with tongs from the altar. {7} With it he touched my mouth and said, "See, this has touched your lips; your guilt is taken away and your sin atoned for." {8} Then I heard the voice of the Lord saying, "Whom shall I send? And who will go for us?" And I said, "Here am I. Send me!" {9} He said, "Go and tell this people: "'Be ever hearing, but never understanding; be ever seeing, but never perceiving.' {10} Make the heart of this people calloused; make their ears dull and close their eyes. Otherwise they might see with their eyes, hear with their ears, understand with their hearts, and turn and be healed." {11} Then I said, "For how long, O Lord?" And he answered: "Until the cities lie ruined and without inhabitant, until the houses are left deserted and the fields ruined and ravaged, {12} until the LORD has sent everyone far away and the land is utterly forsaken.

Isa 8:5-8

The LORD spoke to me again: {6} "Because this people has rejected the gently flowing waters of Shiloah and rejoices over Rezin and the son of Remaliah, {7} therefore the Lord is about to bring against them the mighty floodwaters of the River – the king of Assyria with all his pomp. It will overflow all its channels, run over all its banks {8} and sweep on into Judah, swirling over it, passing through it and reaching up to the neck. Its outspread wings will cover the breadth of your land, O Immanuel!"

THE PROMISE OF THE SAVIOR

Isa 8:18-9:7

Here am I, and the children the LORD has given me. We are signs and symbols in Israel from the LORD Almighty, who dwells on Mount Zion. {19} When men tell you to consult mediums and spiritists, who whisper and mutter, should not a people inquire of their God? Why consult the dead on behalf of the living? {20} To the law and to the testimony! If they do not speak according to this word, they have no light of dawn. {21} Distressed and hungry, they will roam through the land; when they are famished, they will become enraged and, looking upward, will curse their king and their God. {22} Then they will look toward the earth and see only distress and darkness and fearful gloom, and they will be thrust into utter darkness.

{9:1} Nevertheless, there will be no more gloom for those who were in distress. In the past he humbled the land of Zebulun and the land of Naphtali, but in the future he will honor Galilee of the Gentiles, by the way of the sea, along the Jordan– {2} The people walking in darkness have seen a great light; on those living in the land of the shadow of death a light has dawned. {3} You have enlarged the nation and increased their joy; they rejoice before you as people rejoice at the harvest, as men rejoice when dividing the plunder. {4} For as in the day of Midian's defeat, you have shattered the yoke that burdens them, the bar across their shoulders, the rod of their oppressor. {5} Every warrior's boot used in battle and every garment rolled in blood will be destined for burning, will be fuel for the fire. {6} For to us a child is born, to us a son is given, and the government will be on his shoulders. And he will be called Wonderful Counselor, Mighty God, Everlasting Father, Prince of Peace. {7} Of the increase of his government and peace there will be no end. He will reign on David's throne and over his kingdom, establishing and upholding it with justice and righteousness from that time on and forever. The zeal of the LORD Almighty will accomplish this.

WOE TO ASSYRIA

Isa 10:5-19

"Woe to the Assyrian, the rod of my anger, in whose hand is the club of my wrath! {6} I send him against a godless nation, I dispatch him against a people who anger me, to seize loot and snatch plunder, and to trample them down like mud in the streets. {7} But this is not what he intends, this is not what he has in mind; his purpose is to destroy, to put an end to many nations. {8} 'Are not my commanders all kings?' he says. {9} 'Has not Calno fared like Carchemish? Is not Hamath like Arpad, and Samaria like Damascus? {10} As my hand seized the kingdoms of the idols, kingdoms whose images excelled those of Jerusalem and Samaria– {11} shall I not deal with Jerusalem and her images as I dealt with Samaria and her idols?'" {12} When the Lord has finished all his work against Mount Zion and Jerusalem, he will say, "I will punish the king of Assyria for the willful pride of his heart and the haughty look in his eyes. {13} For he says: "'By the strength of my hand I have done this, and by my wisdom, because I have understanding. I removed the boundaries of nations, I plundered their treasures; like a mighty one I subdued their kings. {14} As one reaches into a nest, so my hand reached for the wealth of the nations; as men gather abandoned eggs, so I gathered all the countries; not one flapped a wing, or opened its mouth to chirp.'" {15} Does the ax raise itself above him who swings it, or the saw boast against him who uses it? As if a rod were to wield him who lifts it up, or a club brandish him who is not wood! {16} Therefore, the Lord, the LORD Almighty, will send a wasting disease upon his sturdy warriors; under his pomp a fire will be kindled like a blazing flame. {17} The Light of Israel will become a fire, their Holy One a flame; in a single day it will burn and consume his thorns and his briers. {18} The splendor of his forests and fertile fields it will completely destroy, as when a sick man wastes away. {19} And the remaining trees of his forests will be so few that a child could write them down.

A REMNANT OF ISRAEL WILL TRUST IN GOD

Isa 10:20-25

In that day the remnant of Israel, the survivors of the house of Jacob, will no longer rely on him who struck them down but will truly rely on the LORD, the Holy One of Israel. {21} A remnant will return, a remnant of Jacob will return to the Mighty God. {22} Though your people, O Israel, be like the sand by the sea, only a remnant will return. Destruction has been decreed, overwhelming and righteous. {23} The Lord, the LORD Almighty, will carry out the destruction decreed upon the whole land. {24} Therefore, this is what the Lord, the LORD Almighty, says: "O my people who live in Zion, do not be afraid of the Assyrians, who beat you with a rod and lift up a club against you, as Egypt did. {25} Very soon my anger against you will end and my wrath will be directed to their destruction."

Isa 11:1-11

A shoot will come up from the stump of Jesse; from his roots a Branch will bear fruit. {2} The Spirit of the LORD will rest on him– the Spirit of wisdom and of understanding, the Spirit of counsel and of power, the Spirit of knowledge and of the fear of the LORD– {3} and he will delight in the fear of the LORD. He will not judge by what he sees with his eyes, or decide by what he hears with his ears; {4} but with righteousness he will judge the needy, with justice he will give decisions for the poor of the earth. He will strike the earth with the rod of his mouth; with the breath of his lips he will slay the wicked. {5} Righteousness will be his belt and faithfulness the sash around his waist. {6} The wolf will live with the lamb, the leopard will lie down with the goat, the calf and the lion and the yearling together; and a little child will lead them. {7} The cow will feed with the bear, their young will lie down together, and the lion will eat straw like the ox. {8} The infant will play near the hole of the cobra, and the young child put his hand into the viper's nest. {9} They will neither harm nor destroy on all my holy mountain, for the earth will be full of the knowledge of the LORD as the waters cover the sea. {10} In that day the Root of Jesse will stand as a banner for the peoples; the nations will rally to him, and his place of rest will be glorious. {11} In that day the Lord will reach out his hand a second time to reclaim the remnant that is left of his people from Assyria, from Lower Egypt, from Upper Egypt, from Cush, from Elam, from Babylonia, from Hamath and from the islands of the sea.

BABYLON TOO WILL BE DESTROYED

Isa 14:3-15

On the day the LORD gives you relief from suffering and turmoil and cruel bondage, {4} you will take up this taunt against the king of Babylon: How the oppressor has come to an end! How his fury has ended! {5} The LORD has broken the rod of the wicked, the scepter of the rulers, {6} which in anger struck down peoples with unceasing blows, and in fury subdued nations with relentless aggression. {7} All the lands are at rest and at peace; they break into singing. {8} Even the pine trees and the cedars of Lebanon exult over you and say, "Now that you have been laid low, no woodsman comes to cut us down." {9} The grave below is all astir to meet you at your coming; it rouses the spirits of the departed to greet you– all those who were leaders in the world; it makes them rise from their thrones– all those who were kings over the nations. {10} They will all respond, they will say to you, "You also have become weak, as we are; you have become like us." {11} All your pomp has been brought down to the grave, along with the noise of your harps; maggots are spread out beneath you and worms cover you. {12} How you have fallen from heaven, O morning star, son of the dawn! You have been cast down to the earth, you who once laid low the nations! {13} You said in your heart, "I will ascend to heaven; I will raise my throne above the stars of God; I will sit enthroned on the mount of assembly, on the utmost heights of the sacred mountain. {14} I will ascend above the tops of the clouds; I will make myself like the Most High." {15} But you are brought down to the grave, to the depths of the pit.

SENNECHARIB, KING OF ASSYRIA, THREATENS TO ATTACK

Isa 36:1-10
In the fourteenth year of King Hezekiah's reign, Sennacherib king of Assyria attacked all the fortified cities of Judah and captured them. {2} Then the king of Assyria sent his field commander with a large army from Lachish to King Hezekiah at Jerusalem. When the commander stopped at the aqueduct of the Upper Pool, on the road to the Washerman's Field, {3} Eliakim son of Hilkiah the palace administrator, Shebna the secretary, and Joah son of Asaph the recorder went out to him. {4} The field commander said to them, "Tell Hezekiah, "'This is what the great king, the king of Assyria, says: On what are you basing this confidence of yours? {5} You say you have strategy and military strength–but you speak only empty words. On whom are you depending, that you rebel against me? {6} Look now, you are depending on Egypt, that splintered reed of a staff, which pierces a man's hand and wounds him if he leans on it! Such is Pharaoh king of Egypt to all who depend on him. {7} And if you say to me, "We are depending on the LORD our God"– isn't he the one whose high places and altars Hezekiah removed, saying to Judah and Jerusalem, "You must worship before this altar"? {8} "'Come now, make a bargain with my master, the king of Assyria: I will give you two thousand horses–if you can put riders on them! {9} How then can you repulse one officer of the least of my master's officials, even though you are depending on Egypt for chariots and horsemen? {10} Furthermore, have I come to attack and destroy this land without the LORD? The LORD himself told me to march against this country and destroy it.'"

Isa 37:14-20
Hezekiah received the letter from the messengers and read it. Then he went up to the temple of the LORD and spread it out before the LORD. {15} And Hezekiah prayed to the LORD: {16} "O LORD Almighty, God of Israel, enthroned between the cherubim, you alone are God over all the kingdoms of the earth. You have made heaven and earth. {17} Give ear, O LORD, and hear; open your eyes, O LORD, and see; listen to all the words Sennacherib has sent to insult the living God. {18} "It is true, O LORD, that the Assyrian kings have laid waste all these peoples and their lands. {19} They have thrown their gods into the fire and destroyed them, for they were not gods but only wood and stone, fashioned by human hands. {20} Now, O LORD our God, deliver us from his hand, so that all kingdoms on earth may know that you alone, O LORD, are God."

HEZEKIAH'S LIFE PROLONGED

Isa 38:1-19

In those days Hezekiah became ill and was at the point of death. The prophet Isaiah son of Amoz went to him and said, "This is what the LORD says: Put your house in order, because you are going to die; you will not recover." {2} Hezekiah turned his face to the wall and prayed to the LORD, {3} "Remember, O LORD, how I have walked before you faithfully and with wholehearted devotion and have done what is good in your eyes." And Hezekiah wept bitterly. {4} Then the word of the LORD came to Isaiah: {5} "Go and tell Hezekiah, 'This is what the LORD, the God of your father David, says: I have heard your prayer and seen your tears; I will add fifteen years to your life. {6} And I will deliver you and this city from the hand of the king of Assyria. I will defend this city. {7} "'This is the Lord's sign to you that the LORD will do what he has promised: {8} I will make the shadow cast by the sun go back the ten steps it has gone down on the stairway of Ahaz.'" So the sunlight went back the ten steps it had gone down. {9} A writing of Hezekiah king of Judah after his illness and recovery: {10} I said, "In the prime of my life must I go through the gates of death and be robbed of the rest of my years?" {11} I said, "I will not again see the LORD, the LORD, in the land of the living; no longer will I look on mankind, or be with those who now dwell in this world. {12} Like a shepherd's tent my house has been pulled down and taken from me. Like a weaver I have rolled up my life, and he has cut me off from the loom; day and night you made an end of me. {13} I waited patiently till dawn, but like a lion he broke all my bones; day and night you made an end of me. {14} I cried like a swift or thrush, I moaned like a mourning dove. My eyes grew weak as I looked to the heavens. I am troubled; O Lord, come to my aid!" {15} But what can I say? He has spoken to me, and he himself has done this. I will walk humbly all my years because of this anguish of my soul. {16} Lord, by such things men live; and my spirit finds life in them too. You restored me to health and let me live. {17} Surely it was for my benefit that I suffered such anguish. In your love you kept me from the pit of destruction; you have put all my sins behind your back. {18} For the grave cannot praise you, death cannot sing your praise; those who go down to the pit cannot hope for your faithfulness. {19} The living, the living–they praise you, as I am doing today; fathers tell their children about your faithfulness.

THE MESSIAH WILL COME IN SACRIFICE

Isa 53:1-12

Who has believed our message and to whom has the arm of the LORD been revealed? {2} He grew up before him like a tender shoot, and like a root out of dry ground. He had no beauty or majesty to attract us to him, nothing in his appearance that we should desire him. {3} He was despised and rejected by men, a man of sorrows, and familiar with suffering. Like one from whom men hide their faces he was despised, and we esteemed him not. {4} Surely he took up our infirmities and carried our sorrows, yet we considered him stricken by God, smitten by him, and afflicted. {5} But he was pierced for our transgressions, he was crushed for our iniquities; the punishment that brought us peace was upon him, and by his wounds we are healed. {6} We all, like sheep, have gone astray, each of us has turned to his own way; and the LORD has laid on him the iniquity of us all. {7} He was oppressed and afflicted, yet he did not open his mouth; he was led like a lamb to the slaughter, and as a sheep before her shearers is silent, so he did not open his mouth. {8} By oppression and judgment he was taken away. And who can speak of his descendants? For he was cut off from the land of the living; for the transgression of my people he was stricken. {9} He was assigned a grave with the wicked, and with the rich in his death, though he had done no violence, nor was any deceit in his mouth. {10} Yet it was the Lord's will to crush him and cause him to suffer, and though the LORD makes his life a guilt offering, he will see his offspring and prolong his days, and the will of the LORD will prosper in his hand. {11} After the suffering of his soul, he will see the light <of life> and be satisfied ; by his knowledge my righteous servant will justify many, and he will bear their iniquities. {12} Therefore I will give him a portion among the great, and he will divide the spoils with the strong, because he poured out his life unto death, and was numbered with the transgressors. For he bore the sin of many, and made intercession for the transgressors.

JEREMIAH IS CALLED TO PROPHESY

Jer 1:1-19

The words of Jeremiah son of Hilkiah, one of the priests at Anathoth in the territory of Benjamin. {2} The word of the LORD came to him in the thirteenth year of the reign of Josiah son of Amon king of Judah, {3} and through the reign of Jehoiakim son of Josiah king of Judah, down to the fifth month of the eleventh year of Zedekiah son of Josiah king of Judah, when the people of Jerusalem went into exile. {4} The word of the LORD came to me, saying, {5} "Before I formed you in the womb I knew you, before you were born I set you apart; I appointed you as a prophet to the nations." {6} "Ah, Sovereign LORD," I said, "I do not know how to speak; I am only a child." {7} But the LORD said to me, "Do not say, 'I am only a child.' You must go to everyone I send you to and say whatever I command you. {8} Do not be afraid of them, for I am with you and will rescue you," declares the LORD. {9} Then the LORD reached out his hand and touched my mouth and said to me, "Now, I have put my words in your mouth. {10} See, today I appoint you over nations and kingdoms to uproot and tear down, to destroy and overthrow, to build and to plant." {11} The word of the LORD came to me: "What do you see, Jeremiah?" "I see the branch of an almond tree," I replied. {12} The LORD said to me, "You have seen correctly, for I am watching to see that my word is fulfilled." {13} The word of the LORD came to me again: "What do you see?" "I see a boiling pot, tilting away from the north," I answered. {14} The LORD said to me, "From the north disaster will be poured out on all who live in the land. {15} I am about to summon all the peoples of the northern kingdoms," declares the LORD. "Their kings will come and set up their thrones in the entrance of the gates of Jerusalem; they will come against all her surrounding walls and against all the towns of Judah. {16} I will pronounce my judgments on my people because of their wickedness in forsaking me, in burning incense to other gods and in worshiping what their hands have made. {17} "Get yourself ready! Stand up and say to them whatever I command you. Do not be terrified by them, or I will terrify you before them. {18} Today I have made you a fortified city, an iron pillar and a bronze wall to stand against the whole land–against the kings of Judah, its officials, its priests and the people of the land. {19} They will fight against you but will not overcome you, for I am with you and will rescue you," declares the LORD.

ISRAEL HAS TURNED AWAY FROM GOD

Jer 2:13-26a

"My people have committed two sins: They have forsaken me, the spring of living water, and have dug their own cisterns, broken cisterns that cannot hold water. {14} Is Israel a servant, a slave by birth? Why then has he become plunder? {15} Lions have roared; they have growled at him. They have laid waste his land; his towns are burned and deserted. {16} Also, the men of Memphis and Tahpanhes have shaved the crown of your head. {17} Have you not brought this on yourselves by forsaking the LORD your God when he led you in the way? {18} Now why go to Egypt to drink water from the Shihor ? And why go to Assyria to drink water from the River ? {19} Your wickedness will punish you; your backsliding will rebuke you. Consider then and realize how evil and bitter it is for you when you forsake the LORD your God and have no awe of me," declares the Lord, the LORD Almighty. {20} "Long ago you broke off your yoke and tore off your bonds; you said, 'I will not serve you!' Indeed, on every high hill and under every spreading tree you lay down as a prostitute. {21} I had planted you like a choice vine of sound and reliable stock. How then did you turn against me into a corrupt, wild vine? {22} Although you wash yourself with soda and use an abundance of soap, the stain of your guilt is still before me," declares the Sovereign LORD. {23} "How can you say, 'I am not defiled; I have not run after the Baals'? See how you behaved in the valley; consider what you have done. You are a swift she-camel running here and there, {24} a wild donkey accustomed to the desert, sniffing the wind in her craving– in her heat who can restrain her? Any males that pursue her need not tire themselves; at mating time they will find her. {25} Do not run until your feet are bare and your throat is dry. But you said, 'It's no use! I love foreign gods, and I must go after them.' {26} "As a thief is disgraced when he is caught, so the house of Israel is disgraced– they, their kings and their officials, their priests and their prophets.

A

A

BOTH ISRAEL AND JUDAH HAVE BEEN UNFAITHFUL

Jer 3:6-20

During the reign of King Josiah, the LORD said to me, "Have you seen what faithless Israel has done? She has gone up on every high hill and under every spreading tree and has committed adultery there. {7} I thought that after she had done all this she would return to me but she did not, and her unfaithful sister Judah saw it. {8} I gave faithless Israel her certificate of divorce and sent her away because of all her adulteries. Yet I saw that her unfaithful sister Judah had no fear; she also went out and committed adultery. {9} Because Israel's immorality mattered so little to her, she defiled the land and committed adultery with stone and wood. {10} In spite of all this, her unfaithful sister Judah did not return to me with all her heart, but only in pretense," declares the LORD. {11} The LORD said to me, "Faithless Israel is more righteous than unfaithful Judah. {12} Go, proclaim this message toward the north: "'Return, faithless Israel,' declares the LORD, 'I will frown on you no longer, for I am merciful,' declares the LORD, 'I will not be angry forever. {13} Only acknowledge your guilt— you have rebelled against the LORD your God, you have scattered your favors to foreign gods under every spreading tree, and have not obeyed me,'" declares the LORD. {14} "Return, faithless people," declares the LORD, "for I am your husband. I will choose you—one from a town and two from a clan—and bring you to Zion. {15} Then I will give you shepherds after my own heart, who will lead you with knowledge and understanding. {16} In those days, when your numbers have increased greatly in the land," declares the LORD, "men will no longer say, 'The ark of the covenant of the LORD.' It will never enter their minds or be remembered; it will not be missed, nor will another one be made. {17} At that time they will call Jerusalem The Throne of the LORD, and all nations will gather in Jerusalem to honor the name of the LORD. No longer will they follow the stubbornness of their evil hearts. {18} In those days the house of Judah will join the house of Israel, and together they will come from a northern land to the land I gave your forefathers as an inheritance. {19} "I myself said, "'How gladly would I treat you like sons and give you a desirable land, the most beautiful inheritance of any nation.' I thought you would call me 'Father' and not turn away from following me. {20} But like a woman unfaithful to her husband, so you have been unfaithful to me, O house of Israel," declares the LORD.

GOD WILL HELP IF ISRAEL CHANGES ITS WAYS

Jer 7:8-26

But look, you are trusting in deceptive words that are worthless. {9} "'Will you steal and murder, commit adultery and perjury, burn incense to Baal and follow other gods you have not known, {10} and then come and stand before me in this house, which bears my Name, and say, "We are safe"–safe to do all these detestable things? {11} Has this house, which bears my Name, become a den of robbers to you? But I have been watching! declares the LORD. {12} "'Go now to the place in Shiloh where I first made a dwelling for my Name, and see what I did to it because of the wickedness of my people Israel. {13} While you were doing all these things, declares the LORD, I spoke to you again and again, but you did not listen; I called you, but you did not answer. {14} Therefore, what I did to Shiloh I will now do to the house that bears my Name, the temple you trust in, the place I gave to you and your fathers. {15} I will thrust you from my presence, just as I did all your brothers, the people of Ephraim.' {16} "So do not pray for this people nor offer any plea or petition for them; do not plead with me, for I will not listen to you. {17} Do you not see what they are doing in the towns of Judah and in the streets of Jerusalem? {18} The children gather wood, the fathers light the fire, and the women knead the dough and make cakes of bread for the Queen of Heaven. They pour out drink offerings to other gods to provoke me to anger. {19} But am I the one they are provoking? declares the LORD. Are they not rather harming themselves, to their own shame? {20} "'Therefore this is what the Sovereign LORD says: My anger and my wrath will be poured out on this place, on man and beast, on the trees of the field and on the fruit of the ground, and it will burn and not be quenched. {21} "'This is what the LORD Almighty, the God of Israel, says: Go ahead, add your burnt offerings to your other sacrifices and eat the meat yourselves! {22} For when I brought your forefathers out of Egypt and spoke to them, I did not just give them commands about burnt offerings and sacrifices, {23} but I gave them this command: Obey me, and I will be your God and you will be my people. Walk in all the ways I command you, that it may go well with you. {24} But they did not listen or pay attention; instead, they followed the stubborn inclinations of their evil hearts. They went backward and not forward. {25} From the time your forefathers left Egypt until now, day after day, again and again I sent you my servants the prophets. {26} But they did not listen to me or pay attention. They were stiff-necked and did more evil than their forefathers.'

JUDAH HAS BROKEN THE COVENANT

Jer 11:1-17a

This is the word that came to Jeremiah from the LORD: {2} "Listen to the terms of this covenant and tell them to the people of Judah and to those who live in Jerusalem. {3} Tell them that this is what the LORD, the God of Israel, says: 'Cursed is the man who does not obey the terms of this covenant– {4} the terms I commanded your forefathers when I brought them out of Egypt, out of the iron-smelting furnace.' I said, 'Obey me and do everything I command you, and you will be my people, and I will be your God. {5} Then I will fulfill the oath I swore to your forefathers, to give them a land flowing with milk and honey'–the land you possess today." I answered, "Amen, LORD." {6} The LORD said to me, "Proclaim all these words in the towns of Judah and in the streets of Jerusalem: 'Listen to the terms of this covenant and follow them. {7} From the time I brought your forefathers up from Egypt until today, I warned them again and again, saying, "Obey me." {8} But they did not listen or pay attention; instead, they followed the stubbornness of their evil hearts. So I brought on them all the curses of the covenant I had commanded them to follow but that they did not keep.'" {9} Then the LORD said to me, "There is a conspiracy among the people of Judah and those who live in Jerusalem. {10} They have returned to the sins of their forefathers, who refused to listen to my words. They have followed other gods to serve them. Both the house of Israel and the house of Judah have broken the covenant I made with their forefathers. {11} Therefore this is what the LORD says: 'I will bring on them a disaster they cannot escape. Although they cry out to me, I will not listen to them. {12} The towns of Judah and the people of Jerusalem will go and cry out to the gods to whom they burn incense, but they will not help them at all when disaster strikes. {13} You have as many gods as you have towns, O Judah; and the altars you have set up to burn incense to that shameful god Baal are as many as the streets of Jerusalem.' {14} "Do not pray for this people nor offer any plea or petition for them, because I will not listen when they call to me in the time of their distress. {15} "What is my beloved doing in my temple as she works out her evil schemes with many? Can consecrated meat avert <your punishment>? When you engage in your wickedness, then you rejoice. " {16} The LORD called you a thriving olive tree with fruit beautiful in form. But with the roar of a mighty storm he will set it on fire, and its branches will be broken. {17} The LORD Almighty, who planted you, has decreed disaster for you, because the house of Israel and the house of Judah have done evil....

ZEDEKIAH SEEKS GOD'S HELP AND IS REJECTED

Jer 21:1-14

The word came to Jeremiah from the LORD when King Zedekiah sent to him Pashhur son of Malkijah and the priest Zephaniah son of Maaseiah. They said: {2} "Inquire now of the LORD for us because Nebuchadnezzar king of Babylon is attacking us. Perhaps the LORD will perform wonders for us as in times past so that he will withdraw from us." {3} But Jeremiah answered them, "Tell Zedekiah, {4} 'This is what the LORD, the God of Israel, says: I am about to turn against you the weapons of war that are in your hands, which you are using to fight the king of Babylon and the Babylonians who are outside the wall besieging you. And I will gather them inside this city. {5} I myself will fight against you with an outstretched hand and a mighty arm in anger and fury and great wrath. {6} I will strike down those who live in this city–both men and animals–and they will die of a terrible plague. {7} After that, declares the LORD, I will hand over Zedekiah king of Judah, his officials and the people in this city who survive the plague, sword and famine, to Nebuchadnezzar king of Babylon and to their enemies who seek their lives. He will put them to the sword; he will show them no mercy or pity or compassion.' {8} "Furthermore, tell the people, 'This is what the LORD says: See, I am setting before you the way of life and the way of death. {9} Whoever stays in this city will die by the sword, famine or plague. But whoever goes out and surrenders to the Babylonians who are besieging you will live; he will escape with his life. {10} I have determined to do this city harm and not good, declares the LORD. It will be given into the hands of the king of Babylon, and he will destroy it with fire.' {11} "Moreover, say to the royal house of Judah, 'Hear the word of the LORD; {12} O house of David, this is what the LORD says: "'Administer justice every morning; rescue from the hand of his oppressor the one who has been robbed, or my wrath will break out and burn like fire because of the evil you have done– burn with no one to quench it. {13} I am against you, <Jerusalem>,you who live above this valley on the rocky plateau, declares the LORD– you who say, "Who can come against us? Who can enter our refuge?" {14} I will punish you as your deeds deserve, declares the LORD. I will kindle a fire in your forests that will consume everything around you.'"

PRIESTS WANT JEREMIAH KILLED

Jer 26:5-19

And if you do not listen to the words of my servants the prophets, whom I have sent to you again and again (though you have not listened), {6} then I will make this house like Shiloh and this city an object of cursing among all the nations of the earth.'" {7} The priests, the prophets and all the people heard Jeremiah speak these words in the house of the LORD. {8} But as soon as Jeremiah finished telling all the people everything the LORD had commanded him to say, the priests, the prophets and all the people seized him and said, "You must die! {9} Why do you prophesy in the Lord's name that this house will be like Shiloh and this city will be desolate and deserted?" And all the people crowded around Jeremiah in the house of the LORD. {10} When the officials of Judah heard about these things, they went up from the royal palace to the house of the LORD and took their places at the entrance of the New Gate of the Lord's house. {11} Then the priests and the prophets said to the officials and all the people, "This man should be sentenced to death because he has prophesied against this city. You have heard it with your own ears!" {12} Then Jeremiah said to all the officials and all the people: "The LORD sent me to prophesy against this house and this city all the things you have heard. {13} Now reform your ways and your actions and obey the LORD your God. Then the LORD will relent and not bring the disaster he has pronounced against you. {14} As for me, I am in your hands; do with me whatever you think is good and right. {15} Be assured, however, that if you put me to death, you will bring the guilt of innocent blood on yourselves and on this city and on those who live in it, for in truth the LORD has sent me to you to speak all these words in your hearing." {16} Then the officials and all the people said to the priests and the prophets, "This man should not be sentenced to death! He has spoken to us in the name of the LORD our God." {17} Some of the elders of the land stepped forward and said to the entire assembly of people, {18} "Micah of Moresheth prophesied in the days of Hezekiah king of Judah. He told all the people of Judah, 'This is what the LORD Almighty says: "'Zion will be plowed like a field, Jerusalem will become a heap of rubble, the temple hill a mound overgrown with thickets.' {19} "Did Hezekiah king of Judah or anyone else in Judah put him to death? Did not Hezekiah fear the LORD and seek his favor? And did not the LORD relent, so that he did not bring the disaster he pronounced against them? We are about to bring a terrible disaster on ourselves!"

NEBUCHADNEZZAR WILL CARRY AWAY JUDAH

Jer 27:8-22

"If, however, any nation or kingdom will not serve Nebuchadnezzar king of Babylon or bow its neck under his yoke, I will punish that nation with the sword, famine and plague, declares the LORD, until I destroy it by his hand. {9} So do not listen to your prophets, your diviners, your interpreters of dreams, your mediums or your sorcerers who tell you, 'You will not serve the king of Babylon.' {10} They prophesy lies to you that will only serve to remove you far from your lands; I will banish you and you will perish. {11} But if any nation will bow its neck under the yoke of the king of Babylon and serve him, I will let that nation remain in its own land to till it and to live there, declares the LORD.'" {12} I gave the same message to Zedekiah king of Judah. I said, "Bow your neck under the yoke of the king of Babylon; serve him and his people, and you will live. {13} Why will you and your people die by the sword, famine and plague with which the LORD has threatened any nation that will not serve the king of Babylon? {14} Do not listen to the words of the prophets who say to you, 'You will not serve the king of Babylon,' for they are prophesying lies to you. {15} 'I have not sent them,' declares the LORD. 'They are prophesying lies in my name. Therefore, I will banish you and you will perish, both you and the prophets who prophesy to you.'" {16} Then I said to the priests and all these people, "This is what the LORD says: Do not listen to the prophets who say, 'Very soon now the articles from the Lord's house will be brought back from Babylon.' They are prophesying lies to you. {17} Do not listen to them. Serve the king of Babylon, and you will live. Why should this city become a ruin? {18} If they are prophets and have the word of the LORD, let them plead with the LORD Almighty that the furnishings remaining in the house of the LORD and in the palace of the king of Judah and in Jerusalem not be taken to Babylon. {19} For this is what the LORD Almighty says about the pillars, the Sea, the movable stands and the other furnishings that are left in this city, {20} which Nebuchadnezzar king of Babylon did not take away when he carried Jehoiachin son of Jehoiakim king of Judah into exile from Jerusalem to Babylon, along with all the nobles of Judah and Jerusalem– {21} yes, this is what the LORD Almighty, the God of Israel, says about the things that are left in the house of the LORD and in the palace of the king of Judah and in Jerusalem: {22} 'They will be taken to Babylon and there they will remain until the day I come for them,' declares the LORD. 'Then I will bring them back and restore them to this place.'"

BUT NEBUCHADNEZZAR'S YOKE WILL BE BROKEN

Jer 28:1-17

In the fifth month of that same year, the fourth year, early in the reign of Zedekiah king of Judah, the prophet Hananiah son of Azzur, who was from Gibeon, said to me in the house of the LORD in the presence of the priests and all the people: {2} "This is what the LORD Almighty, the God of Israel, says: 'I will break the yoke of the king of Babylon. {3} Within two years I will bring back to this place all the articles of the Lord's house that Nebuchadnezzar king of Babylon removed from here and took to Babylon. {4} I will also bring back to this place Jehoiachin son of Jehoiakim king of Judah and all the other exiles from Judah who went to Babylon,' declares the LORD, 'for I will break the yoke of the king of Babylon.'" {5} Then the prophet Jeremiah replied to the prophet Hananiah before the priests and all the people who were standing in the house of the LORD. {6} He said, "Amen! May the LORD do so! May the LORD fulfill the words you have prophesied by bringing the articles of the Lord's house and all the exiles back to this place from Babylon. {7} Nevertheless, listen to what I have to say in your hearing and in the hearing of all the people: {8} From early times the prophets who preceded you and me have prophesied war, disaster and plague against many countries and great kingdoms. {9} But the prophet who prophesies peace will be recognized as one truly sent by the LORD only if his prediction comes true." {10} Then the prophet Hananiah took the yoke off the neck of the prophet Jeremiah and broke it, {11} and he said before all the people, "This is what the LORD says: 'In the same way will I break the yoke of Nebuchadnezzar king of Babylon off the neck of all the nations within two years.'" At this, the prophet Jeremiah went on his way. {12} Shortly after the prophet Hananiah had broken the yoke off the neck of the prophet Jeremiah, the word of the LORD came to Jeremiah: {13} "Go and tell Hananiah, 'This is what the LORD says: You have broken a wooden yoke, but in its place you will get a yoke of iron. {14} This is what the LORD Almighty, the God of Israel, says: I will put an iron yoke on the necks of all these nations to make them serve Nebuchadnezzar king of Babylon, and they will serve him. I will even give him control over the wild animals.'" {15} Then the prophet Jeremiah said to Hananiah the prophet, "Listen, Hananiah! The LORD has not sent you, yet you have persuaded this nation to trust in lies. {16} Therefore, this is what the LORD says: 'I am about to remove you from the face of the earth. This very year you are going to die, because you have preached rebellion against the LORD.'" {17} In the seventh month of that same year, Hananiah the prophet died.

JEREMIAH'S LETTER TO THE ELDERS IN EXILE

Jer 29:3-19

He entrusted the letter to Elasah son of Shaphan and to Gemariah son of Hilkiah, whom Zedekiah king of Judah sent to King Nebuchadnezzar in Babylon. It said: {4} This is what the LORD Almighty, the God of Israel, says to all those I carried into exile from Jerusalem to Babylon: {5} "Build houses and settle down; plant gardens and eat what they produce. {6} Marry and have sons and daughters; find wives for your sons and give your daughters in marriage, so that they too may have sons and daughters. Increase in number there; do not decrease. {7} Also, seek the peace and prosperity of the city to which I have carried you into exile. Pray to the LORD for it, because if it prospers, you too will prosper." {8} Yes, this is what the LORD Almighty, the God of Israel, says: "Do not let the prophets and diviners among you deceive you. Do not listen to the dreams you encourage them to have. {9} They are prophesying lies to you in my name. I have not sent them," declares the LORD. {10} This is what the LORD says: "When seventy years are completed for Babylon, I will come to you and fulfill my gracious promise to bring you back to this place. {11} For I know the plans I have for you," declares the LORD, "plans to prosper you and not to harm you, plans to give you hope and a future. {12} Then you will call upon me and come and pray to me, and I will listen to you. {13} You will seek me and find me when you seek me with all your heart. {14} I will be found by you," declares the LORD, "and will bring you back from captivity. I will gather you from all the nations and places where I have banished you," declares the LORD, "and will bring you back to the place from which I carried you into exile." {15} You may say, "The LORD has raised up prophets for us in Babylon," {16} but this is what the LORD says about the king who sits on David's throne and all the people who remain in this city, your countrymen who did not go with you into exile– {17} yes, this is what the LORD Almighty says: "I will send the sword, famine and plague against them and I will make them like poor figs that are so bad they cannot be eaten. {18} I will pursue them with the sword, famine and plague and will make them abhorrent to all the kingdoms of the earth and an object of cursing and horror, of scorn and reproach, among all the nations where I drive them. {19} For they have not listened to my words," declares the LORD, "words that I sent to them again and again by my servants the prophets. And you exiles have not listened either," declares the LORD.

JEHOIAKIM BURNS JEREMIAH'S SCROLL

Jer 36:8

Baruch son of Neriah did everything Jeremiah the prophet told him to do; at the Lord's temple he read the words of the LORD from the scroll.

Jer 36:16-31a

When they heard all these words, they looked at each other in fear and said to Baruch, "We must report all these words to the king." {17} Then they asked Baruch, "Tell us, how did you come to write all this? Did Jeremiah dictate it?" {18} "Yes," Baruch replied, "he dictated all these words to me, and I wrote them in ink on the scroll." {19} Then the officials said to Baruch, "You and Jeremiah, go and hide. Don't let anyone know where you are." {20} After they put the scroll in the room of Elishama the secretary, they went to the king in the courtyard and reported everything to him. {21} The king sent Jehudi to get the scroll, and Jehudi brought it from the room of Elishama the secretary and read it to the king and all the officials standing beside him. {22} It was the ninth month and the king was sitting in the winter apartment, with a fire burning in the firepot in front of him. {23} Whenever Jehudi had read three or four columns of the scroll, the king cut them off with a scribe's knife and threw them into the firepot, until the entire scroll was burned in the fire. {24} The king and all his attendants who heard all these words showed no fear, nor did they tear their clothes. {25} Even though Elnathan, Delaiah and Gemariah urged the king not to burn the scroll, he would not listen to them. {26} Instead, the king commanded Jerahmeel, a son of the king, Seraiah son of Azriel and Shelemiah son of Abdeel to arrest Baruch the scribe and Jeremiah the prophet. But the LORD had hidden them. {27} After the king burned the scroll containing the words that Baruch had written at Jeremiah's dictation, the word of the LORD came to Jeremiah: {28} "Take another scroll and write on it all the words that were on the first scroll, which Jehoiakim king of Judah burned up. {29} Also tell Jehoiakim king of Judah, 'This is what the LORD says: You burned that scroll and said, "Why did you write on it that the king of Babylon would certainly come and destroy this land and cut off both men and animals from it?" {30} Therefore, this is what the LORD says about Jehoiakim king of Judah: He will have no one to sit on the throne of David; his body will be thrown out and exposed to the heat by day and the frost by night. {31} I will punish him and his children and his attendants for their wickedness;

JEREMIAH FORESEES THE FALL OF JERUSALEM

Jer 38:2-4

"This is what the LORD says: 'Whoever stays in this city will die by the sword, famine or plague, but whoever goes over to the Babylonians will live. He will escape with his life; he will live.' {3} And this is what the LORD says: 'This city will certainly be handed over to the army of the king of Babylon, who will capture it.'" {4} Then the officials said to the king, "This man should be put to death. He is discouraging the soldiers who are left in this city, as well as all the people, by the things he is saying to them. This man is not seeking the good of these people but their ruin."

Jer 38:14-23

Then King Zedekiah sent for Jeremiah the prophet and had him brought to the third entrance to the temple of the LORD. "I am going to ask you something," the king said to Jeremiah. "Do not hide anything from me." {15} Jeremiah said to Zedekiah, "If I give you an answer, will you not kill me? Even if I did give you counsel, you would not listen to me." {16} But King Zedekiah swore this oath secretly to Jeremiah: "As surely as the LORD lives, who has given us breath, I will neither kill you nor hand you over to those who are seeking your life." {17} Then Jeremiah said to Zedekiah, "This is what the LORD God Almighty, the God of Israel, says: 'If you surrender to the officers of the king of Babylon, your life will be spared and this city will not be burned down; you and your family will live. {18} But if you will not surrender to the officers of the king of Babylon, this city will be handed over to the Babylonians and they will burn it down; you yourself will not escape from their hands.'" {19} King Zedekiah said to Jeremiah, "I am afraid of the Jews who have gone over to the Babylonians, for the Babylonians may hand me over to them and they will mistreat me." {20} "They will not hand you over," Jeremiah replied. "Obey the LORD by doing what I tell you. Then it will go well with you, and your life will be spared. {21} But if you refuse to surrender, this is what the LORD has revealed to me: {22} All the women left in the palace of the king of Judah will be brought out to the officials of the king of Babylon. Those women will say to you: "'They misled you and overcame you– those trusted friends of yours. Your feet are sunk in the mud; your friends have deserted you.' {23} "All your wives and children will be brought out to the Babylonians. You yourself will not escape from their hands but will be captured by the king of Babylon; and this city will be burned down."

JERUSALEM IS TAKEN BY BABYLON

Jer 39:1-17a

This is how Jerusalem was taken: In the ninth year of Zedekiah king of Judah, in the tenth month, Nebuchadnezzar king of Babylon marched against Jerusalem with his whole army and laid siege to it. {2} And on the ninth day of the fourth month of Zedekiah's eleventh year, the city wall was broken through. {3} Then all the officials of the king of Babylon came and took seats in the Middle Gate: Nergal-Sharezer of Samgar, Nebo-Sarsekim a chief officer, Nergal-Sharezer a high official and all the other officials of the king of Babylon. {4} When Zedekiah king of Judah and all the soldiers saw them, they fled; they left the city at night by way of the king's garden, through the gate between the two walls, and headed toward the Arabah. {5} But the Babylonian army pursued them and overtook Zedekiah in the plains of Jericho. They captured him and took him to Nebuchadnezzar king of Babylon at Riblah in the land of Hamath, where he pronounced sentence on him. {6} There at Riblah the king of Babylon slaughtered the sons of Zedekiah before his eyes and also killed all the nobles of Judah. {7} Then he put out Zedekiah's eyes and bound him with bronze shackles to take him to Babylon. {8} The Babylonians set fire to the royal palace and the houses of the people and broke down the walls of Jerusalem. {9} Nebuzaradan commander of the imperial guard carried into exile to Babylon the people who remained in the city, along with those who had gone over to him, and the rest of the people. {10} But Nebuzaradan the commander of the guard left behind in the land of Judah some of the poor people, who owned nothing; and at that time he gave them vineyards and fields. {11} Now Nebuchadnezzar king of Babylon had given these orders about Jeremiah through Nebuzaradan commander of the imperial guard: {12} "Take him and look after him; don't harm him but do for him whatever he asks." {13} So Nebuzaradan the commander of the guard, Nebushazban a chief officer, Nergal-Sharezer a high official and all the other officers of the king of Babylon {14} sent and had Jeremiah taken out of the courtyard of the guard. They turned him over to Gedaliah son of Ahikam, the son of Shaphan, to take him back to his home. So he remained among his own people. {15} While Jeremiah had been confined in the courtyard of the guard, the word of the LORD came to him: {16} "Go and tell Ebed-Melech the Cushite, 'This is what the LORD Almighty, the God of Israel, says: I am about to fulfill my words against this city through disaster, not prosperity. At that time they will be fulfilled before your eyes. {17} But I will rescue you on that day, declares the LORD;

A REMNANT GOES TO EGYPT IN SPITE OF GOD'S WARNING

Jer 42:5-22

Then they said to Jeremiah, "May the LORD be a true and faithful witness against us if we do not act in accordance with everything the LORD your God sends you to tell us. {6} Whether it is favorable or unfavorable, we will obey the LORD our God, to whom we are sending you, so that it will go well with us, for we will obey the LORD our God." {7} Ten days later the word of the LORD came to Jeremiah. {8} So he called together Johanan son of Kareah and all the army officers who were with him and all the people from the least to the greatest. {9} He said to them, "This is what the LORD, the God of Israel, to whom you sent me to present your petition, says: {10} 'If you stay in this land, I will build you up and not tear you down; I will plant you and not uproot you, for I am grieved over the disaster I have inflicted on you. {11} Do not be afraid of the king of Babylon, whom you now fear. Do not be afraid of him, declares the LORD, for I am with you and will save you and deliver you from his hands. {12} I will show you compassion so that he will have compassion on you and restore you to your land.' {13} "However, if you say, 'We will not stay in this land,' and so disobey the LORD your God, {14} and if you say, 'No, we will go and live in Egypt, where we will not see war or hear the trumpet or be hungry for bread,' {15} then hear the word of the LORD, O remnant of Judah. This is what the LORD Almighty, the God of Israel, says: 'If you are determined to go to Egypt and you do go to settle there, {16} then the sword you fear will overtake you there, and the famine you dread will follow you into Egypt, and there you will die. {17} Indeed, all who are determined to go to Egypt to settle there will die by the sword, famine and plague; not one of them will survive or escape the disaster I will bring on them.' {18} This is what the LORD Almighty, the God of Israel, says: 'As my anger and wrath have been poured out on those who lived in Jerusalem, so will my wrath be poured out on you when you go to Egypt. You will be an object of cursing and horror, of condemnation and reproach; you will never see this place again.' {19} "O remnant of Judah, the LORD has told you, 'Do not go to Egypt.' Be sure of this: I warn you today {20} that you made a fatal mistake when you sent me to the LORD your God and said, 'Pray to the LORD our God for us; tell us everything he says and we will do it.' {21} I have told you today, but you still have not obeyed the LORD your God in all he sent me to tell you. {22} So now, be sure of this: You will die by the sword, famine and plague in the place where you want to go to settle."

THE REMNANT IN EGYPT TO BE DESTROYED

Jer 44:14-27a

None of the remnant of Judah who have gone to live in Egypt will escape or survive to return to the land of Judah, to which they long to return and live; none will return except a few fugitives." {15} Then all the men who knew that their wives were burning incense to other gods, along with all the women who were present–a large assembly–and all the people living in Lower and Upper Egypt, said to Jeremiah, {16} "We will not listen to the message you have spoken to us in the name of the LORD! {17} We will certainly do everything we said we would: We will burn incense to the Queen of Heaven and will pour out drink offerings to her just as we and our fathers, our kings and our officials did in the towns of Judah and in the streets of Jerusalem. At that time we had plenty of food and were well off and suffered no harm. {18} But ever since we stopped burning incense to the Queen of Heaven and pouring out drink offerings to her, we have had nothing and have been perishing by sword and famine." {19} The women added, "When we burned incense to the Queen of Heaven and poured out drink offerings to her, did not our husbands know that we were making cakes like her image and pouring out drink offerings to her?" {20} Then Jeremiah said to all the people, both men and women, who were answering him, {21} "Did not the LORD remember and think about the incense burned in the towns of Judah and the streets of Jerusalem by you and your fathers, your kings and your officials and the people of the land? {22} When the LORD could no longer endure your wicked actions and the detestable things you did, your land became an object of cursing and a desolate waste without inhabitants, as it is today. {23} Because you have burned incense and have sinned against the LORD and have not obeyed him or followed his law or his decrees or his stipulations, this disaster has come upon you, as you now see." {24} Then Jeremiah said to all the people, including the women, "Hear the word of the LORD, all you people of Judah in Egypt. {25} This is what the LORD Almighty, the God of Israel, says: You and your wives have shown by your actions what you promised when you said, 'We will certainly carry out the vows we made to burn incense and pour out drink offerings to the Queen of Heaven.' "Go ahead then, do what you promised! Keep your vows! {26} But hear the word of the LORD, all Jews living in Egypt: 'I swear by my great name,' says the LORD, 'that no one from Judah living anywhere in Egypt will ever again invoke my name or swear, "As surely as the Sovereign LORD lives." {27} For I am watching over them for harm, not for good; the Jews in Egypt will perish by sword and famine....

AND BABYLON WILL ALSO BE DESTROYED

Jer 51:49-64

"Babylon must fall because of Israel's slain, just as the slain in all the earth have fallen because of Babylon. {50} You who have escaped the sword, leave and do not linger! Remember the LORD in a distant land, and think on Jerusalem." {51} "We are disgraced, for we have been insulted and shame covers our faces, because foreigners have entered the holy places of the Lord's house." {52} "But days are coming," declares the LORD, "when I will punish her idols, and throughout her land the wounded will groan. {53} Even if Babylon reaches the sky and fortifies her lofty stronghold, I will send destroyers against her," declares the LORD. {54} "The sound of a cry comes from Babylon, the sound of great destruction from the land of the Babylonians. {55} The LORD will destroy Babylon; he will silence her noisy din. Waves <of enemies> will rage like great waters; the roar of their voices will resound. {56} A destroyer will come against Babylon; her warriors will be captured, and their bows will be broken. For the LORD is a God of retribution; he will repay in full. {57} I will make her officials and wise men drunk, her governors, officers and warriors as well; they will sleep forever and not awake," declares the King, whose name is the LORD Almighty. {58} This is what the LORD Almighty says: "Babylon's thick wall will be leveled and her high gates set on fire; the peoples exhaust themselves for nothing, the nations' labor is only fuel for the flames." {59} This is the message Jeremiah gave to the staff officer Seraiah son of Neriah, the son of Mahseiah, when he went to Babylon with Zedekiah king of Judah in the fourth year of his reign. {60} Jeremiah had written on a scroll about all the disasters that would come upon Babylon–all that had been recorded concerning Babylon. {61} He said to Seraiah, "When you get to Babylon, see that you read all these words aloud. {62} Then say, 'O LORD, you have said you will destroy this place, so that neither man nor animal will live in it; it will be desolate forever.' {63} When you finish reading this scroll, tie a stone to it and throw it into the Euphrates. {64} Then say, 'So will Babylon sink to rise no more because of the disaster I will bring upon her. And her people will fall.'" The words of Jeremiah end here.

JERUSALEM IS DESTROYED

Jer 52:4-16

So in the ninth year of Zedekiah's reign, on the tenth day of the tenth month, Nebuchadnezzar king of Babylon marched against Jerusalem with his whole army. They camped outside the city and built siege works all around it. {5} The city was kept under siege until the eleventh year of King Zedekiah. {6} By the ninth day of the fourth month the famine in the city had become so severe that there was no food for the people to eat. {7} Then the city wall was broken through, and the whole army fled. They left the city at night through the gate between the two walls near the king's garden, though the Babylonians were surrounding the city. They fled toward the Arabah, {8} but the Babylonian army pursued King Zedekiah and overtook him in the plains of Jericho. All his soldiers were separated from him and scattered, {9} and he was captured. He was taken to the king of Babylon at Riblah in the land of Hamath, where he pronounced sentence on him. {10} There at Riblah the king of Babylon slaughtered the sons of Zedekiah before his eyes; he also killed all the officials of Judah. {11} Then he put out Zedekiah's eyes, bound him with bronze shackles and took him to Babylon, where he put him in prison till the day of his death. {12} On the tenth day of the fifth month, in the nineteenth year of Nebuchadnezzar king of Babylon, Nebuzaradan commander of the imperial guard, who served the king of Babylon, came to Jerusalem. {13} He set fire to the temple of the LORD, the royal palace and all the houses of Jerusalem. Every important building he burned down. {14} The whole Babylonian army under the commander of the imperial guard broke down all the walls around Jerusalem. {15} Nebuzaradan the commander of the guard carried into exile some of the poorest people and those who remained in the city, along with the rest of the craftsmen and those who had gone over to the king of Babylon. {16} But Nebuzaradan left behind the rest of the poorest people of the land to work the vineyards and fields.

Jer 52:27b-30

So Judah went into captivity, away from her land. {28} This is the number of the people Nebuchadnezzar carried into exile: in the seventh year, 3,023 Jews; {29} in Nebuchadnezzar's eighteenth year, 832 people from Jerusalem; {30} in his twenty-third year, 745 Jews taken into exile by Nebuzaradan the commander of the imperial guard. There were 4,600 people in all.

GOD'S GLORY APPEARS TO EZEKIEL

Ezek 1:1-3

In the thirtieth year, in the fourth month on the fifth day, while I was among the exiles by the Kebar River, the heavens were opened and I saw visions of God. {2} On the fifth of the month–it was the fifth year of the exile of King Jehoiachin– {3} the word of the LORD came to Ezekiel the priest, the son of Buzi, by the Kebar River in the land of the Babylonians. There the hand of the LORD was upon him.

Ezek 1:19-28

When the living creatures moved, the wheels beside them moved; and when the living creatures rose from the ground, the wheels also rose. {20} Wherever the spirit would go, they would go, and the wheels would rise along with them, because the spirit of the living creatures was in the wheels. {21} When the creatures moved, they also moved; when the creatures stood still, they also stood still; and when the creatures rose from the ground, the wheels rose along with them, because the spirit of the living creatures was in the wheels. {22} Spread out above the heads of the living creatures was what looked like an expanse, sparkling like ice, and awesome. {23} Under the expanse their wings were stretched out one toward the other, and each had two wings covering its body. {24} When the creatures moved, I heard the sound of their wings, like the roar of rushing waters, like the voice of the Almighty, like the tumult of an army. When they stood still, they lowered their wings. {25} Then there came a voice from above the expanse over their heads as they stood with lowered wings. {26} Above the expanse over their heads was what looked like a throne of sapphire, and high above on the throne was a figure like that of a man. {27} I saw that from what appeared to be his waist up he looked like glowing metal, as if full of fire, and that from there down he looked like fire; and brilliant light surrounded him. {28} Like the appearance of a rainbow in the clouds on a rainy day, so was the radiance around him. This was the appearance of the likeness of the glory of the LORD. When I saw it, I fell facedown, and I heard the voice of one speaking.

EZEKIEL IS ASKED TO EAT THE SCROLL AND WARN ISRAEL

Ezek 3:3-19

Then he said to me, "Son of man, eat this scroll I am giving you and fill your stomach with it." So I ate it, and it tasted as sweet as honey in my mouth. {4} He then said to me: "Son of man, go now to the house of Israel and speak my words to them. {5} You are not being sent to a people of obscure speech and difficult language, but to the house of Israel– {6} not to many peoples of obscure speech and difficult language, whose words you cannot understand. Surely if I had sent you to them, they would have listened to you. {7} But the house of Israel is not willing to listen to you because they are not willing to listen to me, for the whole house of Israel is hardened and obstinate. {8} But I will make you as unyielding and hardened as they are. {9} I will make your forehead like the hardest stone, harder than flint. Do not be afraid of them or terrified by them, though they are a rebellious house." {10} And he said to me, "Son of man, listen carefully and take to heart all the words I speak to you. {11} Go now to your countrymen in exile and speak to them. Say to them, 'This is what the Sovereign LORD says,' whether they listen or fail to listen." {12} Then the Spirit lifted me up, and I heard behind me a loud rumbling sound–May the glory of the LORD be praised in his dwelling place!– {13} the sound of the wings of the living creatures brushing against each other and the sound of the wheels beside them, a loud rumbling sound. {14} The Spirit then lifted me up and took me away, and I went in bitterness and in the anger of my spirit, with the strong hand of the LORD upon me. {15} I came to the exiles who lived at Tel Abib near the Kebar River. And there, where they were living, I sat among them for seven days–overwhelmed. {16} At the end of seven days the word of the LORD came to me: {17} "Son of man, I have made you a watchman for the house of Israel; so hear the word I speak and give them warning from me. {18} When I say to a wicked man, 'You will surely die,' and you do not warn him or speak out to dissuade him from his evil ways in order to save his life, that wicked man will die for his sin, and I will hold you accountable for his blood. {19} But if you do warn the wicked man and he does not turn from his wickedness or from his evil ways, he will die for his sin; but you will have saved yourself.

SIEGE OF JERUSALEM IS FORETOLD

Ezek 4:16-5:14

He then said to me: "Son of man, I will cut off the supply of food in Jerusalem. The people will eat rationed food in anxiety and drink rationed water in despair, {17} for food and water will be scarce. They will be appalled at the sight of each other and will waste away because of their sin. {5:1} "Now, son of man, take a sharp sword and use it as a barber's razor to shave your head and your beard. Then take a set of scales and divide up the hair. {2} When the days of your siege come to an end, burn a third of the hair with fire inside the city. Take a third and strike it with the sword all around the city. And scatter a third to the wind. For I will pursue them with drawn sword. {3} But take a few strands of hair and tuck them away in the folds of your garment. {4} Again, take a few of these and throw them into the fire and burn them up. A fire will spread from there to the whole house of Israel. {5} "This is what the Sovereign LORD says: This is Jerusalem, which I have set in the center of the nations, with countries all around her. {6} Yet in her wickedness she has rebelled against my laws and decrees more than the nations and countries around her. She has rejected my laws and has not followed my decrees. {7} "Therefore this is what the Sovereign LORD says: You have been more unruly than the nations around you and have not followed my decrees or kept my laws. You have not even conformed to the standards of the nations around you. {8} "Therefore this is what the Sovereign LORD says: I myself am against you, Jerusalem, and I will inflict punishment on you in the sight of the nations. {9} Because of all your detestable idols, I will do to you what I have never done before and will never do again. {10} Therefore in your midst fathers will eat their children, and children will eat their fathers. I will inflict punishment on you and will scatter all your survivors to the winds. {11} Therefore as surely as I live, declares the Sovereign LORD, because you have defiled my sanctuary with all your vile images and detestable practices, I myself will withdraw my favor; I will not look on you with pity or spare you. {12} A third of your people will die of the plague or perish by famine inside you; a third will fall by the sword outside your walls; and a third I will scatter to the winds and pursue with drawn sword. {13} "Then my anger will cease and my wrath against them will subside, and I will be avenged. And when I have spent my wrath upon them, they will know that I the LORD have spoken in my zeal. {14} "I will make you a ruin and a reproach among the nations around you, in the sight of all who pass by.

THERE IS SIN IN THE TEMPLE

Ezek 8:17-9:8

He said to me, "Have you seen this, son of man? Is it a trivial matter for the house of Judah to do the detestable things they are doing here? Must they also fill the land with violence and continually provoke me to anger? Look at them putting the branch to their nose! {18} Therefore I will deal with them in anger; I will not look on them with pity or spare them. Although they shout in my ears, I will not listen to them."

{9:1} Then I heard him call out in a loud voice, "Bring the guards of the city here, each with a weapon in his hand." {2} And I saw six men coming from the direction of the upper gate, which faces north, each with a deadly weapon in his hand. With them was a man clothed in linen who had a writing kit at his side. They came in and stood beside the bronze altar. {3} Now the glory of the God of Israel went up from above the cherubim, where it had been, and moved to the threshold of the temple. Then the LORD called to the man clothed in linen who had the writing kit at his side {4} and said to him, "Go throughout the city of Jerusalem and put a mark on the foreheads of those who grieve and lament over all the detestable things that are done in it." {5} As I listened, he said to the others, "Follow him through the city and kill, without showing pity or compassion. {6} Slaughter old men, young men and maidens, women and children, but do not touch anyone who has the mark. Begin at my sanctuary." So they began with the elders who were in front of the temple. {7} Then he said to them, "Defile the temple and fill the courts with the slain. Go!" So they went out and began killing throughout the city. {8} While they were killing and I was left alone, I fell facedown, crying out, "Ah, Sovereign LORD! Are you going to destroy the entire remnant of Israel in this outpouring of your wrath on Jerusalem?"

238

ISRAEL WILL BE PUNISHED, THEN RESTORED

Ezek 20:28-42

When I brought them into the land I had sworn to give them and they saw any high hill or any leafy tree, there they offered their sacrifices, made offerings that provoked me to anger, presented their fragrant incense and poured out their drink offerings. {29} Then I said to them: What is this high place you go to?'" (It is called Bamah to this day.) {30} "Therefore say to the house of Israel: 'This is what the Sovereign LORD says: Will you defile yourselves the way your fathers did and lust after their vile images? {31} When you offer your gifts–the sacrifice of your sons in the fire–you continue to defile yourselves with all your idols to this day. Am I to let you inquire of me, O house of Israel? As surely as I live, declares the Sovereign LORD, I will not let you inquire of me. {32} "'You say, "We want to be like the nations, like the peoples of the world, who serve wood and stone." But what you have in mind will never happen. {33} As surely as I live, declares the Sovereign LORD, I will rule over you with a mighty hand and an outstretched arm and with outpoured wrath. {34} I will bring you from the nations and gather you from the countries where you have been scattered–with a mighty hand and an outstretched arm and with outpoured wrath. {35} I will bring you into the desert of the nations and there, face to face, I will execute judgment upon you. {36} As I judged your fathers in the desert of the land of Egypt, so I will judge you, declares the Sovereign LORD. {37} I will take note of you as you pass under my rod, and I will bring you into the bond of the covenant. {38} I will purge you of those who revolt and rebel against me. Although I will bring them out of the land where they are living, yet they will not enter the land of Israel. Then you will know that I am the LORD. {39} "'As for you, O house of Israel, this is what the Sovereign LORD says: Go and serve your idols, every one of you! But afterward you will surely listen to me and no longer profane my holy name with your gifts and idols. {40} For on my holy mountain, the high mountain of Israel, declares the Sovereign LORD, there in the land the entire house of Israel will serve me, and there I will accept them. There I will require your offerings and your choice gifts, along with all your holy sacrifices. {41} I will accept you as fragrant incense when I bring you out from the nations and gather you from the countries where you have been scattered, and I will show myself holy among you in the sight of the nations. {42} Then you will know that I am the LORD, when I bring you into the land of Israel, the land I had sworn with uplifted hand to give to your fathers.

EZEKIEL IS THE WATCHMAN TO WARN ISRAEL

Ezek 33:1-16

The word of the LORD came to me: {2} "Son of man, speak to your countrymen and say to them: 'When I bring the sword against a land, and the people of the land choose one of their men and make him their watchman, {3} and he sees the sword coming against the land and blows the trumpet to warn the people, {4} then if anyone hears the trumpet but does not take warning and the sword comes and takes his life, his blood will be on his own head. {5} Since he heard the sound of the trumpet but did not take warning, his blood will be on his own head. If he had taken warning, he would have saved himself. {6} But if the watchman sees the sword coming and does not blow the trumpet to warn the people and the sword comes and takes the life of one of them, that man will be taken away because of his sin, but I will hold the watchman accountable for his blood.' {7} "Son of man, I have made you a watchman for the house of Israel; so hear the word I speak and give them warning from me. {8} When I say to the wicked, 'O wicked man, you will surely die,' and you do not speak out to dissuade him from his ways, that wicked man will die for his sin, and I will hold you accountable for his blood. {9} But if you do warn the wicked man to turn from his ways and he does not do so, he will die for his sin, but you will have saved yourself. {10} "Son of man, say to the house of Israel, 'This is what you are saying: "Our offenses and sins weigh us down, and we are wasting away because of them. How then can we live?" ' {11} Say to them, 'As surely as I live, declares the Sovereign LORD, I take no pleasure in the death of the wicked, but rather that they turn from their ways and live. Turn! Turn from your evil ways! Why will you die, O house of Israel?' {12} "Therefore, son of man, say to your countrymen, 'The righteousness of the righteous man will not save him when he disobeys, and the wickedness of the wicked man will not cause him to fall when he turns from it. The righteous man, if he sins, will not be allowed to live because of his former righteousness.' {13} If I tell the righteous man that he will surely live, but then he trusts in his righteousness and does evil, none of the righteous things he has done will be remembered; he will die for the evil he has done. {14} And if I say to the wicked man, 'You will surely die,' but he then turns away from his sin and does what is just and right– {15} if he gives back what he took in pledge for a loan, returns what he has stolen, follows the decrees that give life, and does no evil, he will surely live; he will not die. {16} None of the sins he has committed will be remembered against him. He has done what is just and right; he will surely live.

DANIEL AND FRIENDS GO ON VEGETABLE DIET

Dan 1:1-19

In the third year of the reign of Jehoiakim king of Judah, Nebuchadnezzar king of Babylon came to Jerusalem and besieged it. {2} And the Lord delivered Jehoiakim king of Judah into his hand, along with some of the articles from the temple of God. These he carried off to the temple of his god in Babylonia and put in the treasure house of his god. {3} Then the king ordered Ashpenaz, chief of his court officials, to bring in some of the Israelites from the royal family and the nobility– {4} young men without any physical defect, handsome, showing aptitude for every kind of learning, well informed, quick to understand, and qualified to serve in the king's palace. He was to teach them the language and literature of the Babylonians. {5} The king assigned them a daily amount of food and wine from the king's table. They were to be trained for three years, and after that they were to enter the king's service. {6} Among these were some from Judah: Daniel, Hananiah, Mishael and Azariah. {7} The chief official gave them new names: to Daniel, the name Belteshazzar; to Hananiah, Shadrach; to Mishael, Meshach; and to Azariah, Abednego. {8} But Daniel resolved not to defile himself with the royal food and wine, and he asked the chief official for permission not to defile himself this way. {9} Now God had caused the official to show favor and sympathy to Daniel, {10} but the official told Daniel, "I am afraid of my lord the king, who has assigned your food and drink. Why should he see you looking worse than the other young men your age? The king would then have my head because of you." {11} Daniel then said to the guard whom the chief official had appointed over Daniel, Hananiah, Mishael and Azariah, {12} "Please test your servants for ten days: Give us nothing but vegetables to eat and water to drink. {13} Then compare our appearance with that of the young men who eat the royal food, and treat your servants in accordance with what you see." {14} So he agreed to this and tested them for ten days. {15} At the end of the ten days they looked healthier and better nourished than any of the young men who ate the royal food. {16} So the guard took away their choice food and the wine they were to drink and gave them vegetables instead. {17} To these four young men God gave knowledge and understanding of all kinds of literature and learning. And Daniel could understand visions and dreams of all kinds. {18} At the end of the time set by the king to bring them in, the chief official presented them to Nebuchadnezzar. {19} The king talked with them, and he found none equal to Daniel, Hananiah, Mishael and Azariah; so they entered the king's service.

NEBUCHADNEZZAR HAD A DREAM, BUT WOULDN'T SAY WHAT HE DREAMT

Dan 2:3-19a

"I have had a dream that troubles me and I want to know what it means." {4} Then the astrologers answered the king in Aramaic, "O king, live forever! Tell your servants the dream, and we will interpret it." {5} The king replied to the astrologers, "This is what I have firmly decided: If you do not tell me what my dream was and interpret it, I will have you cut into pieces and your houses turned into piles of rubble. {6} But if you tell me the dream and explain it, you will receive from me gifts and rewards and great honor. So tell me the dream and interpret it for me." {7} Once more they replied, "Let the king tell his servants the dream, and we will interpret it." {8} Then the king answered, "I am certain that you are trying to gain time, because you realize that this is what I have firmly decided: {9} If you do not tell me the dream, there is just one penalty for you. You have conspired to tell me misleading and wicked things, hoping the situation will change. So then, tell me the dream, and I will know that you can interpret it for me." {10} The astrologers answered the king, "There is not a man on earth who can do what the king asks! No king, however great and mighty, has ever asked such a thing of any magician or enchanter or astrologer. {11} What the king asks is too difficult. No one can reveal it to the king except the gods, and they do not live among men." {12} This made the king so angry and furious that he ordered the execution of all the wise men of Babylon. {13} So the decree was issued to put the wise men to death, and men were sent to look for Daniel and his friends to put them to death. {14} When Arioch, the commander of the king's guard, had gone out to put to death the wise men of Babylon, Daniel spoke to him with wisdom and tact. {15} He asked the king's officer, "Why did the king issue such a harsh decree?" Arioch then explained the matter to Daniel. {16} At this, Daniel went in to the king and asked for time, so that he might interpret the dream for him. {17} Then Daniel returned to his house and explained the matter to his friends Hananiah, Mishael and Azariah. {18} He urged them to plead for mercy from the God of heaven concerning this mystery, so that he and his friends might not be executed with the rest of the wise men of Babylon. {19} During the night the mystery was revealed to Daniel in a vision.

DANIEL RECOUNTS THE DREAM AND INTERPRETS IT

Dan 2:24-49

Then Daniel went to Arioch, whom the king had appointed to execute the wise men of Babylon, and said to him, "Do not execute the wise men of Babylon. Take me to the king, and I will interpret his dream for him." {25} Arioch took Daniel to the king at once and said, "I have found a man among the exiles from Judah who can tell the king what his dream means." {26} The king asked Daniel (also called Belteshazzar), "Are you able to tell me what I saw in my dream and interpret it?" {27} Daniel replied, "No wise man, enchanter, magician or diviner can explain to the king the mystery he has asked about, {28} but there is a God in heaven who reveals mysteries. He has shown King Nebuchadnezzar what will happen in days to come. Your dream and the visions that passed through your mind as you lay on your bed are these: {29} "As you were lying there, O king, your mind turned to things to come, and the revealer of mysteries showed you what is going to happen. {30} As for me, this mystery has been revealed to me, not because I have greater wisdom than other living men, but so that you, O king, may know the interpretation and that you may understand what went through your mind. {31} "You looked, O king, and there before you stood a large statue–an enormous, dazzling statue, awesome in appearance. {32} The head of the statue was made of pure gold, its chest and arms of silver, its belly and thighs of bronze, {33} its legs of iron, its feet partly of iron and partly of baked clay. {34} While you were watching, a rock was cut out, but not by human hands. It struck the statue on its feet of iron and clay and smashed them. {35} Then the iron, the clay, the bronze, the silver and the gold were broken to pieces at the same time and became like chaff on a threshing floor in the summer. The wind swept them away without leaving a trace. But the rock that struck the statue became a huge mountain and filled the whole earth. {36} "This was the dream, and now we will interpret it to the king. {37} You, O king, are the king of kings. The God of heaven has given you dominion and power and might and glory; {38} in your hands he has placed mankind and the beasts of the field and the birds of the air. Wherever they live, he has made you ruler over them all. You are that head of gold. {39} "After you, another kingdom will rise, inferior to yours. Next, a third kingdom, one of bronze, will rule over the whole earth. {40} Finally, there will be a fourth kingdom, strong as iron–for iron breaks and smashes everything–and as iron breaks things to pieces, so it will crush and break all the others.

NEBUCHADNEZZAR CASTS DANIEL'S FRIENDS
INTO THE FIERY FURNACE

Dan 3:3-19

So the satraps, prefects, governors, advisers, treasurers, judges, magistrates and all the other provincial officials assembled for the dedication of the image that King Nebuchadnezzar had set up, and they stood before it. {4} Then the herald loudly proclaimed, "This is what you are commanded to do, O peoples, nations and men of every language: {5} As soon as you hear the sound of the horn, flute, zither, lyre, harp, pipes and all kinds of music, you must fall down and worship the image of gold that King Nebuchadnezzar has set up. {6} Whoever does not fall down and worship will immediately be thrown into a blazing furnace." {7} Therefore, as soon as they heard the sound of the horn, flute, zither, lyre, harp and all kinds of music, all the peoples, nations and men of every language fell down and worshiped the image of gold that King Nebuchadnezzar had set up. {8} At this time some astrologers came forward and denounced the Jews. {9} They said to King Nebuchadnezzar, "O king, live forever! {10} You have issued a decree, O king, that everyone who hears the sound of the horn, flute, zither, lyre, harp, pipes and all kinds of music must fall down and worship the image of gold, {11} and that whoever does not fall down and worship will be thrown into a blazing furnace. {12} But there are some Jews whom you have set over the affairs of the province of Babylon–Shadrach, Meshach and Abednego–who pay no attention to you, O king. They neither serve your gods nor worship the image of gold you have set up." {13} Furious with rage, Nebuchadnezzar summoned Shadrach, Meshach and Abednego. So these men were brought before the king, {14} and Nebuchadnezzar said to them, "Is it true, Shadrach, Meshach and Abednego, that you do not serve my gods or worship the image of gold I have set up? {15} Now when you hear the sound of the horn, flute, zither, lyre, harp, pipes and all kinds of music, if you are ready to fall down and worship the image I made, very good. But if you do not worship it, you will be thrown immediately into a blazing furnace. Then what god will be able to rescue you from my hand?" {16} Shadrach, Meshach and Abednego replied to the king, "O Nebuchadnezzar, we do not need to defend ourselves before you in this matter. {17} If we are thrown into the blazing furnace, the God we serve is able to save us from it, and he will rescue us from your hand, O king. {18} But even if he does not, we want you to know, O king, that we will not serve your gods or worship the image of gold you have set up." {19} Then Nebuchadnezzar was furious with Shadrach, Meshach and Abednego, and his attitude toward them changed.

NEBUCHADNEZZAR DREAMS OF A TREE

Dan 4:1-18a

King Nebuchadnezzar, To the peoples, nations and men of every language, who live in all the world: May you prosper greatly! {2} It is my pleasure to tell you about the miraculous signs and wonders that the Most High God has performed for me. {3} How great are his signs, how mighty his wonders! His kingdom is an eternal kingdom; his dominion endures from generation to generation. {4} I, Nebuchadnezzar, was at home in my palace, contented and prosperous. {5} I had a dream that made me afraid. As I was lying in my bed, the images and visions that passed through my mind terrified me. {6} So I commanded that all the wise men of Babylon be brought before me to interpret the dream for me. {7} When the magicians, enchanters, astrologers and diviners came, I told them the dream, but they could not interpret it for me. {8} Finally, Daniel came into my presence and I told him the dream. (He is called Belteshazzar, after the name of my god, and the spirit of the holy gods is in him.) {9} I said, "Belteshazzar, chief of the magicians, I know that the spirit of the holy gods is in you, and no mystery is too difficult for you. Here is my dream; interpret it for me. {10} These are the visions I saw while lying in my bed: I looked, and there before me stood a tree in the middle of the land. Its height was enormous. {11} The tree grew large and strong and its top touched the sky; it was visible to the ends of the earth. {12} Its leaves were beautiful, its fruit abundant, and on it was food for all. Under it the beasts of the field found shelter, and the birds of the air lived in its branches; from it every creature was fed. {13} "In the visions I saw while lying in my bed, I looked, and there before me was a messenger, a holy one, coming down from heaven. {14} He called in a loud voice: 'Cut down the tree and trim off its branches; strip off its leaves and scatter its fruit. Let the animals flee from under it and the birds from its branches. {15} But let the stump and its roots, bound with iron and bronze, remain in the ground, in the grass of the field. "'Let him be drenched with the dew of heaven, and let him live with the animals among the plants of the earth. {16} Let his mind be changed from that of a man and let him be given the mind of an animal, till seven times pass by for him. {17} "'The decision is announced by messengers, the holy ones declare the verdict, so that the living may know that the Most High is sovereign over the kingdoms of men and gives them to anyone he wishes and sets over them the lowliest of men.' {18} "This is the dream that I, King Nebuchadnezzar, had. Now, Belteshazzar, tell me what it means....

THE KING'S DREAM COMES TRUE

Dan 4:19b-33

Belteshazzar answered, "My lord, if only the dream applied to your enemies and its meaning to your adversaries! {20} The tree you saw, which grew large and strong, with its top touching the sky, visible to the whole earth, {21} with beautiful leaves and abundant fruit, providing food for all, giving shelter to the beasts of the field, and having nesting places in its branches for the birds of the air– {22} you, O king, are that tree! You have become great and strong; your greatness has grown until it reaches the sky, and your dominion extends to distant parts of the earth. {23} "You, O king, saw a messenger, a holy one, coming down from heaven and saying, 'Cut down the tree and destroy it, but leave the stump, bound with iron and bronze, in the grass of the field, while its roots remain in the ground. Let him be drenched with the dew of heaven; let him live like the wild animals, until seven times pass by for him.' {24} "This is the interpretation, O king, and this is the decree the Most High has issued against my lord the king: {25} You will be driven away from people and will live with the wild animals; you will eat grass like cattle and be drenched with the dew of heaven. Seven times will pass by for you until you acknowledge that the Most High is sovereign over the. kingdoms of men and gives them to anyone he wishes. {26} The command to leave the stump of the tree with its roots means that your kingdom will be restored to you when you acknowledge that Heaven rules. {27} Therefore, O king, be pleased to accept my advice: Renounce your sins by doing what is right, and your wickedness by being kind to the oppressed. It may be that then your prosperity will continue." {28} All this happened to King Nebuchadnezzar. {29} Twelve months later, as the king was walking on the roof of the royal palace of Babylon, {30} he said, "Is not this the great Babylon I have built as the royal residence, by my mighty power and for the glory of my majesty?" {31} The words were still on his lips when a voice came from heaven, "This is what is decreed for you, King Nebuchadnezzar: Your royal authority has been taken from you. {32} You will be driven away from people and will live with the wild animals; you will eat grass like cattle. Seven times will pass by for you until you acknowledge that the Most High is sovereign over the kingdoms of men and gives them to anyone he wishes." {33} Immediately what had been said about Nebuchadnezzar was fulfilled. He was driven away from people and ate grass like cattle. His body was drenched with the dew of heaven until his hair grew like the feathers of an eagle and his nails like the claws of a bird.

A NEW KING, BELSHAZZAR, SEES WRITING ON THE WALL

Dan 5:1-16a

King Belshazzar gave a great banquet for a thousand of his nobles and drank wine with them. {2} While Belshazzar was drinking his wine, he gave orders to bring in the gold and silver goblets that Nebuchadnezzar his father had taken from the temple in Jerusalem, so that the king and his nobles, his wives and his concubines might drink from them. {3} So they brought in the gold goblets that had been taken from the temple of God in Jerusalem, and the king and his nobles, his wives and his concubines drank from them. {4} As they drank the wine, they praised the gods of gold and silver, of bronze, iron, wood and stone. {5} Suddenly the fingers of a human hand appeared and wrote on the plaster of the wall, near the lampstand in the royal palace. The king watched the hand as it wrote. {6} His face turned pale and he was so frightened that his knees knocked together and his legs gave way. {7} The king called out for the enchanters, astrologers and diviners to be brought and said to these wise men of Babylon, "Whoever reads this writing and tells me what it means will be clothed in purple and have a gold chain placed around his neck, and he will be made the third highest ruler in the kingdom." {8} Then all the king's wise men came in, but they could not read the writing or tell the king what it meant. {9} So King Belshazzar became even more terrified and his face grew more pale. His nobles were baffled. {10} The queen, hearing the voices of the king and his nobles, came into the banquet hall. "O king, live forever!" she said. "Don't be alarmed! Don't look so pale! {11} There is a man in your kingdom who has the spirit of the holy gods in him. In the time of your father he was found to have insight and intelligence and wisdom like that of the gods. King Nebuchadnezzar your father—your father the king, I say—appointed him chief of the magicians, enchanters, astrologers and diviners. {12} This man Daniel, whom the king called Belteshazzar, was found to have a keen mind and knowledge and understanding, and also the ability to interpret dreams, explain riddles and solve difficult problems. Call for Daniel, and he will tell you what the writing means." {13} So Daniel was brought before the king, and the king said to him, "Are you Daniel, one of the exiles my father the king brought from Judah? {14} I have heard that the spirit of the gods is in you and that you have insight, intelligence and outstanding wisdom. {15} The wise men and enchanters were brought before me to read this writing and tell me what it means, but they could not explain it. {16} Now I have heard that you are able to give interpretations and to solve difficult problems.

DANIEL INTERPRETS THE WRITING

Dan 5:17-31

Then Daniel answered the king, "You may keep your gifts for yourself and give your rewards to someone else. Nevertheless, I will read the writing for the king and tell him what it means. {18} "O king, the Most High God gave your father Nebuchadnezzar sovereignty and greatness and glory and splendor. {19} Because of the high position he gave him, all the peoples and nations and men of every language dreaded and feared him. Those the king wanted to put to death, he put to death; those he wanted to spare, he spared; those he wanted to promote, he promoted; and those he wanted to humble, he humbled. {20} But when his heart became arrogant and hardened with pride, he was deposed from his royal throne and stripped of his glory. {21} He was driven away from people and given the mind of an animal; he lived with the wild donkeys and ate grass like cattle; and his body was drenched with the dew of heaven, until he acknowledged that the Most High God is sovereign over the kingdoms of men and sets over them anyone he wishes. {22} "But you his son, O Belshazzar, have not humbled yourself, though you knew all this. {23} Instead, you have set yourself up against the Lord of heaven. You had the goblets from his temple brought to you, and you and your nobles, your wives and your concubines drank wine from them. You praised the gods of silver and gold, of bronze, iron, wood and stone, which cannot see or hear or understand. But you did not honor the God who holds in his hand your life and all your ways. {24} Therefore he sent the hand that wrote the inscription. {25} "This is the inscription that was written: MENE, MENE, TEKEL, PARSIN {26} "This is what these words mean: <Mene> : God has numbered the days of your reign and brought it to an end. {27} <Tekel> : You have been weighed on the scales and found wanting. {28} <Peres> : Your kingdom is divided and given to the Medes and Persians." {29} Then at Belshazzar's command, Daniel was clothed in purple, a gold chain was placed around his neck, and he was proclaimed the third highest ruler in the kingdom. {30} That very night Belshazzar, king of the Babylonians, was slain, {31} and Darius the Mede took over the kingdom, at the age of sixty-two.

A NEW KING, DARIUS, THROWS DANIEL TO THE LIONS

Dan 6:7b-23a

...that anyone who prays to any god or man during the next thirty days, except to you, O king, shall be thrown into the lions' den. {8} Now, O king, issue the decree and put it in writing so that it cannot be altered–in accordance with the laws of the Medes and Persians, which cannot be repealed." {9} So King Darius put the decree in writing. {10} Now when Daniel learned that the decree had been published, he went home to his upstairs room where the windows opened toward Jerusalem. Three times a day he got down on his knees and prayed, giving thanks to his God, just as he had done before. {11} Then these men went as a group and found Daniel praying and asking God for help. {12} So they went to the king and spoke to him about his royal decree: "Did you not publish a decree that during the next thirty days anyone who prays to any god or man except to you, O king, would be thrown into the lions' den?" The king answered, "The decree stands–in accordance with the laws of the Medes and Persians, which cannot be repealed." {13} Then they said to the king, "Daniel, who is one of the exiles from Judah, pays no attention to you, O king, or to the decree you put in writing. He still prays three times a day." {14} When the king heard this, he was greatly distressed; he was determined to rescue Daniel and made every effort until sundown to save him. {15} Then the men went as a group to the king and said to him, "Remember, O king, that according to the law of the Medes and Persians no decree or edict that the king issues can be changed." {16} So the king gave the order, and they brought Daniel and threw him into the lions' den. The king said to Daniel, "May your God, whom you serve continually, rescue you!" {17} A stone was brought and placed over the mouth of the den, and the king sealed it with his own signet ring and with the rings of his nobles, so that Daniel's situation might not be changed. {18} Then the king returned to his palace and spent the night without eating and without any entertainment being brought to him. And he could not sleep. {19} At the first light of dawn, the king got up and hurried to the lions' den. {20} When he came near the den, he called to Daniel in an anguished voice, "Daniel, servant of the living God, has your God, whom you serve continually, been able to rescue you from the lions?" {21} Daniel answered, "O king, live forever! {22} My God sent his angel, and he shut the mouths of the lions. They have not hurt me, because I was found innocent in his sight. Nor have I ever done any wrong before you, O king." {23} The king was overjoyed and gave orders to lift Daniel out of the den. And when Daniel was lifted from the den.

HOSEA'S ADULTEROUS WIFE

Hosea 1:1-2:5a

The word of the LORD that came to Hosea son of Beeri during the reigns of Uzziah, Jotham, Ahaz and Hezekiah, kings of Judah, and during the reign of Jeroboam son of Jehoash king of Israel: {2} When the LORD began to speak through Hosea, the LORD said to him, "Go, take to yourself an adulterous wife and children of unfaithfulness, because the land is guilty of the vilest adultery in departing from the LORD." {3} So he married Gomer daughter of Diblaim, and she conceived and bore him a son. {4} Then the LORD said to Hosea, "Call him Jezreel, because I will soon punish the house of Jehu for the massacre at Jezreel, and I will put an end to the kingdom of Israel. {5} In that day I will break Israel's bow in the Valley of Jezreel." {6} Gomer conceived again and gave birth to a daughter. Then the LORD said to Hosea, "Call her Lo-Ruhamah, for I will no longer show love to the house of Israel, that I should at all forgive them. {7} Yet I will show love to the house of Judah; and I will save them—not by bow, sword or battle, or by horses and horsemen, but by the LORD their God." {8} After she had weaned Lo-Ruhamah, Gomer had another son. {9} Then the LORD said, "Call him Lo-Ammi, for you are not my people, and I am not your God. {10} "Yet the Israelites will be like the sand on the seashore, which cannot be measured or counted. In the place where it was said to them, 'You are not my people,' they will be called 'sons of the living God.' {11} The people of Judah and the people of Israel will be reunited, and they will appoint one leader and will come up out of the land, for great will be the day of Jezreel.

{2:1} "Say of your brothers, 'My people,' and of your sisters, 'My loved one.' {2} "Rebuke your mother, rebuke her, for she is not my wife, and I am not her husband. Let her remove the adulterous look from her face and the unfaithfulness from between her breasts. {3} Otherwise I will strip her naked and make her as bare as on the day she was born; I will make her like a desert, turn her into a parched land, and slay her with thirst. {4} I will not show my love to her children, because they are the children of adultery. {5} Their mother has been unfaithful and has conceived them in disgrace. She said, 'I will go after my lovers, who give me my food and my water, my wool and my linen, my oil and my drink.'

JUDAH WILL BE RESTORED, AND THE NATIONS JUDGED

Joel 3:1-2

'In those days and at that time, when I restore the fortunes of Judah and Jerusalem, {2} I will gather all nations and bring them down to the Valley of Jehoshaphat. There I will enter into judgment against them concerning my inheritance, my people Israel, for they scattered my people among the nations and divided up my land.

Joel 3:9-12

Proclaim this among the nations: Prepare for war! Rouse the warriors! Let all the fighting men draw near and attack. {10} Beat your plowshares into swords and your pruning hooks into spears. Let the weakling say, 'I am strong!' {11} Come quickly, all you nations from every side, and assemble there. Bring down your warriors, O LORD! {12} 'Let the nations be roused; let them advance into the Valley of Jehoshaphat, for there I will sit to judge all the nations on every side.

Joel 3:16-21

The LORD will roar from Zion and thunder from Jerusalem; the earth and the sky will tremble. But the LORD will be a refuge for his people, a stronghold for the people of Israel. {17} 'Then you will know that I, the LORD your God, dwell in Zion, my holy hill. Jerusalem will be holy; never again will foreigners invade her. {18} 'In that day the mountains will drip new wine, and the hills will flow with milk; all the ravines of Judah will run with water. A fountain will flow out of the Lord's house and will water the valley of acacias. {19} But Egypt will be desolate, Edom a desert waste, because of violence done to the people of Judah, in whose land they shed innocent blood. {20} Judah will be inhabited forever and Jerusalem through all generations. {21} Their bloodguilt, which I have not pardoned, I will pardon.' The LORD dwells in Zion!

JUDGMENT PRONOUNCED ON JUDAH AND ISRAEL

Amos 2:4-16

This is what the LORD says: "For three sins of Judah, even for four, I will not turn back <my wrath>. Because they have rejected the law of the LORD and have not kept his decrees, because they have been led astray by false gods, the gods their ancestors followed, {5} I will send fire upon Judah that will consume the fortresses of Jerusalem." {6} This is what the LORD says: "For three sins of Israel, even for four, I will not turn back <my wrath>. They sell the righteous for silver, and the needy for a pair of sandals. {7} They trample on the heads of the poor as upon the dust of the ground and deny justice to the oppressed. Father and son use the same girl and so profane my holy name. {8} They lie down beside every altar on garments taken in pledge. In the house of their god they drink wine taken as fines. {9} "I destroyed the Amorite before them, though he was tall as the cedars and strong as the oaks. I destroyed his fruit above and his roots below. {10} "I brought you up out of Egypt, and I led you forty years in the desert to give you the land of the Amorites. {11} I also raised up prophets from among your sons and Nazirites from among your young men. Is this not true, people of Israel?" declares the LORD. {12} "But you made the Nazirites drink wine and commanded the prophets not to prophesy. {13} "Now then, I will crush you as a cart crushes when loaded with grain. {14} The swift will not escape, the strong will not muster their strength, and the warrior will not save his life. {15} The archer will not stand his ground, the fleet-footed soldier will not get away, and the horseman will not save his life. {16} Even the bravest warriors will flee naked on that day," declares the LORD.

GOD'S CHOSEN PEOPLE WILL BE PUNISHED

Amos 3:1-8

Hear this word the LORD has spoken against you, O people of Israel–against the whole family I brought up out of Egypt: {2} "You only have I chosen of all the families of the earth; therefore I will punish you for all your sins." {3} Do two walk together unless they have agreed to do so? {4} Does a lion roar in the thicket when he has no prey? Does he growl in his den when he has caught nothing? {5} Does a bird fall into a trap on the ground where no snare has been set? Does a trap spring up from the earth when there is nothing to catch? {6} When a trumpet sounds in a city, do not the people tremble? When disaster comes to a city, has not the LORD caused it? {7} Surely the Sovereign LORD does nothing without revealing his plan to his servants the prophets. {8} The lion has roared– who will not fear? The Sovereign LORD has spoken– who can but prophesy?

Amos 4:10-13

"I sent plagues among you as I did to Egypt. I killed your young men with the sword, along with your captured horses. I filled your nostrils with the stench of your camps, yet you have not returned to me," declares the LORD. {11} "I overthrew some of you as I overthrew Sodom and Gomorrah. You were like a burning stick snatched from the fire, yet you have not returned to me," declares the LORD. {12} "Therefore this is what I will do to you, Israel, and because I will do this to you, prepare to meet your God, O Israel." {13} He who forms the mountains, creates the wind, and reveals his thoughts to man, he who turns dawn to darkness, and treads the high places of the earth– the LORD God Almighty is his name.

ISRAEL WILL LIVE WHEN IT SEEKS GOD

Amos 5:4-15

This is what the LORD says to the house of Israel: "Seek me and live; {5} do not seek Bethel, do not go to Gilgal, do not journey to Beersheba. For Gilgal will surely go into exile, and Bethel will be reduced to nothing." {6} Seek the LORD and live, or he will sweep through the house of Joseph like a fire; it will devour, and Bethel will have no one to quench it. {7} You who turn justice into bitterness and cast righteousness to the ground {8} (he who made the Pleiades and Orion, who turns blackness into dawn and darkens day into night, who calls for the waters of the sea and pours them out over the face of the land– the LORD is his name– {9} he flashes destruction on the stronghold and brings the fortified city to ruin), {10} you hate the one who reproves in court and despise him who tells the truth. {11} You trample on the poor and force him to give you grain. Therefore, though you have built stone mansions, you will not live in them; though you have planted lush vineyards, you will not drink their wine. {12} For I know how many are your offenses and how great your sins. You oppress the righteous and take bribes and you deprive the poor of justice in the courts. {13} Therefore the prudent man keeps quiet in such times, for the times are evil. {14} Seek good, not evil, that you may live. Then the LORD God Almighty will be with you, just as you say he is. {15} Hate evil, love good; maintain justice in the courts. Perhaps the LORD God Almighty will have mercy on the remnant of Joseph.

Amos 5:21-24

"I hate, I despise your religious feasts; I cannot stand your assemblies. {22} Even though you bring me burnt offerings and grain offerings, I will not accept them. Though you bring choice fellowship offerings, I will have no regard for them. {23} Away with the noise of your songs! I will not listen to the music of your harps. {24} But let justice roll on like a river, righteousness like a never-failing stream!

AMOS THE SHEPHERD REBUKES AMAZIAH THE PRIEST

Amos 7:1-17

This is what the Sovereign LORD showed me: He was preparing swarms of locusts after the king's share had been harvested and just as the second crop was coming up. {2} When they had stripped the land clean, I cried out, "Sovereign LORD, forgive! How can Jacob survive? He is so small!" {3} So the LORD relented. "This will not happen," the LORD said. {4} This is what the Sovereign LORD showed me: The Sovereign LORD was calling for judgment by fire; it dried up the great deep and devoured the land. {5} Then I cried out, "Sovereign LORD, I beg you, stop! How can Jacob survive? He is so small!" {6} So the LORD relented. "This will not happen either," the Sovereign LORD said. {7} This is what he showed me: The Lord was standing by a wall that had been built true to plumb, with a plumb line in his hand. {8} And the LORD asked me, "What do you see, Amos?" "A plumb line," I replied. Then the Lord said, "Look, I am setting a plumb line among my people Israel; I will spare them no longer. {9} "The high places of Isaac will be destroyed and the sanctuaries of Israel will be ruined; with my sword I will rise against the house of Jeroboam." {10} Then Amaziah the priest of Bethel sent a message to Jeroboam king of Israel: "Amos is raising a conspiracy against you in the very heart of Israel. The land cannot bear all his words. {11} For this is what Amos is saying: "'Jeroboam will die by the sword, and Israel will surely go into exile, away from their native land.'" {12} Then Amaziah said to Amos, "Get out, you seer! Go back to the land of Judah. Earn your bread there and do your prophesying there. {13} Don't prophesy anymore at Bethel, because this is the king's sanctuary and the temple of the kingdom." {14} Amos answered Amaziah, "I was neither a prophet nor a prophet's son, but I was a shepherd, and I also took care of sycamore-fig trees. {15} But the LORD took me from tending the flock and said to me, 'Go, prophesy to my people Israel.' {16} Now then, hear the word of the LORD. You say, "'Do not prophesy against Israel, and stop preaching against the house of Isaac.' {17} "Therefore this is what the LORD says: "'Your wife will become a prostitute in the city, and your sons and daughters will fall by the sword. Your land will be measured and divided up, and you yourself will die in a pagan country. And Israel will certainly go into exile, away from their native land.'"

THE LORD WILL TREMBLE BECAUSE OF ISRAEL'S SIN

Amos 8:1-12

This is what the Sovereign LORD showed me: a basket of ripe fruit. {2} "What do you see, Amos?" he asked. "A basket of ripe fruit," I answered. Then the LORD said to me, "The time is ripe for my people Israel; I will spare them no longer. {3} "In that day," declares the Sovereign LORD, "the songs in the temple will turn to wailing. Many, many bodies–flung everywhere! Silence!" {4} Hear this, you who trample the needy and do away with the poor of the land, {5} saying, "When will the New Moon be over that we may sell grain, and the Sabbath be ended that we may market wheat?"– skimping the measure, boosting the price and cheating with dishonest scales, {6} buying the poor with silver and the needy for a pair of sandals, selling even the sweepings with the wheat. {7} The LORD has sworn by the Pride of Jacob: "I will never forget anything they have done. {8} "Will not the land tremble for this, and all who live in it mourn? The whole land will rise like the Nile; it will be stirred up and then sink like the river of Egypt. {9} "In that day," declares the Sovereign LORD, "I will make the sun go down at noon and darken the earth in broad daylight. {10} I will turn your religious feasts into mourning and all your singing into weeping. I will make all of you wear sackcloth and shave your heads. I will make that time like mourning for an only son and the end of it like a bitter day. {11} "The days are coming," declares the Sovereign LORD, "when I will send a famine through the land– not a famine of food or a thirst for water, but a famine of hearing the words of the LORD. {12} Men will stagger from sea to sea and wander from north to east, searching for the word of the LORD, but they will not find it.

256

YET, GOD WILL NOT TOTALLY DESTROY ISRAEL

Amos 9:8-15
     "Surely the eyes of the Sovereign LORD are on the sinful kingdom. I will destroy it from the face of the earth– yet I will not totally destroy the house of Jacob," declares the LORD. {9} "For I will give the command, and I will shake the house of Israel among all the nations as grain is shaken in a sieve, and not a pebble will reach the ground. {10} All the sinners among my people will die by the sword, all those who say, 'Disaster will not overtake or meet us.' {11} "In that day I will restore David's fallen tent. I will repair its broken places, restore its ruins, and build it as it used to be, {12} so that they may possess the remnant of Edom and all the nations that bear my name," declares the LORD, who will do these things. {13} "The days are coming," declares the LORD, "when the reaper will be overtaken by the plowman and the planter by the one treading grapes. New wine will drip from the mountains and flow from all the hills. {14} I will bring back my exiled people Israel; they will rebuild the ruined cities and live in them. They will plant vineyards and drink their wine; they will make gardens and eat their fruit. {15} I will plant Israel in their own land, never again to be uprooted from the land I have given them," says the LORD your God.

PUNISHMENT PROMISED TO ISRAEL, BUT ALSO DELIVERANCE

Micah 1:1-5

The word of the LORD that came to Micah of Moresheth during the reigns of Jotham, Ahaz and Hezekiah, kings of Judah–the vision he saw concerning Samaria and Jerusalem. {2} Hear, O peoples, all of you, listen, O earth and all who are in it, that the Sovereign LORD may witness against you, the Lord from his holy temple. {3} Look! The LORD is coming from his dwelling place; he comes down and treads the high places of the earth. {4} The mountains melt beneath him and the valleys split apart, like wax before the fire, like water rushing down a slope. {5} All this is because of Jacob's transgression, because of the sins of the house of Israel. What is Jacob's transgression? Is it not Samaria? What is Judah's high place? Is it not Jerusalem?

Micah 2:1-5

Woe to those who plan iniquity, to those who plot evil on their beds! At morning's light they carry it out because it is in their power to do it. {2} They covet fields and seize them, and houses, and take them. They defraud a man of his home, a fellowman of his inheritance. {3} Therefore, the LORD says: "I am planning disaster against this people, from which you cannot save yourselves. You will no longer walk proudly, for it will be a time of calamity. {4} In that day men will ridicule you; they will taunt you with this mournful song: 'We are utterly ruined; my people's possession is divided up. He takes it from me! He assigns our fields to traitors.'" {5} Therefore you will have no one in the assembly of the LORD to divide the land by lot.

Micah 2:12-13

"I will surely gather all of you, O Jacob; I will surely bring together the remnant of Israel. I will bring them together like sheep in a pen, like a flock in its pasture; the place will throng with people. {13} One who breaks open the way will go up before them; they will break through the gate and go out. Their king will pass through before them, the LORD at their head."

GOD'S TEMPLE WILL BE RESTORED
AND BETHLEHEM WILL BE PROUD

Micah 4:1-8

In the last days the mountain of the Lord's temple will be established as chief among the mountains; it will be raised above the hills, and peoples will stream to it. {2} Many nations will come and say, "Come, let us go up to the mountain of the LORD, to the house of the God of Jacob. He will teach us his ways, so that we may walk in his paths." The law will go out from Zion, the word of the LORD from Jerusalem. {3} He will judge between many peoples and will settle disputes for strong nations far and wide. They will beat their swords into plowshares and their spears into pruning hooks. Nation will not take up sword against nation, nor will they train for war anymore. {4} Every man will sit under his own vine and under his own fig tree, and no one will make them afraid, for the LORD Almighty has spoken. {5} All the nations may walk in the name of their gods; we will walk in the name of the LORD our God for ever and ever. {6} "In that day," declares the LORD, "I will gather the lame; I will assemble the exiles and those I have brought to grief. {7} I will make the lame a remnant, those driven away a strong nation. The LORD will rule over them in Mount Zion from that day and forever. {8} As for you, O watchtower of the flock, O stronghold of the Daughter of Zion, the former dominion will be restored to you; kingship will come to the Daughter of Jerusalem."

Micah 5:2-5a

"But you, Bethlehem Ephrathah, though you are small among the clans of Judah, out of you will come for me one who will be ruler over Israel, whose origins are from of old, from ancient times. " {3} Therefore Israel will be abandoned until the time when she who is in labor gives birth and the rest of his brothers return to join the Israelites. {4} He will stand and shepherd his flock in the strength of the LORD, in the majesty of the name of the LORD his God. And they will live securely, for then his greatness will reach to the ends of the earth. {5} And he will be their peace.

GOD'S ACCUSATION AGAINST ISRAEL

Micah 6:1-15

Listen to what the LORD says: "Stand up, plead your case before the mountains; let the hills hear what you have to say. {2} Hear, O mountains, the Lord's accusation; listen, you everlasting foundations of the earth. For the LORD has a case against his people; he is lodging a charge against Israel. {3} "My people, what have I done to you? How have I burdened you? Answer me. {4} I brought you up out of Egypt and redeemed you from the land of slavery. I sent Moses to lead you, also Aaron and Miriam. {5} My people, remember what Balak king of Moab counseled and what Balaam son of Beor answered. Remember <your journey> from Shittim to Gilgal, that you may know the righteous acts of the LORD." {6} With what shall I come before the LORD and bow down before the exalted God? Shall I come before him with burnt offerings, with calves a year old? {7} Will the LORD be pleased with thousands of rams, with ten thousand rivers of oil? Shall I offer my firstborn for my transgression, the fruit of my body for the sin of my soul? {8} He has showed you, O man, what is good. And what does the LORD require of you? To act justly and to love mercy and to walk humbly with your God. {9} Listen! The LORD is calling to the city– and to fear your name is wisdom– "Heed the rod and the One who appointed it. {10} Am I still to forget, O wicked house, your ill-gotten treasures and the short ephah, which is accursed? {11} Shall I acquit a man with dishonest scales, with a bag of false weights? {12} Her rich men are violent; her people are liars and their tongues speak deceitfully. {13} Therefore, I have begun to destroy you, to ruin you because of your sins. {14} You will eat but not be satisfied; your stomach will still be empty. You will store up but save nothing, because what you save I will give to the sword. {15} You will plant but not harvest; you will press olives but not use the oil on yourselves, you will crush grapes but not drink the wine.

BUT ISRAEL WILL BE RESTORED

Micah 7:8-13

Do not gloat over me, my enemy! Though I have fallen, I will rise. Though I sit in darkness, the LORD will be my light. {9} Because I have sinned against him, I will bear the Lord's wrath, until he pleads my case and establishes my right. He will bring me out into the light; I will see his righteousness. {10} Then my enemy will see it and will be covered with shame, she who said to me, "Where is the LORD your God?" My eyes will see her downfall; even now she will be trampled underfoot like mire in the streets. {11} The day for building your walls will come, the day for extending your boundaries. {12} In that day people will come to you from Assyria and the cities of Egypt, even from Egypt to the Euphrates and from sea to sea and from mountain to mountain. {13} The earth will become desolate because of its inhabitants, as the result of their deeds.

Micah 7:15-20

"As in the days when you came out of Egypt, I will show them my wonders." {16} Nations will see and be ashamed, deprived of all their power. They will lay their hands on their mouths and their ears will become deaf. {17} They will lick dust like a snake, like creatures that crawl on the ground. They will come trembling out of their dens; they will turn in fear to the LORD our God and will be afraid of you. {18} Who is a God like you, who pardons sin and forgives the transgression of the remnant of his inheritance? You do not stay angry forever but delight to show mercy. {19} You will again have compassion on us; you will tread our sins underfoot and hurl all our iniquities into the depths of the sea. {20} You will be true to Jacob, and show mercy to Abraham, as you pledged on oath to our fathers in days long ago.

CONDEMNATION OF NINEVEH; JUDAH TO BE RESCUED

Nahum 1:1-15

An oracle concerning Nineveh. The book of the vision of Nahum the Elkoshite. {2} The LORD is a jealous and avenging God; the LORD takes vengeance and is filled with wrath. The LORD takes vengeance on his foes and maintains his wrath against his enemies. {3} The LORD is slow to anger and great in power; the LORD will not leave the guilty unpunished. His way is in the whirlwind and the storm, and clouds are the dust of his feet. {4} He rebukes the sea and dries it up; he makes all the rivers run dry. Bashan and Carmel wither and the blossoms of Lebanon fade. {5} The mountains quake before him and the hills melt away. The earth trembles at his presence, the world and all who live in it. {6} Who can withstand his indignation? Who can endure his fierce anger? His wrath is poured out like fire; the rocks are shattered before him. {7} The LORD is good, a refuge in times of trouble. He cares for those who trust in him, {8} but with an overwhelming flood he will make an end of <Nineveh>; he will pursue his foes into darkness. {9} Whatever they plot against the LORD he will bring to an end; trouble will not come a second time. {10} They will be entangled among thorns and drunk from their wine; they will be consumed like dry stubble. {11} From you, <O Nineveh>,has one come forth who plots evil against the LORD and counsels wickedness. {12} This is what the LORD says: "Although they have allies and are numerous, they will be cut off and pass away. Although I have afflicted you, <O Judah>,I will afflict you no more. {13} Now I will break their yoke from your neck and tear your shackles away." {14} The LORD has given a command concerning you, <Nineveh>: "You will have no descendants to bear your name. I will destroy the carved images and cast idols that are in the temple of your gods. I will prepare your grave, for you are vile." {15} Look, there on the mountains, the feet of one who brings good news, who proclaims peace! Celebrate your festivals, O Judah, and fulfill your vows. No more will the wicked invade you; they will be completely destroyed.

WHY, OH LORD, DO YOU TOLERATE THE WICKED?

Hab 1:1-6

The oracle that Habakkuk the prophet received. {2} How long, O LORD, must I call for help, but you do not listen? Or cry out to you, "Violence!" but you do not save? {3} Why do you make me look at injustice? Why do you tolerate wrong? Destruction and violence are before me; there is strife, and conflict abounds. {4} Therefore the law is paralyzed, and justice never prevails. The wicked hem in the righteous, so that justice is perverted. {5} "Look at the nations and watch– and be utterly amazed. For I am going to do something in your days that you would not believe, even if you were told. {6} I am raising up the Babylonians, that ruthless and impetuous people, who sweep across the whole earth to seize dwelling places not their own.

Hab 1:12-13

O LORD, are you not from everlasting? My God, my Holy One, we will not die. O LORD, you have appointed them to execute judgment; O Rock, you have ordained them to punish. {13} Your eyes are too pure to look on evil; you cannot tolerate wrong. Why then do you tolerate the treacherous? Why are you silent while the wicked swallow up those more righteous than themselves?

Hab 2:2-3

Then the LORD replied: "Write down the revelation and make it plain on tablets so that a herald may run with it. {3} For the revelation awaits an appointed time; it speaks of the end and will not prove false. Though it linger, wait for it; it will certainly come and will not delay.

Hab 2:20

But the LORD is in his holy temple; let all the earth be silent before him."

Hab 3:1-2

A prayer of Habakkuk the prophet. On <shigionoth>. {2} LORD, I have heard of your fame; I stand in awe of your deeds, O LORD. Renew them in our day, in our time make them known; in wrath remember mercy.

GOD'S CALL TO REBUILD THE TEMPLE

Hag 1:1-15

In the second year of King Darius, on the first day of the sixth month, the word of the LORD came through the prophet Haggai to Zerubbabel son of Shealtiel, governor of Judah, and to Joshua son of Jehozadak, the high priest: {2} This is what the LORD Almighty says: "These people say, 'The time has not yet come for the Lord's house to be built.'" {3} Then the word of the LORD came through the prophet Haggai: {4} "Is it a time for you yourselves to be living in your paneled houses, while this house remains a ruin?" {5} Now this is what the LORD Almighty says: "Give careful thought to your ways. {6} You have planted much, but have harvested little. You eat, but never have enough. You drink, but never have your fill. You put on clothes, but are not warm. You earn wages, only to put them in a purse with holes in it." {7} This is what the LORD Almighty says: "Give careful thought to your ways. {8} Go up into the mountains and bring down timber and build the house, so that I may take pleasure in it and be honored," says the LORD. {9} "You expected much, but see, it turned out to be little. What you brought home, I blew away. Why?" declares the LORD Almighty. "Because of my house, which remains a ruin, while each of you is busy with his own house. {10} Therefore, because of you the heavens have withheld their dew and the earth its crops. {11} I called for a drought on the fields and the mountains, on the grain, the new wine, the oil and whatever the ground produces, on men and cattle, and on the labor of your hands." {12} Then Zerubbabel son of Shealtiel, Joshua son of Jehozadak, the high priest, and the whole remnant of the people obeyed the voice of the LORD their God and the message of the prophet Haggai, because the LORD their God had sent him. And the people feared the LORD. {13} Then Haggai, the Lord's messenger, gave this message of the LORD to the people: "I am with you," declares the LORD. {14} So the LORD stirred up the spirit of Zerubbabel son of Shealtiel, governor of Judah, and the spirit of Joshua son of Jehozadak, the high priest, and the spirit of the whole remnant of the people. They came and began to work on the house of the LORD Almighty, their God, {15} on the twenty-fourth day of the sixth month in the second year of King Darius.

MEASUREMENTS FOR JERUSALEM;
GARMENTS FOR THE PRIESTS

Zec 2:1-13

Then I looked up–and there before me was a man with a measuring line in his hand! {2} I asked, "Where are you going?" He answered me, "To measure Jerusalem, to find out how wide and how long it is." {3} Then the angel who was speaking to me left, and another angel came to meet him {4} and said to him: "Run, tell that young man, 'Jerusalem will be a city without walls because of the great number of men and livestock in it. {5} And I myself will be a wall of fire around it,' declares the LORD, 'and I will be its glory within.' {6} "Come! Come! Flee from the land of the north," declares the LORD, "for I have scattered you to the four winds of heaven," declares the LORD. {7} "Come, O Zion! Escape, you who live in the Daughter of Babylon!" {8} For this is what the LORD Almighty says: "After he has honored me and has sent me against the nations that have plundered you–for whoever touches you touches the apple of his eye– {9} I will surely raise my hand against them so that their slaves will plunder them. Then you will know that the LORD Almighty has sent me. {10} "Shout and be glad, O Daughter of Zion. For I am coming, and I will live among you," declares the LORD. {11} "Many nations will be joined with the LORD in that day and will become my people. I will live among you and you will know that the LORD Almighty has sent me to you. {12} The LORD will inherit Judah as his portion in the holy land and will again choose Jerusalem. {13} Be still before the LORD, all mankind, because he has roused himself from his holy dwelling."

Zec 3:1-7

Then he showed me Joshua the high priest standing before the angel of the LORD, and Satan standing at his right side to accuse him. {2} The LORD said to Satan, "The LORD rebuke you, Satan! The LORD, who has chosen Jerusalem, rebuke you! Is not this man a burning stick snatched from the fire?" {3} Now Joshua was dressed in filthy clothes as he stood before the angel. {4} The angel said to those who were standing before him, "Take off his filthy clothes." Then he said to Joshua, "See, I have taken away your sin, and I will put rich garments on you." {5} Then I said, "Put a clean turban on his head." So they put a clean turban on his head and clothed him, while the angel of the LORD stood by. {6} The angel of the LORD gave this charge to Joshua: {7} "This is what the LORD Almighty says: 'If you will walk in my ways and keep my requirements, then you will govern my house and have charge of my courts, and I will give you a place among these standing here.

THIRTY PIECES OF SILVER

Zec 11:7-17

So I pastured the flock marked for slaughter, particularly the oppressed of the flock. Then I took two staffs and called one Favor and the other Union, and I pastured the flock. {8} In one month I got rid of the three shepherds. The flock detested me, and I grew weary of them {9} and said, "I will not be your shepherd. Let the dying die, and the perishing perish. Let those who are left eat one another's flesh." {10} Then I took my staff called Favor and broke it, revoking the covenant I had made with all the nations. {11} It was revoked on that day, and so the afflicted of the flock who were watching me knew it was the word of the LORD. {12} I told them, "If you think it best, give me my pay; but if not, keep it." So they paid me thirty pieces of silver. {13} And the LORD said to me, "Throw it to the potter"–the handsome price at which they priced me! So I took the thirty pieces of silver and threw them into the house of the LORD to the potter. {14} Then I broke my second staff called Union, breaking the brotherhood between Judah and Israel. {15} Then the LORD said to me, "Take again the equipment of a foolish shepherd. {16} For I am going to raise up a shepherd over the land who will not care for the lost, or seek the young, or heal the injured, or feed the healthy, but will eat the meat of the choice sheep, tearing off their hoofs. {17} "Woe to the worthless shepherd, who deserts the flock! May the sword strike his arm and his right eye! May his arm be completely withered, his right eye totally blinded!" An Oracle

Zec 12:1-5

This is the word of the LORD concerning Israel. The LORD, who stretches out the heavens, who lays the foundation of the earth, and who forms the spirit of man within him, declares: {2} "I am going to make Jerusalem a cup that sends all the surrounding peoples reeling. Judah will be besieged as well as Jerusalem. {3} On that day, when all the nations of the earth are gathered against her, I will make Jerusalem an immovable rock for all the nations. All who try to move it will injure themselves. {4} On that day I will strike every horse with panic and its rider with madness," declares the LORD. "I will keep a watchful eye over the house of Judah, but I will blind all the horses of the nations. {5} Then the leaders of Judah will say in their hearts, 'The people of Jerusalem are strong, because the LORD Almighty is their God.'

GOD WILL GATHER NATIONS AGAINST JERUSALEM

Zec 14:1-16

A day of the LORD is coming when your plunder will be divided among you. {2} I will gather all the nations to Jerusalem to fight against it; the city will be captured, the houses ransacked, and the women raped. Half of the city will go into exile, but the rest of the people will not be taken from the city. {3} Then the LORD will go out and fight against those nations, as he fights in the day of battle. {4} On that day his feet will stand on the Mount of Olives, east of Jerusalem, and the Mount of Olives will be split in two from east to west, forming a great valley, with half of the mountain moving north and half moving south. {5} You will flee by my mountain valley, for it will extend to Azel. You will flee as you fled from the earthquake in the days of Uzziah king of Judah. Then the LORD my God will come, and all the holy ones with him. {6} On that day there will be no light, no cold or frost. {7} It will be a unique day, without daytime or nighttime—a day known to the LORD. When evening comes, there will be light. {8} On that day living water will flow out from Jerusalem, half to the eastern sea and half to the western sea, in summer and in winter. {9} The LORD will be king over the whole earth. On that day there will be one LORD, and his name the only name. {10} The whole land, from Geba to Rimmon, south of Jerusalem, will become like the Arabah. But Jerusalem will be raised up and remain in its place, from the Benjamin Gate to the site of the First Gate, to the Corner Gate, and from the Tower of Hananel to the royal winepresses. {11} It will be inhabited; never again will it be destroyed. Jerusalem will be secure. {12} This is the plague with which the LORD will strike all the nations that fought against Jerusalem: Their flesh will rot while they are still standing on their feet, their eyes will rot in their sockets, and their tongues will rot in their mouths. {13} On that day men will be stricken by the LORD with great panic. Each man will seize the hand of another, and they will attack each other. {14} Judah too will fight at Jerusalem. The wealth of all the surrounding nations will be collected—great quantities of gold and silver and clothing. {15} A similar plague will strike the horses and mules, the camels and donkeys, and all the animals in those camps. {16} Then the survivors from all the nations that have attacked Jerusalem will go up year after year to worship the King, the LORD Almighty, and to celebrate the Feast of Tabernacles.

SACRIFICES DEFILED

Mal 1:1-14

An oracle: The word of the LORD to Israel through Malachi. {2} "I have loved you," says the LORD. "But you ask, 'How have you loved us?' "Was not Esau Jacob's brother?" the LORD says. "Yet I have loved Jacob, {3} but Esau I have hated, and I have turned his mountains into a wasteland and left his inheritance to the desert jackals." {4} Edom may say, "Though we have been crushed, we will rebuild the ruins." But this is what the LORD Almighty says: "They may build, but I will demolish. They will be called the Wicked Land, a people always under the wrath of the LORD. {5} You will see it with your own eyes and say, 'Great is the LORD– even beyond the borders of Israel!' {6} "A son honors his father, and a servant his master. If I am a father, where is the honor due me? If I am a master, where is the respect due me?" says the LORD Almighty. "It is you, O priests, who show contempt for my name. "But you ask, 'How have we shown contempt for your name?' {7} "You place defiled food on my altar. "But you ask, 'How have we defiled you?' "By saying that the Lord's table is contemptible. {8} When you bring blind animals for sacrifice, is that not wrong? When you sacrifice crippled or diseased animals, is that not wrong? Try offering them to your governor! Would he be pleased with you? Would he accept you?" says the LORD Almighty. {9} "Now implore God to be gracious to us. With such offerings from your hands, will he accept you?"–says the LORD Almighty. {10} "Oh, that one of you would shut the temple doors, so that you would not light useless fires on my altar! I am not pleased with you," says the LORD Almighty, "and I will accept no offering from your hands. {11} My name will be great among the nations, from the rising to the setting of the sun. In every place incense and pure offerings will be brought to my name, because my name will be great among the nations," says the LORD Almighty. {12} "But you profane it by saying of the Lord's table, 'It is defiled,' and of its food, 'It is contemptible.' {13} And you say, 'What a burden!' and you sniff at it contemptuously," says the LORD Almighty. "When you bring injured, crippled or diseased animals and offer them as sacrifices, should I accept them from your hands?" says the LORD. {14} "Cursed is the cheat who has an acceptable male in his flock and vows to give it, but then sacrifices a blemished animal to the Lord. For I am a great king," says the LORD Almighty, "and my name is to be feared among the nations.

HE WILL BE LIKE A REFINER'S FIRE

Mal 2:7-3:4

"For the lips of a priest ought to preserve knowledge, and from his mouth men should seek instruction–because he is the messenger of the LORD Almighty. {8} But you have turned from the way and by your teaching have caused many to stumble; you have violated the covenant with Levi," says the LORD Almighty. {9} "So I have caused you to be despised and humiliated before all the people, because you have not followed my ways but have shown partiality in matters of the law." {10} Have we not all one Father ? Did not one God create us? Why do we profane the covenant of our fathers by breaking faith with one another? {11} Judah has broken faith. A detestable thing has been committed in Israel and in Jerusalem: Judah has desecrated the sanctuary the LORD loves, by marrying the daughter of a foreign god. {12} As for the man who does this, whoever he may be, may the LORD cut him off from the tents of Jacob –even though he brings offerings to the LORD Almighty. {13} Another thing you do: You flood the Lord's altar with tears. You weep and wail because he no longer pays attention to your offerings or accepts them with pleasure from your hands. {14} You ask, "Why?" It is because the LORD is acting as the witness between you and the wife of your youth, because you have broken faith with her, though she is your partner, the wife of your marriage covenant. {15} Has not <the LORD> made them one? In flesh and spirit they are his. And why one? Because he was seeking godly offspring. So guard yourself in your spirit, and do not break faith with the wife of your youth. {16} "I hate divorce," says the LORD God of Israel, "and I hate a man's covering himself with violence as well as with his garment," says the LORD Almighty. So guard yourself in your spirit, and do not break faith. {17} You have wearied the LORD with your words. "How have we wearied him?" you ask. By saying, "All who do evil are good in the eyes of the LORD, and he is pleased with them" or "Where is the God of justice?" {3:1} "See, I will send my messenger, who will prepare the way before me. Then suddenly the Lord you are seeking will come to his temple; the messenger of the covenant, whom you desire, will come," says the LORD Almighty. {2} But who can endure the day of his coming? Who can stand when he appears? For he will be like a refiner's fire or a launderer's soap. {3} He will sit as a refiner and purifier of silver; he will purify the Levites and refine them like gold and silver. Then the LORD will have men who will bring offerings in righteousness, {4} and the offerings of Judah and Jerusalem will be acceptable to the LORD, as in days gone by, as in former years.

JESUS IS BAPTIZED, CALLS HIS FIRST DISCIPLES

Mark 1:1-20

The beginning of the gospel about Jesus Christ, the Son of God. {2} It is written in Isaiah the prophet: "I will send my messenger ahead of you, who will prepare your way" – {3} "a voice of one calling in the desert, 'Prepare the way for the Lord, make straight paths for him.'" {4} And so John came, baptizing in the desert region and preaching a baptism of repentance for the forgiveness of sins. {5} The whole Judean countryside and all the people of Jerusalem went out to him. Confessing their sins, they were baptized by him in the Jordan River. {6} John wore clothing made of camel's hair, with a leather belt around his waist, and he ate locusts and wild honey. {7} And this was his message: "After me will come one more powerful than I, the thongs of whose sandals I am not worthy to stoop down and untie. {8} I baptize you with water, but he will baptize you with the Holy Spirit." {9} At that time Jesus came from Nazareth in Galilee and was baptized by John in the Jordan. {10} As Jesus was coming up out of the water, he saw heaven being torn open and the Spirit descending on him like a dove. {11} And a voice came from heaven: "You are my Son, whom I love; with you I am well pleased." {12} At once the Spirit sent him out into the desert, {13} and he was in the desert forty days, being tempted by Satan. He was with the wild animals, and angels attended him. {14} After John was put in prison, Jesus went into Galilee, proclaiming the good news of God. {15} "The time has come," he said. "The kingdom of God is near. Repent and believe the good news!" {16} As Jesus walked beside the Sea of Galilee, he saw Simon and his brother Andrew casting a net into the lake, for they were fishermen. {17} "Come, follow me," Jesus said, "and I will make you fishers of men." {18} At once they left their nets and followed him. {19} When he had gone a little farther, he saw James son of Zebedee and his brother John in a boat, preparing their nets. {20} Without delay he called them, and they left their father Zebedee in the boat with the hired men and followed him.

JESUS HEALS THE SICK, PRAYS ALONE

Mark 1:21-45

They went to Capernaum, and when the Sabbath came, Jesus went into the synagogue and began to teach. {22} The people were amazed at his teaching, because he taught them as one who had authority, not as the teachers of the law. {23} Just then a man in their synagogue who was possessed by an evil spirit cried out, {24} "What do you want with us, Jesus of Nazareth? Have you come to destroy us? I know who you are–the Holy One of God!" {25} "Be quiet!" said Jesus sternly. "Come out of him!" {26} The evil spirit shook the man violently and came out of him with a shriek. {27} The people were all so amazed that they asked each other, "What is this? A new teaching–and with authority! He even gives orders to evil spirits and they obey him." {28} News about him spread quickly over the whole region of Galilee. {29} As soon as they left the synagogue, they went with James and John to the home of Simon and Andrew. {30} Simon's mother-in-law was in bed with a fever, and they told Jesus about her. {31} So he went to her, took her hand and helped her up. The fever left her and she began to wait on them. {32} That evening after sunset the people brought to Jesus all the sick and demon-possessed. {33} The whole town gathered at the door, {34} and Jesus healed many who had various diseases. He also drove out many demons, but he would not let the demons speak because they knew who he was. {35} Very early in the morning, while it was still dark, Jesus got up, left the house and went off to a solitary place, where he prayed. {36} Simon and his companions went to look for him, {37} and when they found him, they exclaimed: "Everyone is looking for you!" {38} Jesus replied, "Let us go somewhere else–to the nearby villages–so I can preach there also. That is why I have come." {39} So he traveled throughout Galilee, preaching in their synagogues and driving out demons. {40} A man with leprosy came to him and begged him on his knees, "If you are willing, you can make me clean." {41} Filled with compassion, Jesus reached out his hand and touched the man. "I am willing," he said. "Be clean!" {42} Immediately the leprosy left him and he was cured. {43} Jesus sent him away at once with a strong warning: {44} "See that you don't tell this to anyone. But go, show yourself to the priest and offer the sacrifices that Moses commanded for your cleansing, as a testimony to them." {45} Instead he went out and began to talk freely, spreading the news. As a result, Jesus could no longer enter a town openly but stayed outside in lonely places. Yet the people still came to him from everywhere.

JESUS COMMENTS ON FASTING, CALLS TWELVE DISCIPLES

Mark 2:18-27

Now John's disciples and the Pharisees were fasting. Some people came and asked Jesus, "How is it that John's disciples and the disciples of the Pharisees are fasting, but yours are not?" {19} Jesus answered, "How can the guests of the bridegroom fast while he is with them? They cannot, so long as they have him with them. {20} But the time will come when the bridegroom will be taken from them, and on that day they will fast. {21} "No one sews a patch of unshrunk cloth on an old garment. If he does, the new piece will pull away from the old, making the tear worse. {22} And no one pours new wine into old wineskins. If he does, the wine will burst the skins, and both the wine and the wineskins will be ruined. No, he pours new wine into new wineskins." {23} One Sabbath Jesus was going through the grainfields, and as his disciples walked along, they began to pick some heads of grain. {24} The Pharisees said to him, "Look, why are they doing what is unlawful on the Sabbath?" {25} He answered, "Have you never read what David did when he and his companions were hungry and in need? {26} In the days of Abiathar the high priest, he entered the house of God and ate the consecrated bread, which is lawful only for priests to eat. And he also gave some to his companions." {27} Then he said to them, "The Sabbath was made for man, not man for the Sabbath. {28} So the Son of Man is Lord even of the Sabbath."

Mark 3:8-19

When they heard all he was doing, many people came to him from Judea, Jerusalem, Idumea, and the regions across the Jordan and around Tyre and Sidon. {9} Because of the crowd he told his disciples to have a small boat ready for him, to keep the people from crowding him. {10} For he had healed many, so that those with diseases were pushing forward to touch him. {11} Whenever the evil spirits saw him, they fell down before him and cried out, "You are the Son of God." {12} But he gave them strict orders not to tell who he was. {13} Jesus went up on a mountainside and called to him those he wanted, and they came to him. {14} He appointed twelve–designating them apostles –that they might be with him and that he might send them out to preach {15} and to have authority to drive out demons. {16} These are the twelve he appointed: Simon (to whom he gave the name Peter); {17} James son of Zebedee and his brother John (to them he gave the name Boanerges, which means Sons of Thunder); {18} Andrew, Philip, Bartholomew, Matthew, Thomas, James son of Alphaeus, Thaddaeus, Simon the Zealot {19} and Judas Iscariot, who betrayed him.

PARABLE OF THE SOWER AND THE SEED

Mark 4:1-20

Again Jesus began to teach by the lake. The crowd that gathered around him was so large that he got into a boat and sat in it out on the lake, while all the people were along the shore at the water's edge. {2} He taught them many things by parables, and in his teaching said: {3} "Listen ! A farmer went out to sow his seed. {4} As he was scattering the seed, some fell along the path, and the birds came and ate it up. {5} Some fell on rocky places, where it did not have much soil. It sprang up quickly, because the soil was shallow. {6} But when the sun came up, the plants were scorched, and they withered because they had no root. {7} Other seed fell among thorns, which grew up and choked the plants, so that they did not bear grain. {8} Still other seed fell on good soil. It came up, grew and produced a crop, multiplying thirty, sixty, or even a hundred times." {9} Then Jesus said, "He who has ears to hear, let him hear." {10} When he was alone, the Twelve and the others around him asked him about the parables. {11} He told them, "The secret of the kingdom of God has been given to you. But to those on the outside everything is said in parables {12} so that, "'they may be ever seeing but never perceiving, and ever hearing but never understanding; otherwise they might turn and be forgiven!' " {13} Then Jesus said to them, "Don't you understand this parable? How then will you understand any parable? {14} The farmer sows the word. {15} Some people are like seed along the path, where the word is sown. As soon as they hear it, Satan comes and takes away the word that was sown in them. {16} Others , like seed sown on rocky places, hear the word and at once receive it with joy. {17} But since they have no root, they last only a short time. When trouble or persecution comes because of the word, they quickly fall away. {18} Still others, like seed sown among thorns, hear the word; {19} but the worries of this life, the deceitfulness of wealth and the desires for other things come in and choke the word, making it unfruitful. {20} Others, like seed sown on good soil, hear the word, accept it, and produce a crop– thirty, sixty or even a hundred times what was sown."

JESUS HEALS DEMON-POSSESSED

Mark 5:1-20

They went across the lake to the region of the Gerasenes. {2} When Jesus got out of the boat, a man with an evil spirit came from the tombs to meet him. {3} This man lived in the tombs, and no one could bind him any more, not even with a chain. {4} For he had often been chained hand and foot, but he tore the chains apart and broke the irons on his feet. No one was strong enough to subdue him. {5} Night and day among the tombs and in the hills he would cry out and cut himself with stones. {6} When he saw Jesus from a distance, he ran and fell on his knees in front of him. {7} He shouted at the top of his voice, "What do you want with me, Jesus, Son of the Most High God? Swear to God that you won't torture me!" {8} For Jesus had said to him, "Come out of this man, you evil spirit!" {9} Then Jesus asked him, "What is your name?" "My name is Legion," he replied, "for we are many." {10} And he begged Jesus again and again not to send them out of the area. {11} A large herd of pigs was feeding on the nearby hillside. {12} The demons begged Jesus, "Send us among the pigs; allow us to go into them." {13} He gave them permission, and the evil spirits came out and went into the pigs. The herd, about two thousand in number, rushed down the steep bank into the lake and were drowned. {14} Those tending the pigs ran off and reported this in the town and countryside, and the people went out to see what had happened. {15} When they came to Jesus, they saw the man who had been possessed by the legion of demons, sitting there, dressed and in his right mind; and they were afraid. {16} Those who had seen it told the people what had happened to the demon-possessed man–and told about the pigs as well. {17} Then the people began to plead with Jesus to leave their region. {18} As Jesus was getting into the boat, the man who had been demon-possessed begged to go with him. {19} Jesus did not let him, but said, "Go home to your family and tell them how much the Lord has done for you, and how he has had mercy on you." {20} So the man went away and began to tell in the Decapolis how much Jesus had done for him. And all the people were amazed.

JESUS SENDS OUT HIS DISCIPLES
JOHN THE BAPTIST IS BEHEADED

Mark 6:7-28

Calling the Twelve to him, he sent them out two by two and gave them authority over evil spirits. {8} These were his instructions: "Take nothing for the journey except a staff–no bread, no bag, no money in your belts. {9} Wear sandals but not an extra tunic. {10} Whenever you enter a house, stay there until you leave that town. {11} And if any place will not welcome you or listen to you, shake the dust off your feet when you leave, as a testimony against them." {12} They went out and preached that people should repent. {13} They drove out many demons and anointed many sick people with oil and healed them. {14} King Herod heard about this, for Jesus' name had become well known. Some were saying, "John the Baptist has been raised from the dead, and that is why miraculous powers are at work in him." {15} Others said, "He is Elijah." And still others claimed, "He is a prophet, like one of the prophets of long ago."

{16} But when Herod heard this, he said, "John, the man I beheaded, has been raised from the dead!" {17} For Herod himself had given orders to have John arrested, and he had him bound and put in prison. He did this because of Herodias, his brother Philip's wife, whom he had married. {18} For John had been saying to Herod, "It is not lawful for you to have your brother's wife." {19} So Herodias nursed a grudge against John and wanted to kill him. But she was not able to, {20} because Herod feared John and protected him, knowing him to be a righteous and holy man. When Herod heard John, he was greatly puzzled; yet he liked to listen to him. {21} Finally the opportune time came. On his birthday Herod gave a banquet for his high officials and military commanders and the leading men of Galilee. {22} When the daughter of Herodias came in and danced, she pleased Herod and his dinner guests. The king said to the girl, "Ask me for anything you want, and I'll give it to you." {23} And he promised her with an oath, "Whatever you ask I will give you, up to half my kingdom." {24} She went out and said to her mother, "What shall I ask for?" "The head of John the Baptist," she answered. {25} At once the girl hurried in to the king with the request: "I want you to give me right now the head of John the Baptist on a platter." {26} The king was greatly distressed, but because of his oaths and his dinner guests, he did not want to refuse her. {27} So he immediately sent an executioner with orders to bring John's head. The man went, beheaded John in the prison, {28} and brought back his head on a platter. He presented it to the girl, and she gave it to her mother.

JESUS FEEDS FIVE THOUSAND, WALKS ON WATER

Mark 6:30-51

The apostles gathered around Jesus and reported to him all they had done and taught. {31} Then, because so many people were coming and going that they did not even have a chance to eat, he said to them, "Come with me by yourselves to a quiet place and get some rest." {32} So they went away by themselves in a boat to a solitary place. {33} But many who saw them leaving recognized them and ran on foot from all the towns and got there ahead of them. {34} When Jesus landed and saw a large crowd, he had compassion on them, because they were like sheep without a shepherd. So he began teaching them many things. {35} By this time it was late in the day, so his disciples came to him. "This is a remote place," they said, "and it's already very late. {36} Send the people away so they can go to the surrounding countryside and villages and buy themselves something to eat." {37} But he answered, "You give them something to eat." They said to him, "That would take eight months of a man's wages ! Are we to go and spend that much on bread and give it to them to eat?" {38} "How many loaves do you have?" he asked. "Go and see." When they found out, they said, "Five—and two fish." {39} Then Jesus directed them to have all the people sit down in groups on the green grass. {40} So they sat down in groups of hundreds and fifties. {41} Taking the five loaves and the two fish and looking up to heaven, he gave thanks and broke the loaves. Then he gave them to his disciples to set before the people. He also divided the two fish among them all. {42} They all ate and were satisfied, {43} and the disciples picked up twelve basketfuls of broken pieces of bread and fish. {44} The number of the men who had eaten was five thousand.

{45} Immediately Jesus made his disciples get into the boat and go on ahead of him to Bethsaida, while he dismissed the crowd. {46} After leaving them, he went up on a mountainside to pray. {47} When evening came, the boat was in the middle of the lake, and he was alone on land. {48} He saw the disciples straining at the oars, because the wind was against them. About the fourth watch of the night he went out to them, walking on the lake. He was about to pass by them, {49} but when they saw him walking on the lake, they thought he was a ghost. They cried out, {50} because they all saw him and were terrified. Immediately he spoke to them and said, "Take courage! It is I. Don't be afraid." {51} Then he climbed into the boat with them, and the wind died down. They were completely amazed,

THE PHARISEES' LAWS CONDEMNED;
EXEMPLARY FAITH OF THE PHOENICIAN WOMAN

Mark 7:7-30

They worship me in vain; their teachings are but rules taught by men.' {8} You have let go of the commands of God and are holding on to the traditions of men." {9} And he said to them: "You have a fine way of setting aside the commands of God in order to observe your own traditions! {10} For Moses said, 'Honor your father and your mother,' and, 'Anyone who curses his father or mother must be put to death.' {11} But you say that if a man says to his father or mother: 'Whatever help you might otherwise have received from me is Corban' (that is, a gift devoted to God), {12} then you no longer let him do anything for his father or mother. {13} Thus you nullify the word of God by your tradition that you have handed down. And you do many things like that." {14} Again Jesus called the crowd to him and said, "Listen to me, everyone, and understand this. {15} Nothing outside a man can make him 'unclean' by going into him. Rather, it is what comes out of a man that makes him 'unclean.'" {16} {17} After he had left the crowd and entered the house, his disciples asked him about this parable. {18} "Are you so dull?" he asked. "Don't you see that nothing that enters a man from the outside can make him 'unclean'? {19} For it doesn't go into his heart but into his stomach, and then out of his body." (In saying this, Jesus declared all foods "clean.") {20} He went on: "What comes out of a man is what makes him 'unclean.' {21} For from within, out of men's hearts, come evil thoughts, sexual immorality, theft, murder, adultery, {22} greed, malice, deceit, lewdness, envy, slander, arrogance and folly. {23} All these evils come from inside and make a man 'unclean.'" {24} Jesus left that place and went to the vicinity of Tyre. He entered a house and did not want anyone to know it; yet he could not keep his presence secret.

{25} In fact, as soon as she heard about him, a woman whose little daughter was possessed by an evil spirit came and fell at his feet. {26} The woman was a Greek, born in Syrian Phoenicia. She begged Jesus to drive the demon out of her daughter. {27} "First let the children eat all they want," he told her, "for it is not right to take the children's bread and toss it to their dogs." {28} "Yes, Lord," she replied, "but even the dogs under the table eat the children's crumbs." {29} Then he told her, "For such a reply, you may go; the demon has left your daughter." {30} She went home and found her child lying on the bed, and the demon gone.

THE PHARISEES' LEAVEN; JESUS HEALS A BLIND MAN; PETER'S WITNESS

Mark 8:14-36

The disciples had forgotten to bring bread, except for one loaf they had with them in the boat. {15} "Be careful," Jesus warned them. "Watch out for the yeast of the Pharisees and that of Herod." {16} They discussed this with one another and said, "It is because we have no bread." {17} Aware of their discussion, Jesus asked them: "Why are you talking about having no bread? Do you still not see or understand? Are your hearts hardened? {18} Do you have eyes but fail to see, and ears but fail to hear? And don't you remember? {19} When I broke the five loaves for the five thousand, how many basketfuls of pieces did you pick up?" "Twelve," they replied. {20} "And when I broke the seven loaves for the four thousand, how many basketfuls of pieces did you pick up?" They answered, "Seven." {21} He said to them, "Do you still not understand?"

{22} They came to Bethsaida, and some people brought a blind man and begged Jesus to touch him. {23} He took the blind man by the hand and led him outside the village. When he had spit on the man's eyes and put his hands on him, Jesus asked, "Do you see anything?" {24} He looked up and said, "I see people; they look like trees walking around." {25} Once more Jesus put his hands on the man's eyes. Then his eyes were opened, his sight was restored, and he saw everything clearly. {26} Jesus sent him home, saying, "Don't go into the village."

{27} Jesus and his disciples went on to the villages around Caesarea Philippi. On the way he asked them, "Who do people say I am?" {28} They replied, "Some say John the Baptist; others say Elijah; and still others, one of the prophets." {29} "But what about you?" he asked. "Who do you say I am?" Peter answered, "You are the Christ." {30} Jesus warned them not to tell anyone about him. {31} He then began to teach them that the Son of Man must suffer many things and be rejected by the elders, chief priests and teachers of the law, and that he must be killed and after three days rise again. {32} He spoke plainly about this, and Peter took him aside and began to rebuke him. {33} But when Jesus turned and looked at his disciples, he rebuked Peter. "Get behind me, Satan!" he said. "You do not have in mind the things of God, but the things of men." {34} Then he called the crowd to him along with his disciples and said: "If anyone would come after me, he must deny himself and take up his cross and follow me. {35} For whoever wants to save his life will lose it, but whoever loses his life for me and for the gospel will save it. {36} What good is it for a man to gain the whole world, yet forfeit his soul?

JESUS' TRANSFIGURATION

Mark 9:2-9

After six days Jesus took Peter, James and John with him and led them up a high mountain, where they were all alone. There he was transfigured before them. {3} His clothes became dazzling white, whiter than anyone in the world could bleach them. {4} And there appeared before them Elijah and Moses, who were talking with Jesus. {5} Peter said to Jesus, "Rabbi, it is good for us to be here. Let us put up three shelters—one for you, one for Moses and one for Elijah." {6} (He did not know what to say, they were so frightened.) {7} Then a cloud appeared and enveloped them, and a voice came from the cloud: "This is my Son, whom I love. Listen to him!" {8} Suddenly, when they looked around, they no longer saw anyone with them except Jesus. {9} As they were coming down the mountain, Jesus gave them orders not to tell anyone what they had seen until the Son of Man had risen from the dead.

JESUS HEALS BOY WITH EVIL SPIRIT

Mark 9:17-27

"Teacher, I brought you my son, who is possessed by a spirit that has robbed him of speech. {18} Whenever it seizes him, it throws him to the ground. He foams at the mouth, gnashes his teeth and becomes rigid. I asked your disciples to drive out the spirit, but they could not." {19} "O unbelieving generation," Jesus replied, "how long shall I stay with you? How long shall I put up with you? Bring the boy to me." {20} So they brought him. When the spirit saw Jesus, it immediately threw the boy into a convulsion. He fell to the ground and rolled around, foaming at the mouth. {21} Jesus asked the boy's father, "How long has he been like this?" "From childhood," he answered. {22} "It has often thrown him into fire or water to kill him. But if you can do anything, take pity on us and help us." {23} "'If you can'?" said Jesus. "Everything is possible for him who believes." {24} Immediately the boy's father exclaimed, "I do believe; help me overcome my unbelief!" {25} When Jesus saw that a crowd was running to the scene, he rebuked the evil spirit. "You deaf and mute spirit," he said, "I command you, come out of him and never enter him again." {26} The spirit shrieked, convulsed him violently and came out. The boy looked so much like a corpse that many said, "He's dead." {27} But Jesus took him by the hand and lifted him to his feet, and he stood up.

JESUS' COMMENTS ON DIVORCE, AND LITTLE CHILDREN; AND HAS CONVERSATION WITH RICH YOUNG MAN

Mark 10:1-25

Jesus then left that place and went into the region of Judea and across the Jordan. Again crowds of people came to him, and as was his custom, he taught them. {2} Some Pharisees came and tested him by asking, "Is it lawful for a man to divorce his wife?" {3} "What did Moses command you?" he replied. {4} They said, "Moses permitted a man to write a certificate of divorce and send her away." {5} "It was because your hearts were hard that Moses wrote you this law," Jesus replied. {6} "But at the beginning of creation God 'made them male and female.' {7} 'For this reason a man will leave his father and mother and be united to his wife, {8} and the two will become one flesh.' So they are no longer two, but one. {9} Therefore what God has joined together, let man not separate." {10} When they were in the house again, the disciples asked Jesus about this. {11} He answered, "Anyone who divorces his wife and marries another woman commits adultery against her. {12} And if she divorces her husband and marries another man, she commits adultery."

{13} People were bringing little children to Jesus to have him touch them, but the disciples rebuked them. {14} When Jesus saw this, he was indignant. He said to them, "Let the little children come to me, and do not hinder them, for the kingdom of God belongs to such as these. {15} I tell you the truth, anyone who will not receive the kingdom of God like a little child will never enter it." {16} And he took the children in his arms, put his hands on them and blessed them.

{17} As Jesus started on his way, a man ran up to him and fell on his knees before him. "Good teacher," he asked, "what must I do to inherit eternal life?" {18} "Why do you call me good?" Jesus answered. "No one is good–except God alone. {19} You know the commandments: 'Do not murder, do not commit adultery, do not steal, do not give false testimony, do not defraud, honor your father and mother.' " {20} "Teacher," he declared, "all these I have kept since I was a boy." {21} Jesus looked at him and loved him. "One thing you lack," he said. "Go , sell everything you have and give to the poor, and you will have treasure in heaven. Then come, follow me." {22} At this the man's face fell. He went away sad, because he had great wealth. {23} Jesus looked around and said to his disciples, "How hard it is for the rich to enter the kingdom of God!" {24} The disciples were amazed at his words. But Jesus said again, "Children , how hard it is to enter the kingdom of God! {25} It is easier for a camel to go through the eye of a needle than for a rich man to enter the kingdom of God."

JESUS PREDICTS HIS DEATH;
JOHN AND JAMES WANT PRVILEGES;
BARTIMAEUS IS HEALED

Mark 10:32-52

They were on their way up to Jerusalem, with Jesus leading the way, and the disciples were astonished, while those who followed were afraid. Again he took the Twelve aside and told them what was going to happen to him. {33} "We are going up to Jerusalem," he said, "and the Son of Man will be betrayed to the chief priests and teachers of the law. They will condemn him to death and will hand him over to the Gentiles, {34} who will mock him and spit on him, flog him and kill him. Three days later he will rise."

{35} Then James and John, the sons of Zebedee, came to him. "Teacher," they said, "we want you to do for us whatever we ask." {36} "What do you want me to do for you?" he asked. {37} They replied, "Let one of us sit at your right and the other at your left in your glory." {38} "You don't know what you are asking," Jesus said. "Can you drink the cup I drink or be baptized with the baptism I am baptized with?" {39} "We can," they answered. Jesus said to them, "You will drink the cup I drink and be baptized with the baptism I am baptized with, {40} but to sit at my right or left is not for me to grant. These places belong to those for whom they have been prepared." {41} When the ten heard about this, they became indignant with James and John. {42} Jesus called them together and said, "You know that those who are regarded as rulers of the Gentiles lord it over them, and their high officials exercise authority over them. {43} Not so with you. Instead, whoever wants to become great among you must be your servant, {44} and whoever wants to be first must be slave of all. {45} For even the Son of Man did not come to be served, but to serve, and to give his life as a ransom for many."

{46} Then they came to Jericho. As Jesus and his disciples, together with a large crowd, were leaving the city, a blind man, Bartimaeus (that is, the Son of Timaeus), was sitting by the roadside begging. {47} When he heard that it was Jesus of Nazareth, he began to shout, "Jesus, Son of David, have mercy on me!" {48} Many rebuked him and told him to be quiet, but he shouted all the more, "Son of David, have mercy on me!" {49} Jesus stopped and said, "Call him." So they called to the blind man, "Cheer up! On your feet! He's calling you." {50} Throwing his cloak aside, he jumped to his feet and came to Jesus. {51} "What do you want me to do for you?" Jesus asked him. The blind man said, "Rabbi, I want to see." {52} "Go," said Jesus, "your faith has healed you." Immediately he received his sight and followed Jesus along the road.

JESUS ENTERS JERUSALEM IN TRIUMPH, AND CLEARS THE TEMPLE

Mark 11:1-19

As they approached Jerusalem and came to Bethphage and Bethany at the Mount of Olives, Jesus sent two of his disciples, {2} saying to them, "Go to the village ahead of you, and just as you enter it, you will find a colt tied there, which no one has ever ridden. Untie it and bring it here. {3} If anyone asks you, 'Why are you doing this?' tell him, 'The Lord needs it and will send it back here shortly.'" {4} They went and found a colt outside in the street, tied at a doorway. As they untied it, {5} some people standing there asked, "What are you doing, untying that colt?" {6} They answered as Jesus had told them to, and the people let them go. {7} When they brought the colt to Jesus and threw their cloaks over it, he sat on it. {8} Many people spread their cloaks on the road, while others spread branches they had cut in the fields. {9} Those who went ahead and those who followed shouted, "Hosanna!" "Blessed is he who comes in the name of the Lord!" {10} "Blessed is the coming kingdom of our father David!" "Hosanna in the highest!" {11} Jesus entered Jerusalem and went to the temple. He looked around at everything, but since it was already late, he went out to Bethany with the Twelve. {12} The next day as they were leaving Bethany, Jesus was hungry. {13} Seeing in the distance a fig tree in leaf, he went to find out if it had any fruit. When he reached it, he found nothing but leaves, because it was not the season for figs. {14} Then he said to the tree, "May no one ever eat fruit from you again." And his disciples heard him say it.

{15} On reaching Jerusalem, Jesus entered the temple area and began driving out those who were buying and selling there. He overturned the tables of the money changers and the benches of those selling doves, {16} and would not allow anyone to carry merchandise through the temple courts. {17} And as he taught them, he said, "Is it not written: "'My house will be called a house of prayer for all nations' ? But you have made it 'a den of robbers.'" {18} The chief priests and the teachers of the law heard this and began looking for a way to kill him, for they feared him, because the whole crowd was amazed at his teaching. {19} When evening came, they went out of the city.

CHIEF PRIESTS QUESTION JESUS' AUTHORITY; PARABLE OF TENANTS; ON PAYING TAXES

Mark 11:28b-12:11

"And who gave you authority to do this?" {29} Jesus replied, "I will ask you one question. Answer me, and I will tell you by what authority I am doing these things. {30} John's baptism—was it from heaven, or from men? Tell me!" {31} They discussed it among themselves and said, "If we say, 'From heaven,' he will ask, 'Then why didn't you believe him?' {32} But if we say, 'From men' . . . ." (They feared the people, for everyone held that John really was a prophet.) {33} So they answered Jesus, "We don't know." Jesus said, "Neither will I tell you by what authority I am doing these things."

{12:1} He then began to speak to them in parables: "A man planted a vineyard. He put a wall around it, dug a pit for the winepress and built a watchtower. Then he rented the vineyard to some farmers and went away on a journey. {2} At harvest time he sent a servant to the tenants to collect from them some of the fruit of the vineyard. {3} But they seized him, beat him and sent him away empty-handed. {4} Then he sent another servant to them; they struck this man on the head and treated him shamefully. {5} He sent still another, and that one they killed. He sent many others; some of them they beat, others they killed. {6} "He had one left to send, a son, whom he loved. He sent him last of all, saying, 'They will respect my son.' {7} "But the tenants said to one another, 'This is the heir. Come, let's kill him, and the inheritance will be ours.' {8} So they took him and killed him, and threw him out of the vineyard. {9} "What then will the owner of the vineyard do? He will come and kill those tenants and give the vineyard to others. {10} Haven't you read this scripture: '"The stone the builders rejected has become the capstone; {11} the Lord has done this, and it is marvelous in our eyes'?"

Mark 12:13-17

Later they sent some of the Pharisees and Herodians to Jesus to catch him in his words. {14} They came to him and said, "Teacher, we know you are a man of integrity. You aren't swayed by men, because you pay no attention to who they are; but you teach the way of God in accordance with the truth. Is it right to pay taxes to Caesar or not? {15} Should we pay or shouldn't we?" But Jesus knew their hypocrisy. "Why are you trying to trap me?" he asked. "Bring me a denarius and let me look at it." {16} They brought the coin, and he asked them, "Whose portrait is this? And whose inscription?" "Caesar's," they replied. {17} Then Jesus said to them, "Give to Caesar what is Caesar's and to God what is God's." And they were amazed at him.

THE GREAT COMMANDMENT; A WIDOW'S OFFERING

Mark 12:28-44

One of the teachers of the law came and heard them debating. Noticing that Jesus had given them a good answer, he asked him, "Of all the commandments, which is the most important?" {29} "The most important one," answered Jesus, "is this: 'Hear, O Israel, the Lord our God, the Lord is one. {30} Love the Lord your God with all your heart and with all your soul and with all your mind and with all your strength.' {31} The second is this: 'Love your neighbor as yourself.' There is no commandment greater than these." {32} "Well said, teacher," the man replied. "You are right in saying that God is one and there is no other but him. {33} To love him with all your heart, with all your understanding and with all your strength, and to love your neighbor as yourself is more important than all burnt offerings and sacrifices." {34} When Jesus saw that he had answered wisely, he said to him, "You are not far from the kingdom of God." And from then on no one dared ask him any more questions. {35} While Jesus was teaching in the temple courts, he asked, "How is it that the teachers of the law say that the Christ is the son of David? {36} David himself, speaking by the Holy Spirit, declared: "'The Lord said to my Lord: "Sit at my right hand until I put your enemies under your feet."' {37} David himself calls him 'Lord.' How then can he be his son?" The large crowd listened to him with delight. {38} As he taught, Jesus said, "Watch out for the teachers of the law. They like to walk around in flowing robes and be greeted in the marketplaces, {39} and have the most important seats in the synagogues and the places of honor at banquets. {40} They devour widows' houses and for a show make lengthy prayers. Such men will be punished most severely."

{41} Jesus sat down opposite the place where the offerings were put and watched the crowd putting their money into the temple treasury. Many rich people threw in large amounts. {42} But a poor widow came and put in two very small copper coins, worth only a fraction of a penny. {43} Calling his disciples to him, Jesus said, "I tell you the truth, this poor widow has put more into the treasury than all the others. {44} They all gave out of their wealth; but she, out of her poverty, put in everything–all she had to live on."

THE END DAYS

Mark 13:4-27

"Tell us, when will these things happen? And what will be the sign that they are all about to be fulfilled?" {5} Jesus said to them: "Watch out that no one deceives you. {6} Many will come in my name, claiming, 'I am he,' and will deceive many. {7} When you hear of wars and rumors of wars, do not be alarmed. Such things must happen, but the end is still to come. {8} Nation will rise against nation, and kingdom against kingdom. There will be earthquakes in various places, and famines. These are the beginning of birth pains. {9} "You must be on your guard. You will be handed over to the local councils and flogged in the synagogues. On account of me you will stand before governors and kings as witnesses to them. {10} And the gospel must first be preached to all nations. {11} Whenever you are arrested and brought to trial, do not worry beforehand about what to say. Just say whatever is given you at the time, for it is not you speaking, but the Holy Spirit. {12} "Brother will betray brother to death, and a father his child. Children will rebel against their parents and have them put to death. {13} All men will hate you because of me, but he who stands firm to the end will be saved. {14} "When you see 'the abomination that causes desolation' standing where it does not belong–let the reader understand–then let those who are in Judea flee to the mountains. {15} Let no one on the roof of his house go down or enter the house to take anything out. {16} Let no one in the field go back to get his cloak. {17} How dreadful it will be in those days for pregnant women and nursing mothers! {18} Pray that this will not take place in winter, {19} because those will be days of distress unequaled from the beginning, when God created the world, until now–and never to be equaled again. {20} If the Lord had not cut short those days, no one would survive. But for the sake of the elect, whom he has chosen, he has shortened them. {21} At that time if anyone says to you, 'Look, here is the Christ!' or, 'Look, there he is!' do not believe it. {22} For false Christs and false prophets will appear and perform signs and miracles to deceive the elect–if that were possible. {23} So be on your guard; I have told you everything ahead of time. {24} "But in those days, following that distress, "'the sun will be darkened, and the moon will not give its light; {25} the stars will fall from the sky, and the heavenly bodies will be shaken.' {26} "At that time men will see the Son of Man coming in clouds with great power and glory. {27} And he will send his angels and gather his elect from the four winds, from the ends of the earth to the ends of the heavens.

JESUS ANOINTED;THE LAST SUPPER

Mark 14:3-24

While he was in Bethany, reclining at the table in the home of a man known as Simon the Leper, a woman came with an alabaster jar of very expensive perfume, made of pure nard. She broke the jar and poured the perfume on his head. {4} Some of those present were saying indignantly to one another, "Why this waste of perfume? {5} It could have been sold for more than a year's wages and the money given to the poor." And they rebuked her harshly. {6} "Leave her alone," said Jesus. "Why are you bothering her? She has done a beautiful thing to me. {7} The poor you will always have with you, and you can help them any time you want. But you will not always have me. {8} She did what she could. She poured perfume on my body beforehand to prepare for my burial. {9} I tell you the truth, wherever the gospel is preached throughout the world, what she has done will also be told, in memory of her." {10} Then Judas Iscariot, one of the Twelve, went to the chief priests to betray Jesus to them. {11} They were delighted to hear this and promised to give him money. So he watched for an opportunity to hand him over.

{12} On the first day of the Feast of Unleavened Bread, when it was customary to sacrifice the Passover lamb, Jesus' disciples asked him, "Where do you want us to go and make preparations for you to eat the Passover?" {13} So he sent two of his disciples, telling them, "Go into the city, and a man carrying a jar of water will meet you. Follow him. {14} Say to the owner of the house he enters, 'The Teacher asks: Where is my guest room, where I may eat the Passover with my disciples?' {15} He will show you a large upper room, furnished and ready. Make preparations for us there." {16} The disciples left, went into the city and found things just as Jesus had told them. So they prepared the Passover. {17} When evening came, Jesus arrived with the Twelve. {18} While they were reclining at the table eating, he said, "I tell you the truth, one of you will betray me—one who is eating with me." {19} They were saddened, and one by one they said to him, "Surely not I?" {20} "It is one of the Twelve," he replied, "one who dips bread into the bowl with me. {21} The Son of Man will go just as it is written about him. But woe to that man who betrays the Son of Man! It would be better for him if he had not been born." {22} While they were eating, Jesus took bread, gave thanks and broke it, and gave it to his disciples, saying, "Take it; this is my body." {23} Then he took the cup, gave thanks and offered it to them, and they all drank from it. {24} "This is my blood of the covenant, which is poured out for many," he said to them.

285

PETER'S DENIAL PREDICTED; GETHSEMANE; JESUS ARRESTED

Mark 14:29-51

Peter declared, "Even if all fall away, I will not." {30} "I tell you the truth," Jesus answered, "today –yes, tonight–before the rooster crows twice you yourself will disown me three times." {31} But Peter insisted emphatically, "Even if I have to die with you, I will never disown you." And all the others said the same.

{32} They went to a place called Gethsemane, and Jesus said to his disciples, "Sit here while I pray." {33} He took Peter, James and John along with him, and he began to be deeply distressed and troubled. {34} "My soul is overwhelmed with sorrow to the point of death," he said to them. "Stay here and keep watch." {35} Going a little farther, he fell to the ground and prayed that if possible the hour might pass from him. {36} "<Abba> , Father," he said, "everything is possible for you. Take this cup from me. Yet not what I will, but what you will." {37} Then he returned to his disciples and found them sleeping. "Simon," he said to Peter, "are you asleep? Could you not keep watch for one hour? {38} Watch and pray so that you will not fall into temptation. The spirit is willing, but the body is weak." {39} Once more he went away and prayed the same thing. {40} When he came back, he again found them sleeping, because their eyes were heavy. They did not know what to say to him. {41} Returning the third time, he said to them, "Are you still sleeping and resting? Enough! The hour has come. Look, the Son of Man is betrayed into the hands of sinners. {42} Rise! Let us go! Here comes my betrayer!"

{43} Just as he was speaking, Judas, one of the Twelve, appeared. With him was a crowd armed with swords and clubs, sent from the chief priests, the teachers of the law, and the elders. {44} Now the betrayer had arranged a signal with them: "The one I kiss is the man; arrest him and lead him away under guard." {45} Going at once to Jesus, Judas said, "Rabbi!" and kissed him. {46} The men seized Jesus and arrested him. {47} Then one of those standing near drew his sword and struck the servant of the high priest, cutting off his ear. {48} "Am I leading a rebellion," said Jesus, "that you have come out with swords and clubs to capture me? {49} Every day I was with you, teaching in the temple courts, and you did not arrest me. But the Scriptures must be fulfilled." {50} Then everyone deserted him and fled. {51} A young man, wearing nothing but a linen garment, was following Jesus. When they seized him,

CRUCIFIXION AND BURIAL OF JESUS

Mark 15:22-46

They brought Jesus to the place called Golgotha (which means The Place of the Skull). {23} Then they offered him wine mixed with myrrh, but he did not take it. {24} And they crucified him. Dividing up his clothes, they cast lots to see what each would get. {25} It was the third hour when they crucified him. {26} The written notice of the charge against him read: THE KING OF THE JEWS. {27} They crucified two robbers with him, one on his right and one on his left. {28} {29} Those who passed by hurled insults at him, shaking their heads and saying, "So! You who are going to destroy the temple and build it in three days, {30} come down from the cross and save yourself!" {31} In the same way the chief priests and the teachers of the law mocked him among themselves. "He saved others," they said, "but he can't save himself! {32} Let this Christ, this King of Israel, come down now from the cross, that we may see and believe." Those crucified with him also heaped insults on him. {33} At the sixth hour darkness came over the whole land until the ninth hour. {34} And at the ninth hour Jesus cried out in a loud voice, <"Eloi> , <Eloi>, <lama sabachthani>?"–which means, "My God, my God, why have you forsaken me?" {35} When some of those standing near heard this, they said, "Listen, he's calling Elijah." {36} One man ran, filled a sponge with wine vinegar, put it on a stick, and offered it to Jesus to drink. "Now leave him alone. Let's see if Elijah comes to take him down," he said. {37} With a loud cry, Jesus breathed his last. {38} The curtain of the temple was torn in two from top to bottom. {39} And when the centurion, who stood there in front of Jesus, heard his cry and saw how he died, he said, "Surely this man was the Son of God!" {40} Some women were watching from a distance. Among them were Mary Magdalene, Mary the mother of James the younger and of Joses, and Salome. {41} In Galilee these women had followed him and cared for his needs. Many other women who had come up with him to Jerusalem were also there. {42} It was Preparation Day (that is, the day before the Sabbath). So as evening approached, {43} Joseph of Arimathea, a prominent member of the Council, who was himself waiting for the kingdom of God, went boldly to Pilate and asked for Jesus' body. {44} Pilate was surprised to hear that he was already dead. Summoning the centurion, he asked him if Jesus had already died. {45} When he learned from the centurion that it was so, he gave the body to Joseph. {46} So Joseph bought some linen cloth, took down the body, wrapped it in the linen, and placed it in a tomb cut out of rock. Then he rolled a stone against the entrance of the tomb.

RESURRECTION OF JESUS

Mark 16:1-20

When the Sabbath was over, Mary Magdalene, Mary the mother of James, and Salome bought spices so that they might go to anoint Jesus' body. {2} Very early on the first day of the week, just after sunrise, they were on their way to the tomb {3} and they asked each other, "Who will roll the stone away from the entrance of the tomb?" {4} But when they looked up, they saw that the stone, which was very large, had been rolled away. {5} As they entered the tomb, they saw a young man dressed in a white robe sitting on the right side, and they were alarmed. {6} "Don't be alarmed," he said. "You are looking for Jesus the Nazarene, who was crucified. He has risen! He is not here. See the place where they laid him. {7} But go, tell his disciples and Peter, 'He is going ahead of you into Galilee. There you will see him, just as he told you.'" {8} Trembling and bewildered, the women went out and fled from the tomb. They said nothing to anyone, because they were afraid. {9} When Jesus rose early on the first day of the week, he appeared first to Mary Magdalene, out of whom he had driven seven demons. {10} She went and told those who had been with him and who were mourning and weeping. {11} When they heard that Jesus was alive and that she had seen him, they did not believe it. {12} Afterward Jesus appeared in a different form to two of them while they were walking in the country. {13} These returned and reported it to the rest; but they did not believe them either. {14} Later Jesus appeared to the Eleven as they were eating; he rebuked them for their lack of faith and their stubborn refusal to believe those who had seen him after he had risen. {15} He said to them, "Go into all the world and preach the good news to all creation. {16} Whoever believes and is baptized will be saved, but whoever does not believe will be condemned. {17} And these signs will accompany those who believe: In my name they will drive out demons; they will speak in new tongues; {18} they will pick up snakes with their hands; and when they drink deadly poison, it will not hurt them at all; they will place their hands on sick people, and they will get well." {19} After the Lord Jesus had spoken to them, he was taken up into heaven and he sat at the right hand of God. {20} Then the disciples went out and preached everywhere, and the Lord worked with them and confirmed his word by the signs that accompanied it.

THE WORD BECAME FLESH;
MINISTRY OF JOHN THE BAPTIST

John 1:1-27

In the beginning was the Word, and the Word was with God, and the Word was God. {2} He was with God in the beginning. {3} Through him all things were made; without him nothing was made that has been made. {4} In him was life, and that life was the light of men. {5} The light shines in the darkness, but the darkness has not understood it. {6} There came a man who was sent from God; his name was John. {7} He came as a witness to testify concerning that light, so that through him all men might believe. {8} He himself was not the light; he came only as a witness to the light. {9} The true light that gives light to every man was coming into the world. {10} He was in the world, and though the world was made through him, the world did not recognize him. {11} He came to that which was his own, but his own did not receive him. {12} Yet to all who received him, to those who believed in his name, he gave the right to become children of God– {13} children born not of natural descent, nor of human decision or a husband's will, but born of God. {14} The Word became flesh and made his dwelling among us. We have seen his glory, the glory of the One and Only, who came from the Father, full of grace and truth.

{15} John testifies concerning him. He cries out, saying, "This was he of whom I said, 'He who comes after me has surpassed me because he was before me.'" {16} From the fullness of his grace we have all received one blessing after another. {17} For the law was given through Moses; grace and truth came through Jesus Christ. {18} No one has ever seen God, but God the One and Only, who is at the Father's side, has made him known. {19} Now this was John's testimony when the Jews of Jerusalem sent priests and Levites to ask him who he was. {20} He did not fail to confess, but confessed freely, "I am not the Christ." {21} They asked him, "Then who are you? Are you Elijah?" He said, "I am not." "Are you the Prophet?" He answered, "No." {22} Finally they said, "Who are you? Give us an answer to take back to those who sent us. What do you say about yourself?" {23} John replied in the words of Isaiah the prophet, "I am the voice of one calling in the desert, 'Make straight the way for the Lord.'" {24} Now some Pharisees who had been sent {25} questioned him, "Why then do you baptize if you are not the Christ, nor Elijah, nor the Prophet?" {26} "I baptize with water," John replied, "but among you stands one you do not know. {27} He is the one who comes after me, the thongs of whose sandals I am not worthy to untie."

JESUS' FIRST DISCIPLES

John 1:35-51

The next day John was there again with two of his disciples. {36} When he saw Jesus passing by, he said, "Look, the Lamb of God!" {37} When the two disciples heard him say this, they followed Jesus. {38} Turning around, Jesus saw them following and asked, "What do you want?" They said, "Rabbi" (which means Teacher), "where are you staying?" {39} "Come," he replied, "and you will see." So they went and saw where he was staying, and spent that day with him. It was about the tenth hour. {40} Andrew, Simon Peter's brother, was one of the two who heard what John had said and who had followed Jesus. {41} The first thing Andrew did was to find his brother Simon and tell him, "We have found the Messiah" (that is, the Christ). {42} And he brought him to Jesus. Jesus looked at him and said, "You are Simon son of John. You will be called Cephas" (which, when translated, is Peter). {43} The next day Jesus decided to leave for Galilee. Finding Philip, he said to him, "Follow me." {44} Philip, like Andrew and Peter, was from the town of Bethsaida. {45} Philip found Nathanael and told him, "We have found the one Moses wrote about in the Law, and about whom the prophets also wrote–Jesus of Nazareth, the son of Joseph." {46} "Nazareth! Can anything good come from there?" Nathanael asked. "Come and see," said Philip. {47} When Jesus saw Nathanael approaching, he said of him, "Here is a true Israelite, in whom there is nothing false." {48} "How do you know me?" Nathanael asked. Jesus answered, "I saw you while you were still under the fig tree before Philip called you." {49} Then Nathanael declared, "Rabbi, you are the Son of God; you are the King of Israel." {50} Jesus said, "You believe because I told you I saw you under the fig tree. You shall see greater things than that." {51} He then added, "I tell you the truth, you shall see heaven open, and the angels of God ascending and descending on the Son of Man."

JESUS AT A WEDDING; AND CLEARS OUT THE TEMPLE

John 2:1-23

On the third day a wedding took place at Cana in Galilee. Jesus' mother was there, {2} and Jesus and his disciples had also been invited to the wedding. {3} When the wine was gone, Jesus' mother said to him, "They have no more wine." {4} "Dear woman, why do you involve me?" Jesus replied. "My time has not yet come." {5} His mother said to the servants, "Do whatever he tells you." {6} Nearby stood six stone water jars, the kind used by the Jews for ceremonial washing, each holding from twenty to thirty gallons. {7} Jesus said to the servants, "Fill the jars with water"; so they filled them to the brim. {8} Then he told them, "Now draw some out and take it to the master of the banquet." They did so, {9} and the master of the banquet tasted the water that had been turned into wine. He did not realize where it had come from, though the servants who had drawn the water knew. Then he called the bridegroom aside {10} and said, "Everyone brings out the choice wine first and then the cheaper wine after the guests have had too much to drink; but you have saved the best till now." {11} This, the first of his miraculous signs, Jesus performed at Cana in Galilee. He thus revealed his glory, and his disciples put their faith in him. {12} After this he went down to Capernaum with his mother and brothers and his disciples. There they stayed for a few days.

{13} When it was almost time for the Jewish Passover, Jesus went up to Jerusalem. {14} In the temple courts he found men selling cattle, sheep and doves, and others sitting at tables exchanging money. {15} So he made a whip out of cords, and drove all from the temple area, both sheep and cattle; he scattered the coins of the money changers and overturned their tables. {16} To those who sold doves he said, "Get these out of here! How dare you turn my Father's house into a market!" {17} His disciples remembered that it is written: "Zeal for your house will consume me." {18} Then the Jews demanded of him, "What miraculous sign can you show us to prove your authority to do all this?" {19} Jesus answered them, "Destroy this temple, and I will raise it again in three days." {20} The Jews replied, "It has taken forty-six years to build this temple, and you are going to raise it in three days?" {21} But the temple he had spoken of was his body. {22} After he was raised from the dead, his disciples recalled what he had said. Then they believed the Scripture and the words that Jesus had spoken. {23} Now while he was in Jerusalem at the Passover Feast, many people saw the miraculous signs he was doing and believed in his name.

JESUS AND NICODEMUS

John 3:1-22

Now there was a man of the Pharisees named Nicodemus, a member of the Jewish ruling council. {2} He came to Jesus at night and said, "Rabbi, we know you are a teacher who has come from God. For no one could perform the miraculous signs you are doing if God were not with him." {3} In reply Jesus declared, "I tell you the truth, no one can see the kingdom of God unless he is born again." {4} "How can a man be born when he is old?" Nicodemus asked. "Surely he cannot enter a second time into his mother's womb to be born!" {5} Jesus answered, "I tell you the truth, no one can enter the kingdom of God unless he is born of water and the Spirit. {6} Flesh gives birth to flesh, but the Spirit gives birth to spirit. {7} You should not be surprised at my saying, 'You must be born again.' {8} The wind blows wherever it pleases. You hear its sound, but you cannot tell where it comes from or where it is going. So it is with everyone born of the Spirit." {9} "How can this be?" Nicodemus asked. {10} "You are Israel's teacher," said Jesus, "and do you not understand these things? {11} I tell you the truth, we speak of what we know, and we testify to what we have seen, but still you people do not accept our testimony. {12} I have spoken to you of earthly things and you do not believe; how then will you believe if I speak of heavenly things? {13} No one has ever gone into heaven except the one who came from heaven–the Son of Man. {14} Just as Moses lifted up the snake in the desert, so the Son of Man must be lifted up, {15} that everyone who believes in him may have eternal life. {16} "For God so loved the world that he gave his one and only Son, that whoever believes in him shall not perish but have eternal life. {17} For God did not send his Son into the world to condemn the world, but to save the world through him. {18} Whoever believes in him is not condemned, but whoever does not believe stands condemned already because he has not believed in the name of God's one and only Son. {19} This is the verdict: Light has come into the world, but men loved darkness instead of light because their deeds were evil. {20} Everyone who does evil hates the light, and will not come into the light for fear that his deeds will be exposed. {21} But whoever lives by the truth comes into the light, so that it may be seen plainly that what he has done has been done through God." {22} After this, Jesus and his disciples went out into the Judean countryside, where he spent some time with them, and baptized.

JESUS TALKS TO SAMARITAN WOMAN

John 4:5-26

So he came to a town in Samaria called Sychar, near the plot of ground Jacob had given to his son Joseph. {6} Jacob's well was there, and Jesus, tired as he was from the journey, sat down by the well. It was about the sixth hour. {7} When a Samaritan woman came to draw water, Jesus said to her, "Will you give me a drink?" {8} (His disciples had gone into the town to buy food.) {9} The Samaritan woman said to him, "You are a Jew and I am a Samaritan woman. How can you ask me for a drink?" (For Jews do not associate with Samaritans.) {10} Jesus answered her, "If you knew the gift of God and who it is that asks you for a drink, you would have asked him and he would have given you living water." {11} "Sir," the woman said, "you have nothing to draw with and the well is deep. Where can you get this living water? {12} Are you greater than our father Jacob, who gave us the well and drank from it himself, as did also his sons and his flocks and herds?" {13} Jesus answered, "Everyone who drinks this water will be thirsty again, {14} but whoever drinks the water I give him will never thirst. Indeed, the water I give him will become in him a spring of water welling up to eternal life." {15} The woman said to him, "Sir, give me this water so that I won't get thirsty and have to keep coming here to draw water." {16} He told her, "Go, call your husband and come back." {17} "I have no husband," she replied. Jesus said to her, "You are right when you say you have no husband. {18} The fact is, you have had five husbands, and the man you now have is not your husband. What you have just said is quite true." {19} "Sir," the woman said, "I can see that you are a prophet. {20} Our fathers worshiped on this mountain, but you Jews claim that the place where we must worship is in Jerusalem." {21} Jesus declared, "Believe me, woman, a time is coming when you will worship the Father neither on this mountain nor in Jerusalem. {22} You Samaritans worship what you do not know; we worship what we do know, for salvation is from the Jews. {23} Yet a time is coming and has now come when the true worshipers will worship the Father in spirit and truth, for they are the kind of worshipers the Father seeks. {24} God is spirit, and his worshipers must worship in spirit and in truth." {25} The woman said, "I know that Messiah" (called Christ) "is coming. When he comes, he will explain everything to us." {26} Then Jesus declared, "I who speak to you am he."

JESUS HEALS OFFICIAL'S SON,
AND HEALS AN INVALID ON THE SABBATH

John 4:45-5:14

When he arrived in Galilee, the Galileans welcomed him. They had seen all that he had done in Jerusalem at the Passover Feast, for they also had been there. {46} Once more he visited Cana in Galilee, where he had turned the water into wine. And there was a certain royal official whose son lay sick at Capernaum. {47} When this man heard that Jesus had arrived in Galilee from Judea, he went to him and begged him to come and heal his son, who was close to death. {48} "Unless you people see miraculous signs and wonders," Jesus told him, "you will never believe." {49} The royal official said, "Sir, come down before my child dies." {50} Jesus replied, "You may go. Your son will live." The man took Jesus at his word and departed. {51} While he was still on the way, his servants met him with the news that his boy was living. {52} When he inquired as to the time when his son got better, they said to him, "The fever left him yesterday at the seventh hour." {53} Then the father realized that this was the exact time at which Jesus had said to him, "Your son will live." So he and all his household believed. {54} This was the second miraculous sign that Jesus performed, having come from Judea to Galilee.

{5:1} Some time later, Jesus went up to Jerusalem for a feast of the Jews. {2} Now there is in Jerusalem near the Sheep Gate a pool, which in Aramaic is called Bethesda and which is surrounded by five covered colonnades. {3} Here a great number of disabled people used to lie–the blind, the lame, the paralyzed. {4} {5} One who was there had been an invalid for thirty-eight years. {6} When Jesus saw him lying there and learned that he had been in this condition for a long time, he asked him, "Do you want to get well?" {7} "Sir," the invalid replied, "I have no one to help me into the pool when the water is stirred. While I am trying to get in, someone else goes down ahead of me." {8} Then Jesus said to him, "Get up! Pick up your mat and walk." {9} At once the man was cured; he picked up his mat and walked. The day on which this took place was a Sabbath, {10} and so the Jews said to the man who had been healed, "It is the Sabbath; the law forbids you to carry your mat." {11} But he replied, "The man who made me well said to me, 'Pick up your mat and walk.'" {12} So they asked him, "Who is this fellow who told you to pick it up and walk?" {13} The man who was healed had no idea who it was, for Jesus had slipped away into the crowd that was there. {14} Later Jesus found him at the temple and said to him, "See , you are well again. Stop sinning or something worse may happen to you."

ETERNAL LIFE THROUGH JESUS

John 5:17-39

Jesus said to them, "My Father is always at his work to this very day, and I, too, am working." {18} For this reason the Jews tried all the harder to kill him; not only was he breaking the Sabbath, but he was even calling God his own Father, making himself equal with God. {19} Jesus gave them this answer: "I tell you the truth, the Son can do nothing by himself; he can do only what he sees his Father doing, because whatever the Father does the Son also does. {20} For the Father loves the Son and shows him all he does. Yes, to your amazement he will show him even greater things than these. {21} For just as the Father raises the dead and gives them life, even so the Son gives life to whom he is pleased to give it. {22} Moreover, the Father judges no one, but has entrusted all judgment to the Son, {23} that all may honor the Son just as they honor the Father. He who does not honor the Son does not honor the Father, who sent him. {24} "I tell you the truth, whoever hears my word and believes him who sent me has eternal life and will not be condemned; he has crossed over from death to life. {25} I tell you the truth, a time is coming and has now come when the dead will hear the voice of the Son of God and those who hear will live. {26} For as the Father has life in himself, so he has granted the Son to have life in himself. {27} And he has given him authority to judge because he is the Son of Man. {28} "Do not be amazed at this, for a time is coming when all who are in their graves will hear his voice {29} and come out–those who have done good will rise to live, and those who have done evil will rise to be condemned. {30} By myself I can do nothing; I judge only as I hear, and my judgment is just, for I seek not to please myself but him who sent me. {31} "If I testify about myself, my testimony is not valid. {32} There is another who testifies in my favor, and I know that his testimony about me is valid. {33} "You have sent to John and he has testified to the truth. {34} Not that I accept human testimony; but I mention it that you may be saved. {35} John was a lamp that burned and gave light, and you chose for a time to enjoy his light. {36} "I have testimony weightier than that of John. For the very work that the Father has given me to finish, and which I am doing, testifies that the Father has sent me. {37} And the Father who sent me has himself testified concerning me. You have never heard his voice nor seen his form, {38} nor does his word dwell in you, for you do not believe the one he sent. {39} You diligently study the Scriptures because you think that by them you possess eternal life. These are the Scriptures that testify about me,

JESUS FEEDS FIVE THOUSAND, WALKS ON WATER

John 6:2-24

And a great crowd of people followed him because they saw the miraculous signs he had performed on the sick. {3} Then Jesus went up on a mountainside and sat down with his disciples. {4} The Jewish Passover Feast was near. {5} When Jesus looked up and saw a great crowd coming toward him, he said to Philip, "Where shall we buy bread for these people to eat?" {6} He asked this only to test him, for he already had in mind what he was going to do. {7} Philip answered him, "Eight months' wages would not buy enough bread for each one to have a bite!" {8} Another of his disciples, Andrew, Simon Peter's brother, spoke up, {9} "Here is a boy with five small barley loaves and two small fish, but how far will they go among so many?" {10} Jesus said, "Have the people sit down." There was plenty of grass in that place, and the men sat down, about five thousand of them. {11} Jesus then took the loaves, gave thanks, and distributed to those who were seated as much as they wanted. He did the same with the fish. {12} When they had all had enough to eat, he said to his disciples, "Gather the pieces that are left over. Let nothing be wasted." {13} So they gathered them and filled twelve baskets with the pieces of the five barley loaves left over by those who had eaten. {14} After the people saw the miraculous sign that Jesus did, they began to say, "Surely this is the Prophet who is to come into the world." {15} Jesus, knowing that they intended to come and make him king by force, withdrew again to a mountain by himself. {16} When evening came, his disciples went down to the lake, {17} where they got into a boat and set off across the lake for Capernaum. By now it was dark, and Jesus had not yet joined them. {18} A strong wind was blowing and the waters grew rough. {19} When they had rowed three or three and a half miles, they saw Jesus approaching the boat, walking on the water; and they were terrified. {20} But he said to them, "It is I; don't be afraid." {21} Then they were willing to take him into the boat, and immediately the boat reached the shore where they were heading. {22} The next day the crowd that had stayed on the opposite shore of the lake realized that only one boat had been there, and that Jesus had not entered it with his disciples, but that they had gone away alone. {23} Then some boats from Tiberias landed near the place where the people had eaten the bread after the Lord had given thanks. {24} Once the crowd realized that neither Jesus nor his disciples were there, they got into the boats and went to Capernaum in search of Jesus.

JESUS THE BREAD OF LIFE

John 6:32b-58

It is my Father who gives you the true bread from heaven. {33} For the bread of God is he who comes down from heaven and gives life to the world." {34} "Sir," they said, "from now on give us this bread." {35} Then Jesus declared, "I am the bread of life. He who comes to me will never go hungry, and he who believes in me will never be thirsty. {36} But as I told you, you have seen me and still you do not believe. {37} All that the Father gives me will come to me, and whoever comes to me I will never drive away. {38} For I have come down from heaven not to do my will but to do the will of him who sent me. {39} And this is the will of him who sent me, that I shall lose none of all that he has given me, but raise them up at the last day. {40} For my Father's will is that everyone who looks to the Son and believes in him shall have eternal life, and I will raise him up at the last day." {41} At this the Jews began to grumble about him because he said, "I am the bread that came down from heaven." {42} They said, "Is this not Jesus, the son of Joseph, whose father and mother we know? How can he now say, 'I came down from heaven'?" {43} "Stop grumbling among yourselves," Jesus answered. {44} "No one can come to me unless the Father who sent me draws him, and I will raise him up at the last day. {45} It is written in the Prophets: 'They will all be taught by God.' Everyone who listens to the Father and learns from him comes to me. {46} No one has seen the Father except the one who is from God; only he has seen the Father. {47} I tell you the truth, he who believes has everlasting life. {48} I am the bread of life. {49} Your forefathers ate the manna in the desert, yet they died. {50} But here is the bread that comes down from heaven, which a man may eat and not die. {51} I am the living bread that came down from heaven. If anyone eats of this bread, he will live forever. This bread is my flesh, which I will give for the life of the world." {52} Then the Jews began to argue sharply among themselves, "How can this man give us his flesh to eat?" {53} Jesus said to them, "I tell you the truth, unless you eat the flesh of the Son of Man and drink his blood, you have no life in you. {54} Whoever eats my flesh and drinks my blood has eternal life, and I will raise him up at the last day. {55} For my flesh is real food and my blood is real drink. {56} Whoever eats my flesh and drinks my blood remains in me, and I in him. {57} Just as the living Father sent me and I live because of the Father, so the one who feeds on me will live because of me. {58} This is the bread that came down from heaven. Your forefathers ate manna and died, but he who feeds on this bread will live forever."

JESUS AT FEAST OF THE TABERNACLE

John 7:1-24

After this, Jesus went around in Galilee, purposely staying away from Judea because the Jews there were waiting to take his life. {2} But when the Jewish Feast of Tabernacles was near, {3} Jesus' brothers said to him, "You ought to leave here and go to Judea, so that your disciples may see the miracles you do. {4} No one who wants to become a public figure acts in secret. Since you are doing these things, show yourself to the world." {5} For even his own brothers did not believe in him. {6} Therefore Jesus told them, "The right time for me has not yet come; for you any time is right. {7} The world cannot hate you, but it hates me because I testify that what it does is evil. {8} You go to the Feast. I am not yet going up to this Feast, because for me the right time has not yet come." {9} Having said this, he stayed in Galilee. {10} However, after his brothers had left for the Feast, he went also, not publicly, but in secret. {11} Now at the Feast the Jews were watching for him and asking, "Where is that man?" {12} Among the crowds there was widespread whispering about him. Some said, "He is a good man." Others replied, "No, he deceives the people." {13} But no one would say anything publicly about him for fear of the Jews. {14} Not until halfway through the Feast did Jesus go up to the temple courts and begin to teach. {15} The Jews were amazed and asked, "How did this man get such learning without having studied?" {16} Jesus answered, "My teaching is not my own. It comes from him who sent me. {17} If anyone chooses to do God's will, he will find out whether my teaching comes from God or whether I speak on my own. {18} He who speaks on his own does so to gain honor for himself, but he who works for the honor of the one who sent him is a man of truth; there is nothing false about him. {19} Has not Moses given you the law? Yet not one of you keeps the law. Why are you trying to kill me?" {20} "You are demon-possessed," the crowd answered. "Who is trying to kill you?" {21} Jesus said to them, "I did one miracle, and you are all astonished. {22} Yet , because Moses gave you circumcision (though actually it did not come from Moses, but from the patriarchs), you circumcise a child on the Sabbath. {23} Now if a child can be circumcised on the Sabbath so that the law of Moses may not be broken, why are you angry with me for healing the whole man on the Sabbath? {24} Stop judging by mere appearances, and make a right judgment."

"IS THIS THE CHRIST?"

John 7:31-52

Still, many in the crowd put their faith in him. They said, "When the Christ comes, will he do more miraculous signs than this man?" {32} The Pharisees heard the crowd whispering such things about him. Then the chief priests and the Pharisees sent temple guards to arrest him. {33} Jesus said, "I am with you for only a short time, and then I go to the one who sent me. {34} You will look for me, but you will not find me; and where I am, you cannot come." {35} The Jews said to one another, "Where does this man intend to go that we cannot find him? Will he go where our people live scattered among the Greeks, and teach the Greeks? {36} What did he mean when he said, 'You will look for me, but you will not find me,' and 'Where I am, you cannot come'?" {37} On the last and greatest day of the Feast, Jesus stood and said in a loud voice, "If anyone is thirsty, let him come to me and drink. {38} Whoever believes in me, as the Scripture has said, streams of living water will flow from within him." {39} By this he meant the Spirit, whom those who believed in him were later to receive. Up to that time the Spirit had not been given, since Jesus had not yet been glorified. {40} On hearing his words, some of the people said, "Surely this man is the Prophet." {41} Others said, "He is the Christ." Still others asked, "How can the Christ come from Galilee? {42} Does not the Scripture say that the Christ will come from David's family and from Bethlehem, the town where David lived?" {43} Thus the people were divided because of Jesus. {44} Some wanted to seize him, but no one laid a hand on him. {45} Finally the temple guards went back to the chief priests and Pharisees, who asked them, "Why didn't you bring him in?" {46} "No one ever spoke the way this man does," the guards declared. {47} "You mean he has deceived you also?" the Pharisees retorted. {48} "Has any of the rulers or of the Pharisees believed in him? {49} No! But this mob that knows nothing of the law— there is a curse on them." {50} Nicodemus, who had gone to Jesus earlier and who was one of their own number, asked, {51} "Does our law condemn anyone without first hearing him to find out what he is doing?" {52} They replied, "Are you from Galilee, too? Look into it, and you will find that a prophet does not come out of Galilee."

JESUS' TESTIMONY IS TRUE

John 8:13-36

The Pharisees challenged him, "Here you are, appearing as your own witness; your testimony is not valid." {14} Jesus answered, "Even if I testify on my own behalf, my testimony is valid, for I know where I came from and where I am going. But you have no idea where I come from or where I am going. {15} You judge by human standards; I pass judgment on no one. {16} But if I do judge, my decisions are right, because I am not alone. I stand with the Father, who sent me. {17} In your own Law it is written that the testimony of two men is valid. {18} I am one who testifies for myself; my other witness is the Father, who sent me." {19} Then they asked him, "Where is your father?" "You do not know me or my Father," Jesus replied. "If you knew me, you would know my Father also." {20} He spoke these words while teaching in the temple area near the place where the offerings were put. Yet no one seized him, because his time had not yet come. {21} Once more Jesus said to them, "I am going away, and you will look for me, and you will die in your sin. Where I go, you cannot come." {22} This made the Jews ask, "Will he kill himself? Is that why he says, 'Where I go, you cannot come'?" {23} But he continued, "You are from below; I am from above. You are of this world; I am not of this world. {24} I told you that you would die in your sins; if you do not believe that I am <the one I claim to be>, you will indeed die in your sins." {25} "Who are you?" they asked. "Just what I have been claiming all along," Jesus replied. {26} "I have much to say in judgment of you. But he who sent me is reliable, and what I have heard from him I tell the world." {27} They did not understand that he was telling them about his Father. {28} So Jesus said, "When you have lifted up the Son of Man, then you will know that I am <the one I claim to be> and that I do nothing on my own but speak just what the Father has taught me. {29} The one who sent me is with me; he has not left me alone, for I always do what pleases him." {30} Even as he spoke, many put their faith in him. {31} To the Jews who had believed him, Jesus said, "If you hold to my teaching, you are really my disciples. {32} Then you will know the truth, and the truth will set you free." {33} They answered him, "We are Abraham's descendants and have never been slaves of anyone. How can you say that we shall be set free?" {34} Jesus replied, "I tell you the truth, everyone who sins is a slave to sin. {35} Now a slave has no permanent place in the family, but a son belongs to it forever. {36} So if the Son sets you free, you will be free indeed.

MAN BORN BLIND IS HEALED

John 9:2-25

His disciples asked him, "Rabbi, who sinned, this man or his parents, that he was born blind?" {3} "Neither this man nor his parents sinned," said Jesus, "but this happened so that the work of God might be displayed in his life. {4} As long as it is day, we must do the work of him who sent me. Night is coming, when no one can work. {5} While I am in the world, I am the light of the world." {6} Having said this, he spit on the ground, made some mud with the saliva, and put it on the man's eyes. {7} "Go," he told him, "wash in the Pool of Siloam" (this word means Sent). So the man went and washed, and came home seeing. {8} His neighbors and those who had formerly seen him begging asked, "Isn't this the same man who used to sit and beg?" {9} Some claimed that he was. Others said, "No, he only looks like him." But he himself insisted, "I am the man." {10} "How then were your eyes opened?" they demanded. {11} He replied, "The man they call Jesus made some mud and put it on my eyes. He told me to go to Siloam and wash. So I went and washed, and then I could see." {12} "Where is this man?" they asked him. "I don't know," he said. {13} They brought to the Pharisees the man who had been blind. {14} Now the day on which Jesus had made the mud and opened the man's eyes was a Sabbath. {15} Therefore the Pharisees also asked him how he had received his sight. "He put mud on my eyes," the man replied, "and I washed, and now I see." {16} Some of the Pharisees said, "This man is not from God, for he does not keep the Sabbath." But others asked, "How can a sinner do such miraculous signs?" So they were divided. {17} Finally they turned again to the blind man, "What have you to say about him? It was your eyes he opened." The man replied, "He is a prophet." {18} The Jews still did not believe that he had been blind and had received his sight until they sent for the man's parents. {19} "Is this your son?" they asked. "Is this the one you say was born blind? How is it that now he can see?" {20} "We know he is our son," the parents answered, "and we know he was born blind. {21} But how he can see now, or who opened his eyes, we don't know. Ask him. He is of age; he will speak for himself." {22} His parents said this because they were afraid of the Jews, for already the Jews had decided that anyone who acknowledged that Jesus was the Christ would be put out of the synagogue. {23} That was why his parents said, "He is of age; ask him." {24} A second time they summoned the man who had been blind. "Give glory to God, " they said. "We know this man is a sinner." {25} He replied, "Whether he is a sinner or not, I don't know. One thing I do know. I was blind but now I see!"

JESUS, SHEPHERD OF HIS FLOCK

John 10:1b-27

"The man who does not enter the sheep pen by the gate, but climbs in by some other way, is a thief and a robber. {2} The man who enters by the gate is the shepherd of his sheep. {3} The watchman opens the gate for him, and the sheep listen to his voice. He calls his own sheep by name and leads them out. {4} When he has brought out all his own, he goes on ahead of them, and his sheep follow him because they know his voice. {5} But they will never follow a stranger; in fact, they will run away from him because they do not recognize a stranger's voice." {6} Jesus used this figure of speech, but they did not understand what he was telling them. {7} Therefore Jesus said again, "I tell you the truth, I am the gate for the sheep. {8} All who ever came before me were thieves and robbers, but the sheep did not listen to them. {9} I am the gate; whoever enters through me will be saved. He will come in and go out, and find pasture. {10} The thief comes only to steal and kill and destroy; I have come that they may have life, and have it to the full. {11} "I am the good shepherd. The good shepherd lays down his life for the sheep. {12} The hired hand is not the shepherd who owns the sheep. So when he sees the wolf coming, he abandons the sheep and runs away. Then the wolf attacks the flock and scatters it. {13} The man runs away because he is a hired hand and cares nothing for the sheep. {14} "I am the good shepherd; I know my sheep and my sheep know me– {15} just as the Father knows me and I know the Father–and I lay down my life for the sheep. {16} I have other sheep that are not of this sheep pen. I must bring them also. They too will listen to my voice, and there shall be one flock and one shepherd. {17} The reason my Father loves me is that I lay down my life–only to take it up again. {18} No one takes it from me, but I lay it down of my own accord. I have authority to lay it down and authority to take it up again. This command I received from my Father." {19} At these words the Jews were again divided. {20} Many of them said, "He is demon-possessed and raving mad. Why listen to him?" {21} But others said, "These are not the sayings of a man possessed by a demon. Can a demon open the eyes of the blind?" {22} Then came the Feast of Dedication at Jerusalem. It was winter, {23} and Jesus was in the temple area walking in Solomon's Colonnade. {24} The Jews gathered around him, saying, "How long will you keep us in suspense? If you are the Christ, tell us plainly." {25} Jesus answered, "I did tell you, but you do not believe. The miracles I do in my Father's name speak for me, {26} but you do not believe because you are not my sheep. {27} My sheep listen to my voice; I know them, and they follow me.

DEATH AND RAISING OF LAZARUS

John 11:1-27

Now a man named Lazarus was sick. He was from Bethany, the village of Mary and her sister Martha. {2} This Mary, whose brother Lazarus now lay sick, was the same one who poured perfume on the Lord and wiped his feet with her hair. {3} So the sisters sent word to Jesus, "Lord, the one you love is sick." {4} When he heard this, Jesus said, "This sickness will not end in death. No, it is for God's glory so that God's Son may be glorified through it." {5} Jesus loved Martha and her sister and Lazarus. {6} Yet when he heard that Lazarus was sick, he stayed where he was two more days. {7} Then he said to his disciples, "Let us go back to Judea." {8} "But Rabbi," they said, "a short while ago the Jews tried to stone you, and yet you are going back there?" {9} Jesus answered, "Are there not twelve hours of daylight? A man who walks by day will not stumble, for he sees by this world's light. {10} It is when he walks by night that he stumbles, for he has no light." {11} After he had said this, he went on to tell them, "Our friend Lazarus has fallen asleep; but I am going there to wake him up." {12} His disciples replied, "Lord, if he sleeps, he will get better." {13} Jesus had been speaking of his death, but his disciples thought he meant natural sleep. {14} So then he told them plainly, "Lazarus is dead, {15} and for your sake I am glad I was not there, so that you may believe. But let us go to him." {16} Then Thomas (called Didymus) said to the rest of the disciples, "Let us also go, that we may die with him." {17} On his arrival, Jesus found that Lazarus had already been in the tomb for four days. {18} Bethany was less than two miles from Jerusalem, {19} and many Jews had come to Martha and Mary to comfort them in the loss of their brother. {20} When Martha heard that Jesus was coming, she went out to meet him, but Mary stayed at home. {21} "Lord," Martha said to Jesus, "if you had been here, my brother would not have died. {22} But I know that even now God will give you whatever you ask." {23} Jesus said to her, "Your brother will rise again." {24} Martha answered, "I know he will rise again in the resurrection at the last day." {25} Jesus said to her, "I am the resurrection and the life. He who believes in me will live, even though he dies; {26} and whoever lives and believes in me will never die. Do you believe this?" {27} "Yes, Lord," she told him, "I believe that you are the Christ, the Son of God, who was to come into the world."

John 11:43-44a

When he had said this, Jesus called in a loud voice, "Lazarus, come out!" {44} The dead man came out.

JESUS' ANOINTING AT BETHANY;
JESUS' TRIUMPHAL ENTRY INTO JERUSALEM

John 12:1-19

Six days before the Passover, Jesus arrived at Bethany, where Lazarus lived, whom Jesus had raised from the dead. {2} Here a dinner was given in Jesus' honor. Martha served, while Lazarus was among those reclining at the table with him. {3} Then Mary took about a pint of pure nard, an expensive perfume; she poured it on Jesus' feet and wiped his feet with her hair. And the house was filled with the fragrance of the perfume. {4} But one of his disciples, Judas Iscariot, who was later to betray him, objected, {5} "Why wasn't this perfume sold and the money given to the poor? It was worth a year's wages." {6} He did not say this because he cared about the poor but because he was a thief; as keeper of the money bag, he used to help himself to what was put into it. {7} "Leave her alone," Jesus replied. <"It was intended> that she should save this perfume for the day of my burial. {8} You will always have the poor among you, but you will not always have me." {9} Meanwhile a large crowd of Jews found out that Jesus was there and came, not only because of him but also to see Lazarus, whom he had raised from the dead. {10} So the chief priests made plans to kill Lazarus as well, {11} for on account of him many of the Jews were going over to Jesus and putting their faith in him.

{12} The next day the great crowd that had come for the Feast heard that Jesus was on his way to Jerusalem. {13} They took palm branches and went out to meet him, shouting, "Hosanna!" "Blessed is he who comes in the name of the Lord!" "Blessed is the King of Israel!" {14} Jesus found a young donkey and sat upon it, as it is written, {15} "Do not be afraid, O Daughter of Zion; see, your king is coming, seated on a donkey's colt." {16} At first his disciples did not understand all this. Only after Jesus was glorified did they realize that these things had been written about him and that they had done these things to him. {17} Now the crowd that was with him when he called Lazarus from the tomb and raised him from the dead continued to spread the word. {18} Many people, because they had heard that he had given this miraculous sign, went out to meet him. {19} So the Pharisees said to one another, "See, this is getting us nowhere. Look how the whole world has gone after him!"

JESUS WASHES DISCIPLES FEET, FORESEES HIS BETRAYAL

John 13:5-28

After that, he poured water into a basin and began to wash his disciples' feet, drying them with the towel that was wrapped around him. {6} He came to Simon Peter, who said to him, "Lord, are you going to wash my feet?" {7} Jesus replied, "You do not realize now what I am doing, but later you will understand." {8} "No," said Peter, "you shall never wash my feet." Jesus answered, "Unless I wash you, you have no part with me." {9} "Then, Lord," Simon Peter replied, "not just my feet but my hands and my head as well!" {10} Jesus answered, "A person who has had a bath needs only to wash his feet; his whole body is clean. And you are clean, though not every one of you." {11} For he knew who was going to betray him, and that was why he said not every one was clean. {12} When he had finished washing their feet, he put on his clothes and returned to his place. "Do you understand what I have done for you?" he asked them. {13} "You call me 'Teacher' and 'Lord,' and rightly so, for that is what I am. {14} Now that I, your Lord and Teacher, have washed your feet, you also should wash one another's feet. {15} I have set you an example that you should do as I have done for you. {16} I tell you the truth, no servant is greater than his master, nor is a messenger greater than the one who sent him. {17} Now that you know these things, you will be blessed if you do them. {18} "I am not referring to all of you; I know those I have chosen. But this is to fulfill the scripture: 'He who shares my bread has lifted up his heel against me.' {19} "I am telling you now before it happens, so that when it does happen you will believe that I am He. {20} I tell you the truth, whoever accepts anyone I send accepts me; and whoever accepts me accepts the one who sent me."

{21} After he had said this, Jesus was troubled in spirit and testified, "I tell you the truth, one of you is going to betray me." {22} His disciples stared at one another, at a loss to know which of them he meant. {23} One of them, the disciple whom Jesus loved, was reclining next to him. {24} Simon Peter motioned to this disciple and said, "Ask him which one he means." {25} Leaning back against Jesus, he asked him, "Lord, who is it?" {26} Jesus answered, "It is the one to whom I will give this piece of bread when I have dipped it in the dish." Then , dipping the piece of bread, he gave it to Judas Iscariot, son of Simon. {27} As soon as Judas took the bread, Satan entered into him. "What you are about to do, do quickly," Jesus told him, {28} but no one at the meal understood why Jesus said this to him.

JESUS PROMISES THE COMFORTER, THE HOLY SPIRIT

John 14:4-27a

You know the way to the place where I am going." {5} Thomas said to him, "Lord, we don't know where you are going, so how can we know the way?" {6} Jesus answered, "I am the way and the truth and the life. No one comes to the Father except through me. {7} If you really knew me, you would know my Father as well. From now on, you do know him and have seen him." {8} Philip said, "Lord, show us the Father and that will be enough for us." {9} Jesus answered: "Don't you know me, Philip, even after I have been among you such a long time? Anyone who has seen me has seen the Father. How can you say, 'Show us the Father'? {10} Don't you believe that I am in the Father, and that the Father is in me? The words I say to you are not just my own. Rather, it is the Father, living in me, who is doing his work. {11} Believe me when I say that I am in the Father and the Father is in me; or at least believe on the evidence of the miracles themselves. {12} I tell you the truth, anyone who has faith in me will do what I have been doing. He will do even greater things than these, because I am going to the Father. {13} And I will do whatever you ask in my name, so that the Son may bring glory to the Father. {14} You may ask me for anything in my name, and I will do it. {15} "If you love me, you will obey what I command. {16} And I will ask the Father, and he will give you another Counselor to be with you forever– {17} the Spirit of truth. The world cannot accept him, because it neither sees him nor knows him. But you know him, for he lives with you and will be in you. {18} I will not leave you as orphans; I will come to you. {19} Before long, the world will not see me anymore, but you will see me. Because I live, you also will live. {20} On that day you will realize that I am in my Father, and you are in me, and I am in you. {21} Whoever has my commands and obeys them, he is the one who loves me. He who loves me will be loved by my Father, and I too will love him and show myself to him." {22} Then Judas (not Judas Iscariot) said, "But, Lord, why do you intend to show yourself to us and not to the world?" {23} Jesus replied, "If anyone loves me, he will obey my teaching. My Father will love him, and we will come to him and make our home with him. {24} He who does not love me will not obey my teaching. These words you hear are not my own; they belong to the Father who sent me. {25} "All this I have spoken while still with you. {26} But the Counselor, the Holy Spirit, whom the Father will send in my name, will teach you all things and will remind you of everything I have said to you. {27} Peace I leave with you; my peace I give you.

VINE AND BRANCHES

John 15:1-24

"I am the true vine, and my Father is the gardener. {2} He cuts off every branch in me that bears no fruit, while every branch that does bear fruit he prunes so that it will be even more fruitful. {3} You are already clean because of the word I have spoken to you. {4} Remain in me, and I will remain in you. No branch can bear fruit by itself; it must remain in the vine. Neither can you bear fruit unless you remain in me. {5} "I am the vine; you are the branches. If a man remains in me and I in him, he will bear much fruit; apart from me you can do nothing. {6} If anyone does not remain in me, he is like a branch that is thrown away and withers; such branches are picked up, thrown into the fire and burned. {7} If you remain in me and my words remain in you, ask whatever you wish, and it will be given you. {8} This is to my Father's glory, that you bear much fruit, showing yourselves to be my disciples. {9} "As the Father has loved me, so have I loved you. Now remain in my love. {10} If you obey my commands, you will remain in my love, just as I have obeyed my Father's commands and remain in his love. {11} I have told you this so that my joy may be in you and that your joy may be complete. {12} My command is this: Love each other as I have loved you. {13} Greater love has no one than this, that he lay down his life for his friends. {14} You are my friends if you do what I command. {15} I no longer call you servants, because a servant does not know his master's business. Instead, I have called you friends, for everything that I learned from my Father I have made known to you. {16} You did not choose me, but I chose you and appointed you to go and bear fruit–fruit that will last. Then the Father will give you whatever you ask in my name. {17} This is my command: Love each other. {18} "If the world hates you, keep in mind that it hated me first. {19} If you belonged to the world, it would love you as its own. As it is, you do not belong to the world, but I have chosen you out of the world. That is why the world hates you. {20} Remember the words I spoke to you: 'No servant is greater than his master.' If they persecuted me, they will persecute you also. If they obeyed my teaching, they will obey yours also. {21} They will treat you this way because of my name, for they do not know the One who sent me. {22} If I had not come and spoken to them, they would not be guilty of sin. Now, however, they have no excuse for their sin. {23} He who hates me hates my Father as well. {24} If I had not done among them what no one else did, they would not be guilty of sin. But now they have seen these miracles, and yet they have hated both me and my Father.

SORROW WILL TURN TO JOY

John 16:15-33

All that belongs to the Father is mine. That is why I said the Spirit will take from what is mine and make it known to you. {16} "In a little while you will see me no more, and then after a little while you will see me." {17} Some of his disciples said to one another, "What does he mean by saying, 'In a little while you will see me no more, and then after a little while you will see me,' and 'Because I am going to the Father'?" {18} They kept asking, "What does he mean by 'a little while'? We don't understand what he is saying." {19} Jesus saw that they wanted to ask him about this, so he said to them, "Are you asking one another what I meant when I said, 'In a little while you will see me no more, and then after a little while you will see me'? {20} I tell you the truth, you will weep and mourn while the world rejoices. You will grieve, but your grief will turn to joy. {21} A woman giving birth to a child has pain because her time has come; but when her baby is born she forgets the anguish because of her joy that a child is born into the world. {22} So with you: Now is your time of grief, but I will see you again and you will rejoice, and no one will take away your joy. {23} In that day you will no longer ask me anything. I tell you the truth, my Father will give you whatever you ask in my name. {24} Until now you have not asked for anything in my name. Ask and you will receive, and your joy will be complete. {25} "Though I have been speaking figuratively, a time is coming when I will no longer use this kind of language but will tell you plainly about my Father. {26} In that day you will ask in my name. I am not saying that I will ask the Father on your behalf. {27} No , the Father himself loves you because you have loved me and have believed that I came from God. {28} I came from the Father and entered the world; now I am leaving the world and going back to the Father." {29} Then Jesus' disciples said, "Now you are speaking clearly and without figures of speech. {30} Now we can see that you know all things and that you do not even need to have anyone ask you questions. This makes us believe that you came from God." {31} "You believe at last!" Jesus answered. {32} "But a time is coming, and has come, when you will be scattered, each to his own home. You will leave me all alone. Yet I am not alone, for my Father is with me. {33} "I have told you these things, so that in me you may have peace. In this world you will have trouble. But take heart! I have overcome the world."

JESUS PRAYS FOR HIS OWN

John 17:1b-24

"Father, the time has come. Glorify your Son, that your Son may glorify you. {2} For you granted him authority over all people that he might give eternal life to all those you have given him. {3} Now this is eternal life: that they may know you, the only true God, and Jesus Christ, whom you have sent. {4} I have brought you glory on earth by completing the work you gave me to do. {5} And now, Father, glorify me in your presence with the glory I had with you before the world began. {6} "I have revealed you to those whom you gave me out of the world. They were yours; you gave them to me and they have obeyed your word. {7} Now they know that everything you have given me comes from you. {8} For I gave them the words you gave me and they accepted them. They knew with certainty that I came from you, and they believed that you sent me. {9} I pray for them. I am not praying for the world, but for those you have given me, for they are yours. {10} All I have is yours, and all you have is mine. And glory has come to me through them. {11} I will remain in the world no longer, but they are still in the world, and I am coming to you. Holy Father, protect them by the power of your name–the name you gave me–so that they may be one as we are one. {12} While I was with them, I protected them and kept them safe by that name you gave me. None has been lost except the one doomed to destruction so that Scripture would be fulfilled. {13} "I am coming to you now, but I say these things while I am still in the world, so that they may have the full measure of my joy within them. {14} I have given them your word and the world has hated them, for they are not of the world any more than I am of the world. {15} My prayer is not that you take them out of the world but that you protect them from the evil one. {16} They are not of the world, even as I am not of it. {17} Sanctify them by the truth; your word is truth. {18} As you sent me into the world, I have sent them into the world. {19} For them I sanctify myself, that they too may be truly sanctified. {20} "My prayer is not for them alone. I pray also for those who will believe in me through their message, {21} that all of them may be one, Father, just as you are in me and I am in you. May they also be in us so that the world may believe that you have sent me. {22} I have given them the glory that you gave me, that they may be one as we are one: {23} I in them and you in me. May they be brought to complete unity to let the world know that you sent me and have loved them even as you have loved me. {24} "Father, I want those you have given me to be with me where I am, and to see my glory, the glory you have given me because you loved me before the creation of the world.

JESUS ARRESTED, DENIED BY PETER

John 18:1-11

When he had finished praying, Jesus left with his disciples and crossed the Kidron Valley. On the other side there was an olive grove, and he and his disciples went into it. {2} Now Judas, who betrayed him, knew the place, because Jesus had often met there with his disciples. {3} So Judas came to the grove, guiding a detachment of soldiers and some officials from the chief priests and Pharisees. They were carrying torches, lanterns and weapons. {4} Jesus, knowing all that was going to happen to him, went out and asked them, "Who is it you want?" {5} "Jesus of Nazareth," they replied. "I am he," Jesus said. (And Judas the traitor was standing there with them.) {6} When Jesus said, "I am he," they drew back and fell to the ground. {7} Again he asked them, "Who is it you want?" And they said, "Jesus of Nazareth." {8} "I told you that I am he," Jesus answered. "If you are looking for me, then let these men go." {9} This happened so that the words he had spoken would be fulfilled: "I have not lost one of those you gave me." {10} Then Simon Peter, who had a sword, drew it and struck the high priest's servant, cutting off his right ear. (The servant's name was Malchus.) {11} Jesus commanded Peter, "Put your sword away! Shall I not drink the cup the Father has given me?"

John 18:17-27

"You are not one of his disciples, are you?" the girl at the door asked Peter. He replied, "I am not." {18} It was cold, and the servants and officials stood around a fire they had made to keep warm. Peter also was standing with them, warming himself. {19} Meanwhile, the high priest questioned Jesus about his disciples and his teaching. {20} "I have spoken openly to the world," Jesus replied. "I always taught in synagogues or at the temple, where all the Jews come together. I said nothing in secret. {21} Why question me? Ask those who heard me. Surely they know what I said." {22} When Jesus said this, one of the officials nearby struck him in the face. "Is this the way you answer the high priest?" he demanded. {23} "If I said something wrong," Jesus replied, "testify as to what is wrong. But if I spoke the truth, why did you strike me?" {24} Then Annas sent him, still bound, to Caiaphas the high priest. {25} As Simon Peter stood warming himself, he was asked, "You are not one of his disciples, are you?" He denied it, saying, "I am not." {26} One of the high priest's servants, a relative of the man whose ear Peter had cut off, challenged him, "Didn't I see you with him in the olive grove?" {27} Again Peter denied it, and at that moment a rooster began to crow.

JESUS BEFORE PILATE

John 18:35b-19:14

"It was your people and your chief priests who handed you over to me. What is it you have done?" {36} Jesus said, "My kingdom is not of this world. If it were, my servants would fight to prevent my arrest by the Jews. But now my kingdom is from another place." {37} "You are a king, then!" said Pilate. Jesus answered, "You are right in saying I am a king. In fact, for this reason I was born, and for this I came into the world, to testify to the truth. Everyone on the side of truth listens to me." {38} "What is truth?" Pilate asked. With this he went out again to the Jews and said, "I find no basis for a charge against him. {39} But it is your custom for me to release to you one prisoner at the time of the Passover. Do you want me to release 'the king of the Jews'?" {40} They shouted back, "No, not him! Give us Barabbas!" Now Barabbas had taken part in a rebellion. {19:1} Then Pilate took Jesus and had him flogged. {2} The soldiers twisted together a crown of thorns and put it on his head. They clothed him in a purple robe {3} and went up to him again and again, saying, "Hail, king of the Jews!" And they struck him in the face. {4} Once more Pilate came out and said to the Jews, "Look, I am bringing him out to you to let you know that I find no basis for a charge against him." {5} When Jesus came out wearing the crown of thorns and the purple robe, Pilate said to them, "Here is the man!" {6} As soon as the chief priests and their officials saw him, they shouted, "Crucify! Crucify!" But Pilate answered, "You take him and crucify him. As for me, I find no basis for a charge against him." {7} The Jews insisted, "We have a law, and according to that law he must die, because he claimed to be the Son of God." {8} When Pilate heard this, he was even more afraid, {9} and he went back inside the palace. "Where do you come from?" he asked Jesus, but Jesus gave him no answer. {10} "Do you refuse to speak to me?" Pilate said. "Don't you realize I have power either to free you or to crucify you?" {11} Jesus answered, "You would have no power over me if it were not given to you from above. Therefore the one who handed me over to you is guilty of a greater sin." {12} From then on, Pilate tried to set Jesus free, but the Jews kept shouting, "If you let this man go, you are no friend of Caesar. Anyone who claims to be a king opposes Caesar." {13} When Pilate heard this, he brought Jesus out and sat down on the judge's seat at a place known as the Stone Pavement (which in Aramaic is Gabbatha). {14} It was the day of Preparation of Passover Week, about the sixth hour. "Here is your king," Pilate said to the Jews.

CRUCIFIXION, DEATH AND BURIAL OF JESUS

John 19:23-40

When the soldiers crucified Jesus, they took his clothes, dividing them into four shares, one for each of them, with the undergarment remaining. This garment was seamless, woven in one piece from top to bottom. {24} "Let's not tear it," they said to one another. "Let's decide by lot who will get it." This happened that the scripture might be fulfilled which said, "They divided my garments among them and cast lots for my clothing." So this is what the soldiers did. {25} Near the cross of Jesus stood his mother, his mother's sister, Mary the wife of Clopas, and Mary Magdalene. {26} When Jesus saw his mother there, and the disciple whom he loved standing nearby, he said to his mother, "Dear woman, here is your son," {27} and to the disciple, "Here is your mother." From that time on, this disciple took her into his home. {28} Later, knowing that all was now completed, and so that the Scripture would be fulfilled, Jesus said, "I am thirsty." {29} A jar of wine vinegar was there, so they soaked a sponge in it, put the sponge on a stalk of the hyssop plant, and lifted it to Jesus' lips. {30} When he had received the drink, Jesus said, "It is finished." With that, he bowed his head and gave up his spirit. {31} Now it was the day of Preparation, and the next day was to be a special Sabbath. Because the Jews did not want the bodies left on the crosses during the Sabbath, they asked Pilate to have the legs broken and the bodies taken down. {32} The soldiers therefore came and broke the legs of the first man who had been crucified with Jesus, and then those of the other. {33} But when they came to Jesus and found that he was already dead, they did not break his legs. {34} Instead, one of the soldiers pierced Jesus' side with a spear, bringing a sudden flow of blood and water. {35} The man who saw it has given testimony, and his testimony is true. He knows that he tells the truth, and he testifies so that you also may believe. {36} These things happened so that the scripture would be fulfilled: "Not one of his bones will be broken," {37} and, as another scripture says, "They will look on the one they have pierced." {38} Later, Joseph of Arimathea asked Pilate for the body of Jesus. Now Joseph was a disciple of Jesus, but secretly because he feared the Jews. With Pilate's permission, he came and took the body away. {39} He was accompanied by Nicodemus, the man who earlier had visited Jesus at night. Nicodemus brought a mixture of myrrh and aloes, about seventy-five pounds. {40} Taking Jesus' body, the two of them wrapped it, with the spices, in strips of linen. This was in accordance with Jewish burial customs.

RESURRECTION OF JESUS;
HE APPEARS TO MARY MAGDALENE AND TO DISCIPLES

John 20:1-22

Early on the first day of the week, while it was still dark, Mary Magdalene went to the tomb and saw that the stone had been removed from the entrance. {2} So she came running to Simon Peter and the other disciple, the one Jesus loved, and said, "They have taken the Lord out of the tomb, and we don't know where they have put him!" {3} So Peter and the other disciple started for the tomb. {4} Both were running, but the other disciple outran Peter and reached the tomb first. {5} He bent over and looked in at the strips of linen lying there but did not go in. {6} Then Simon Peter, who was behind him, arrived and went into the tomb. He saw the strips of linen lying there, {7} as well as the burial cloth that had been around Jesus' head. The cloth was folded up by itself, separate from the linen. {8} Finally the other disciple, who had reached the tomb first, also went inside. He saw and believed. {9} (They still did not understand from Scripture that Jesus had to rise from the dead.) {10} Then the disciples went back to their homes, {11} but Mary stood outside the tomb crying. As she wept, she bent over to look into the tomb {12} and saw two angels in white, seated where Jesus' body had been, one at the head and the other at the foot. {13} They asked her, "Woman, why are you crying?" "They have taken my Lord away," she said, "and I don't know where they have put him."

{14} At this, she turned around and saw Jesus standing there, but she did not realize that it was Jesus. {15} "Woman," he said, "why are you crying? Who is it you are looking for?" Thinking he was the gardener, she said, "Sir, if you have carried him away, tell me where you have put him, and I will get him." {16} Jesus said to her, "Mary." She turned toward him and cried out in Aramaic, "Rabboni!" (which means Teacher). {17} Jesus said, "Do not hold on to me, for I have not yet returned to the Father. Go instead to my brothers and tell them, 'I am returning to my Father and your Father, to my God and your God.'" {18} Mary Magdalene went to the disciples with the news: "I have seen the Lord!" And she told them that he had said these things to her. {19} On the evening of that first day of the week, when the disciples were together, with the doors locked for fear of the Jews, Jesus came and stood among them and said, "Peace be with you!" {20} After he said this, he showed them his hands and side. The disciples were overjoyed when they saw the Lord. {21} Again Jesus said, "Peace be with you! As the Father has sent me, I am sending you." {22} And with that he breathed on them and said, "Receive the Holy Spirit.

JESUS TALKS TO THOMAS, AND HELPS PETER COOK FISH

John 20:24-21:12

Now Thomas (called Didymus), one of the Twelve, was not with the disciples when Jesus came. {25} So the other disciples told him, "We have seen the Lord!" But he said to them, "Unless I see the nail marks in his hands and put my finger where the nails were, and put my hand into his side, I will not believe it." {26} A week later his disciples were in the house again, and Thomas was with them. Though the doors were locked, Jesus came and stood among them and said, "Peace be with you!" {27} Then he said to Thomas, "Put your finger here; see my hands. Reach out your hand and put it into my side. Stop doubting and believe." {28} Thomas said to him, "My Lord and my God!" {29} Then Jesus told him, "Because you have seen me, you have believed; blessed are those who have not seen and yet have believed." {30} Jesus did many other miraculous signs in the presence of his disciples, which are not recorded in this book. {31} But these are written that you may believe that Jesus is the Christ, the Son of God, and that by believing you may have life in his name.

{21:1} Afterward Jesus appeared again to his disciples, by the Sea of Tiberias. It happened this way: {2} Simon Peter, Thomas (called Didymus), Nathanael from Cana in Galilee, the sons of Zebedee, and two other disciples were together. {3} "I'm going out to fish," Simon Peter told them, and they said, "We'll go with you." So they went out and got into the boat, but that night they caught nothing. {4} Early in the morning, Jesus stood on the shore, but the disciples did not realize that it was Jesus. {5} He called out to them, "Friends, haven't you any fish?" "No," they answered. {6} He said, "Throw your net on the right side of the boat and you will find some." When they did, they were unable to haul the net in because of the large number of fish. {7} Then the disciple whom Jesus loved said to Peter, "It is the Lord!" As soon as Simon Peter heard him say, "It is the Lord," he wrapped his outer garment around him (for he had taken it off) and jumped into the water. {8} The other disciples followed in the boat, towing the net full of fish, for they were not far from shore, about a hundred yards. {9} When they landed, they saw a fire of burning coals there with fish on it, and some bread. {10} Jesus said to them, "Bring some of the fish you have just caught." {11} Simon Peter climbed aboard and dragged the net ashore. It was full of large fish, 153, but even with so many the net was not torn. {12} Jesus said to them, "Come and have breakfast." None of the disciples dared ask him, "Who are you?" They knew it was the Lord.

FELLOWSHIP OF JESUS AND PETER RESTORED

John 21:15-25

When they had finished eating, Jesus said to Simon Peter, "Simon son of John, do you truly love me more than these?" "Yes , Lord," he said, "you know that I love you." Jesus said, "Feed my lambs." {16} Again Jesus said, "Simon son of John, do you truly love me?" He answered, "Yes, Lord, you know that I love you." Jesus said, "Take care of my sheep." {17} The third time he said to him, "Simon son of John, do you love me?" Peter was hurt because Jesus asked him the third time, "Do you love me?" He said, "Lord, you know all things; you know that I love you." Jesus said, "Feed my sheep. {18} I tell you the truth, when you were younger you dressed yourself and went where you wanted; but when you are old you will stretch out your hands, and someone else will dress you and lead you where you do not want to go." {19} Jesus said this to indicate the kind of death by which Peter would glorify God. Then he said to him, "Follow me!" {20} Peter turned and saw that the disciple whom Jesus loved was following them. (This was the one who had leaned back against Jesus at the supper and had said, "Lord, who is going to betray you?") {21} When Peter saw him, he asked, "Lord, what about him?" {22} Jesus answered, "If I want him to remain alive until I return, what is that to you? You must follow me." {23} Because of this, the rumor spread among the brothers that this disciple would not die. But Jesus did not say that he would not die; he only said, "If I want him to remain alive until I return, what is that to you?" {24} This is the disciple who testifies to these things and who wrote them down. We know that his testimony is true. {25} Jesus did many other things as well. If every one of them were written down, I suppose that even the whole world would not have room for the books that would be written.

JESUS IS TAKEN TO HEAVEN; THE HOLY SPIRIT COMES

Acts 1:1-11

In my former book, Theophilus, I wrote about all that Jesus began to do and to teach {2} until the day he was taken up to heaven, after giving instructions through the Holy Spirit to the apostles he had chosen. {3} After his suffering, he showed himself to these men and gave many convincing proofs that he was alive. He appeared to them over a period of forty days and spoke about the kingdom of God. {4} On one occasion, while he was eating with them, he gave them this command: "Do not leave Jerusalem, but wait for the gift my Father promised, which you have heard me speak about. {5} For John baptized with water, but in a few days you will be baptized with the Holy Spirit." {6} So when they met together, they asked him, "Lord, are you at this time going to restore the kingdom to Israel?" {7} He said to them: "It is not for you to know the times or dates the Father has set by his own authority. {8} But you will receive power when the Holy Spirit comes on you; and you will be my witnesses in Jerusalem, and in all Judea and Samaria, and to the ends of the earth." {9} After he said this, he was taken up before their very eyes, and a cloud hid him from their sight. {10} They were looking intently up into the sky as he was going, when suddenly two men dressed in white stood beside them. {11} "Men of Galilee," they said, "why do you stand here looking into the sky? This same Jesus, who has been taken from you into heaven, will come back in the same way you have seen him go into heaven."

Acts 2:1-11

When the day of Pentecost came, they were all together in one place. {2} Suddenly a sound like the blowing of a violent wind came from heaven and filled the whole house where they were sitting. {3} They saw what seemed to be tongues of fire that separated and came to rest on each of them. {4} All of them were filled with the Holy Spirit and began to speak in other tongues as the Spirit enabled them. {5} Now there were staying in Jerusalem God-fearing Jews from every nation under heaven. {6} When they heard this sound, a crowd came together in bewilderment, because each one heard them speaking in his own language. {7} Utterly amazed, they asked: "Are not all these men who are speaking Galileans? {8} Then how is it that each of us hears them in his own native language? {9} Parthians, Medes and Elamites; residents of Mesopotamia, Judea and Cappadocia, Pontus and Asia, {10} Phrygia and Pamphylia, Egypt and the parts of Libya near Cyrene; visitors from Rome {11} (both Jews and converts to Judaism); Cretans and Arabs—we hear them declaring the wonders of God in our own tongues!"

PETER'S SERMON IN JERUSALEM

Acts 2:14-24

Then Peter stood up with the Eleven, raised his voice and addressed the crowd: "Fellow Jews and all of you who live in Jerusalem, let me explain this to you; listen carefully to what I say. {15} These men are not drunk, as you suppose. It's only nine in the morning! {16} No, this is what was spoken by the prophet Joel: {17} "'In the last days, God says, I will pour out my Spirit on all people. Your sons and daughters will prophesy, your young men will see visions, your old men will dream dreams. {18} Even on my servants, both men and women, I will pour out my Spirit in those days, and they will prophesy. {19} I will show wonders in the heaven above and signs on the earth below, blood and fire and billows of smoke. {20} The sun will be turned to darkness and the moon to blood before the coming of the great and glorious day of the Lord. {21} And everyone who calls on the name of the Lord will be saved.' {22} "Men of Israel, listen to this: Jesus of Nazareth was a man accredited by God to you by miracles, wonders and signs, which God did among you through him, as you yourselves know. {23} This man was handed over to you by God's set purpose and foreknowledge; and you, with the help of wicked men, put him to death by nailing him to the cross. {24} But God raised him from the dead, freeing him from the agony of death, because it was impossible for death to keep its hold on him.

Acts 2:36-41

"Therefore let all Israel be assured of this: God has made this Jesus, whom you crucified, both Lord and Christ." {37} When the people heard this, they were cut to the heart and said to Peter and the other apostles, "Brothers, what shall we do?" {38} Peter replied, "Repent and be baptized, every one of you, in the name of Jesus Christ for the forgiveness of your sins. And you will receive the gift of the Holy Spirit. {39} The promise is for you and your children and for all who are far off—for all whom the Lord our God will call." {40} With many other words he warned them; and he pleaded with them, "Save yourselves from this corrupt generation." {41} Those who accepted his message were baptized, and about three thousand were added to their number that day.

THE WORKS AND PREACHING OF THE NEW BELIEVERS

Acts 2:44-3:19a

All the believers were together and had everything in common. {45} Selling their possessions and goods, they gave to anyone as he had need. {46} Every day they continued to meet together in the temple courts. They broke bread in their homes and ate together with glad and sincere hearts, {47} praising God and enjoying the favor of all the people. And the Lord added to their number daily those who were being saved. {3:1} One day Peter and John were going up to the temple at the time of prayer–at three in the afternoon. {2} Now a man crippled from birth was being carried to the temple gate called Beautiful, where he was put every day to beg from those going into the temple courts. {3} When he saw Peter and John about to enter, he asked them for money. {4} Peter looked straight at him, as did John. Then Peter said, "Look at us!" {5} So the man gave them his attention, expecting to get something from them. {6} Then Peter said, "Silver or gold I do not have, but what I have I give you. In the name of Jesus Christ of Nazareth, walk." {7} Taking him by the right hand, he helped him up, and instantly the man's feet and ankles became strong. {8} He jumped to his feet and began to walk. Then he went with them into the temple courts, walking and jumping, and praising God. {9} When all the people saw him walking and praising God, {10} they recognized him as the same man who used to sit begging at the temple gate called Beautiful, and they were filled with wonder and amazement at what had happened to him. {11} While the beggar held on to Peter and John, all the people were astonished and came running to them in the place called Solomon's Colonnade. {12} When Peter saw this, he said to them: "Men of Israel, why does this surprise you? Why do you stare at us as if by our own power or godliness we had made this man walk? {13} The God of Abraham, Isaac and Jacob, the God of our fathers, has glorified his servant Jesus. You handed him over to be killed, and you disowned him before Pilate, though he had decided to let him go. {14} You disowned the Holy and Righteous One and asked that a murderer be released to you. {15} You killed the author of life, but God raised him from the dead. We are witnesses of this. {16} By faith in the name of Jesus, this man whom you see and know was made strong. It is Jesus' name and the faith that comes through him that has given this complete healing to him, as you can all see. {17} "Now, brothers, I know that you acted in ignorance, as did your leaders. {18} But this is how God fulfilled what he had foretold through all the prophets, saying that his Christ would suffer. {19} Repent, then, and turn to God, so that your sins may be wiped out....

PETER AND JOHN TESTIFY BEFORE THE SANHEDRIN

Acts 4:7-23

They had Peter and John brought before them and began to question them: "By what power or what name did you do this?" {8} Then Peter, filled with the Holy Spirit, said to them: "Rulers and elders of the people! {9} If we are being called to account today for an act of kindness shown to a cripple and are asked how he was healed, {10} then know this, you and all the people of Israel: It is by the name of Jesus Christ of Nazareth, whom you crucified but whom God raised from the dead, that this man stands before you healed. {11} He is "'the stone you builders rejected, which has become the capstone.' {12} Salvation is found in no one else, for there is no other name under heaven given to men by which we must be saved." {13} When they saw the courage of Peter and John and realized that they were unschooled, ordinary men, they were astonished and they took note that these men had been with Jesus. {14} But since they could see the man who had been healed standing there with them, there was nothing they could say. {15} So they ordered them to withdraw from the Sanhedrin and then conferred together. {16} "What are we going to do with these men?" they asked. "Everybody living in Jerusalem knows they have done an outstanding miracle, and we cannot deny it. {17} But to stop this thing from spreading any further among the people, we must warn these men to speak no longer to anyone in this name." {18} Then they called them in again and commanded them not to speak or teach at all in the name of Jesus. {19} But Peter and John replied, "Judge for yourselves whether it is right in God's sight to obey you rather than God. {20} For we cannot help speaking about what we have seen and heard." {21} After further threats they let them go. They could not decide how to punish them, because all the people were praising God for what had happened. {22} For the man who was miraculously healed was over forty years old. {23} On their release, Peter and John went back to their own people and reported all that the chief priests and elders had said to them.

THE BELIEVERS SHARE EVERYTHING

Acts 4:32-5:15

All the believers were one in heart and mind. No one claimed that any of his possessions was his own, but they shared everything they had. {33} With great power the apostles continued to testify to the resurrection of the Lord Jesus, and much grace was upon them all. {34} There were no needy persons among them. For from time to time those who owned lands or houses sold them, brought the money from the sales {35} and put it at the apostles' feet, and it was distributed to anyone as he had need. {36} Joseph, a Levite from Cyprus, whom the apostles called Barnabas (which means Son of Encouragement), {37} sold a field he owned and brought the money and put it at the apostles' feet. {5:1} Now a man named Ananias, together with his wife Sapphira, also sold a piece of property. {2} With his wife's full knowledge he kept back part of the money for himself, but brought the rest and put it at the apostles' feet. {3} Then Peter said, "Ananias, how is it that Satan has so filled your heart that you have lied to the Holy Spirit and have kept for yourself some of the money you received for the land? {4} Didn't it belong to you before it was sold? And after it was sold, wasn't the money at your disposal? What made you think of doing such a thing? You have not lied to men but to God." {5} When Ananias heard this, he fell down and died. And great fear seized all who heard what had happened. {6} Then the young men came forward, wrapped up his body, and carried him out and buried him. {7} About three hours later his wife came in, not knowing what had happened. {8} Peter asked her, "Tell me, is this the price you and Ananias got for the land?" "Yes," she said, "that is the price." {9} Peter said to her, "How could you agree to test the Spirit of the Lord? Look! The feet of the men who buried your husband are at the door, and they will carry you out also." {10} At that moment she fell down at his feet and died. Then the young men came in and, finding her dead, carried her out and buried her beside her husband. {11} Great fear seized the whole church and all who heard about these events. {12} The apostles performed many miraculous signs and wonders among the people. And all the believers used to meet together in Solomon's Colonnade. {13} No one else dared join them, even though they were highly regarded by the people. {14} Nevertheless, more and more men and women believed in the Lord and were added to their number. {15} As a result, people brought the sick into the streets and laid them on beds and mats so that at least Peter's shadow might fall on some of them as he passed by.

APOSTLES ARRESTED AGAIN

Acts 5:22-41

On arriving at the jail, the officers did not find them there. So they went back and reported, {23} "We found the jail securely locked, with the guards standing at the doors; but when we opened them, we found no one inside." {24} On hearing this report, the captain of the temple guard and the chief priests were puzzled, wondering what would come of this. {25} Then someone came and said, "Look! The men you put in jail are standing in the temple courts teaching the people." {26} At that, the captain went with his officers and brought the apostles. They did not use force, because they feared that the people would stone them. {27} Having brought the apostles, they made them appear before the Sanhedrin to be questioned by the high priest. {28} "We gave you strict orders not to teach in this name," he said. "Yet you have filled Jerusalem with your teaching and are determined to make us guilty of this man's blood." {29} Peter and the other apostles replied: "We must obey God rather than men! {30} The God of our fathers raised Jesus from the dead–whom you had killed by hanging him on a tree. {31} God exalted him to his own right hand as Prince and Savior that he might give repentance and forgiveness of sins to Israel. {32} We are witnesses of these things, and so is the Holy Spirit, whom God has given to those who obey him." {33} When they heard this, they were furious and wanted to put them to death. {34} But a Pharisee named Gamaliel, a teacher of the law, who was honored by all the people, stood up in the Sanhedrin and ordered that the men be put outside for a little while. {35} Then he addressed them: "Men of Israel, consider carefully what you intend to do to these men. {36} Some time ago Theudas appeared, claiming to be somebody, and about four hundred men rallied to him. He was killed, all his followers were dispersed, and it all came to nothing. {37} After him, Judas the Galilean appeared in the days of the census and led a band of people in revolt. He too was killed, and all his followers were scattered. {38} Therefore, in the present case I advise you: Leave these men alone! Let them go! For if their purpose or activity is of human origin, it will fail. {39} But if it is from God, you will not be able to stop these men; you will only find yourselves fighting against God." {40} His speech persuaded them. They called the apostles in and had them flogged. Then they ordered them not to speak in the name of Jesus, and let them go. {41} The apostles left the Sanhedrin, rejoicing because they had been counted worthy of suffering disgrace for the Name.

322

STEPHEN AND OTHER DEACONS CHOSEN

Acts 6:1-15

In those days when the number of disciples was increasing, the Grecian Jews among them complained against the Hebraic Jews because their widows were being overlooked in the daily distribution of food. {2} So the Twelve gathered all the disciples together and said, "It would not be right for us to neglect the ministry of the word of God in order to wait on tables. {3} Brothers, choose seven men from among you who are known to be full of the Spirit and wisdom. We will turn this responsibility over to them {4} and will give our attention to prayer and the ministry of the word." {5} This proposal pleased the whole group. They chose Stephen, a man full of faith and of the Holy Spirit; also Philip, Procorus, Nicanor, Timon, Parmenas, and Nicolas from Antioch, a convert to Judaism. {6} They presented these men to the apostles, who prayed and laid their hands on them. {7} So the word of God spread. The number of disciples in Jerusalem increased rapidly, and a large number of priests became obedient to the faith. {8} Now Stephen, a man full of God's grace and power, did great wonders and miraculous signs among the people. {9} Opposition arose, however, from members of the Synagogue of the Freedmen (as it was called)–Jews of Cyrene and Alexandria as well as the provinces of Cilicia and Asia. These men began to argue with Stephen, {10} but they could not stand up against his wisdom or the Spirit by whom he spoke. {11} Then they secretly persuaded some men to say, "We have heard Stephen speak words of blasphemy against Moses and against God." {12} So they stirred up the people and the elders and the teachers of the law. They seized Stephen and brought him before the Sanhedrin. {13} They produced false witnesses, who testified, "This fellow never stops speaking against this holy place and against the law. {14} For we have heard him say that this Jesus of Nazareth will destroy this place and change the customs Moses handed down to us." {15} All who were sitting in the Sanhedrin looked intently at Stephen, and they saw that his face was like the face of an angel.

STEPHEN PREACHES TO SANHEDRIN

Acts 7:1-18

Then the high priest asked him, "Are these charges true?" {2} To this he replied: "Brothers and fathers, listen to me! The God of glory appeared to our father Abraham while he was still in Mesopotamia, before he lived in Haran. {3} 'Leave your country and your people,' God said, 'and go to the land I will show you.' {4} "So he left the land of the Chaldeans and settled in Haran. After the death of his father, God sent him to this land where you are now living. {5} He gave him no inheritance here, not even a foot of ground. But God promised him that he and his descendants after him would possess the land, even though at that time Abraham had no child. {6} God spoke to him in this way: 'Your descendants will be strangers in a country not their own, and they will be enslaved and mistreated four hundred years. {7} But I will punish the nation they serve as slaves,' God said, 'and afterward they will come out of that country and worship me in this place.' {8} Then he gave Abraham the covenant of circumcision. And Abraham became the father of Isaac and circumcised him eight days after his birth. Later Isaac became the father of Jacob, and Jacob became the father of the twelve patriarchs. {9} "Because the patriarchs were jealous of Joseph, they sold him as a slave into Egypt. But God was with him {10} and rescued him from all his troubles. He gave Joseph wisdom and enabled him to gain the goodwill of Pharaoh king of Egypt; so he made him ruler over Egypt and all his palace. {11} "Then a famine struck all Egypt and Canaan, bringing great suffering, and our fathers could not find food. {12} When Jacob heard that there was grain in Egypt, he sent our fathers on their first visit. {13} On their second visit, Joseph told his brothers who he was, and Pharaoh learned about Joseph's family. {14} After this, Joseph sent for his father Jacob and his whole family, seventy-five in all. {15} Then Jacob went down to Egypt, where he and our fathers died. {16} Their bodies were brought back to Shechem and placed in the tomb that Abraham had bought from the sons of Hamor at Shechem for a certain sum of money. {17} "As the time drew near for God to fulfill his promise to Abraham, the number of our people in Egypt greatly increased. {18} Then another king, who knew nothing about Joseph, became ruler of Egypt.

Acts 7:51

"You stiff-necked people, with uncircumcised hearts and ears! You are just like your fathers: You always resist the Holy Spirit!

MINISTRY OF PHILIP

Acts 8:4-8

Those who had been scattered preached the word wherever they went. {5} Philip went down to a city in Samaria and proclaimed the Christ there. {6} When the crowds heard Philip and saw the miraculous signs he did, they all paid close attention to what he said. {7} With shrieks, evil spirits came out of many, and many paralytics and cripples were healed. {8} So there was great joy in that city.

Acts 8:26-40

Now an angel of the Lord said to Philip, "Go south to the road–the desert road–that goes down from Jerusalem to Gaza." {27} So he started out, and on his way he met an Ethiopian eunuch, an important official in charge of all the treasury of Candace, queen of the Ethiopians. This man had gone to Jerusalem to worship, {28} and on his way home was sitting in his chariot reading the book of Isaiah the prophet. {29} The Spirit told Philip, "Go to that chariot and stay near it." {30} Then Philip ran up to the chariot and heard the man reading Isaiah the prophet. "Do you understand what you are reading?" Philip asked. {31} "How can I," he said, "unless someone explains it to me?" So he invited Philip to come up and sit with him. {32} The eunuch was reading this passage of Scripture: "He was led like a sheep to the slaughter, and as a lamb before the shearer is silent, so he did not open his mouth. {33} In his humiliation he was deprived of justice. Who can speak of his descendants? For his life was taken from the earth." {34} The eunuch asked Philip, "Tell me, please, who is the prophet talking about, himself or someone else?" {35} Then Philip began with that very passage of Scripture and told him the good news about Jesus. {36} As they traveled along the road, they came to some water and the eunuch said, "Look, here is water. Why shouldn't I be baptized?" {37} {38} And he gave orders to stop the chariot. Then both Philip and the eunuch went down into the water and Philip baptized him. {39} When they came up out of the water, the Spirit of the Lord suddenly took Philip away, and the eunuch did not see him again, but went on his way rejoicing. {40} Philip, however, appeared at Azotus and traveled about, preaching the gospel in all the towns until he reached Caesarea.

SAUL BECOMES A CHRISTIAN

Acts 9:3-26

As he neared Damascus on his journey, suddenly a light from heaven flashed around him. {4} He fell to the ground and heard a voice say to him, "Saul , Saul, why do you persecute me?" {5} "Who are you, Lord?" Saul asked. "I am Jesus, whom you are persecuting," he replied. {6} "Now get up and go into the city, and you will be told what you must do." {7} The men traveling with Saul stood there speechless; they heard the sound but did not see anyone. {8} Saul got up from the ground, but when he opened his eyes he could see nothing. So they led him by the hand into Damascus. {9} For three days he was blind, and did not eat or drink anything. {10} In Damascus there was a disciple named Ananias. The Lord called to him in a vision, "Ananias!" "Yes, Lord," he answered. {11} The Lord told him, "Go to the house of Judas on Straight Street and ask for a man from Tarsus named Saul, for he is praying. {12} In a vision he has seen a man named Ananias come and place his hands on him to restore his sight." {13} "Lord," Ananias answered, "I have heard many reports about this man and all the harm he has done to your saints in Jerusalem. {14} And he has come here with authority from the chief priests to arrest all who call on your name." {15} But the Lord said to Ananias, "Go! This man is my chosen instrument to carry my name before the Gentiles and their kings and before the people of Israel. {16} I will show him how much he must suffer for my name." {17} Then Ananias went to the house and entered it. Placing his hands on Saul, he said, "Brother Saul, the Lord–Jesus, who appeared to you on the road as you were coming here–has sent me so that you may see again and be filled with the Holy Spirit." {18} Immediately, something like scales fell from Saul's eyes, and he could see again. He got up and was baptized, {19} and after taking some food, he regained his strength. Saul spent several days with the disciples in Damascus. {20} At once he began to preach in the synagogues that Jesus is the Son of God. {21} All those who heard him were astonished and asked, "Isn't he the man who raised havoc in Jerusalem among those who call on this name? And hasn't he come here to take them as prisoners to the chief priests?" {22} Yet Saul grew more and more powerful and baffled the Jews living in Damascus by proving that Jesus is the Christ. {23} After many days had gone by, the Jews conspired to kill him, {24} but Saul learned of their plan. Day and night they kept close watch on the city gates in order to kill him. {25} But his followers took him by night and lowered him in a basket through an opening in the wall. {26} When he came to Jerusalem, he tried to join the disciples, but they were all afraid of him....

CORNELIUS SENDS FOR PETER

Acts 10:1-23a

At Caesarea there was a man named Cornelius, a centurion in what was known as the Italian Regiment. {2} He and all his family were devout and God-fearing; he gave generously to those in need and prayed to God regularly. {3} One day at about three in the afternoon he had a vision. He distinctly saw an angel of God, who came to him and said, "Cornelius!" {4} Cornelius stared at him in fear. "What is it, Lord?" he asked. The angel answered, "Your prayers and gifts to the poor have come up as a memorial offering before God. {5} Now send men to Joppa to bring back a man named Simon who is called Peter. {6} He is staying with Simon the tanner, whose house is by the sea." {7} When the angel who spoke to him had gone, Cornelius called two of his servants and a devout soldier who was one of his attendants. {8} He told them everything that had happened and sent them to Joppa. {9} About noon the following day as they were on their journey and approaching the city, Peter went up on the roof to pray. {10} He became hungry and wanted something to eat, and while the meal was being prepared, he fell into a trance. {11} He saw heaven opened and something like a large sheet being let down to earth by its four corners. {12} It contained all kinds of four-footed animals, as well as reptiles of the earth and birds of the air. {13} Then a voice told him, "Get up, Peter. Kill and eat." {14} "Surely not, Lord!" Peter replied. "I have never eaten anything impure or unclean." {15} The voice spoke to him a second time, "Do not call anything impure that God has made clean." {16} This happened three times, and immediately the sheet was taken back to heaven. {17} While Peter was wondering about the meaning of the vision, the men sent by Cornelius found out where Simon's house was and stopped at the gate. {18} They called out, asking if Simon who was known as Peter was staying there. {19} While Peter was still thinking about the vision, the Spirit said to him, "Simon, three men are looking for you. {20} So get up and go downstairs. Do not hesitate to go with them, for I have sent them." {21} Peter went down and said to the men, "I'm the one you're looking for. Why have you come?" {22} The men replied, "We have come from Cornelius the centurion. He is a righteous and God-fearing man, who is respected by all the Jewish people. A holy angel told him to have you come to his house so that he could hear what you have to say." {23} Then Peter invited the men into the house to be his guests.

PETER BAPTIZES CORNELIUS

Acts 10:28-48a

"You are well aware that it is against our law for a Jew to associate with a Gentile or visit him. But God has shown me that I should not call any man impure or unclean. {29} So when I was sent for, I came without raising any objection. May I ask why you sent for me?" {30} Cornelius answered: "Four days ago I was in my house praying at this hour, at three in the afternoon. Suddenly a man in shining clothes stood before me {31} and said, 'Cornelius, God has heard your prayer and remembered your gifts to the poor. {32} Send to Joppa for Simon who is called Peter. He is a guest in the home of Simon the tanner, who lives by the sea.' {33} So I sent for you immediately, and it was good of you to come. Now we are all here in the presence of God to listen to everything the Lord has commanded you to tell us." {34} Then Peter began to speak: "I now realize how true it is that God does not show favoritism {35} but accepts men from every nation who fear him and do what is right. {36} You know the message God sent to the people of Israel, telling the good news of peace through Jesus Christ, who is Lord of all. {37} You know what has happened throughout Judea, beginning in Galilee after the baptism that John preached– {38} how God anointed Jesus of Nazareth with the Holy Spirit and power, and how he went around doing good and healing all who were under the power of the devil, because God was with him. {39} "We are witnesses of everything he did in the country of the Jews and in Jerusalem. They killed him by hanging him on a tree, {40} but God raised him from the dead on the third day and caused him to be seen. {41} He was not seen by all the people, but by witnesses whom God had already chosen–by us who ate and drank with him after he rose from the dead. {42} He commanded us to preach to the people and to testify that he is the one whom God appointed as judge of the living and the dead. {43} All the prophets testify about him that everyone who believes in him receives forgiveness of sins through his name." {44} While Peter was still speaking these words, the Holy Spirit came on all who heard the message. {45} The circumcised believers who had come with Peter were astonished that the gift of the Holy Spirit had been poured out even on the Gentiles. {46} For they heard them speaking in tongues and praising God. Then Peter said, {47} "Can anyone keep these people from being baptized with water? They have received the Holy Spirit just as we have." {48} So he ordered that they be baptized in the name of Jesus Christ.

PETER DEFENDS HIS ACTIONS

Acts 11:1-24

The apostles and the brothers throughout Judea heard that the Gentiles also had received the word of God. {2} So when Peter went up to Jerusalem, the circumcised believers criticized him {3} and said, "You went into the house of uncircumcised men and ate with them." {4} Peter began and explained everything to them precisely as it had happened: {5} "I was in the city of Joppa praying, and in a trance I saw a vision. I saw something like a large sheet being let down from heaven by its four corners, and it came down to where I was. {6} I looked into it and saw four-footed animals of the earth, wild beasts, reptiles, and birds of the air. {7} Then I heard a voice telling me, 'Get up, Peter. Kill and eat.' {8} "I replied, 'Surely not, Lord! Nothing impure or unclean has ever entered my mouth.' {9} "The voice spoke from heaven a second time, 'Do not call anything impure that God has made clean.' {10} This happened three times, and then it was all pulled up to heaven again. {11} "Right then three men who had been sent to me from Caesarea stopped at the house where I was staying. {12} The Spirit told me to have no hesitation about going with them. These six brothers also went with me, and we entered the man's house. {13} He told us how he had seen an angel appear in his house and say, 'Send to Joppa for Simon who is called Peter. {14} He will bring you a message through which you and all your household will be saved.' {15} "As I began to speak, the Holy Spirit came on them as he had come on us at the beginning. {16} Then I remembered what the Lord had said: 'John baptized with water, but you will be baptized with the Holy Spirit.' {17} So if God gave them the same gift as he gave us, who believed in the Lord Jesus Christ, who was I to think that I could oppose God?" {18} When they heard this, they had no further objections and praised God, saying, "So then, God has granted even the Gentiles repentance unto life." {19} Now those who had been scattered by the persecution in connection with Stephen traveled as far as Phoenicia, Cyprus and Antioch, telling the message only to Jews. {20} Some of them, however, men from Cyprus and Cyrene, went to Antioch and began to speak to Greeks also, telling them the good news about the Lord Jesus. {21} The Lord's hand was with them, and a great number of people believed and turned to the Lord. {22} News of this reached the ears of the church at Jerusalem, and they sent Barnabas to Antioch. {23} When he arrived and saw the evidence of the grace of God, he was glad and encouraged them all to remain true to the Lord with all their hearts. {24} He was a good man, full of the Holy Spirit and faith, and a great number of people were brought to the Lord.

PETER ESCAPES FROM PRISON

Acts 12:1-19a

It was about this time that King Herod arrested some who belonged to the church, intending to persecute them. {2} He had James, the brother of John, put to death with the sword. {3} When he saw that this pleased the Jews, he proceeded to seize Peter also. This happened during the Feast of Unleavened Bread. {4} After arresting him, he put him in prison, handing him over to be guarded by four squads of four soldiers each. Herod intended to bring him out for public trial after the Passover. {5} So Peter was kept in prison, but the church was earnestly praying to God for him. {6} The night before Herod was to bring him to trial, Peter was sleeping between two soldiers, bound with two chains, and sentries stood guard at the entrance. {7} Suddenly an angel of the Lord appeared and a light shone in the cell. He struck Peter on the side and woke him up. "Quick, get up!" he said, and the chains fell off Peter's wrists. {8} Then the angel said to him, "Put on your clothes and sandals." And Peter did so. "Wrap your cloak around you and follow me," the angel told him. {9} Peter followed him out of the prison, but he had no idea that what the angel was doing was really happening; he thought he was seeing a vision. {10} They passed the first and second guards and came to the iron gate leading to the city. It opened for them by itself, and they went through it. When they had walked the length of one street, suddenly the angel left him. {11} Then Peter came to himself and said, "Now I know without a doubt that the Lord sent his angel and rescued me from Herod's clutches and from everything the Jewish people were anticipating." {12} When this had dawned on him, he went to the house of Mary the mother of John, also called Mark, where many people had gathered and were praying. {13} Peter knocked at the outer entrance, and a servant girl named Rhoda came to answer the door. {14} When she recognized Peter's voice, she was so overjoyed she ran back without opening it and exclaimed, "Peter is at the door!" {15} "You're out of your mind," they told her. When she kept insisting that it was so, they said, "It must be his angel." {16} But Peter kept on knocking, and when they opened the door and saw him, they were astonished. {17} Peter motioned with his hand for them to be quiet and described how the Lord had brought him out of prison. "Tell James and the brothers about this," he said, and then he left for another place. {18} In the morning, there was no small commotion among the soldiers as to what had become of Peter. {19} After Herod had a thorough search made for him and did not find him, he cross-examined the guards and ordered that they be executed.

BARNABAS AND PAUL GO WEST AND PREACH

Acts 13:7b-25

The proconsul, an intelligent man, sent for Barnabas and Saul because he wanted to hear the word of God. {8} But Elymas the sorcerer (for that is what his name means) opposed them and tried to turn the proconsul from the faith. {9} Then Saul, who was also called Paul, filled with the Holy Spirit, looked straight at Elymas and said, {10} "You are a child of the devil and an enemy of everything that is right! You are full of all kinds of deceit and trickery. Will you never stop perverting the right ways of the Lord? {11} Now the hand of the Lord is against you. You are going to be blind, and for a time you will be unable to see the light of the sun." Immediately mist and darkness came over him, and he groped about, seeking someone to lead him by the hand. {12} When the proconsul saw what had happened, he believed, for he was amazed at the teaching about the Lord. {13} From Paphos, Paul and his companions sailed to Perga in Pamphylia, where John left them to return to Jerusalem. {14} From Perga they went on to Pisidian Antioch. On the Sabbath they entered the synagogue and sat down. {15} After the reading from the Law and the Prophets, the synagogue rulers sent word to them, saying, "Brothers, if you have a message of encouragement for the people, please speak." {16} Standing up, Paul motioned with his hand and said: "Men of Israel and you Gentiles who worship God, listen to me! {17} The God of the people of Israel chose our fathers; he made the people prosper during their stay in Egypt, with mighty power he led them out of that country, {18} he endured their conduct for about forty years in the desert, {19} he overthrew seven nations in Canaan and gave their land to his people as their inheritance. {20} All this took about 450 years. "After this, God gave them judges until the time of Samuel the prophet. {21} Then the people asked for a king, and he gave them Saul son of Kish, of the tribe of Benjamin, who ruled forty years. {22} After removing Saul, he made David their king. He testified concerning him: 'I have found David son of Jesse a man after my own heart; he will do everything I want him to do.' {23} "From this man's descendants God has brought to Israel the Savior Jesus, as he promised. {24} Before the coming of Jesus, John preached repentance and baptism to all the people of Israel. {25} As John was completing his work, he said: 'Who do you think I am? I am not that one. No, but he is coming after me, whose sandals I am not worthy to untie.'

PAUL CONTINUES SERMON IN ANTIOCH

Acts 13:32-52

"We tell you the good news: What God promised our fathers {33} he has fulfilled for us, their children, by raising up Jesus. As it is written in the second Psalm: "'You are my Son; today I have become your Father.' {34} The fact that God raised him from the dead, never to decay, is stated in these words: "'I will give you the holy and sure blessings promised to David.' {35} So it is stated elsewhere: "'You will not let your Holy One see decay.' {36} "For when David had served God's purpose in his own generation, he fell asleep; he was buried with his fathers and his body decayed. {37} But the one whom God raised from the dead did not see decay. {38} "Therefore, my brothers, I want you to know that through Jesus the forgiveness of sins is proclaimed to you. {39} Through him everyone who believes is justified from everything you could not be justified from by the law of Moses. {40} Take care that what the prophets have said does not happen to you: {41} "'Look, you scoffers, wonder and perish, for I am going to do something in your days that you would never believe, even if someone told you.' " {42} As Paul and Barnabas were leaving the synagogue, the people invited them to speak further about these things on the next Sabbath. {43} When the congregation was dismissed, many of the Jews and devout converts to Judaism followed Paul and Barnabas, who talked with them and urged them to continue in the grace of God. {44} On the next Sabbath almost the whole city gathered to hear the word of the Lord. {45} When the Jews saw the crowds, they were filled with jealousy and talked abusively against what Paul was saying. {46} Then Paul and Barnabas answered them boldly: "We had to speak the word of God to you first. Since you reject it and do not consider yourselves worthy of eternal life, we now turn to the Gentiles. {47} For this is what the Lord has commanded us: "'I have made you a light for the Gentiles, that you may bring salvation to the ends of the earth.' " {48} When the Gentiles heard this, they were glad and honored the word of the Lord; and all who were appointed for eternal life believed. {49} The word of the Lord spread through the whole region. {50} But the Jews incited the God-fearing women of high standing and the leading men of the city. They stirred up persecution against Paul and Barnabas, and expelled them from their region. {51} So they shook the dust from their feet in protest against them and went to Iconium. {52} And the disciples were filled with joy and with the Holy Spirit.

PAUL AND BARNABAS VISIT OTHER TOWNS IN ASIA MINOR

Acts 14:2-22a

But the Jews who refused to believe stirred up the Gentiles and poisoned their minds against the brothers. {3} So Paul and Barnabas spent considerable time there, speaking boldly for the Lord, who confirmed the message of his grace by enabling them to do miraculous signs and wonders. {4} The people of the city were divided; some sided with the Jews, others with the apostles. {5} There was a plot afoot among the Gentiles and Jews, together with their leaders, to mistreat them and stone them. {6} But they found out about it and fled to the Lycaonian cities of Lystra and Derbe and to the surrounding country, {7} where they continued to preach the good news. {8} In Lystra there sat a man crippled in his feet, who was lame from birth and had never walked. {9} He listened to Paul as he was speaking. Paul looked directly at him, saw that he had faith to be healed {10} and called out, "Stand up on your feet!" At that, the man jumped up and began to walk. {11} When the crowd saw what Paul had done, they shouted in the Lycaonian language, "The gods have come down to us in human form!" {12} Barnabas they called Zeus, and Paul they called Hermes because he was the chief speaker. {13} The priest of Zeus, whose temple was just outside the city, brought bulls and wreaths to the city gates because he and the crowd wanted to offer sacrifices to them. {14} But when the apostles Barnabas and Paul heard of this, they tore their clothes and rushed out into the crowd, shouting: {15} "Men, why are you doing this? We too are only men, human like you. We are bringing you good news, telling you to turn from these worthless things to the living God, who made heaven and earth and sea and everything in them. {16} In the past, he let all nations go their own way. {17} Yet he has not left himself without testimony: He has shown kindness by giving you rain from heaven and crops in their seasons; he provides you with plenty of food and fills your hearts with joy." {18} Even with these words, they had difficulty keeping the crowd from sacrificing to them. {19} Then some Jews came from Antioch and Iconium and won the crowd over. They stoned Paul and dragged him outside the city, thinking he was dead. {20} But after the disciples had gathered around him, he got up and went back into the city. The next day he and Barnabas left for Derbe. {21} They preached the good news in that city and won a large number of disciples. Then they returned to Lystra, Iconium and Antioch, {22} strengthening the disciples and encouraging them to remain true to the faith.

JERUSALEM COUNCIL ACCEPTS GENTILE BELIEVERS

Acts 15:1-20

Some men came down from Judea to Antioch and were teaching the brothers: "Unless you are circumcised, according to the custom taught by Moses, you cannot be saved." {2} This brought Paul and Barnabas into sharp dispute and debate with them. So Paul and Barnabas were appointed, along with some other believers, to go up to Jerusalem to see the apostles and elders about this question. {3} The church sent them on their way, and as they traveled through Phoenicia and Samaria, they told how the Gentiles had been converted. This news made all the brothers very glad. {4} When they came to Jerusalem, they were welcomed by the church and the apostles and elders, to whom they reported everything God had done through them. {5} Then some of the believers who belonged to the party of the Pharisees stood up and said, "The Gentiles must be circumcised and required to obey the law of Moses." {6} The apostles and elders met to consider this question. {7} After much discussion, Peter got up and addressed them: "Brothers, you know that some time ago God made a choice among you that the Gentiles might hear from my lips the message of the gospel and believe. {8} God, who knows the heart, showed that he accepted them by giving the Holy Spirit to them, just as he did to us. {9} He made no distinction between us and them, for he purified their hearts by faith. {10} Now then, why do you try to test God by putting on the necks of the disciples a yoke that neither we nor our fathers have been able to bear? {11} No! We believe it is through the grace of our Lord Jesus that we are saved, just as they are." {12} The whole assembly became silent as they listened to Barnabas and Paul telling about the miraculous signs and wonders God had done among the Gentiles through them. {13} When they finished, James spoke up: "Brothers, listen to me. {14} Simon has described to us how God at first showed his concern by taking from the Gentiles a people for himself. {15} The words of the prophets are in agreement with this, as it is written: {16} "'After this I will return and rebuild David's fallen tent. Its ruins I will rebuild, and I will restore it, {17} that the remnant of men may seek the Lord, and all the Gentiles who bear my name, says the Lord, who does these things' {18} that have been known for ages. {19} "It is my judgment, therefore, that we should not make it difficult for the Gentiles who are turning to God. {20} Instead we should write to them, telling them to abstain from food polluted by idols, from sexual immorality, from the meat of strangled animals and from blood.

LETTER FROM JERUSALEM COUNCIL TO GENTILE BELIEVERS

Acts 15:22-35

Then the apostles and elders, with the whole church, decided to choose some of their own men and send them to Antioch with Paul and Barnabas. They chose Judas (called Barsabbas) and Silas, two men who were leaders among the brothers. {23} With them they sent the following letter: The apostles and elders, your brothers, To the Gentile believers in Antioch, Syria and Cilicia: Greetings. {24} We have heard that some went out from us without our authorization and disturbed you, troubling your minds by what they said. {25} So we all agreed to choose some men and send them to you with our dear friends Barnabas and Paul– {26} men who have risked their lives for the name of our Lord Jesus Christ. {27} Therefore we are sending Judas and Silas to confirm by word of mouth what we are writing. {28} It seemed good to the Holy Spirit and to us not to burden you with anything beyond the following requirements: {29} You are to abstain from food sacrificed to idols, from blood, from the meat of strangled animals and from sexual immorality. You will do well to avoid these things. Farewell. {30} The men were sent off and went down to Antioch, where they gathered the church together and delivered the letter. {31} The people read it and were glad for its encouraging message. {32} Judas and Silas, who themselves were prophets, said much to encourage and strengthen the brothers. {33} After spending some time there, they were sent off by the brothers with the blessing of peace to return to those who had sent them. {34} {35} But Paul and Barnabas remained in Antioch, where they and many others taught and preached the word of the Lord.

DISAGREEMENT BETWEEN PAUL AND BARNABAS;
PAUL HAS VISION TO GO TO MACEDONIA

Acts 15:36-41

Some time later Paul said to Barnabas, "Let us go back and visit the brothers in all the towns where we preached the word of the Lord and see how they are doing." {37} Barnabas wanted to take John, also called Mark, with them, {38} but Paul did not think it wise to take him, because he had deserted them in Pamphylia and had not continued with them in the work. {39} They had such a sharp disagreement that they parted company. Barnabas took Mark and sailed for Cyprus, {40} but Paul chose Silas and left, commended by the brothers to the grace of the Lord. {41} He went through Syria and Cilicia, strengthening the churches.

Acts 16:1-10

He came to Derbe and then to Lystra, where a disciple named Timothy lived, whose mother was a Jewess and a believer, but whose father was a Greek. {2} The brothers at Lystra and Iconium spoke well of him. {3} Paul wanted to take him along on the journey, so he circumcised him because of the Jews who lived in that area, for they all knew that his father was a Greek. {4} As they traveled from town to town, they delivered the decisions reached by the apostles and elders in Jerusalem for the people to obey. {5} So the churches were strengthened in the faith and grew daily in numbers. {6} Paul and his companions traveled throughout the region of Phrygia and Galatia, having been kept by the Holy Spirit from preaching the word in the province of Asia. {7} When they came to the border of Mysia, they tried to enter Bithynia, but the Spirit of Jesus would not allow them to. {8} So they passed by Mysia and went down to Troas. {9} During the night Paul had a vision of a man of Macedonia standing and begging him, "Come over to Macedonia and help us." {10} After Paul had seen the vision, we got ready at once to leave for Macedonia, concluding that God had called us to preach the gospel to them.

LYDIA BECOMES A BELIEVER IN PHILIPPI; PAUL AND SILAS IN PRISON

Acts 16:14-33a

One of those listening was a woman named Lydia, a dealer in purple cloth from the city of Thyatira, who was a worshiper of God. The Lord opened her heart to respond to Paul's message. {15} When she and the members of her household were baptized, she invited us to her home. "If you consider me a believer in the Lord," she said, "come and stay at my house." And she persuaded us. {16} Once when we were going to the place of prayer, we were met by a slave girl who had a spirit by which she predicted the future. She earned a great deal of money for her owners by fortune-telling. {17} This girl followed Paul and the rest of us, shouting, "These men are servants of the Most High God, who are telling you the way to be saved." {18} She kept this up for many days. Finally Paul became so troubled that he turned around and said to the spirit, "In the name of Jesus Christ I command you to come out of her!" At that moment the spirit left her.

{19} When the owners of the slave girl realized that their hope of making money was gone, they seized Paul and Silas and dragged them into the marketplace to face the authorities. {20} They brought them before the magistrates and said, "These men are Jews, and are throwing our city into an uproar {21} by advocating customs unlawful for us Romans to accept or practice." {22} The crowd joined in the attack against Paul and Silas, and the magistrates ordered them to be stripped and beaten. {23} After they had been severely flogged, they were thrown into prison, and the jailer was commanded to guard them carefully. {24} Upon receiving such orders, he put them in the inner cell and fastened their feet in the stocks. {25} About midnight Paul and Silas were praying and singing hymns to God, and the other prisoners were listening to them. {26} Suddenly there was such a violent earthquake that the foundations of the prison were shaken. At once all the prison doors flew open, and everybody's chains came loose. {27} The jailer woke up, and when he saw the prison doors open, he drew his sword and was about to kill himself because he thought the prisoners had escaped. {28} But Paul shouted, "Don't harm yourself! We are all here!" {29} The jailer called for lights, rushed in and fell trembling before Paul and Silas. {30} He then brought them out and asked, "Sirs, what must I do to be saved?" {31} They replied, "Believe in the Lord Jesus, and you will be saved—you and your household." {32} Then they spoke the word of the Lord to him and to all the others in his house. {33} At that hour of the night the jailer took them and washed their wounds....

PAUL AND SILAS RELEASED FROM PRISON, AND GO TO THESSALONICA AND BEREA

Acts 16:35-17:12

When it was daylight, the magistrates sent their officers to the jailer with the order: "Release those men." {36} The jailer told Paul, "The magistrates have ordered that you and Silas be released. Now you can leave. Go in peace." {37} But Paul said to the officers: "They beat us publicly without a trial, even though we are Roman citizens, and threw us into prison. And now do they want to get rid of us quietly? No! Let them come themselves and escort us out." {38} The officers reported this to the magistrates, and when they heard that Paul and Silas were Roman citizens, they were alarmed. {39} They came to appease them and escorted them from the prison, requesting them to leave the city. {40} After Paul and Silas came out of the prison, they went to Lydia's house, where they met with the brothers and encouraged them. Then they left. {17:1} When they had passed through Amphipolis and Apollonia, they came to Thessalonica, where there was a Jewish synagogue. {2} As his custom was, Paul went into the synagogue, and on three Sabbath days he reasoned with them from the Scriptures, {3} explaining and proving that the Christ had to suffer and rise from the dead. "This Jesus I am proclaiming to you is the Christ, " he said. {4} Some of the Jews were persuaded and joined Paul and Silas, as did a large number of God-fearing Greeks and not a few prominent women. {5} But the Jews were jealous; so they rounded up some bad characters from the marketplace, formed a mob and started a riot in the city. They rushed to Jason's house in search of Paul and Silas in order to bring them out to the crowd. {6} But when they did not find them, they dragged Jason and some other brothers before the city officials, shouting: "These men who have caused trouble all over the world have now come here, {7} and Jason has welcomed them into his house. They are all defying Caesar's decrees, saying that there is another king, one called Jesus." {8} When they heard this, the crowd and the city officials were thrown into turmoil. {9} Then they made Jason and the others post bond and let them go. {10} As soon as it was night, the brothers sent Paul and Silas away to Berea. On arriving there, they went to the Jewish synagogue. {11} Now the Bereans were of more noble character than the Thessalonians, for they received the message with great eagerness and examined the Scriptures every day to see if what Paul said was true. {12} Many of the Jews believed, as did also a number of prominent Greek women and many Greek men.

PAUL PREACHES IN ATHENS

Acts 17:15-32

The men who escorted Paul brought him to Athens and then left with instructions for Silas and Timothy to join him as soon as possible. {16} While Paul was waiting for them in Athens, he was greatly distressed to see that the city was full of idols. {17} So he reasoned in the synagogue with the Jews and the God-fearing Greeks, as well as in the marketplace day by day with those who happened to be there. {18} A group of Epicurean and Stoic philosophers began to dispute with him. Some of them asked, "What is this babbler trying to say?" Others remarked, "He seems to be advocating foreign gods." They said this because Paul was preaching the good news about Jesus and the resurrection. {19} Then they took him and brought him to a meeting of the Areopagus, where they said to him, "May we know what this new teaching is that you are presenting? {20} You are bringing some strange ideas to our ears, and we want to know what they mean." {21} (All the Athenians and the foreigners who lived there spent their time doing nothing but talking about and listening to the latest ideas.) {22} Paul then stood up in the meeting of the Areopagus and said: "Men of Athens! I see that in every way you are very religious. {23} For as I walked around and looked carefully at your objects of worship, I even found an altar with this inscription: TO AN UNKNOWN GOD. Now what you worship as something unknown I am going to proclaim to you. {24} "The God who made the world and everything in it is the Lord of heaven and earth and does not live in temples built by hands. {25} And he is not served by human hands, as if he needed anything, because he himself gives all men life and breath and everything else. {26} From one man he made every nation of men, that they should inhabit the whole earth; and he determined the times set for them and the exact places where they should live. {27} God did this so that men would seek him and perhaps reach out for him and find him, though he is not far from each one of us. {28} 'For in him we live and move and have our being.' As some of your own poets have said, 'We are his offspring.' {29} "Therefore since we are God's offspring, we should not think that the divine being is like gold or silver or stone—an image made by man's design and skill. {30} In the past God overlooked such ignorance, but now he commands all people everywhere to repent. {31} For he has set a day when he will judge the world with justice by the man he has appointed. He has given proof of this to all men by raising him from the dead." {32} When they heard about the resurrection of the dead, some of them sneered, but others said, "We want to hear you again on this subject."

PAUL STAYS WITH PRISCILLA AND AQUILA IN CORINTH;

Acts 18:1-22

After this, Paul left Athens and went to Corinth. {2} There he met a Jew named Aquila, a native of Pontus, who had recently come from Italy with his wife Priscilla, because Claudius had ordered all the Jews to leave Rome. Paul went to see them, {3} and because he was a tentmaker as they were, he stayed and worked with them. {4} Every Sabbath he reasoned in the synagogue, trying to persuade Jews and Greeks. {5} When Silas and Timothy came from Macedonia, Paul devoted himself exclusively to preaching, testifying to the Jews that Jesus was the Christ. {6} But when the Jews opposed Paul and became abusive, he shook out his clothes in protest and said to them, "Your blood be on your own heads! I am clear of my responsibility. From now on I will go to the Gentiles." {7} Then Paul left the synagogue and went next door to the house of Titius Justus, a worshiper of God. {8} Crispus, the synagogue ruler, and his entire household believed in the Lord; and many of the Corinthians who heard him believed and were baptized. {9} One night the Lord spoke to Paul in a vision: "Do not be afraid; keep on speaking, do not be silent. {10} For I am with you, and no one is going to attack and harm you, because I have many people in this city." {11} So Paul stayed for a year and a half, teaching them the word of God. {12} While Gallio was proconsul of Achaia, the Jews made a united attack on Paul and brought him into court. {13} "This man," they charged, "is persuading the people to worship God in ways contrary to the law." {14} Just as Paul was about to speak, Gallio said to the Jews, "If you Jews were making a complaint about some misdemeanor or serious crime, it would be reasonable for me to listen to you. {15} But since it involves questions about words and names and your own law—settle the matter yourselves. I will not be a judge of such things." {16} So he had them ejected from the court. {17} Then they all turned on Sosthenes the synagogue ruler and beat him in front of the court. But Gallio showed no concern whatever. {18} Paul stayed on in Corinth for some time. Then he left the brothers and sailed for Syria, accompanied by Priscilla and Aquila. Before he sailed, he had his hair cut off at Cenchrea because of a vow he had taken. {19} They arrived at Ephesus, where Paul left Priscilla and Aquila. He himself went into the synagogue and reasoned with the Jews. {20} When they asked him to spend more time with them, he declined. {21} But as he left, he promised, "I will come back if it is God's will." Then he set sail from Ephesus. {22} When he landed at Caesarea, he went up and greeted the church and then went down to Antioch.

PAUL AT EPHESUS

Acts 19:1-21

While Apollos was at Corinth, Paul took the road through the interior and arrived at Ephesus. There he found some disciples {2} and asked them, "Did you receive the Holy Spirit when you believed?" They answered, "No, we have not even heard that there is a Holy Spirit." {3} So Paul asked, "Then what baptism did you receive?" "John's baptism," they replied. {4} Paul said, "John's baptism was a baptism of repentance. He told the people to believe in the one coming after him, that is, in Jesus." {5} On hearing this, they were baptized into the name of the Lord Jesus. {6} When Paul placed his hands on them, the Holy Spirit came on them, and they spoke in tongues and prophesied. {7} There were about twelve men in all. {8} Paul entered the synagogue and spoke boldly there for three months, arguing persuasively about the kingdom of God. {9} But some of them became obstinate; they refused to believe and publicly maligned the Way. So Paul left them. He took the disciples with him and had discussions daily in the lecture hall of Tyrannus. {10} This went on for two years, so that all the Jews and Greeks who lived in the province of Asia heard the word of the Lord. {11} God did extraordinary miracles through Paul, {12} so that even handkerchiefs and aprons that had touched him were taken to the sick, and their illnesses were cured and the evil spirits left them. {13} Some Jews who went around driving out evil spirits tried to invoke the name of the Lord Jesus over those who were demon-possessed. They would say, "In the name of Jesus, whom Paul preaches, I command you to come out." {14} Seven sons of Sceva, a Jewish chief priest, were doing this. {15} <One day> the evil spirit answered them, "Jesus I know, and I know about Paul, but who are you?" {16} Then the man who had the evil spirit jumped on them and overpowered them all. He gave them such a beating that they ran out of the house naked and bleeding. {17} When this became known to the Jews and Greeks living in Ephesus, they were all seized with fear, and the name of the Lord Jesus was held in high honor. {18} Many of those who believed now came and openly confessed their evil deeds. {19} A number who had practiced sorcery brought their scrolls together and burned them publicly. When they calculated the value of the scrolls, the total came to fifty thousand drachmas. {20} In this way the word of the Lord spread widely and grew in power. {21} After all this had happened, Paul decided to go to Jerusalem, passing through Macedonia and Achaia. "After I have been there," he said, "I must visit Rome also."

DEMETRIUS, THE SILVERSMITH, STIRS UP A RIOT

Acts 19:23-41

About that time there arose a great disturbance about the Way. {24} A silversmith named Demetrius, who made silver shrines of Artemis, brought in no little business for the craftsmen. {25} He called them together, along with the workmen in related trades, and said: "Men, you know we receive a good income from this business. {26} And you see and hear how this fellow Paul has convinced and led astray large numbers of people here in Ephesus and in practically the whole province of Asia. He says that man-made gods are no gods at all. {27} There is danger not only that our trade will lose its good name, but also that the temple of the great goddess Artemis will be discredited, and the goddess herself, who is worshiped throughout the province of Asia and the world, will be robbed of her divine majesty." {28} When they heard this, they were furious and began shouting: "Great is Artemis of the Ephesians!" {29} Soon the whole city was in an uproar. The people seized Gaius and Aristarchus, Paul's traveling companions from Macedonia, and rushed as one man into the theater. {30} Paul wanted to appear before the crowd, but the disciples would not let him. {31} Even some of the officials of the province, friends of Paul, sent him a message begging him not to venture into the theater. {32} The assembly was in confusion: Some were shouting one thing, some another. Most of the people did not even know why they were there. {33} The Jews pushed Alexander to the front, and some of the crowd shouted instructions to him. He motioned for silence in order to make a defense before the people. {34} But when they realized he was a Jew, they all shouted in unison for about two hours: "Great is Artemis of the Ephesians!" {35} The city clerk quieted the crowd and said: "Men of Ephesus, doesn't all the world know that the city of Ephesus is the guardian of the temple of the great Artemis and of her image, which fell from heaven? {36} Therefore, since these facts are undeniable, you ought to be quiet and not do anything rash. {37} You have brought these men here, though they have neither robbed temples nor blasphemed our goddess. {38} If, then, Demetrius and his fellow craftsmen have a grievance against anybody, the courts are open and there are proconsuls. They can press charges. {39} If there is anything further you want to bring up, it must be settled in a legal assembly. {40} As it is, we are in danger of being charged with rioting because of today's events. In that case we would not be able to account for this commotion, since there is no reason for it." {41} After he had said this, he dismissed the assembly.

342

PAUL SAYS FAREWELL TO EPHESIAN BELIEVERS

Acts 20:17-38

From Miletus, Paul sent to Ephesus for the elders of the church. {18} When they arrived, he said to them: "You know how I lived the whole time I was with you, from the first day I came into the province of Asia. {19} I served the Lord with great humility and with tears, although I was severely tested by the plots of the Jews. {20} You know that I have not hesitated to preach anything that would be helpful to you but have taught you publicly and from house to house. {21} I have declared to both Jews and Greeks that they must turn to God in repentance and have faith in our Lord Jesus. {22} "And now, compelled by the Spirit, I am going to Jerusalem, not knowing what will happen to me there. {23} I only know that in every city the Holy Spirit warns me that prison and hardships are facing me. {24} However, I consider my life worth nothing to me, if only I may finish the race and complete the task the Lord Jesus has given me–the task of testifying to the gospel of God's grace. {25} "Now I know that none of you among whom I have gone about preaching the kingdom will ever see me again. {26} Therefore, I declare to you today that I am innocent of the blood of all men. {27} For I have not hesitated to proclaim to you the whole will of God. {28} Keep watch over yourselves and all the flock of which the Holy Spirit has made you overseers. Be shepherds of the church of God, which he bought with his own blood. {29} I know that after I leave, savage wolves will come in among you and will not spare the flock. {30} Even from your own number men will arise and distort the truth in order to draw away disciples after them. {31} So be on your guard! Remember that for three years I never stopped warning each of you night and day with tears. {32} "Now I commit you to God and to the word of his grace, which can build you up and give you an inheritance among all those who are sanctified. {33} I have not coveted anyone's silver or gold or clothing. {34} You yourselves know that these hands of mine have supplied my own needs and the needs of my companions. {35} In everything I did, I showed you that by this kind of hard work we must help the weak, remembering the words the Lord Jesus himself said: 'It is more blessed to give than to receive.'" {36} When he had said this, he knelt down with all of them and prayed. {37} They all wept as they embraced him and kissed him. {38} What grieved them most was his statement that they would never see his face again. Then they accompanied him to the ship.

PAUL GOES TO JERUSALEM

Acts 21:3-24a

After sighting Cyprus and passing to the south of it, we sailed on to Syria. We landed at Tyre, where our ship was to unload its cargo. {4} Finding the disciples there, we stayed with them seven days. Through the Spirit they urged Paul not to go on to Jerusalem. {5} But when our time was up, we left and continued on our way. All the disciples and their wives and children accompanied us out of the city, and there on the beach we knelt to pray. {6} After saying good-by to each other, we went aboard the ship, and they returned home. {7} We continued our voyage from Tyre and landed at Ptolemais, where we greeted the brothers and stayed with them for a day. {8} Leaving the next day, we reached Caesarea and stayed at the house of Philip the evangelist, one of the Seven. {9} He had four unmarried daughters who prophesied. {10} After we had been there a number of days, a prophet named Agabus came down from Judea. {11} Coming over to us, he took Paul's belt, tied his own hands and feet with it and said, "The Holy Spirit says, 'In this way the Jews of Jerusalem will bind the owner of this belt and will hand him over to the Gentiles.'" {12} When we heard this, we and the people there pleaded with Paul not to go up to Jerusalem. {13} Then Paul answered, "Why are you weeping and breaking my heart? I am ready not only to be bound, but also to die in Jerusalem for the name of the Lord Jesus." {14} When he would not be dissuaded, we gave up and said, "The Lord's will be done." {15} After this, we got ready and went up to Jerusalem. {16} Some of the disciples from Caesarea accompanied us and brought us to the home of Mnason, where we were to stay. He was a man from Cyprus and one of the early disciples. {17} When we arrived at Jerusalem, the brothers received us warmly. {18} The next day Paul and the rest of us went to see James, and all the elders were present. {19} Paul greeted them and reported in detail what God had done among the Gentiles through his ministry. {20} When they heard this, they praised God. Then they said to Paul: "You see, brother, how many thousands of Jews have believed, and all of them are zealous for the law. {21} They have been informed that you teach all the Jews who live among the Gentiles to turn away from Moses, telling them not to circumcise their children or live according to our customs. {22} What shall we do? They will certainly hear that you have come, {23} so do what we tell you. There are four men with us who have made a vow. {24} Take these men, join in their purification rites and pay their expenses, so that they can have their heads shaved. Then everybody will know there is no truth in these reports about you....

ANGRY CROWD INCITES PAUL'S ARREST IN JERUSALEM

Acts 21:27-22:2a

When the seven days were nearly over, some Jews from the province of Asia saw Paul at the temple. They stirred up the whole crowd and seized him, {28} shouting, "Men of Israel, help us! This is the man who teaches all men everywhere against our people and our law and this place. And besides, he has brought Greeks into the temple area and defiled this holy place." {29} (They had previously seen Trophimus the Ephesian in the city with Paul and assumed that Paul had brought him into the temple area.) {30} The whole city was aroused, and the people came running from all directions. Seizing Paul, they dragged him from the temple, and immediately the gates were shut. {31} While they were trying to kill him, news reached the commander of the Roman troops that the whole city of Jerusalem was in an uproar. {32} He at once took some officers and soldiers and ran down to the crowd. When the rioters saw the commander and his soldiers, they stopped beating Paul. {33} The commander came up and arrested him and ordered him to be bound with two chains. Then he asked who he was and what he had done. {34} Some in the crowd shouted one thing and some another, and since the commander could not get at the truth because of the uproar, he ordered that Paul be taken into the barracks. {35} When Paul reached the steps, the violence of the mob was so great he had to be carried by the soldiers. {36} The crowd that followed kept shouting, "Away with him!" {37} As the soldiers were about to take Paul into the barracks, he asked the commander, "May I say something to you?" "Do you speak Greek?" he replied. {38} "Aren't you the Egyptian who started a revolt and led four thousand terrorists out into the desert some time ago?" {39} Paul answered, "I am a Jew, from Tarsus in Cilicia, a citizen of no ordinary city. Please let me speak to the people." {40} Having received the commander's permission, Paul stood on the steps and motioned to the crowd. When they were all silent, he said to them in Aramaic : {22:1} "Brothers and fathers, listen now to my defense." {2} When they heard him speak to them in Aramaic, they became very quiet. Then Paul said:

PAUL TELLS OF HIS CONVERSION

Acts 22:2-22

When they heard him speak to them in Aramaic, they became very quiet. Then Paul said: {3} "I am a Jew, born in Tarsus of Cilicia, but brought up in this city. Under Gamaliel I was thoroughly trained in the law of our fathers and was just as zealous for God as any of you are today. {4} I persecuted the followers of this Way to their death, arresting both men and women and throwing them into prison, {5} as also the high priest and all the Council can testify. I even obtained letters from them to their brothers in Damascus, and went there to bring these people as prisoners to Jerusalem to be punished. {6} "About noon as I came near Damascus, suddenly a bright light from heaven flashed around me. {7} I fell to the ground and heard a voice say to me, 'Saul! Saul! Why do you persecute me?' {8} "'Who are you, Lord?' I asked. "'I am Jesus of Nazareth, whom you are persecuting,' he replied. {9} My companions saw the light, but they did not understand the voice of him who was speaking to me. {10} "'What shall I do, Lord?' I asked. "'Get up,' the Lord said, 'and go into Damascus. There you will be told all that you have been assigned to do.' {11} My companions led me by the hand into Damascus, because the brilliance of the light had blinded me. {12} "A man named Ananias came to see me. He was a devout observer of the law and highly respected by all the Jews living there. {13} He stood beside me and said, 'Brother Saul, receive your sight!' And at that very moment I was able to see him. {14} "Then he said: 'The God of our fathers has chosen you to know his will and to see the Righteous One and to hear words from his mouth. {15} You will be his witness to all men of what you have seen and heard. {16} And now what are you waiting for? Get up, be baptized and wash your sins away, calling on his name.' {17} "When I returned to Jerusalem and was praying at the temple, I fell into a trance {18} and saw the Lord speaking. 'Quick!' he said to me. 'Leave Jerusalem immediately, because they will not accept your testimony about me.' {19} "'Lord,' I replied, 'these men know that I went from one synagogue to another to imprison and beat those who believe in you. {20} And when the blood of your martyr Stephen was shed, I stood there giving my approval and guarding the clothes of those who were killing him.' {21} "Then the Lord said to me, 'Go; I will send you far away to the Gentiles.'" {22} The crowd listened to Paul until he said this. Then they raised their voices and shouted, "Rid the earth of him! He's not fit to live!"

PAUL BEFORE THE SANHEDRIN

Acts 22:30-23:11

The next day, since the commander wanted to find out exactly why Paul was being accused by the Jews, he released him and ordered the chief priests and all the Sanhedrin to assemble. Then he brought Paul and had him stand before them. {23:1} Paul looked straight at the Sanhedrin and said, "My brothers, I have fulfilled my duty to God in all good conscience to this day." {2} At this the high priest Ananias ordered those standing near Paul to strike him on the mouth. {3} Then Paul said to him, "God will strike you, you whitewashed wall! You sit there to judge me according to the law, yet you yourself violate the law by commanding that I be struck!" {4} Those who were standing near Paul said, "You dare to insult God's high priest?" {5} Paul replied, "Brothers, I did not realize that he was the high priest; for it is written: 'Do not speak evil about the ruler of your people.'" {6} Then Paul, knowing that some of them were Sadducees and the others Pharisees, called out in the Sanhedrin, "My brothers, I am a Pharisee, the son of a Pharisee. I stand on trial because of my hope in the resurrection of the dead." {7} When he said this, a dispute broke out between the Pharisees and the Sadducees, and the assembly was divided. {8} (The Sadducees say that there is no resurrection, and that there are neither angels nor spirits, but the Pharisees acknowledge them all.) {9} There was a great uproar, and some of the teachers of the law who were Pharisees stood up and argued vigorously. "We find nothing wrong with this man," they said. "What if a spirit or an angel has spoken to him?" {10} The dispute became so violent that the commander was afraid Paul would be torn to pieces by them. He ordered the troops to go down and take him away from them by force and bring him into the barracks. {11} The following night the Lord stood near Paul and said, "Take courage! As you have testified about me in Jerusalem, so you must also testify in Rome."

JEWS PLOT TO KILL PAUL

Acts 23:12-32

The next morning the Jews formed a conspiracy and bound themselves with an oath not to eat or drink until they had killed Paul. {13} More than forty men were involved in this plot. {14} They went to the chief priests and elders and said, "We have taken a solemn oath not to eat anything until we have killed Paul. {15} Now then, you and the Sanhedrin petition the commander to bring him before you on the pretext of wanting more accurate information about his case. We are ready to kill him before he gets here." {16} But when the son of Paul's sister heard of this plot, he went into the barracks and told Paul. {17} Then Paul called one of the centurions and said, "Take this young man to the commander; he has something to tell him." {18} So he took him to the commander. The centurion said, "Paul, the prisoner, sent for me and asked me to bring this young man to you because he has something to tell you." {19} The commander took the young man by the hand, drew him aside and asked, "What is it you want to tell me?" {20} He said: "The Jews have agreed to ask you to bring Paul before the Sanhedrin tomorrow on the pretext of wanting more accurate information about him. {21} Don't give in to them, because more than forty of them are waiting in ambush for him. They have taken an oath not to eat or drink until they have killed him. They are ready now, waiting for your consent to their request." {22} The commander dismissed the young man and cautioned him, "Don't tell anyone that you have reported this to me." {23} Then he called two of his centurions and ordered them, "Get ready a detachment of two hundred soldiers, seventy horsemen and two hundred spearmen to go to Caesarea at nine tonight. {24} Provide mounts for Paul so that he may be taken safely to Governor Felix." {25} He wrote a letter as follows: {26} Claudius Lysias, To His Excellency, Governor Felix: Greetings. {27} This man was seized by the Jews and they were about to kill him, but I came with my troops and rescued him, for I had learned that he is a Roman citizen. {28} I wanted to know why they were accusing him, so I brought him to their Sanhedrin. {29} I found that the accusation had to do with questions about their law, but there was no charge against him that deserved death or imprisonment. {30} When I was informed of a plot to be carried out against the man, I sent him to you at once. I also ordered his accusers to present to you their case against him. {31} So the soldiers, carrying out their orders, took Paul with them during the night and brought him as far as Antipatris. {32} The next day they let the cavalry go on with him, while they returned to the barracks.

PAUL BEFORE GOVERNOR FELIX

Acts 24:1-22

Five days later the high priest Ananias went down to Caesarea with some of the elders and a lawyer named Tertullus, and they brought their charges against Paul before the governor. {2} When Paul was called in, Tertullus presented his case before Felix: "We have enjoyed a long period of peace under you, and your foresight has brought about reforms in this nation. {3} Everywhere and in every way, most excellent Felix, we acknowledge this with profound gratitude. {4} But in order not to weary you further, I would request that you be kind enough to hear us briefly. {5} "We have found this man to be a troublemaker, stirring up riots among the Jews all over the world. He is a ringleader of the Nazarene sect {6} and even tried to desecrate the temple; so we seized him. {7} {8} By examining him yourself you will be able to learn the truth about all these charges we are bringing against him." {9} The Jews joined in the accusation, asserting that these things were true. {10} When the governor motioned for him to speak, Paul replied: "I know that for a number of years you have been a judge over this nation; so I gladly make my defense. {11} You can easily verify that no more than twelve days ago I went up to Jerusalem to worship. {12} My accusers did not find me arguing with anyone at the temple, or stirring up a crowd in the synagogues or anywhere else in the city. {13} And they cannot prove to you the charges they are now making against me. {14} However, I admit that I worship the God of our fathers as a follower of the Way, which they call a sect. I believe everything that agrees with the Law and that is written in the Prophets, {15} and I have the same hope in God as these men, that there will be a resurrection of both the righteous and the wicked. {16} So I strive always to keep my conscience clear before God and man. {17} "After an absence of several years, I came to Jerusalem to bring my people gifts for the poor and to present offerings. {18} I was ceremonially clean when they found me in the temple courts doing this. There was no crowd with me, nor was I involved in any disturbance. {19} But there are some Jews from the province of Asia, who ought to be here before you and bring charges if they have anything against me. {20} Or these who are here should state what crime they found in me when I stood before the Sanhedrin– {21} unless it was this one thing I shouted as I stood in their presence: 'It is concerning the resurrection of the dead that I am on trial before you today.'" {22} Then Felix, who was well acquainted with the Way, adjourned the proceedings. "When Lysias the commander comes," he said, "I will decide your case."

PAUL IS TRIED BEFORE FESTUS WHO CONSULTS AGRIPPA

Acts 25:4-22

Festus answered, "Paul is being held at Caesarea, and I myself am going there soon. {5} Let some of your leaders come with me and press charges against the man there, if he has done anything wrong." {6} After spending eight or ten days with them, he went down to Caesarea, and the next day he convened the court and ordered that Paul be brought before him. {7} When Paul appeared, the Jews who had come down from Jerusalem stood around him, bringing many serious charges against him, which they could not prove. {8} Then Paul made his defense: "I have done nothing wrong against the law of the Jews or against the temple or against Caesar." {9} Festus, wishing to do the Jews a favor, said to Paul, "Are you willing to go up to Jerusalem and stand trial before me there on these charges?" {10} Paul answered: "I am now standing before Caesar's court, where I ought to be tried. I have not done any wrong to the Jews, as you yourself know very well. {11} If, however, I am guilty of doing anything deserving death, I do not refuse to die. But if the charges brought against me by these Jews are not true, no one has the right to hand me over to them. I appeal to Caesar!" {12} After Festus had conferred with his council, he declared: "You have appealed to Caesar. To Caesar you will go!" {13} A few days later King Agrippa and Bernice arrived at Caesarea to pay their respects to Festus. {14} Since they were spending many days there, Festus discussed Paul's case with the king. He said: "There is a man here whom Felix left as a prisoner. {15} When I went to Jerusalem, the chief priests and elders of the Jews brought charges against him and asked that he be condemned. {16} "I told them that it is not the Roman custom to hand over any man before he has faced his accusers and has had an opportunity to defend himself against their charges. {17} When they came here with me, I did not delay the case, but convened the court the next day and ordered the man to be brought in. {18} When his accusers got up to speak, they did not charge him with any of the crimes I had expected. {19} Instead, they had some points of dispute with him about their own religion and about a dead man named Jesus who Paul claimed was alive. {20} I was at a loss how to investigate such matters; so I asked if he would be willing to go to Jerusalem and stand trial there on these charges. {21} When Paul made his appeal to be held over for the Emperor's decision, I ordered him held until I could send him to Caesar." {22} Then Agrippa said to Festus, "I would like to hear this man myself." He replied, "Tomorrow you will hear him."

PAUL BEGINS TESTIMONY BEFORE KING AGRIPPA

Acts 25:23-26:11

The next day Agrippa and Bernice came with great pomp and entered the audience room with the high ranking officers and the leading men of the city. At the command of Festus, Paul was brought in. {24} Festus said: "King Agrippa, and all who are present with us, you see this man! The whole Jewish community has petitioned me about him in Jerusalem and here in Caesarea, shouting that he ought not to live any longer. {25} I found he had done nothing deserving of death, but because he made his appeal to the Emperor I decided to send him to Rome. {26} But I have nothing definite to write to His Majesty about him. Therefore I have brought him before all of you, and especially before you, King Agrippa, so that as a result of this investigation I may have something to write. {27} For I think it is unreasonable to send on a prisoner without specifying the charges against him." {26:1} Then Agrippa said to Paul, "You have permission to speak for yourself." So Paul motioned with his hand and began his defense: {2} "King Agrippa, I consider myself fortunate to stand before you today as I make my defense against all the accusations of the Jews, {3} and especially so because you are well acquainted with all the Jewish customs and controversies. Therefore, I beg you to listen to me patiently. {4} "The Jews all know the way I have lived ever since I was a child, from the beginning of my life in my own country, and also in Jerusalem. {5} They have known me for a long time and can testify, if they are willing, that according to the strictest sect of our religion, I lived as a Pharisee. {6} And now it is because of my hope in what God has promised our fathers that I am on trial today. {7} This is the promise our twelve tribes are hoping to see fulfilled as they earnestly serve God day and night. O king, it is because of this hope that the Jews are accusing me. {8} Why should any of you consider it incredible that God raises the dead? {9} "I too was convinced that I ought to do all that was possible to oppose the name of Jesus of Nazareth. {10} And that is just what I did in Jerusalem. On the authority of the chief priests I put many of the saints in prison, and when they were put to death, I cast my vote against them. {11} Many a time I went from one synagogue to another to have them punished, and I tried to force them to blaspheme. In my obsession against them, I even went to foreign cities to persecute them.

PAUL ENDS TESTIMONY BEFORE KING AGRIPPA

Acts 26:12-31

"On one of these journeys I was going to Damascus with the authority and commission of the chief priests. {13} About noon, O king, as I was on the road, I saw a light from heaven, brighter than the sun, blazing around me and my companions. {14} We all fell to the ground, and I heard a voice saying to me in Aramaic, 'Saul, Saul, why do you persecute me? It is hard for you to kick against the goads.' {15} "Then I asked, 'Who are you, Lord?' "'I am Jesus, whom you are persecuting,' the Lord replied. {16} 'Now get up and stand on your feet. I have appeared to you to appoint you as a servant and as a witness of what you have seen of me and what I will show you. {17} I will rescue you from your own people and from the Gentiles. I am sending you to them {18} to open their eyes and turn them from darkness to light, and from the power of Satan to God, so that they may receive forgiveness of sins and a place among those who are sanctified by faith in me.' {19} "So then, King Agrippa, I was not disobedient to the vision from heaven. {20} First to those in Damascus, then to those in Jerusalem and in all Judea, and to the Gentiles also, I preached that they should repent and turn to God and prove their repentance by their deeds. {21} That is why the Jews seized me in the temple courts and tried to kill me. {22} But I have had God's help to this very day, and so I stand here and testify to small and great alike. I am saying nothing beyond what the prophets and Moses said would happen– {23} that the Christ would suffer and, as the first to rise from the dead, would proclaim light to his own people and to the Gentiles." {24} At this point Festus interrupted Paul's defense. "You are out of your mind, Paul!" he shouted. "Your great learning is driving you insane." {25} "I am not insane, most excellent Festus," Paul replied. "What I am saying is true and reasonable. {26} The king is familiar with these things, and I can speak freely to him. I am convinced that none of this has escaped his notice, because it was not done in a corner. {27} King Agrippa, do you believe the prophets? I know you do." {28} Then Agrippa said to Paul, "Do you think that in such a short time you can persuade me to be a Christian?" {29} Paul replied, "Short time or long–I pray God that not only you but all who are listening to me today may become what I am, except for these chains." {30} The king rose, and with him the governor and Bernice and those sitting with them. {31} They left the room, and while talking with one another, they said, "This man is not doing anything that deserves death or imprisonment."

PAUL SAILS FOR ROME

Acts 27:3-22

The next day we landed at Sidon; and Julius, in kindness to Paul, allowed him to go to his friends so they might provide for his needs. {4} From there we put out to sea again and passed to the lee of Cyprus because the winds were against us. {5} When we had sailed across the open sea off the coast of Cilicia and Pamphylia, we landed at Myra in Lycia. {6} There the centurion found an Alexandrian ship sailing for Italy and put us on board. {7} We made slow headway for many days and had difficulty arriving off Cnidus. When the wind did not allow us to hold our course, we sailed to the lee of Crete, opposite Salmone. {8} We moved along the coast with difficulty and came to a place called Fair Havens, near the town of Lasea. {9} Much time had been lost, and sailing had already become dangerous because by now it was after the Fast. So Paul warned them, {10} "Men, I can see that our voyage is going to be disastrous and bring great loss to ship and cargo, and to our own lives also." {11} But the centurion, instead of listening to what Paul said, followed the advice of the pilot and of the owner of the ship. {12} Since the harbor was unsuitable to winter in, the majority decided that we should sail on, hoping to reach Phoenix and winter there. This was a harbor in Crete, facing both southwest and northwest. {13} When a gentle south wind began to blow, they thought they had obtained what they wanted; so they weighed anchor and sailed along the shore of Crete. {14} Before very long, a wind of hurricane force, called the "northeaster," swept down from the island. {15} The ship was caught by the storm and could not head into the wind; so we gave way to it and were driven along. {16} As we passed to the lee of a small island called Cauda, we were hardly able to make the lifeboat secure. {17} When the men had hoisted it aboard, they passed ropes under the ship itself to hold it together. Fearing that they would run aground on the sandbars of Syrtis, they lowered the sea anchor and let the ship be driven along. {18} We took such a violent battering from the storm that the next day they began to throw the cargo overboard. {19} On the third day, they threw the ship's tackle overboard with their own hands. {20} When neither sun nor stars appeared for many days and the storm continued raging, we finally gave up all hope of being saved. {21} After the men had gone a long time without food, Paul stood up before them and said: "Men, you should have taken my advice not to sail from Crete; then you would have spared yourselves this damage and loss. {22} But now I urge you to keep up your courage, because not one of you will be lost; only the ship will be destroyed.

PAUL SHIPWRECKED ON MALTA

Acts 27:29-28:5
Fearing that we would be dashed against the rocks, they dropped four anchors from the stern and prayed for daylight. {30} In an attempt to escape from the ship, the sailors let the lifeboat down into the sea, pretending they were going to lower some anchors from the bow. {31} Then Paul said to the centurion and the soldiers, "Unless these men stay with the ship, you cannot be saved." {32} So the soldiers cut the ropes that held the lifeboat and let it fall away. {33} Just before dawn Paul urged them all to eat. "For the last fourteen days," he said, "you have been in constant suspense and have gone without food–you haven't eaten anything. {34} Now I urge you to take some food. You need it to survive. Not one of you will lose a single hair from his head." {35} After he said this, he took some bread and gave thanks to God in front of them all. Then he broke it and began to eat. {36} They were all encouraged and ate some food themselves. {37} Altogether there were 276 of us on board. {38} When they had eaten as much as they wanted, they lightened the ship by throwing the grain into the sea. {39} When daylight came, they did not recognize the land, but they saw a bay with a sandy beach, where they decided to run the ship aground if they could. {40} Cutting loose the anchors, they left them in the sea and at the same time untied the ropes that held the rudders. Then they hoisted the foresail to the wind and made for the beach. {41} But the ship struck a sandbar and ran aground. The bow stuck fast and would not move,2 and the stern was broken to pieces by the pounding of the surf. {42} The soldiers planned to kill the prisoners to prevent any of them from swimming away and escaping. {43} But the centurion wanted to spare Paul's life and kept them from carrying out their plan. He ordered those who could swim to jump overboard first and get to land. {44} The rest were to get there on planks or on pieces of the ship. In this way everyone reached land in safety. {28:1} Once safely on shore, we found out that the island was called Malta. {2} The islanders showed us unusual kindness. They built a fire and welcomed us all because it was raining and cold. {3} Paul gathered a pile of brushwood and, as he put it on the fire, a viper, driven out by the heat, fastened itself on his hand. {4} When the islanders saw the snake hanging from his hand, they said to each other, "This man must be a murderer; for though he escaped from the sea, Justice has not allowed him to live." {5} But Paul shook the snake off into the fire and suffered no ill effects.

PAUL PREACHES IN ROME

Acts 28:13-31

From there we set sail and arrived at Rhegium. The next day the south wind came up, and on the following day we reached Puteoli. {14} There we found some brothers who invited us to spend a week with them. And so we came to Rome. {15} The brothers there had heard that we were coming, and they traveled as far as the Forum of Appius and the Three Taverns to meet us. At the sight of these men Paul thanked God and was encouraged. {16} When we got to Rome, Paul was allowed to live by himself, with a soldier to guard him. {17} Three days later he called together the leaders of the Jews. When they had assembled, Paul said to them: "My brothers, although I have done nothing against our people or against the customs of our ancestors, I was arrested in Jerusalem and handed over to the Romans. {18} They examined me and wanted to release me, because I was not guilty of any crime deserving death. {19} But when the Jews objected, I was compelled to appeal to Caesar–not that I had any charge to bring against my own people. {20} For this reason I have asked to see you and talk with you. It is because of the hope of Israel that I am bound with this chain." {21} They replied, "We have not received any letters from Judea concerning you, and none of the brothers who have come from there has reported or said anything bad about you. {22} But we want to hear what your views are, for we know that people everywhere are talking against this sect." {23} They arranged to meet Paul on a certain day, and came in even larger numbers to the place where he was staying. From morning till evening he explained and declared to them the kingdom of God and tried to convince them about Jesus from the Law of Moses and from the Prophets. {24} Some were convinced by what he said, but others would not believe. {25} They disagreed among themselves and began to leave after Paul had made this final statement: "The Holy Spirit spoke the truth to your forefathers when he said through Isaiah the prophet: {26} "'Go to this people and say, "You will be ever hearing but never understanding; you will be ever seeing but never perceiving." {27} For this people's heart has become calloused; they hardly hear with their ears, and they have closed their eyes. Otherwise they might see with their eyes, hear with their ears, understand with their hearts and turn, and I would heal them.' {28} "Therefore I want you to know that God's salvation has been sent to the Gentiles, and they will listen!" {29} {30} For two whole years Paul stayed there in his own rented house and welcomed all who came to see him. {31} Boldly and without hindrance he preached the kingdom of God and taught about the Lord Jesus Christ.

PAUL CALLED TO PREACH TO JEWS AND GENTILES

Rom 1:1-20

Paul, a servant of Christ Jesus, called to be an apostle and set apart for the gospel of God– {2} the gospel he promised beforehand through his prophets in the Holy Scriptures {3} regarding his Son, who as to his human nature was a descendant of David, {4} and who through the Spirit of holiness was declared with power to be the Son of God by his resurrection from the dead: Jesus Christ our Lord. {5} Through him and for his name's sake, we received grace and apostleship to call people from among all the Gentiles to the obedience that comes from faith. {6} And you also are among those who are called to belong to Jesus Christ. {7} To all in Rome who are loved by God and called to be saints: Grace and peace to you from God our Father and from the Lord Jesus Christ. {8} First, I thank my God through Jesus Christ for all of you, because your faith is being reported all over the world. {9} God, whom I serve with my whole heart in preaching the gospel of his Son, is my witness how constantly I remember you {10} in my prayers at all times; and I pray that now at last by God's will the way may be opened for me to come to you. {11} I long to see you so that I may impart to you some spiritual gift to make you strong– {12} that is, that you and I may be mutually encouraged by each other's faith. {13} I do not want you to be unaware, brothers, that I planned many times to come to you (but have been prevented from doing so until now) in order that I might have a harvest among you, just as I have had among the other Gentiles. {14} I am obligated both to Greeks and non-Greeks, both to the wise and the foolish. {15} That is why I am so eager to preach the gospel also to you who are at Rome. {16} I am not ashamed of the gospel, because it is the power of God for the salvation of everyone who believes: first for the Jew, then for the Gentile. {17} For in the gospel a righteousness from God is revealed, a righteousness that is by faith from first to last, just as it is written: "The righteous will live by faith." {18} The wrath of God is being revealed from heaven against all the godlessness and wickedness of men who suppress the truth by their wickedness, {19} since what may be known about God is plain to them, because God has made it plain to them. {20} For since the creation of the world God's invisible qualities– his eternal power and divine nature–have been clearly seen, being understood from what has been made, so that men are without excuse.

JESUS IS LIKE A BROTHER

Heb 2:1-18

We must pay more careful attention, therefore, to what we have heard, so that we do not drift away. {2} For if the message spoken by angels was binding, and every violation and disobedience received its just punishment, {3} how shall we escape if we ignore such a great salvation? This salvation, which was first announced by the Lord, was confirmed to us by those who heard him. {4} God also testified to it by signs, wonders and various miracles, and gifts of the Holy Spirit distributed according to his will. {5} It is not to angels that he has subjected the world to come, about which we are speaking. {6} But there is a place where someone has testified: "What is man that you are mindful of him, the son of man that you care for him? {7} You made him a little lower than the angels; you crowned him with glory and honor {8} and put everything under his feet." In putting everything under him, God left nothing that is not subject to him. Yet at present we do not see everything subject to him. {9} But we see Jesus, who was made a little lower than the angels, now crowned with glory and honor because he suffered death, so that by the grace of God he might taste death for everyone. {10} In bringing many sons to glory, it was fitting that God, for whom and through whom everything exists, should make the author of their salvation perfect through suffering. {11} Both the one who makes men holy and those who are made holy are of the same family. So Jesus is not ashamed to call them brothers. {12} He says, "I will declare your name to my brothers; in the presence of the congregation I will sing your praises." {13} And again, "I will put my trust in him." And again he says, "Here am I, and the children God has given me." {14} Since the children have flesh and blood, he too shared in their humanity so that by his death he might destroy him who holds the power of death–that is, the devil– {15} and free those who all their lives were held in slavery by their fear of death. {16} For surely it is not angels he helps, but Abraham's descendants. {17} For this reason he had to be made like his brothers in every way, in order that he might become a merciful and faithful high priest in service to God, and that he might make atonement for the sins of the people. {18} Because he himself suffered when he was tempted, he is able to help those who are being tempted.

JESUS, THE APOSTLE AND HIGH PRIEST

Heb 3:1-6

Therefore, holy brothers, who share in the heavenly calling, fix your thoughts on Jesus, the apostle and high priest whom we confess. {2} He was faithful to the one who appointed him, just as Moses was faithful in all God's house. {3} Jesus has been found worthy of greater honor than Moses, just as the builder of a house has greater honor than the house itself. {4} For every house is built by someone, but God is the builder of everything. {5} Moses was faithful as a servant in all God's house, testifying to what would be said in the future. {6} But Christ is faithful as a son over God's house. And we are his house, if we hold on to our courage and the hope of which we boast.

Heb 4:14-5:10

Therefore, since we have a great high priest who has gone through the heavens, Jesus the Son of God, let us hold firmly to the faith we profess. {15} For we do not have a high priest who is unable to sympathize with our weaknesses, but we have one who has been tempted in every way, just as we are–yet was without sin. {16} Let us then approach the throne of grace with confidence, so that we may receive mercy and find grace to help us in our time of need. {5:1} Every high priest is selected from among men and is appointed to represent them in matters related to God, to offer gifts and sacrifices for sins. {2} He is able to deal gently with those who are ignorant and are going astray, since he himself is subject to weakness. {3} This is why he has to offer sacrifices for his own sins, as well as for the sins of the people. {4} No one takes this honor upon himself; he must be called by God, just as Aaron was. {5} So Christ also did not take upon himself the glory of becoming a high priest. But God said to him, "You are my Son; today I have become your Father. " {6} And he says in another place, "You are a priest forever, in the order of Melchizedek." {7} During the days of Jesus' life on earth, he offered up prayers and petitions with loud cries and tears to the one who could save him from death, and he was heard because of his reverent submission. {8} Although he was a son, he learned obedience from what he suffered {9} and, once made perfect, he became the source of eternal salvation for all who obey him {10} and was designated by God to be high priest in the order of Melchizedek.

GO ON TO MATURITY

Heb 6:1-20

Therefore let us leave the elementary teachings about Christ and go on to maturity, not laying again the foundation of repentance from acts that lead to death, and of faith in God, {2} instruction about baptisms, the laying on of hands, the resurrection of the dead, and eternal judgment. {3} And God permitting, we will do so. {4} It is impossible for those who have once been enlightened, who have tasted the heavenly gift, who have shared in the Holy Spirit, {5} who have tasted the goodness of the word of God and the powers of the coming age, {6} if they fall away, to be brought back to repentance, because to their loss they are crucifying the Son of God all over again and subjecting him to public disgrace. {7} Land that drinks in the rain often falling on it and that produces a crop useful to those for whom it is farmed receives the blessing of God. {8} But land that produces thorns and thistles is worthless and is in danger of being cursed. In the end it will be burned. {9} Even though we speak like this, dear friends, we are confident of better things in your case—things that accompany salvation. {10} God is not unjust; he will not forget your work and the love you have shown him as you have helped his people and continue to help them. {11} We want each of you to show this same diligence to the very end, in order to make your hope sure. {12} We do not want you to become lazy, but to imitate those who through faith and patience inherit what has been promised. {13} When God made his promise to Abraham, since there was no one greater for him to swear by, he swore by himself, {14} saying, "I will surely bless you and give you many descendants." {15} And so after waiting patiently, Abraham received what was promised. {16} Men swear by someone greater than themselves, and the oath confirms what is said and puts an end to all argument. {17} Because God wanted to make the unchanging nature of his purpose very clear to the heirs of what was promised, he confirmed it with an oath. {18} God did this so that, by two unchangeable things in which it is impossible for God to lie, we who have fled to take hold of the hope offered to us may be greatly encouraged. {19} We have this hope as an anchor for the soul, firm and secure. It enters the inner sanctuary behind the curtain, {20} where Jesus, who went before us, has entered on our behalf. He has become a high priest forever, in the order of Melchizedek.

JESUS IS LIKE MELCHIZEDEK

Heb 7:1-22

This Melchizedek was king of Salem and priest of God Most High. He met Abraham returning from the defeat of the kings and blessed him, {2} and Abraham gave him a tenth of everything. First, his name means "king of righteousness"; then also, "king of Salem" means "king of peace." {3} Without father or mother, without genealogy, without beginning of days or end of life, like the Son of God he remains a priest forever. {4} Just think how great he was: Even the patriarch Abraham gave him a tenth of the plunder! {5} Now the law requires the descendants of Levi who become priests to collect a tenth from the people–that is, their brothers–even though their brothers are descended from Abraham. {6} This man, however, did not trace his descent from Levi, yet he collected a tenth from Abraham and blessed him who had the promises. {7} And without doubt the lesser person is blessed by the greater. {8} In the one case, the tenth is collected by men who die; but in the other case, by him who is declared to be living. {9} One might even say that Levi, who collects the tenth, paid the tenth through Abraham, {10} because when Melchizedek met Abraham, Levi was still in the body of his ancestor. {11} If perfection could have been attained through the Levitical priesthood (for on the basis of it the law was given to the people), why was there still need for another priest to come–one in the order of Melchizedek, not in the order of Aaron? {12} For when there is a change of the priesthood, there must also be a change of the law. {13} He of whom these things are said belonged to a different tribe, and no one from that tribe has ever served at the altar. {14} For it is clear that our Lord descended from Judah, and in regard to that tribe Moses said nothing about priests. {15} And what we have said is even more clear if another priest like Melchizedek appears, {16} one who has become a priest not on the basis of a regulation as to his ancestry but on the basis of the power of an indestructible life. {17} For it is declared: "You are a priest forever, in the order of Melchizedek." {18} The former regulation is set aside because it was weak and useless {19} (for the law made nothing perfect), and a better hope is introduced, by which we draw near to God. {20} And it was not without an oath! Others became priests without any oath, {21} but he became a priest with an oath when God said to him: "The Lord has sworn and will not change his mind: 'You are a priest forever.'" {22} Because of this oath, Jesus has become the guarantee of a better covenant.

JESUS, THE HIGH PRIEST OF A NEW COVENANT

Heb 8:1-13

The point of what we are saying is this: We do have such a high priest, who sat down at the right hand of the throne of the Majesty in heaven, {2} and who serves in the sanctuary, the true tabernacle set up by the Lord, not by man. {3} Every high priest is appointed to offer both gifts and sacrifices, and so it was necessary for this one also to have something to offer. {4} If he were on earth, he would not be a priest, for there are already men who offer the gifts prescribed by the law. {5} They serve at a sanctuary that is a copy and shadow of what is in heaven. This is why Moses was warned when he was about to build the tabernacle: "See to it that you make everything according to the pattern shown you on the mountain." {6} But the ministry Jesus has received is as superior to theirs as the covenant of which he is mediator is superior to the old one, and it is founded on better promises. {7} For if there had been nothing wrong with that first covenant, no place would have been sought for another. {8} But God found fault with the people and said : "The time is coming, declares the Lord, when I will make a new covenant with the house of Israel and with the house of Judah. {9} It will not be like the covenant I made with their forefathers when I took them by the hand to lead them out of Egypt, because they did not remain faithful to my covenant, and I turned away from them, declares the Lord. {10} This is the covenant I will make with the house of Israel after that time, declares the Lord. I will put my laws in their minds and write them on their hearts. I will be their God, and they will be my people. {11} No longer will a man teach his neighbor, or a man his brother, saying, 'Know the Lord,' because they will all know me, from the least of them to the greatest. {12} For I will forgive their wickedness and will remember their sins no more." {13} By calling this covenant "new," he has made the first one obsolete; and what is obsolete and aging will soon disappear.

CHRIST, THE MEDIATOR OF A NEW COVENANT

Heb 9:12-28

He did not enter by means of the blood of goats and calves; but he entered the Most Holy Place once for all by his own blood, having obtained eternal redemption. {13} The blood of goats and bulls and the ashes of a heifer sprinkled on those who are ceremonially unclean sanctify them so that they are outwardly clean. {14} How much more, then, will the blood of Christ, who through the eternal Spirit offered himself unblemished to God, cleanse our consciences from acts that lead to death, so that we may serve the living God! {15} For this reason Christ is the mediator of a new covenant, that those who are called may receive the promised eternal inheritance—now that he has died as a ransom to set them free from the sins committed under the first covenant. {16} In the case of a will, it is necessary to prove the death of the one who made it, {17} because a will is in force only when somebody has died; it never takes effect while the one who made it is living. {18} This is why even the first covenant was not put into effect without blood. {19} When Moses had proclaimed every commandment of the law to all the people, he took the blood of calves, together with water, scarlet wool and branches of hyssop, and sprinkled the scroll and all the people. {20} He said, "This is the blood of the covenant, which God has commanded you to keep." {21} In the same way, he sprinkled with the blood both the tabernacle and everything used in its ceremonies. {22} In fact, the law requires that nearly everything be cleansed with blood, and without the shedding of blood there is no forgiveness. {23} It was necessary, then, for the copies of the heavenly things to be purified with these sacrifices, but the heavenly things themselves with better sacrifices than these. {24} For Christ did not enter a man-made sanctuary that was only a copy of the true one; he entered heaven itself, now to appear for us in God's presence. {25} Nor did he enter heaven to offer himself again and again, the way the high priest enters the Most Holy Place every year with blood that is not his own. {26} Then Christ would have had to suffer many times since the creation of the world. But now he has appeared once for all at the end of the ages to do away with sin by the sacrifice of himself. {27} Just as man is destined to die once, and after that to face judgment, {28} so Christ was sacrificed once to take away the sins of many people; and he will appear a second time, not to bear sin, but to bring salvation to those who are waiting for him.

HEROES OF THE FAITH

Heb 11:1-19a

Now faith is being sure of what we hope for and certain of what we do not see. {2} This is what the ancients were commended for. {3} By faith we understand that the universe was formed at God's command, so that what is seen was not made out of what was visible. {4} By faith Abel offered God a better sacrifice than Cain did. By faith he was commended as a righteous man, when God spoke well of his offerings. And by faith he still speaks, even though he is dead. {5} By faith Enoch was taken from this life, so that he did not experience death; he could not be found, because God had taken him away. For before he was taken, he was commended as one who pleased God. {6} And without faith it is impossible to please God, because anyone who comes to him must believe that he exists and that he rewards those who earnestly seek him. {7} By faith Noah, when warned about things not yet seen, in holy fear built an ark to save his family. By his faith he condemned the world and became heir of the righteousness that comes by faith. {8} By faith Abraham, when called to go to a place he would later receive as his inheritance, obeyed and went, even though he did not know where he was going. {9} By faith he made his home in the promised land like a stranger in a foreign country; he lived in tents, as did Isaac and Jacob, who were heirs with him of the same promise. {10} For he was looking forward to the city with foundations, whose architect and builder is God. {11} By faith Abraham, even though he was past age–and Sarah herself was barren–was enabled to become a father because he considered him faithful who had made the promise. {12} And so from this one man, and he as good as dead, came descendants as numerous as the stars in the sky and as countless as the sand on the seashore. {13} All these people were still living by faith when they died. They did not receive the things promised; they only saw them and welcomed them from a distance. And they admitted that they were aliens and strangers on earth. {14} People who say such things show that they are looking for a country of their own. {15} If they had been thinking of the country they had left, they would have had opportunity to return. {16} Instead, they were longing for a better country–a heavenly one. Therefore God is not ashamed to be called their God, for he has prepared a city for them. {17} By faith Abraham, when God tested him, offered Isaac as a sacrifice. He who had received the promises was about to sacrifice his one and only son, {18} even though God had said to him, "It is through Isaac that your offspring will be reckoned." {19} Abraham reasoned that God could raise the dead....

MORE HEROES OF THE FAITH

Heb 11:20-40

By faith Isaac blessed Jacob and Esau in regard to their future. {21} By faith Jacob, when he was dying, blessed each of Joseph's sons, and worshiped as he leaned on the top of his staff. {22} By faith Joseph, when his end was near, spoke about the exodus of the Israelites from Egypt and gave instructions about his bones. {23} By faith Moses' parents hid him for three months after he was born, because they saw he was no ordinary child, and they were not afraid of the king's edict. {24} By faith Moses, when he had grown up, refused to be known as the son of Pharaoh's daughter. {25} He chose to be mistreated along with the people of God rather than to enjoy the pleasures of sin for a short time. {26} He regarded disgrace for the sake of Christ as of greater value than the treasures of Egypt, because he was looking ahead to his reward. {27} By faith he left Egypt, not fearing the king's anger; he persevered because he saw him who is invisible. {28} By faith he kept the Passover and the sprinkling of blood, so that the destroyer of the firstborn would not touch the firstborn of Israel. {29} By faith the people passed through the Red Sea as on dry land; but when the Egyptians tried to do so, they were drowned. {30} By faith the walls of Jericho fell, after the people had marched around them for seven days. {31} By faith the prostitute Rahab, because she welcomed the spies, was not killed with those who were disobedient. {32} And what more shall I say? I do not have time to tell about Gideon, Barak, Samson, Jephthah, David, Samuel and the prophets, {33} who through faith conquered kingdoms, administered justice, and gained what was promised; who shut the mouths of lions, {34} quenched the fury of the flames, and escaped the edge of the sword; whose weakness was turned to strength; and who became powerful in battle and routed foreign armies. {35} Women received back their dead, raised to life again. Others were tortured and refused to be released, so that they might gain a better resurrection. {36} Some faced jeers and flogging, while still others were chained and put in prison. {37} They were stoned ; they were sawed in two; they were put to death by the sword. They went about in sheepskins and goatskins, destitute, persecuted and mistreated– {38} the world was not worthy of them. They wandered in deserts and mountains, and in caves and holes in the ground. {39} These were all commended for their faith, yet none of them received what had been promised. {40} God had planned something better for us so that only together with us would they be made perfect.

LIVE AT PEACE WITH ALL MEN

Heb 12:4-25a

In your struggle against sin, you have not yet resisted to the point of shedding your blood. {5} And you have forgotten that word of encouragement that addresses you as sons: "My son, do not make light of the Lord's discipline, and do not lose heart when he rebukes you, {6} because the Lord disciplines those he loves, and he punishes everyone he accepts as a son." {7} Endure hardship as discipline; God is treating you as sons. For what son is not disciplined by his father? {8} If you are not disciplined (and everyone undergoes discipline), then you are illegitimate children and not true sons. {9} Moreover, we have all had human fathers who disciplined us and we respected them for it. How much more should we submit to the Father of our spirits and live! {10} Our fathers disciplined us for a little while as they thought best; but God disciplines us for our good, that we may share in his holiness. {11} No discipline seems pleasant at the time, but painful. Later on, however, it produces a harvest of righteousness and peace for those who have been trained by it. {12} Therefore, strengthen your feeble arms and weak knees. {13} "Make level paths for your feet," so that the lame may not be disabled, but rather healed. {14} Make every effort to live in peace with all men and to be holy; without holiness no one will see the Lord. {15} See to it that no one misses the grace of God and that no bitter root grows up to cause trouble and defile many. {16} See that no one is sexually immoral, or is godless like Esau, who for a single meal sold his inheritance rights as the oldest son. {17} Afterward, as you know, when he wanted to inherit this blessing, he was rejected. He could bring about no change of mind, though he sought the blessing with tears. {18} You have not come to a mountain that can be touched and that is burning with fire; to darkness, gloom and storm; {19} to a trumpet blast or to such a voice speaking words that those who heard it begged that no further word be spoken to them, {20} because they could not bear what was commanded: "If even an animal touches the mountain, it must be stoned." {21} The sight was so terrifying that Moses said, "I am trembling with fear." {22} But you have come to Mount Zion, to the heavenly Jerusalem, the city of the living God. You have come to thousands upon thousands of angels in joyful assembly, {23} to the church of the firstborn, whose names are written in heaven. You have come to God, the judge of all men, to the spirits of righteous men made perfect, {24} to Jesus the mediator of a new covenant, and to the sprinkled blood that speaks a better word than the blood of Abel. {25} See to it that you do not refuse him who speaks.

KEEP ON LOVING EACH OTHER

Heb 13:1-21

Keep on loving each other as brothers. {2} Do not forget to entertain strangers, for by so doing some people have entertained angels without knowing it. {3} Remember those in prison as if you were their fellow prisoners, and those who are mistreated as if you yourselves were suffering. {4} Marriage should be honored by all, and the marriage bed kept pure, for God will judge the adulterer and all the sexually immoral. {5} Keep your lives free from the love of money and be content with what you have, because God has said, "Never will I leave you; never will I forsake you." {6} So we say with confidence, "The Lord is my helper; I will not be afraid. What can man do to me?" {7} Remember your leaders, who spoke the word of God to you. Consider the outcome of their way of life and imitate their faith. {8} Jesus Christ is the same yesterday and today and forever. {9} Do not be carried away by all kinds of strange teachings. It is good for our hearts to be strengthened by grace, not by ceremonial foods, which are of no value to those who eat them. {10} We have an altar from which those who minister at the tabernacle have no right to eat. {11} The high priest carries the blood of animals into the Most Holy Place as a sin offering, but the bodies are burned outside the camp. {12} And so Jesus also suffered outside the city gate to make the people holy through his own blood. {13} Let us, then, go to him outside the camp, bearing the disgrace he bore. {14} For here we do not have an enduring city, but we are looking for the city that is to come. {15} Through Jesus, therefore, let us continually offer to God a sacrifice of praise–the fruit of lips that confess his name. {16} And do not forget to do good and to share with others, for with such sacrifices God is pleased. {17} Obey your leaders and submit to their authority. They keep watch over you as men who must give an account. Obey them so that their work will be a joy, not a burden, for that would be of no advantage to you. {18} Pray for us. We are sure that we have a clear conscience and desire to live honorably in every way. {19} I particularly urge you to pray so that I may be restored to you soon. {20} May the God of peace, who through the blood of the eternal covenant brought back from the dead our Lord Jesus, that great Shepherd of the sheep, {21} equip you with everything good for doing his will, and may he work in us what is pleasing to him, through Jesus Christ, to whom be glory for ever and ever. Amen.

NOTES